JOURNAL FOR THE STUDY OF THE OLD TESTAMENT
SUPPLEMENT SERIES
198

Sheffield Academic Press

Aramaic Daniel and Greek Daniel

A Literary Comparison

T.J. Meadowcroft

Journal for the Study of the Old Testament
Supplement Series 198

For Sue

'Facts,' murmured Basil, like one mentioning some strange, far-off animals, 'how facts obscure the truth... Every detail points to something, certainly; but generally to the wrong thing. Facts point in all directions, it seems to me, like the thousands of twigs on a tree. It's only the life of the tree that has unity and goes up—only the green blood that springs, like a fountain, at the stars.'

G.K. Chesterton in 'The Tremendous Adventure of Major Brown'

Published by
Sheffield Academic Press Ltd
Mansion House
19 Kingfield Road
Sheffield, S11 9AS
England

Typeset by Sheffield Academic Press
and
Printed on acid-free paper in Great Britain
by Bookcraft
Midsomer Norton, Somerset

British Library Cataloguing in Publication Data

A catalogue record for this book is available
from the British Library

ISBN 1-85075-551-5

CONTENTS

PREFACE

The work herein is the result of minor revisions to a doctoral thesis submitted to the Faculty of Divinity at New College, University of Edinburgh, in 1993. I wish to express my gratitude to the St Johns College Trust, Auckland, and the New College Faculty of Divinity, whose funding made my research possible. During the course of that research, the encouragement, interest and criticism of my two supervisors, Dr Peter Hayman and Professor Graeme Auld, were invaluable, and the models of scholarship they embodied were formative. Since my return to New Zealand, the environment created by library staff and faculty colleagues at the Bible College of New Zealand has assisted in the preparation of this manuscript. My greatest debt is to my family. Anna, Sarah, Katie and Elizabeth have endured two international shifts brought about by their father's work, always with courage and usually with good humour and tolerance. I thank them. And most important of all has been the flexibility, love and support of my wife, Sue, to whom I dedicate this book.

ABBREVIATIONS

ANEP	J.B. Pritchard (ed.), *Ancient Near East in Pictures*
ANET	J.B. Pritchard (ed.), *Ancient Near Eastern Texts*
AUSS	*Andrews University Seminary Studies*
BASOR	*Bulletin of the American Schools of Oriental Research*
BDB	F. Brown, S.R. Driver and C.A. Briggs, *Hebrew and English Lexicon of the Old Testament*
BHS	*Biblia hebraica stuttgartensia*
Bib	*Biblica*
BIOSCS	*Bulletin of the International Organization for Septuagint and Cognate Studies*
BR	*Biblical Research*
BZ	*Biblische Zeitschrift*
CBQ	*Catholic Biblical Quarterly*
CSR	*Christian Scholars Review*
ETL	*Ephemerides theologicae lovaniensis*
EvQ	*Evangelical Quarterly*
ExpTim	*Expository Times*
HAR	*Hebrew Annual Review*
Hen	*Henoch*
HUCA	*Hebrew Union College Annual*
Int	*Interpretation*
ITQ	*Irish Theological Quarterly*
JAOS	*Journal of the American Oriental Society*
Jastrow	M. Jastrow, *A Dictionary of the Targumim, The Talmud Babli and Yerushalmi, and the Midrashic Literature*
JBL	*Journal of Biblical Literature*
JCS	*Journal of Cuneiform Studies*
JETS	*Journal of the Evangelical Theological Society*
JJS	*Journal of Jewish Studies*
JNES	*Journal of Near Eastern Studies*
JSOT	*Journal for the Study of the Old Testament*
JSS	*Journal of Semitic Studies*
JTS	*Journal of Theological Studies*
LSJ	Liddell–Scott–Jones, *Greek–English Lexicon*
LV	*Lumière et Vie*
NEB	*New English Bible*

NLH	*New Literary History*
NRT	*La nouvelle revue théologique*
Or	*Orientalia*
OTS	*Oudtestamentische Studiën*
PSBA	*Proceedings of the Society of Biblical Archeology*
PT	*Poetics Today*
RB	*Revue biblique*
RelS	*Religious Studies*
RevQ	*Revue de Qumran*
RHR	*Revue de l'histoire des religions*
RR	*Reformed Review*
RSV	Revised Standard Version
Sef	*Sefarad*
TCAAS	*Transactions of the Connecticut Academy of Arts and Sciences*
TLZ	*Theologische Literaturzeitung*
TynBul	*Tyndale Bulletin*
UF	*Ugarit-Forschungen*
VT	*Vetus Testamentum*
VTSup	*Vetus Testamentum*, Supplements
WTJ	*Westminster Theological Journal*
ZAW	*Zeitschrift für die alttestamentliche Wissenschaft*
ZDMG	*Zeitschrift der deutschen morgenländischen Gesellschaft*

Chapter 1

INTRODUCTION

One of the challenges of the book of Daniel is that the Septuagint (LXX)
version of the book, diverges from the Masoretic Text (MT) in significant
ways, especially, but not only, in chs. 3–6. At the same time, another
version known as Theodotion (θ) has become the well-known and better
attested Greek version of Daniel. Neither of these phenomena on their
own are unique in the Greek Bible. The apparent freedom of the translators of Job or Proverbs is well known, as are the substantial differences
in length of other texts, such as Jeremiah and portions of the former
prophets.[1] The presence of a differing Greek tradition is also a feature of
the history of the book of Esther.[2] What is unique about the Greek
translation of Daniel is that somewhere in the history of the Greek Bible
the LXX of Daniel was replaced by θ, which is much closer to the MT, as
the authoritative Greek version.

How and why this situation came about is uncertain. What can be
determined is that the two Greek versions jostled with each other for
many years from possibly the early first century BCE until at least the
time of Origen, who was aware of both.[3] By then θ was the Greek text

1.   S. Jellicoe, *The Septuagint and Modern Study* (Oxford: Oxford University
Press, 1968), pp. 316-18.
2.   Jellicoe, *The Septuagint*, p. 68.
3.   See the summaries on Theodotion in E. Würthwein, *The Text of the Old
Testament* (Oxford: Basil Blackwell, 1957), pp. 54-55, and Jellicoe, *The Septuagint*,
pp. 83-94. R.H. Charles, *A Critical and Exegetical Commentary on The Revelation
of St John* (2 vols.; Edinburgh: T. and T. Clark, 1920), I, pp. lxxx-lxxxi, demonstrates the presence of both θ and LXX influence in Revelation. G.K. Beale, 'A
Reconsideration of the Text of Daniel in the Apocalypse', *Bib* 67 (1986), pp. 540-
41, and L.P. Trudinger, 'Some Observations concerning the Text of the Old
Testament in the Book of Revelation', *JTS* 17 (1966), p. 83, argue that there is more
LXX and less θ in Revelation than Charles has allowed for. See also the summary of
L.F. Hartman and A.A. DiLella, *The Book of Daniel* (New York: Doubleday, 1978),

of Daniel favoured by Christians. Jewish opinion during the period in question is less accessible, since by the stage that Daniel was accepted into the Jewish canon, greater authority was attributed by Jews to the original Semitic languages of Scripture.

My purpose is to explore the curious situation outlined above by applying the tools of literary criticism to a comparison of the MT and the LXX of Daniel 2–7. I will do this by comparing the versions of each chapter first as discrete narratives. For form-critical reasons, which are spelled out in more detail below, I work with the chapters in the following order: 4, 5, 6, 3, 2 and 7. At each stage the links with stories already treated in each version will be explored, so gradually building up a picture of the MT and LXX, both as collections of individual narratives and as larger literary units. Finally I will undertake a brief survey of the differences between the LXX and the Hebrew in chs. 1 and 8–12 as a check on the trends detected in chs. 2–7. Two appendices supplement the argument. The first contains a survey of characteristics of θ for each chapter, although that version also receives regular mention in the main body of the book. The second appendix provides a literal English translation of the LXX in Rahlfs's edition. When I quote the LXX in English I quote from the translation of Appendix 2.

The literary approach as outlined yields results that are both literary and historical. We will see that the two versions differ markedly in the way they tell their stories as well as in the concerns that motivate them, and in the process we will gain further insight into the nature of biblical narrative and the quality of the work that resulted in the MT of Daniel.

We will also find that some light has been shed on the historical puzzles posed by these texts. The historical evidence is tantalizing for the student in that at one point it suggests a LXX which is later than the MT while at another the position is reversed. Gradually a picture emerges into focus of differing, if not competing, wisdom circles witnessed to by the two versions of Daniel 2–7 under scrutiny. These divergent outlooks,

---

pp. 76-83. Behind this lies a wider debate on the relationship of θ to the καίγε recension identified by Barthélemy. See D. Barthélemy, *Les devanciers d'Aquila* (Leiden: Brill, 1963), pp. 147-57. S. Jellicoe, 'Some Reflections on the καίγε Recension', *VT* 23 (1973), p. 24, prefers Ur-Theodotion as an explanation of early witnesses to θ. A. Schmitt, 'Die griechischen Danieltexte ("θ'" und o') und das Theodotionproblem', *BZ* 36 (1992), pp. 12-20, also differs with Barthélemy and one of Barthélemy's supporters, J.R. Busto Saiz, 'El texto teodocionico de Daniel y la traduccion de Simaco', *Sef* 40 (1980), pp. 43-49.

possibly originating as early as the Persian period, are hinted at by such things as the way the different kings are viewed, how Daniel and his friends are understood, the use made of symbols, and the picture painted of the interaction between heaven and earth.

The exact structure of each chapter will be determined by the literary form and content of the story being treated, but certain topics will recur regularly. Narrative features, such as the use of dialogue, the stance of the narrator, manipulation of perspective, and the employment of phrases, words or syntactic structures for thematic purposes, are normally treated first.[4] Then follows a discussion of differences in content between the versions, such as attitudes towards wisdom and the Gentile kings. It is there that some of the historical issues begin to emerge. In the context of my treatment of Daniel 4, the first story dealt with, I pause several times to discuss issues or define terms which are germane to the work as a whole. But before then, the remainder of this introductory section is devoted to some methodological questions raised above, and to further matters of terminology.

Limits

There are a number of areas of research upon which this study will impinge that can only be alluded to. The border drawn between them and a literary-critical comparison of Daniel 2–7 is arbitrary, but necessary to keep the discussion to manageable proportions. For example, I do not deal in depth with θ, because its closeness to the MT means that there are few differences of narrative consequence. I do not explore the textual issues in either version to the depth which they demand, as a necessary supplement to the literary criticism. The work of others on the nature of the LXX as translation is drawn on but not added to. The differences between versions in the way symbolism is handled call for a more comprehensive treatment of the relationship of texts to meaning. Most obviously, the links in the book of Daniel across all the form divisions make it clear that any treatment of less than all 12 chapters (14 if Susanna and Bel and the Dragon are included) is incomplete. I acknowledge all these areas, but am not able to include their treatment amongst

---

4.   The position of the narrator within his narration affects the reader's perception of the story. The word 'stance' pertains to that position adopted by the narrator. See S.S. Lanser, *The Narrative Act* (Princeton, NJ: Princeton University Press), p. 9, on stance.

the purposes of the present discussion. I do, however, conclude with an indication of several areas of thematic and text-historical research which would be worth revisiting in the light of the present work.

Literary or Historical Approaches

In undertaking a literary study I use the word 'literary' as the adjective from the noun 'literature', and do not intend it to denote the study of sources and 'history of literature', an earlier usage in biblical criticism.[5] Such an approach takes the LXX seriously both as a literary creation with its own integrity, and as a collection of writings that at some stage has possibly been accorded authoritative status. The LXX, particularly in Daniel, has often been treated simply as a mine of historical-critical information to be quarried in assessing the MT.[6] The results can be a confusing plethora of detail pointing in no direction and many directions at once. By approaching the text from the literary end of the literary–historical axis I seek to discover more about the LXX and its relationship to the MT, and about the world behind both versions.[7] In the imagery of Chesterton from the epigraph, the LXX version is seen as a living tree rather than a collection of twigs pointing in many directions.[8] To put it another way, textual criticism is a servant of the literary study, rather than the reverse. Fewell, in introducing her literary reading of Daniel 1–6 MT, points to such an approach to the Greek versions of the same stories as potentially 'an interesting and helpful study'.[9] In adopting this particular approach I do not deny the validity of other encounters with the text from different angles.

The application of literary criteria to scriptural material raises large questions about the respective natures of literature and sacred texts, and

5. See J. Barton, *Reading the Old Testament* (London: Darton, Longman & Todd, 1984), pp. 20-26 and 154-56, for a discussion of the difference.

6. See the comments of A. Berlin, 'Book Review of *The Redaction of the Books of Esther*', *Bib* 75 (1994), pp. 110-11, on the question of 'whether it is legitimate to read a redacted text as a monolith'.

7. Long, in his introduction to B.O. Long (ed.), *Images of Man and God* (Sheffield: Almond Press, 1981), p. 7, speaks of de-emphasizing more usual 'philological and historical concerns' in order to highlight the material 'as story'.

8. G.K. Chesterton, 'The Tremendous Adventures of Major Brown', in *Thirteen Detectives* (London: Xanadu, 1987), pp. 41-42.

9. D.N. Fewell, *Circle of Sovereignty* (Sheffield: Almond Press, 1988), p. 9.

the relationship between the two.[10] Without attempting to address those issues in a formal way, the 'literary' approach of my discussion displays two chief characteristics. First, it deals primarily with the received forms of the versions as we have them in the LXX and MT, although of course issues of composition history must impinge on that approach in places. The manner in which the stories relate to one another is part of that consideration of the received form. Secondly, it seeks to appreciate such things as 'the beauty of the text, the narrative and poetic skill of its writers, and the richness of metaphor and other figurative language which it contains'.[11] However the versions of Daniel came to be, and whatever the intentions of those involved with their compilation and creation, they contain stories that can be appreciated as literary creations within a collection that owes something of its shape to literary craftsmanship.

In a sense, what I am doing is a denial of Westcott and Hort's famous dictum 'final decision on documents should precede final decision on readings'.[12] An opposite perspective could be that literary texts should not be asked to answer the historical questions that have dominated biblical criticism.[13] Therefore, the only questions that ought to be asked of texts are those concerning their literary form. There is something of such a reaction against a historicist attitude towards the LXX in my own approach. But I also take the view expressed by Thompson that historiographical reconstruction and literary interpretation should be inseparable.[14] Just as text reconstruction is sometimes a necessary precursor to literary appreciation, so at times a literary approach can point beyond the immediate questions to the history of the texts.

As far as LXX studies are concerned, the historical–literary debate is

10. For a helpful summary, see R. Coggins, 'The Literary Approach to the Bible', *ExpTim* 96 (1984), pp. 12-14.

11. Coggins, 'Literary Approach', p. 13.

12. Cited in S.P. Cowe, *The Armenian Version of Daniel* (Atlanta: Scholars Press, 1992), p. 59.

13. M. Sternberg, *The Poetics of Biblical Narrative* (Bloomington: Indiana University Press, 1985), p. 13, reacts against 'the excesses and fruitlessness of traditional source criticism' but warns against ignoring the data it provides. See B.O. Long, 'The "New" Biblical Poetics of Alter and Sternberg', *JSOT* 51 (1991), pp. 79-83, on the attitudes of Sternberg and Alter in this field.

14. These are the terms used by T.L. Thompson, *The Origin Tradition of Ancient Israel* (Sheffield: JSOT Press, 1987), p. 39. See also the discussion by T. Longman, *Literary Approaches to Biblical Interpretation* (Grand Rapids: Zondervan, 1987), pp. 49-61, on the strengths and weaknesses of literary approaches.

epitomized in the Joint Research Venture undertaken by Barthélemy, Gooding, Lust and Tov, which resulted in *The Story of David and Goliath*. In their debate over methodology, Barthélemy and Gooding, who hold to the priority of the MT, allow the literary study to feed into their textual work on 1 Samuel 16–18, while Lust and Tov, who are for the priority of the LXX, insist that the more objective work of textual criticism must be done first, and allowed to inform the literary study.[15] More recently Auld and Ho return to the same discussion and attempt to show a way through the impasse encountered by the Joint Venture scholars by arguing that the MT is 'the recomposition of an original story'.[16] They affirm the methodological views of Lust, but at the same time espouse a position in favour of the priority of the LXX that is highly dependent on literary considerations.[17] This unfinished debate demonstrates Thompson's views on the dependence on one another of the literary and historical.

The work of Clines in *The Esther Scroll* is a widely lauded example of scholarship which holds the two aspects together. He compares the MT of Esther with the two Greek versions of the book, one similar to MT and one significantly different. His method combines a comparative literary appreciation of the three versions with source-critical work, in order to reach conclusions about how the canonical text of Esther was built up.[18] I have been influenced by Clines's approach, but place a stronger emphasis on the literary side of the equation, and am less

15. See Lust in D. Barthélemy, D.W. Gooding, J. Lust and E. Tov, *The Story of David and Goliath* (Göttingen: Editions Universitaires, 1986), pp. 121-26, on the methodological issues.

16. A.G. Auld and C.Y.S. Ho, 'The Making of David and Goliath', *JSOT* 56 (1992), p. 24.

17. Auld and Ho, 'David and Goliath', pp. 24 and 38, ask 'What about literary creation by a redactor out of existing material in 1 Samuel?' and partly conclude that their approach 'explains the literary function of all the major MT pluses...', and takes account of 'the artistic quality of the MT story'.

18. D.J.A. Clines, *The Esther Scroll* (Sheffield: JSOT Press, 1984), p. 15, says that 'we should first attempt to seize the narrative shape and direction before asking what purpose the narrative shaped in this way may be supposed to have served. The literary question must precede the historical.' Compare another recent treatment of Esther by M.V. Fox, *The Redaction of the Books of Esther* (Atlanta: Scholars Press, 1991), pp. 6 and 127-35, whose work is centred on the redactional process and whose tools are source and redaction criticism. His literary treatment of the texts is secondary.

interested in the search for a sequence of stories.[19] As a result my historical conclusions are more to do with the background to the versions than with a detailed picture of the composition of the texts.

'Literary' or 'Narrative' Criticism

In recent times a discipline known as 'narrative criticism' has been identified and begun to be codified. It is important to be clear what is meant by 'narrative criticism' as opposed to 'literary criticism'. Confusion arises because in one sense the 'narrative' may be thought of as only one aspect of the many that together form a 'literary' entity. In that respect, my work is literary because the narrative shape and the role of the narrator in the story are not the only concerns treated, even if they do form a major part. I have chosen to use the word 'literary' in the sub-title to avoid the suggestion that I do not also deal with matters such as plot, characterization, theme and pace. However, the present study owes much to the categories identified by Powell as central to the narrative-critical approach, and they go beyond the simple study of narrative aspects as part of the literary craft.[20] The starting point provided by narrative criticism also leads into treatment of other aspects of the story. In particular, because the operation of point of view is so important to an appreciation of the particular stories in question, the concept of an implied reader and an implied narrator within the text informs much of what I do.[21] So this volume could accurately be called 'narrative critical' in concern, were it not for problems of definition created by such a description.

At the same time I acknowledge the work of a number of diverse authors, such as Sternberg, Bar-Efrat, Berlin and Alter, who undertake a treatment of what they generally call biblical narrative. They do not appear to be self-consciously members of a 'narrative criticism' school yet their central concern as espoused in the titles of their books is with

---

19. Contrast L.M. Wills, *The Jew in the Court of the Foreign King* (Minneapolis: Fortress Press, 1990), p. 87, whose approach to Dan. 4–6 and Bel and the Dragon relies on genre distinction in order to identify stages in the redaction of the stories. Within this limited range of chapters he builds a detailed picture of the layers of tradition that are evident in them.

20. M.A. Powell, *What is Narrative Criticism?* (Minneapolis: Fortress Press, 1990), pp. 36-44.

21. Powell, *Narrative Criticism*, p. 19.

the narrative.[22] What they mean by narrative is clearly wider than one aspect of a literary treatment. My indebtedness to their insights is another reason why the use of the phrase 'narrative criticism' would be an inappropriate description of this study. It should be noted that most of the work of such critics has been done with the Pentateuchal and historical narratives of the Hebrew Bible, and very little in texts such as Daniel.

Form-Critical Considerations

Any work on the stories of Daniel and his friends must first define the boundaries of the text. Some deal with the Aramaic stories (chs. 2–6), some deal with all the stories (chs. 1–6), some treat the Aramaic chapters (chs. 2–7), and a few work with chs. 1–7. I have chosen to treat chs. 2–7 for various form-critical reasons. They are taken largely from the work of others and are by no means definitive, but they do provide a necessary way into the present study. The most obvious reason is that those chapters constitute the Aramaic material in the MT, but there are other factors which complement that reason.

One such factor is that there are strong echoes in ch. 7 of material that precedes it. To leave off before the first vision would be to leave the tale partly untold.[23] At the same time, there is some evidence that chs. 8–12 are a development of ch. 7 and therefore in some sense separate from it, although an exploration of that issue is beyond the scope of this book.[24] The affinity of ch. 7 with the other Aramaic material in Daniel suggests that chs. 2–7 can be treated as a unit. That leaves the question of what to do with ch. 1, which is not in Aramaic but is a story rather than a vision. It is commonly accepted that the Aramaic material of

22. Sternberg, *Poetics*; S. Bar-Efrat, *Narrative Art in the Bible* (Sheffield: Almond Press, 1989); A. Berlin, *Poetics and Interpretation of Biblical Narrative* (Sheffield: Almond Press, 1983); R. Alter, *The Art of Biblical Narrative* (London: George Allen & Unwin, 1981).

23. Fewell (*Circle of Sovereignty*) and Wills (*The Jew in the Court*) provide examples of treatments which end at ch. 6.

24. See, for example, J.A. Montgomery, *Daniel* (Edinburgh: T. & T. Clark, 1927), pp. 325-27, or L. Dequeker, 'The "Saints of the Most High" in Qumran and Daniel', *OTS* 18 (1973), p. 109. The distinction is as much literary as historical. Contrast H.H. Rowley, 'The Unity of the Book of Daniel', in *The Servant of the Lord* (London: Lutterworth Press, 1952), pp. 249-50, for whom chs. 7 and 8 are closely bound together. At the same time he sees chs. 8–12 as from a single hand.

chs. 2–7 was subsequently redacted into the Hebrew framework, which places ch. 1 as a later introduction to the final form of the book.[25] It is on the basis of that form-critical judgment that I have left ch. 1 out of consideration.

An influential point of view on the structure of chs. 2–7 in the MT has been that of Lenglet. He argues that the Aramaic stories are arranged as a chiasm with chs. 4–5 as the central pairing. Beyond this are chs. 3 and 6 as mirrors of each other in the chiasm, and chs. 3–6 together are flanked by chs. 2 and 7.[26] A number of literary factors also emerge during the course of my argument in support of Lenglet's view.[27] The chiastic structure informs the order in which I treat the narratives, beginning at the centre and moving outwards, without denying that there is also a progression between the chapters.[28]

The Septuagint as a Translation

Wherever a difference between the versions occurs, a fundamental but complex historical question arises. Does the variant represent a *Vorlage* different from the MT, or did it come about in the course of translation? To the extent that I am interested in the literary form of the

---

25. J.E. Miller, 'The Redaction of Daniel', *JSOT* 52 (1991), pp. 115-21, treats ch. 1 as part of a Hebrew collection distinct from the Aramaic Daniel collection. J.G. Gammie, 'The Classification, Stages of Growth, and Changing Intentions in the Book of Daniel', *JBL* 95 (1976), p. 195, also accepts an early form of chs. 2–7 as a distinct unit. See also the conclusion of P.A. David, 'The Composition and Structure of the Book of Daniel: A Synchronic and Diachronic Reading' (unpublished D.S.T. thesis, Katholieke Universiteit Leuven, 1991), p. 396, on ch. 1 as the work of a Maccabean editor. J.G. Baldwin, *Daniel* (Leicester: Inter-Varsity Press, 1978), p. 154, argues from a quite different perspective that chs. 2–7 are 'the nucleus of the book'.

26. A. Lenglet, 'La structure littéraire de Daniel 2–7', *Bib* 53 (1972), pp. 170-89.

27. Some genre analyses support this structure by linking chs. 4 and 5 and chs. 3 and 6 by a shared genre. That analysis also has the effect of distinguishing the pairs from each other. See, for example, the distinction of W.L Humphreys, 'A Lifestyle for Diaspora: A Study of the Tales of Esther and Daniel', *JBL* 92 (1973), pp. 217-18, between court contest and court conflict, and of H.-P. Müller, 'Märchen, Legende und Enderwartung', *VT* 26 (1976), pp. 338-41, between *Märchen* ('fairy tale') and *Legende* ('legend'). But these distinctions must be treated with caution.

28. E.M. Good, 'Apocalyptic as Comedy: The Book of Daniel', *Semeia* 32 (1984), p. 66, warns that the presence of a chiastic structure in MT should not blind us to the progression between chapters as they now stand.

LXX regardless of how it came to be, the question is not relevant. But since an awareness of the theological and political interests of each version is part and parcel of the literary study, it is important to be conscious of the different levels at which divergence could have occurred without necessarily being able to identify the reason for each one. I do not set out to produce a comprehensive treatment of every difference, but an awareness of the possibilities is an important part of the backdrop to this study.[29]

It has been amply demonstrated that the ancients were aware of the distinction between free and literal translation.[30] The LXX has been reckoned to occupy various positions on the free–literal spectrum in different books. The Pentateuch is thought of as the most literal and the opposite end of the range is reckoned to be occupied by various writings, such as Job or Proverbs.[31] In the wake of a number of studies of translation technique in the LXX, some doubt is cast on the usefulness of the distinction between free and literal translation. Instead, it is now argued that the LXX translator is always literal in intent, but in varying degrees.[32]

29. S.P. Jeansonne, *The Old Greek Translation of Daniel 7–12* (Washington, DC: Catholic Biblical Association, 1988) is an example of one who does engage in such a comprehensive treatment. See also the thesis by D.O. Wenthe, 'The Old Greek Translation of Daniel 1–6' (unpublished PhD thesis, Notre Dame University, 1991). This work came to hand too late to be incorporated into my research, but note Wenthe's conclusion (p. 247) that 'the OG can be favorably compared with Theodotion in terms of fidelity'.

30. See, for example, S.P. Brock, 'The Phenomenon of Biblical Translation in Antiquity', in S. Jellicoe (ed.), *Studies in the Septuagint: Origins, Recensions, and Interpretations* (New York: Ktav, 1974), pp. 555-56.

31. This relates to the thesis that earlier translations formed a Greek tradition that informed later translation. See I.L. Seeligmann, *The Septuagint Version of Isaiah: A Discussion of its Problems* (Leiden: Brill, 1948), p. 46, on the LXX of Isaiah influencing the translator of Daniel. See also R. Hanhart, 'The Translation of the Septuagint in Light of Earlier Tradition and Subsequent Influences', in G.J. Brooke and B. Lindars (eds.), *Septuagint, Scrolls and Cognate Writings* (Atlanta: Scholars Press, 1992), p. 363, and C. Rabin, 'The Translation Process and the Character of the Septuagint', *Textus* 6 (1968), p. 22, on the influence of the Greek Pentateuch.

32. J. Barr, *The Typology of Literalism in Ancient Biblical Translations* (Göttingen: Vandenhoeck & Ruprecht), pp. 281-84, has been especially influential. Others to note are Hanhart, 'The Translation of the Septuagint', p. 342, and A. Aejmelaeus, 'Septuagintal Translation Techniques—A Solution to the Problem of the Tabernacle Account', in Brooke and Lindars (eds.), *Septuagint, Scrolls and Cognate Writings*, p. 381. E. Tov has also worked extensively in this area: see, for

As such, his version deserves to be taken seriously as a reliable witness to his *Vorlage*.[33]

One early translator from Hebrew into Greek who articulated his thoughts on translation was the grandson of Sirach.[34] He acknowledges that his grandfather's work is different in kind from 'the law and the prophets and the rest of the books' (Sir. Prol. 24-25, ὁ νόμος καὶ αἱ προφητεῖαι καὶ τὰ λοιπὰ βιβλίων), but still struggles to find precise equivalents in the Greek. He laments his own imprecision in the face of a requirement of great precision (Sir. Prol. 20) by setting the verbs ἀδυναμέω and ἰσοδυναμέω against one another.[35] How important then must an accurate translation even of the writings have been? It seems inherently unlikely therefore that the Septuagintal translator of Daniel would have been translating a MT-like *Vorlage* at points where the versions diverge substantially.

Wright's work on the parent text of Sirach has provided us with a modern piece of research to back up that supposition. He begins with the assertion of Barr that the LXX is a literal translation, and takes up the aspects of literalism defined by Barr and Tov.[36] From there he does a computer-based comparison of several indicators of literalness in different biblical books of the LXX, as a lead in to his work on Ben Sira. His measure of word-order variations is of particular interest to us because it embraces the whole of the Old Testament including both Daniel θ and Daniel LXX. Wright measures the percentage variation of word order between the translation and its original, both including and excluding the

example, 'Loan Words, Homophony and Transliterations in the Septuagint', *Bib* 60 (1979), pp. 216-36; 'Did the Septuagint Translators always Understand their Hebrew Text?', in A. Piertsma and C. Cox (eds.), *De Septuaginta* (Mississauga: Benben Publications, 1984), pp. 53-70; and 'Three Dimensions of LXX Words', *RB* 83 (1976), pp. 529-44.

33. Note also the argument of E. Ulrich, 'The Septuagint Manuscripts from Qumran: A Reappraisal of their Value', in Brooke and Lindars (eds.), *Septuagint, Scrolls and Cognate Writings*, p. 65, that findings at Qumran confirm the importance of the LXX as a faithful witness.

34. See Brock, 'The Phenomenon of Biblical Translation', p. 555, on Sirach.

35. His lament is rounded out with the advice that could well be heeded by moderns: read it in the original.

36. B.G. Wright, *No Small Difference: Sirach's Relationship to its Hebrew Parent Text* (Atlanta: Scholars Press, 1989), pp. 27 and 270 n. 18, draws on Barr, *Typology of Literalism*, pp. 281-325, and E. Tov, *The Text Critical Use of the Septuagint in Biblical Research* (Jerusalem: Simor, 1981), pp. 53-55.

particle δέ. In the inclusive measure the most literal books in terms of word order are Song of Songs and Qohelet, with a variation of under 0.1%. Esther, Proverbs and Job, all in the 7-12% range, show the greatest variation. Daniel LXX shows a variation in word order of 2.16%, which is less than books such as Exodus, Genesis and Isaiah, and not very different from Leviticus.[37] While this measure is a crude and limited one, it is a further indicator that Daniel LXX provides a literal translation of the material in its *Vorlage*.[38]

This has a couple of consequences for the comparison I am undertaking. It suggests that the LXX, for all its apparent freedom in parts, is the work of a translator rather than a redactor. It also allows for the assumption that substantial pluses or minuses in the Greek reflect a different *Vorlage*.[39] It does not deny, though, that the Septuagintal translator conveys something of his own understanding and interests within the constraints of his search for a literal equivalent. Sometimes this comes through in a conscious attempt to clarify the original text, sometimes it is evident in an unconscious choice of synonyms, and sometimes his choice reflects the translation tradition in which he stands. While care will be taken not to read more into the text than is there, this study will be alert to differences that have more than technical significance.[40]

Some Important Terms

When wisdom in the book of Daniel is discussed a distinction is often made between 'mantic' and 'aphoristic' or 'logoic' wisdom.[41] Mantic

37. See Wright, *No Small Difference*, pp. 43-54, especially the tables on pp. 46-49.

38. Wright, *No Small Difference*, p. 33, himself cautions on the limitations of a statistical study.

39. P. Grelot, 'La Septante de Daniel 4 et son substrat sémitique', *RB* 81 (1974), pp. 19-22, argues that this *Vorlage* was Hebrew rather than Aramaic, but his view has received little support. My working assumption is that the LXX *Vorlage* was an Aramaic one.

40. Seeligmann, *The Septuagint Version of Isaiah*, p. 8, cautions against 'overrating the extent and importance of intentional changes in the text, and underestimating the part that accident may have played... in the vicissitudes leading to (the text's) final version'.

41. See, for example, A. Lacocque, *Daniel in his Time* (Columbia: University of South Carolina Press), pp. 189-92. See also the extended discussion by J.C. VanderKam, *Enoch and the Growth of an Apocalyptic Tradition* (Washington,

wisdom seeks to divine the future or is dependent on external or divine revelation for its operation. Aphoristic wisdom refers to such things as wise judgment and the exercise of statecraft. Müller expresses the difference with the terms 'mantische Weisheit' and 'Bildungsweisheit'.[42] He argues that both types of wisdom were exercised in Israel. Indeed they were combined in the person of Joseph.[43] However it is described, the distinction is reasonably clear.

Nevertheless, there is a problem in applying the term 'mantic' to Jewish wisdom, as biblical reference to it is at best ambivalent. The family of Greek words related to μαντεία almost inevitably translates קסם or one of its cognate forms (Ezek. 13.8, where חזה is so represented, is the sole exception). Sometimes the 'divination', as the RSV normally translates the term, is explicitly forbidden (Num. 23.23 and Deut. 18.10). Often it is accompanied by unflattering adjectives, such as 'worthless' or 'false' (Jer. 14.14 and Ezek. 21.23). Only on one occasion in the Hebrew scriptures is קסם used in an unreservedly positive sense. That is at Prov. 16.10 where the king is said to possess קסם. Yet there is also a strand that suggests some ambiguity about the term. The most famous instance is the story of Saul's encounter with the medium at Endor in 1 Sam. 28.8-25. In response to Saul's command to her to 'divine for me' (קסומי־נא לי), the medium called up the spirit of Samuel which produced a word from the Lord that is unquestioned by the narrative. In some of the prophets the 'diviners' are figures in Israel who exercise a harmful ministry, but there is a hint that it need not be so (for example Mic. 3.7-11). In Jeremiah's letter to the remaining elders of Jerusalem 'your prophets' (Jer. 29/36.8, נביאיכם) are spoken of in the same breath as 'your diviners' (קסמיכם).

The generally negative view of wisdom that is described as 'mantic', if not of the function itself, means that the wisdom of Daniel ideally ought not to be so described. To a certain extent it has been imposed by the secondary literature. Nevertheless, it serves a useful function, and a more neutral alternative does not appear to be available to us. At the same

DC: Catholic Biblical Association of America, 1984), pp. 52-75, on mantic divination and Jewish apocalypticism.

42. H.-P. Müller, 'Mantische Weisheit und Apocalyptic', in J.A. Emerton *et al.* (eds.), *Congress Volume Uppsala 1971* (VTSup, 22; Leiden: Brill, 1972), pp. 271-79 etc. See also Wills, *The Jew in the Court*, p. 80, who speaks of courtly wisdom (in chs. 3 and 6) and mantic wisdom (in chs. 2, 4 and 5).

43. Müller, 'Mantische Weisheit', pp. 274-75.

time, it does express what seems to be the MT understanding of Daniel's function as not so very different in kind from that of his Babylonian counterparts. Accordingly, I follow the lead of others in using 'mantic' to describe a type of Israelite wisdom, but with caution.

A number of genre analyses have been applied to Daniel in recent times, most of which have some problems.[44] Milne has applied morphological categories to the stories with limited success, the influential distinction made by Humphreys between court conflict and contest breaks down at some points under literary analysis, and Müller's delineations are heavily dependent on his historical approach to the texts.[45] Sometimes also assumptions about genre can limit the literary analysis, as will become clear at one or two points in our discussion of the texts. Consequently I do not seek to provide well-defined genre classifications for each story where others have tried and failed to agree.[46] I do, however, work with an awareness that the stories differ from one another, and that the differences may at least partly be understood in terms of genre.

The description of material in either of the versions as 'plus' or 'minus' will be employed as a shorthand way of denoting text in one version that is absent in the other. The terms should not be taken to imply any views on the priority of one of the versions over another.

Reference to the translator in the third person singular is another shorthand usage which does not address the question of how many people worked on the LXX translation of Daniel 2–7. There may have been one translator or many separate ones, or the translation may have been the result of the activity of a school. For ease of expression, all the possibilities are present in the term 'the translator'.

The historicity or otherwise of the book of Daniel is not a subject of

---

44. See the summary of Wills, *The Jew in the Court*, pp. 3-19, and the discussion in Gammie, 'The Classification', p. 192, on sub-genres within what he terms the 'composite literary genre' of apocalyptic literature.

45. See P.J. Milne, *Vladimir Propp and the Study of Structure in Hebrew Biblical Narrative* (Sheffield: Almond Press, 1988), pp. 126-59, on the difficulties in agreeing on morphological functions in the Daniel stories. See Humphreys, 'Lifestyle', pp. 217-18, on court contest and conflict, and Müller, 'Märchen, Legende', pp. 338-39. Note also S. Niditch and R. Doran, 'The Success Story of the Wise Courtier: A Formal Approach', *JBL* 96 (1977), p. 180, on the literary type of the story in Dan. 2.

46. Longman, *Literary Approaches*, p. 81, while stressing the importance of genre identification, warns against pigeon-holing texts.

this monograph. Reference to events in the lives of Daniel and his companions as 'stories' is not intended as a judgment on that particular issue. A story is simply a crafted account of events.[47] I use 'story' roughly synonymously with 'narrative', although ch. 7 also proves to be a narrative of sorts whereas stories are distinguished from visions.

The 'Old Greek' is not quite the same thing as the 'LXX'. Jeansonne defines the Old Greek as 'the oldest recoverable form of the first translation into Greek' of the Semitic texts.[48] The LXX as we have it is largely based on the Old Greek but also has its own transmission history. The two terms can be used synonymously, but there are times when a distinction must be preserved.

There is considerable diversity in the way the terms 'version', 'revision' and 'recension' are used. I refer throughout to both the MT and the LXX as 'versions' rather than 'revisions' or 'recensions'. I base my usage on Würthwein who says that a version is a translation from another language, whereas a recension is a revision of a previously translated version.[49] I suspect that he uses the word 'recension' synonymously with 'revision'. The key distinction is between 'version' and 'recension/revision'.[50] It is clear that the LXX can be spoken of as a version. However, if a version is a translation then the MT cannot be so described. At that point I take refuge in non-technical English usage where a version can be a variant or a form of something else. In that respect, the MT and LXX are both versions, in that they are both variations on a common tradition. So 'version' functions as a useful generic term which includes the MT and LXX for the purposes of my argument.

Textual Witnesses to the Septuagint

Because the LXX of Daniel was eclipsed so early in the present era, there are only three manuscript witnesses to it. The first is manuscript R. vii.45 in the Chigi library in Rome, known to us as 88, according to

---

47. See the discussion of R.W.L. Moberly, *From Eden to Golgotha* (Atlanta: Scholars Press, 1992), p. 113, on 'story, history and truth' in the Old Testament.

48. Jeansonne, *Daniel 7–12*, p. 8.

49. Würthwein, *The Text of the Old Testament*, pp. 49 and 57. But contrast Jellicoe in *The Septuagint*, who seems to understand revision and recension in different ways but never defines exactly how.

50. In light of this distinction, there is obviously debate over whether θ is a version in its own right or a revision. See Würthwein, *The Text of the Old Testament*, p. 54. For convenience I refer to θ as a version.

the manuscript numbering system of Göttingen (87 according to Field and Swete). Other evidence is in the Codex Syro-hexaplaris Ambrosianus, a Syriac translation of the Hexaplaric Greek, preserving the asterisks and obeli of Origen. This is referred to as Syh. Largely confirming the Chigi manuscript 88 is the Chester Beatty Papyrus known as 967.[51] Daniel is incomplete in 967, but since the work of Geissen and Hamm on the portions at Cologne, there is much more available than there used to be.[52] The ordering of chapters in the Chester Beatty Papyrus differs from the other witnesses in that chs. 7 and 8 appear between chs. 4 and 5, a fact that has some bearing on the discussion that follows.

The two major modern editions of the LXX of Daniel are contained in Rahlfs and the volume edited by Ziegler in the Göttingen project. Both present the LXX and θ in parallel to one another. Because it is beyond the scope and purpose of the present study to assess all the textual variants in the Greek, unless indicated otherwise, the Rahlfs edition is the basis of what follows in the main body of the book as well as the translation of Appendix 2. Differences between the Rahlfs and Göttingen editions are noted where appropriate. Most disagreements arise from the availability to Ziegler of Kenyon's earlier less complete edition of 967. Because of its more eclectic approach, Göttingen shows a preference for the pre-hexaplaric evidence of 967 in a number of places. Since Ziegler did his work on the Göttingen edition (1954), the Cologne portions of the papyrus have become available and there are points in the text at which I accept the Cologne witness of 967 against both Rahlfs and Göttingen. The LXX versification in Rahlfs is the one that I shall observe. Where this differs from the MT, both options will be cited unless it is plain from the context that the reference is to one version in particular.

51. F.C. Kenyon, *The Chester Beatty Biblical Papyri* (London: Emery Walker, 1937), p. xi.

52. A. Geissen (ed.), *Der Septuaginta-Text des Buches Daniel 5–12 sowie Esther 1–2.15 nach dem Kölner Teil des Papyrus 967* (Bonn: Rudolf Habelt Verlag, 1968); W. Hamm (ed.), *Der Septuaginta-Text des Buches Daniel Kap 1-2 nach dem Teil des Papyrus 967* (Bonn: Rudolf Habelt Verlag, 1969); and W. Hamm (ed.), *Der Septuaginta-Text des Buches Daniel Kap 3-4 nach dem Teil des Papyrus 967* (Bonn: Rudolf Habelt Verlag, 1977). There is also a portion of Daniel in 967 in a fragment in Barcelona published by R. Roca-Puig, 'Daniele: Due semifogli del codice 967: P.Barc. inv. nn. 42 e 43', *Aegyptus* 56 (1976), pp. 3-18, as cited in J.J. Collins, *Daniel* (Minneapolis: Fortress Press, 1993), p. 4.

Chapter 2

DANIEL 4

Apart from form-critical considerations, the story of Daniel and Nebuchadnezzar's dream of the great tree (3.31–4.34 MT, 4.1-37 in Rahlfs's edition of both Greek versions) is a good place to begin the literary comparison, because the greatest surface divergence between the MT and the Old Greek in Daniel 2–7 is found in this story. A comparison of the two accounts reveals a number of literary and theological points that will recur in our study of other chapters in Daniel.

The MT and LXX tell the same story to markedly different effect and for different purposes. I begin with a look at the different ways in which each version of the story arranges its material and, as part of that, the different characterization of Daniel. From there I consider narrative person and the use of dialogue, and how these aspects affect point of view.[1] Relevant to that part of the argument is a consideration of the events that lie behind the tradition. I then explore the difference between symbol and allegory with respect to the two stories. In doing so I notice variations in the way the myth of the great tree is applied, and additions to the telling and the application on the part of the LXX version. The discussion ends with a comment on literary merit in the LXX version.

---

1. F.K. Stanzel, *A Theory of Narrative* (trans. C. Goedsche; Cambridge: Cambridge University Press, 1984), p. 9, identifies two overlapping functions of point of view or viewpoint. One denotes the attitude of a narrator or character towards a question. The other concerns the standpoint from which a story is narrated. Lanser, *The Narrative Act*, p. 18, expresses the concept similarly when she says point of view combines ideology and technique. While the complexities of some modern analyses of point of view in a text, such as that by J.M. Lotman (trans. L.M. O'Toole), 'Point of View in a Text', *NLH* 6 (1975), pp. 339-52, are not so applicable to biblical narrative, the different aspects highlighted by Lanser and Stanzel are borne in mind by the present treatment. I employ the word 'perspective' almost synonymously with point of view, but with a tendency to use it more to denote standpoint, Stanzel's second function of point of view.

On occasions in this chapter, I pause to consider issues that have some application to the immediate context of Daniel 4 but are also foundational to my discussion as a whole. The first of these looks at literary questions concerning the place and function of the narrator in biblical narrative, his reliability or otherwise, the extent of his knowledge, his relationship to the implied author, and the relationship between God and the narrator. These are matters particularly highlighted by the use of a first person narrator in ch. 4. The second cluster of questions is theological or thematic, and relates to the different types of wisdom evident in the versions of the Daniel stories. It contains such topics as the distinction between allegory and symbol, the nature of interpretation, and the relationship between mantic wisdom and apocalyptic. Coverage of the second group of questions begins with Daniel 4, but will emerge with greater clarity as we work through Daniel 2–7.

Arrangement of Material

The surface level of the stories told is the same in essentials. A relaxed King Nebuchadnezzar is upset by a frightening dream about a great tree which shelters and sustains many. By some agency of heavenly beings the tree is destroyed but its root-stock is left in the ground. Daniel is called to interpret the dream, and to his horror he discerns that it applies to the king himself. He interprets, then begs the king to reconsider his attitudes and life-style in the light of the interpretation. Twelve months after the dream and its interpretation Nebuchadnezzar suffers the predicted fate and endures seven units of time as an outcast from human society. Upon his acknowledgment of God's sovereignty, he is reinstated and declares throughout the empire his submission to God.

These matters are agreed upon between the versions, but there are two ways in which the arrangement of the material is different. First, the material in vv. 3-6 MT is not represented in the LXX. This comprises an introduction to the person of Daniel, the beginning of an account of the dream, and the failure of the wise men of the kingdom to interpret it. In the LXX version the magicians do not appear at all, and are not even mentioned at the entrance of Daniel in v. 18. The aspect of the court contest is thus entirely absent.[2]

---

2. Note in Humphreys, 'Lifestyle', p. 217, the difference between a court contest and a court conflict. See also J.J. Collins, *The Apocalyptic Vision of the Book of Daniel* (Ann Arbor: Scholars Press, 1977), p. 33. In a contest an unknown figure

In the MT this material serves as a link with the other court stories in Daniel. The tension builds until 'finally' (v. 5, עד אחרין) Daniel makes his appearance.[3] Immediately the reader is put in mind of the figure from ch. 2 who vied at greater length with the same group of functionaries, and ultimately prevailed to become 'chief' (רב) of all of them. On his first appearance in ch. 4 the link is made by introducing him in that capacity as 'chief of the magicians' (v. 6, רב חרטמיא). In contrast, the story of Nebuchadnezzar and the dream of the great tree stands alone in the LXX. This could reflect a reluctance on the part of the LXX to see Daniel in the same category as the mantic officials, hence a lack of interest in the court contest form. Or it could be that the LXX witnesses to a stage of transmission when the stories in the Daniel cycle were still relatively independent of each other. A third option is that both possibilities obtain. The form of the story in its *Vorlage* points to an early stage in its composition history, but at the same time the treatment of that *Vorlage* shows the interests of the translator.

The second major difference is in the placing of the epistolary material. In the MT the events are presented as if recounted in a letter to the subjects of Nebuchadnezzar. There are greetings and a statement of purpose at the beginning. In the final verse the phrase 'Now I, Nebuchadnezzar...' (v. 34, כען אנה נבוכדנצר) functions as a kind of signing off. At times in between, the letter form becomes incidental to the flow of narrative and dialogue but the first-person narrator serves as a reminder of its presence. There is a sense that the epistle is a deliberately crafted form. Moreover, the device of the epistle provides a reason for the sovereign to speak autobiographically in this chapter, as opposed to the other stories about kings in the first part of Daniel. In that sense it contributes to the continuity of narrative with what precedes and what follows ch. 4.

The epistolary form does not inform the narrative of the LXX version in the same way. The story starts straight in with 'In the eighteenth year of King Nebuchadnezzar, he said:' (῎Ετους ὀκτωκαιδεκάτου τῆς βασιλείας Ναβουχοδονοσορ εἶπεν). There is no hint of an encyclical at this stage, and it is not clear exactly who is being spoken to by the first-person narrator, or for what purpose. Only in the last two verses

---

bests the established courtiers and is granted rank, whereas a conflict is between courtly figures as a result of which the victor is confirmed in his position.

3.   C.C. Torrey, 'Notes on the Aramaic Part of Daniel', *TCAAS* 15 (1909), p. 267, translates עד אחרין as 'But at last'.

(vv. 37b-38) does the suggestion of a letter come in, yet even here the situation is confused. The narrative does not take the form of a letter but tells that King Nebuchadnezzar wrote an 'encyclical' (v. 37b, ἐπιστολὴν ἐγκύκλιον), then follows with a report of its contents in direct speech. Verse 37b is an approximation of the concluding remarks in v. 34 MT. However, v. 37c represents, somewhat more closely, the salutation in 3.31-33 MT. The words ἔθνεσι, χώραις, and οἰκοῦσιν correspond to MT, with the datives reflecting the prefixed ל of the Aramaic. In a turn of phrase strongly reminiscent of 3.32 MT, v. 37c LXX even states, 'now I will show you the works...' (νῦν ὑποδείξω ὑμῖν τὰς πράξεις), yet it comes in after the summing up of v. 37b. In the present form of the narrative the final verse of the LXX appears misplaced. Possibly the redactor or translator was more interested in its confessional material than its place in the story, and so placed it with v. 37b as an extension of Nebuchadnezzar's confession.[4]

Person of the Narrator

The MT plus material of vv. 3-6 and the different uses made of the epistolary form are substantial variations in the material of the MT and the LXX. But below the surface of the stories there are other important differences. Reference has already been made to the use of the first-person narrator. In the MT Nebuchadnezzar reports in the first person through the device of the letter, but this is not sustained throughout the story. At the moment that Daniel is called to interpret the king's dream (v. 16), there is a shift to the third person which continues until Nebuchadnezzar emerges from his madness and his understanding returns (v. 31). The final four verses are in the first person. Much ink has been spilled over the reasons for the change. Earlier commentators tended towards the view that this was merely due to carelessness on the part of 'the story-teller'.[5] Others, such as Delcor, take more account of the story's

---

4. R.H. Charles, *A Commentary on Daniel* (Oxford: Clarendon Press, 1929), p. 80, believes the LXX retains the original order. Grelot, 'La Septante', p. 17, turns Charles's argument on its head. Collins, *Daniel*, p. 221, steers a middle path with the comment that 'both the MT and the OG appear to have undergone redactional development'.

5. For example, Charles, *Daniel*, p. 81, and C.C. Torrey, *Ezra Studies* (Chicago: University of Chicago Press, 1910), p. 146 n. 13. Montgomery, *Daniel*, p. 223, an exception in his era, disagreed. More recently, Collins, *Daniel*, p. 229, has spoken of authorial 'failure'.

plot.[6] He notes three main sections—the dream, its interpretation and its fulfillment—and connects the third-person material with the middle section in his plot structure. A limitation of that analysis is that it does not explain why the third-person narration continues to v. 31 where we would have expected it to end at v. 24 after the interpretation. However, the value of his approach is that it treats the material in literary terms, and in that respect points towards more recent narrative critical treatments of the shift between first and third person.[7]

It is appropriate that Nebuchadnezzar's madness is recounted by another. Within the framework of the letter, it allows the king to acknowledge it, but spares him the telling of it.[8] However, if that were the only reason for the shift, we would expect it to occur at v. 25, 'All this came upon Nebuchadnezzar' (כלא מטא על־נבוכדנצר). But it comes earlier, at the moment that Daniel begins to respond to the king's request for an interpretation. This allows the narrator to convey the otherwise unknowable information that Daniel's 'thoughts frightened him' (v. 16, רעינהי יבהלנה). At the same time it provides a change in perspective from Nebuchadnezzar to Daniel. The retelling of the dream, the interpretation, and the diplomatic problem of its application are all viewed through Daniel's eyes, although he himself is not telling the story. An analogy may be drawn from the medium of film, in which a change in point of view can be represented by changing the camera angle.[9] Once Nebuchadnezzar recovers, the story is his again, the camera angle changes, and the first person is restored. Such a shift in point of view is made possible through the introduction of the third person, without destroying the effect of the wider narrative framework. Had Nebuchadnezzar spoken autobiographically of Daniel's response and interpretation, the importance of Daniel's viewpoint, as distinct from the king's, would have been diminished.[10]

6. M. Delcor, *Le livre de Daniel* (Paris: Gabalda, 1971), p. 108.

7. Fewell, *Circle of Sovereignty*, p. 97, for example.

8. Montgomery, *Daniel*, p. 223, recognizes this and attributes it to 'an unconscious dramatic sense'. Hartman and DiLella, *Daniel*, p. 174, take up the same point.

9. See Berlin, *Poetics*, p. 44. This analogy will prove useful in my analyses of other Daniel stories also. It is not dissimilar to the concept of camera-eye technique sometimes employed by novelists. See the discussion by Stanzel, *A Theory of Narrative*, pp. 232-34, who observes that the 'camera-eye technique does not permit a distinction between first- and third-person reference'.

10. W.C. Booth, *The Rhetoric of Fiction* (Chicago: University of Chicago Press, 1961), p. 282, describes the same phenomenon in modern fiction thus: 'If granting

The use of narrative person in the LXX is more complicated. We have seen that there are two elements of the story conveyed in the third-person segment of the MT: Daniel's interpretation, and the king's madness. The LXX preserves the perspective of Nebuchadnezzar, the first-person narrator, for both elements. The reader does not see Daniel interpreting a dream so much as the king receiving an interpretation. Editorial omniscience is permitted Nebuchadnezzar at the point where he says that 'Daniel marvelled' (v. 19, ἐθαύμασεν) and the real meaning 'dismayed' (v. 19, κατέσπευδεν) him.[11] But there is also more description of Daniel's outward aspect, which would have struck the eye-witness narrator: fearful trembling seized him, and the sight of him changed, and his head 'shook for a moment' (v. 19, φοβηθεὶς τρόμου λαβόντος αὐτὸν καὶ ἀλλοιωθείσης τῆς ὁράσεως αὐτοῦ κινήσας τὴν κεφαλήν). The second element is the description of the king's madness. The MT narrator describes it in v. 30 briefly and baldly, almost as an anticlimax. The LXX here also retains the first person for Nebuchadnezzar to describe his own experience (v. 33a), and in more detail than the MT narrator. This may not be inappropriate to a story-teller who perceived Nebuchadnezzar's banishment to be as much a political exile as a personal illness.

The third-person segment in the LXX occurs at vv. 28-33, and coincides with the interval between Daniel's plea to Nebuchadnezzar to reform his ways in the light of the dream, and the onset of the king's troubles. Thus it functions differently from the MT segment of third person. Whether by design or by accident of textual history, it simply links two parts of the story as told by the king. It does not serve to manipulate point of view, nor does it relieve Nebuchadnezzar of having to describe his own period in exile.

The difference may partly be explained by the composite nature of the LXX or its *Vorlage*.[12] Material appears to have been used in vv. 25/28-28/31 common to the MT and LXX, with the insertion by the LXX of the theme of usurpation and imprisonment (vv. 31-32). These verses are part of the third-person section in the MT. If this common material has

---

the hero the right to reflect his own story can insure the reader's sympathy, with-holding it from him and giving it to another character can prevent too much identification...'

11. Bar-Efrat, *Narrative Art*, pp. 23-45, distinguishes between overt and covert narration and editorial and neutral omniscience.

12. Montgomery, *Daniel*, p. 248, calls it 'manifestly composite'.

been inserted at some stage by another tradition represented in the LXX, the join occurs in the middle of a reported speech where Daniel is addressing King Nebuchadnezzar, just as in the MT equivalent (v. 24). The LXX narrator continues the story in v. 28 at the end of the speech and simply retains the third person of the material it is incorporating. When the LXX diverges again from the MT the voice from heaven is being reported. The change in narrative person of the different source is not apparent until the end of that speech and the return of the narrator with the phrase 'I, Nebuchadnezzar' (v. 33a, ἐγὼ Ναβουχοδονοσορ). Rather than the third person of the MT narrative being a sign of a forgetful redactor, it is more likely that the smaller piece of third person in LXX (vv. 28-33) is the result of editorial activity.[13]

The Narrator in Biblical Literature

The matters discussed and terms used so far raise wide-ranging questions about the nature of the biblical narrator. To what extent is his point of view identified with God's? What is meant by omniscience when we speak of biblical narrative? Is God a character within or a narrator of the story? The questions come more sharply than usual into focus in a study of Daniel 4 because this is an extended piece of first-person narrative, a rarity in biblical literature, and it contains direct speech within the first-person narrative. Answers to these questions will inform our study of the text throughout, and a summary of the issues involved is in order at this point. In the process it will be possible to make some useful distinctions.

The first one is between 'story' and 'discourse'.[14] Story constitutes characters and events, and the world in which those characters exist and events happen. Discourse, on the other hand, is the means by which the narrator invests the story with meaning and conveys that to the reader. Discourse analysis therefore considers how a story is used by a particular narrator. In making the distinction between discourse and story we are able to distinguish between the point of view of the narrator and that of characters within the story. A particular character may reflect the narrative perspective or may be the subject of critique by the narrator. There are also characters employed simply to facilitate plot development.

---

13. Note again Grelot, 'La Septante', p. 17, and Charles, *Daniel*, p. 81.

14. G. Savran, *Telling and Retelling: Quotation in Biblical Narrative* (Bloomington: Indiana University Press, 1988), pp. 15-16.

In the context of Daniel we will see various ways by which the narrator
identifies Daniel's outlook as his own and leads the reader to do the
same. In observing these things we are differentiating between story and
discourse, whether or not the terminology is used.[15]

This raises the question of the different ways in which the narrator
functions within the story. In answering it, Bar-Efrat makes a distinction
between the 'covert' and 'overt' narrator.[16] These may be thought of as
extremes at either end of a continuum rather than absolute categories.
Every story contains a narrative presence of some sort, however mini-
mal, but the profile of the narrator varies. At the discourse level, the
activity of the narrator is in some degree covert or overt in the measures
he takes to manipulate the story and thus to influence the reader.
Biblical narrators are generally more covert than overt in their activity.
Little knowledge is shared with the reader that cannot be deduced from
the speech and actions of the characters, or particular aspects of the setting highlighted by the narrator, or devices such as repetition or shifts in
perspective. Scholars have spoken of this phenomenon in various ways.
For Alter this type of narrative is intrinsic to the monotheism of the
Bible.[17] For Bar-Efrat it means that the reader of the Bible must perceive things as we do in real life, so that a picture gradually and dynami-
cally emerges.[18] In that respect biblical narrative can be said to be
'realistic'.[19] Bar-Efrat says the value of the covert narratorial stance is
that it enables a more effective transmission of the narrator's values,

15. See Powell, *Narrative Criticism*, p. 23, on the importance of the
story/discourse distinction when handling point of view.

16. Bar-Efrat, *Narrative Art*, p. 32. Berlin, *Poetics*, p. 99, uses the less neutral
term 'intrusion' to signify a more overt narrator

17. This quote in Alter, *Biblical Narrative*, p. 155, summarizes his attitude to the
story-tellers of the Bible: 'Habitants of a tiny and often imperfectly monotheistic
island in a vast and alluring sea of paganism, they wrote with an intent... of fulfilling
or perpetuating through the act of writing a momentous revolution in consciousness'.

18. Bar-Efrat, *Narrative Art*, p. 89. Booth, *Rhetoric*, pp. 211-12, calls this
'telling as showing'.

19. E. Auerbach, *Mimesis: The Representation of Reality in Western Literature*
(trans. W.R. Trask; Princeton, NJ: Princeton University Press, 1953), pp. 15 and
23, speaks of biblical literature as 'representation of reality', and says the Bible
claims of itself that it is 'the only real world'. But S. Prickett, 'Poetics and Narrative,
Biblical Criticism and the Nineteenth-Century Novel', in D. Jaspar and T.R. Wright
(eds.), *The Critical Spirit and the Will to Believe* (London: MacMillan Press, 1989),
p. 15, cautions against making analogies with prose realism.

although he does not attach the same theological significance to the method as Alter.[20] We have begun to see that the MT narrator of Daniel is more covert than his LXX counterpart, and this results in a more multi-faceted story. This is a difference that also pertains in other stories of Daniel.

Closely connected to the distinction between the covert and overt narrator is a further distinction between 'neutral' and 'editorial' LXX omniscience.[21] These too should not be thought of as absolute categories.[22] It is in the nature of storytelling that narrators are omniscient, but there are different ways that the omniscience is experienced by the story's readers. More overt narrators display their omniscience editorially from outside the story and thus enable readers to share their omniscient perspective. The omniscience of covert narrators is more neutral. They remain largely within their story and draw readers to their point of view by various arts, which it is part of the purpose of this book to explore.[23] In the process alert readers gain more knowledge than any of the characters within the story. Again, generally speaking the omniscience of the MT narrator of Daniel is more neutral while that of the LXX is more editorial. This point will become more obvious as our literary comparison of the Daniel stories proceeds.

Any attempt to produce a modern theory of narrative has to face the fact that some narrators are reliable and others are not, while some are more fallible than others.[24] There is no unanimity on the question of whether or not the biblical narrator may be relied on. A number of scholars would say that the narrator's perspective can be identified with God's. In the preliminary stages of his study, Booth asserts that the narrator of Job, and by implication the biblical narrator generally, is utterly reliable.[25] Savran speaks of the trustworthiness of the narrator while Sternberg emphasizes the narrator's authority.[26] For Alter, the narrator knows what God knows.[27] Gunn, however, disagrees on the grounds

20. Bar-Efrat, *Narrative Art*, p. 33.

21. Bar-Efrat, *Narrative Art*, p. 23.

22. Booth, *Rhetoric*, p. 150, is an example of a critic of modern realistic literature who recognizes the inadequacy of the term 'omniscience' as an absolute category.

23. Booth, *Rhetoric*, p. 282, calls them 'major devices of disclosure and evaluation'.

24. See for example the analysis of Booth, *Rhetoric*, pp. 158-59.

25. Booth, *Rhetoric*, p. 4.

26. Savran, *Telling and Retelling*, p. 76, and Sternberg, *Poetics*, pp. 77 and 98.

27. Alter, *Biblical Narrative*, p. 157.

that the narrator neither is nor claims to be all-knowing.[28] No evidence
emerges during the course of this study that the perspective of the narrator in Daniel is in any sense unreliable. By that I mean that the attitude
which the narrator induces in the reader towards events and characters
in the stories is that of the implied author.[29]

The implied author is a construct in the reader's mind and as such
plays a part within the narrative.[30] The attitudes and perspectives so
displayed by the implied author need not coincide with those of the
actual author. However, since we cannot be certain of the actual authors
of the ancient texts of Daniel, no distinction can be made between them.
Because the narrator is reliable, he or she is also virtually identical to the
implied author. The fact that Nebuchadnezzar tells the story of his own
dream and its subsequent interpretation places a strain on that coincidence, and for the only time in the stories of Daniel a gap appears
between narrator and implied author. The problem for the implied
author in Daniel 4 is how to ensure that his or her own point of view
rather than Nebuchadnezzar's prevails. That end is achieved in the MT
through the inclusion of a third-person section and the device of the
epistle, aspects that are discussed above. In addition, the appearance and
speech of the angel (v. 14) shifts responsibility for the story away from
Nebuchadnezzar and onto the implied author. By way of contrast,
Nebuchadnezzar does seem to be given considerable responsibility for
his own story in the LXX and the smaller amount of third-person material is not sufficient to disturb that.

None of this articulates the relationship between God and the implied
author or his reliable narrator, a problem peculiar to biblical literature.
The working proposition generally adopted is that the narrator's perspective can be identified with that of God, and therefore God is understood to be the implied author. However, there is a tendency for critics
to find solace in theological assertions when addressing this question.[31]
The tension is inherent in the fact that God not only functions effectively

28. D.M. Gunn, 'Reading Right, Reliable and Omniscient Narrator, Omniscient
God, and Foolproof Composition in the Hebrew Bible', in D.J.A. Clines,
S.E. Fowl and S.E. Porter (eds.), *The Bible in Three Dimensions* (Sheffield: JSOT
Press, 1990), pp. 60-61.

29. See Bar-Efrat, *Narrative Art*, p. 14, on the distinction between narrator and
implied author.

30. Powell, *Narrative Criticism*, pp. 19-21.

31. Savran, p. 88, *Telling and Retelling*, for example.

as the narrator but he also sometimes enters the story as one of the characters to be encountered by the reader as other characters are encountered.[32] Whether or not the literary phenomenon of God's presence within and outside biblical narrative will ever be able to be reduced to a proposition, it is a paradox evident in Daniel 4, as becomes clear when the use of dialogue in each version is considered.

The Nature of the King's Exile

Aside from literary considerations, the differing use of the third-person narrator may partly be explained as a consequence of the different views of the versions on what happened in the seven 'times' (עִדָּנִין, MT; καιροί, θ) or 'years' (ἔτη, LXX). The MT sees this as a period of some sort of mental derangement on the part of the king. His heart was altered 'from that of men' (v. 13, מִן־אֲנוֹשָׁא יְשַׁנּוֹן), and at the end of the time Nebuchadnezzar's 'understanding returned' (v. 31, מַנְדְּעִי...יְתוּב). Consequent on that was his confirmation in the kingdom (v. 33). This bears some likeness to the 'Prayer of Nabonidus', which tells of the king's exile in Teiman, although there it is a result of some sort of physical rather than mental suffering (שַׁחְנָא).[33] In the LXX view there is also an element of mental illness or distress as vividly described in the phrase 'My flesh was changed, as well as my heart' (v. 33b, ἠλλοιώθη ἡ σάρξ μου καὶ ἡ καρδία μου). It is impossible to say whether mental suffering followed on physical banishment or brought it about, but both aspects are present. There is a strong suggestion as well that Nebuchadnezzar was usurped and imprisoned. This is expressed most clearly in v. 25. In the allegory of the great tree the felling represents a banishment, and eating 'the grass of the earth with the beasts of the earth' (v. 17a, τὸν χόρτον τῆς γῆς μετὰ τῶν θηρίων τῆς γῆς) represents the time in the wilderness.

These events suggested by the LXX account recall the 'Nabonidus

32. See, for example, Bar-Efrat, *Narrative Art*, p. 19. Gunn, 'Reading Right', pp. 60-61, also notes that at such moments God can seem neither omnipotent nor omniscient. But that particular quandary is not encountered in Daniel.

33. J.T. Milik, 'Prière de Nabonide', *RB* 63 (1956), p. 408. Lacocque, *Daniel in his Time*, p. 63, suggests that 4QPrNab points to a 'remote common source'. But note the doubts expressed by F. García Martínez, *Qumran and Apocalyptic: Studies on the Aramaic Texts from Qumran* (Leiden: Brill, 1992), pp. 129-35, about the dependence of Daniel on the Prayer of Nabonidus. See also D.J. Wiseman, *Nebuchadrezzar and Babylon* (Oxford: Oxford University Press, 1985), p. 104.

Chronicle' and 'The Verse Account of Nabonidus', in which sources the king is absent for long periods of time in the city of Teiman.[34] His exile was to some extent self-imposed, but there also appears to have been conflict between the king and the Babylonian establishment. This possibly related to Nabonidus's espousal of the cult of Sin, the moon god, which resulted in opposition to the king from the priests and helps explain their reference to his madness.[35] Leaving aside for the moment the question of whether or not Nabonidus is to be found in the Daniel tales, these ancient Near Eastern sources suggest a common tradition of some sort of royal exile, which has received divergent interpretations by the two versions of Daniel 4. The LXX seems to take us a little closer to the political events behind the fulfillment of Nebuchadnezzar's dream.

From a literary perspective the emphasis of the LXX account on exile, rather than madness, makes it more appropriate for Nebuchadnezzar to retain the narrative point of view in the way that he does. His words thus become a kind of apologia and it is not so necessary as in the MT to spare him the recounting of his madness. This also has a bearing on the characterization of Daniel in the two stories. In effect he has little more personality in the LXX than the mysterious Jew in the 'Prayer of Nabonidus'. In both versions he is portrayed as having a collegial rather than adversarial relationship with the king, but he plays a more prominent role in the MT because God's judgment is conveyed to Nebuchadnezzar from Daniel's point of view. In the LXX he is a functionary in the king's personal account of what happened to him.

Wisdom in Daniel

This raises a point that is central to the characterization of Daniel in the stories of his interactions with different kings. What is the nature of wisdom evident in Daniel and his relationship with the Babylonian officials? Lacocque distinguishes between mantic and aphoristic wisdom. He does not define mantic wisdom but seems to associate it with the ecstatic experiences of the visionary. Ezekiel is cited as an example of such wisdom, and the experience of Daniel in 7.28 and 8.27 is thought of in the same terms.[36] Müller and VanderKam go farther and link

34. *ANET*, pp. 305-306 and 312-15.

35. J. Lewy, 'The Late Assyro-Babylonian Cult of the Moon and its Culmination at the Time of Nabonidus', *HUCA* 19 (1945–46), p. 437.

36. Lacocque, *Daniel in his Time*, pp. 185-89.

mantic wisdom to divination, the seer's claim to special enlightenment, and the encoding of reality in symbols.[37]

Lacocque thinks of the distinction in chronological terms.[38] As prophecy shifted from shamanic or mystical to 'logoic', so wisdom shifted from mantic or 'primitive' to aphoristic. He sees the precursor of Daniel in the mystical experiences of Ezekiel.[39] For him the visions show Daniel as both mantic sage and prophet, whereas in the stories he is more an aphoristic originator of wisdom. The problem with this point of view is that even in the oldest stories about him Daniel is portrayed as a mantic sage.[40] Whether or not the identification of different types of wisdom can answer historical questions is raised in more detail in the concluding chapter. In the meantime it is perhaps more helpful to think in terms of 'trajectories' of wisdom without requiring each to be mutually exclusive of the other. This is the approach of Hayman, who identifies three trajectories in evidence about the time that the versions of Daniel would have been finding their final form.[41] After Qohelet, wisdom either became identified with the Torah on a cosmic scale, or became involved in reshaping the ancient myth of secret heavenly wisdom, or married the speculative and the philosophical with Jewish wisdom. These three developments may well have rubbed up against each other if not been positively hostile to one another. Certainly a conflict between Torah wisdom and the apocalyptic wisdom of heavenly secrets was later reflected in a tension between developing orthodoxy and popular religion.[42]

One of the concerns of this discussion will be to see whether the differences in characterization of the sage between the MT and LXX in the stories reflects a consistently different type of wisdom in the terms outlined above. It is too early to draw conclusions but it is noteworthy that the MT of Daniel 4, by including the court contest aspect and Daniel's position as chief of the mantic officials, places him in the same category as those officials. In the LXX his wisdom lies simply in the interpretation of the dreams (v. 18). However, the evidence is contradictory as v. 19

---

37. VanderKam, *Enoch*, pp. 6-7, and Müller, 'Mantische Weisheit', pp. 285-86.
38. Lacocque, *Daniel in his Time*, p. 189.
39. See also Delcor, *Daniel*, p. 167, on the link with Ezek. 17.
40. VanderKam, *Enoch*, p. 6.
41. A.P. Hayman, 'Qohelet and the Book of Creation', *JSOT* 50 (1991), pp. 106-108.
42. Hayman, 'Qohelet', p. 108.

LXX speaks of the 'true meaning' (ὑπόνοια) being revealed to Daniel, which has mantic connotations more appropriate to the visions. Incidentally, as we will see in the discussion below on the dream's interpretation, this is not the only place where the vocabulary of the LXX seems to have links with the later chapters of Daniel. At this stage it must suffice to say that a distinction that will recur has been made between different types of wisdom.

Use of Dialogue

The changes in narrative person in each version are part of the wider question of the presence of the narrator and the use of dialogue in the two versions. A characteristic of Old Testament narrative is the primacy of dialogue.[43] Visual details tend to be sparsely reported, and the essence of the story and its characters revealed through dialogue.[44] Repetition of material in both narrative and dialogue, or by different speakers, is manipulated for various effects.[45] In the telling of the stories, the narrative skill is in being able to keep the persona of the narrator distinct from the speaker of dialogue.[46] Failure to do so means that the impact of the use of reported speech is diluted. This characteristic use of dialogue can be seen in the MT version of Daniel 4.

Excluding the first-person sections, just under 60 per cent of the material is direct speech, the two most important blocks being the king's long speech to Daniel (vv. 6-15) and the latter's reply (vv. 17-24). In addition there is a brief interchange between the two (v. 16), Nebuchadnezzar's boastful soliloquy (v. 27) and the voice from heaven (vv. 28-29). Within the chapter there are three accounts of the dream, its interpretation and its purpose to demonstrate that God rules (vv. 7-14, 17-22, 29). Each time, the material is conveyed by dialogue, an indicator of its importance as a narrative tool.

The potential for confusion when dialogue is reported by a first-

43. R.W.L. Moberly, *Genesis 12–50* (Sheffield: JSOT Press, 1992), p. 40, writes that the 'points at which the story-teller usually places what he considers most important are usually the speeches made by the main characters at the dramatically crucial moments'.

44. Alter, *Biblical Narrative*, pp. 65 and 70.

45. Alter, *Biblical Narrative*, pp. 70-74.

46. Sternberg, *Poetics*, p. 73. On this point the view of Savran, *Telling and Retelling*, p. 37, that 'quoted direct speech involves a temporary transfer of the role of narrator to the quoting character' is contradictory.

person narrator is considerable. The complexity increases with the reported speech of the watcher (vv. 10-11) within the king's account of the dream to Daniel.[47] Moreover, the recipient of the watcher's command (v. 11) is an unseen presence. Indeed by v. 14 of the MT the reader wonders who is telling the story, the watcher or Nebuchadnezzar. For a brief moment it does not seem to matter because the dream and its reason ('so that the living might know...', v. 14) has taken over the form of the narrative. The effect is heightened by the cryptic message at the start of v. 14, roughly translated 'By a decree of the watchers is the message, and a word of the holy ones is the question'. This consists of two nominal clauses containing four words, each with a wide range of meaning (גזרת, פתגמא, מאמר, and שאלתא), with the first word prefixed by the multi-purpose ב. The Greek of θ is similarly ambiguous. These words are spoken neither by the watcher, nor by the watcher's agent, nor by Nebuchadnezzar. A new level of authority and mystery is thereby introduced into the narrative, necessary to the statement of purpose that follows.[48] At that point the implied author of the story has taken over from the narrator. If Nebuchadnezzar himself were reporting it with any degree of understanding, Daniel's interpretation would be quite unnecessary. Yet for a brief moment a protagonist is doubling as commentator.[49]

The different levels of narration can be thought of as operating parenthetically. A bracket opens with the watcher's speech (v. 11), and another is opened by the mysterious statement of v. 14a. Within these brackets the story is permitted a limited life of its own, distinct from the wider narrative form. Just when the storyteller threatens to lose control of his form altogether, the brackets close and he re-asserts himself with 'I, King Nebuchadnezzar saw... And you, Belteshazzar, tell...' (v. 15,

---

47. R. Murray, 'The Origin of Aramaic 'îr, Angel', *Or* 53 (1984), p. 304, considers the 'watcher' (עיר) to be an angelic being, and the term is in apposition to 'holy one' (קדיש) in 4.10. I accept that view for the present context, but the question must be addressed further in relation to the 'holy ones' of ch. 7. See J.A. Fitzmyer, *The Genesis Apocryphon of Qumran Cave 1* (Rome: Pontifical Biblical Institute, 1966), pp. 43 and 72, for a similar parallelism in 1QGenAp.

48. A.A. Bevan, *A Short Commentary on the Book of Daniel* (Cambridge: Cambridge University Press, 1892), p. 91, suggests the cryptic nature of the verse reflects an inscrutable judgment. According to Auerbach, *Mimesis*, p. 11, an important characteristic of biblical narrative is that it is 'fraught with background'. The present instance typifies that.

49. Sternberg, *Poetics*, p. 112.

חזית אנה מלכא נבוכדנצר ואנתה בלטשאצר...אמר). The reader is jolted back into
the first-person narrative, into the dialogue between Nebuchadnezzar
and Daniel, and into the setting of the court contest. The emphatics 'I'
and 'you' serve as important markers in this process. Through the rest
of the MT of ch. 4 the distinction between speaker and narrator is preserved.

The storyteller of the LXX version manipulates the dialogue in quite a
different way. The narrative, which is about one fifth longer than in the
MT, is almost entirely reported speech. In fact the only narrator presence
is in the six-word introduction of v. 4, the description of the interlude
between vision and fulfillment (vv. 28-31), and 'King Nebuchadnezzar
wrote an encyclical...' (v. 37b). Effectively, Nebuchadnezzar is the narrator and it is his perspective that prevails throughout. Within that broad
framework there are different layers of reported speech. By v. 15 there
are no less than four layers alive in the narrative. The narrator reports
the speech of King Nebuchadnezzar, who reports his dream and within
it the words of the angel, who orders another being to 'Hew it down...'
(v. 14, ἐκκόψατε αὐτό) and records the words that that being is commanded to say. In addition, there is a recipient of the commands of
vv. 15-16, who does not speak. By now, several speakers are sharing the
stage, and point of view has become unclear. Verse 17a, and more particularly v. 18, point the reader back to Nebuchadnezzar and re-establish
the setting of the king recounting a dream.

The style is reminiscent of some talmudic literature where the distinctions between different speakers, and between speakers and the compil-
ers, are maintained in the mind of the reader only with difficulty. The
concern is not with narrative flow, but with an accurate reporting of the
views of different speakers.[50] A similar effect may be seen in vv. 13-15

---

50. An example from *b. Meg.* 3a: 'R. Jeremiah—or some say R. Hiyya b.
Abba—also said: The *Targum* of the Pentateuch was composed by Onkelos the
proselyte under the guidance of R. Eleazer and R. Joshua. The *Targum* of the
prophets was composed by Jonathan ben Uzziel under the guidance of Haggai,
Zechariah, and Malachi, and the land of Israel [thereupon] quaked over an area of
four hundred parasangs by four hundred parasangs and a *Bath Kol* came forth and
exclaimed, Who is this that has revealed My secrets to mankind? Jonathan b. Uzziel
thereupon arose and said, It is I who have revealed Thy secrets to mankind. It is fully
known to Thee that I have not done this for my own honour or for the honour of my
father's house, but for Thy honour I have done it, that dissension may not increase in
Israel. He further sought to reveal [by] a *targum* [the inner meaning] of the
Hagiographa, but a *Bath Kol* went forth and said, Enough! What was the reason?—

of the LXX, where the report of speech becomes more important than the quality of narrative. The writer or editor has been more concerned with presenting the dream and its meaning than with a carefully crafted dialogue, or subtlety in characterization. Consequently there is a sense of unfinished business about this section. The lack of multiple points of view, here and elsewhere in the LXX version, results in a more monochrome narrative. The depth and ambiguity that more than one point of view permits is not present to the same extent.[51]

Symbol or Allegory?

So far our focus has been on narrative person and the use of dialogue, and their effect on point of view in the MT and LXX versions. But there are also differences in content, and in treatment of that content. The central symbol of the great tree is an important case in point. At one level it functions in the same way in both stories. It is a myth of cosmic security, drawing on a number of biblical uses of tree imagery and mythology.[52] At another level the symbol is interpreted in different ways.

In vv. 8 and 17 the MT describes the greatness of the tree in terms of its beauty, its cosmic proportions, and its provision of food and shelter for the world. It then focuses on one basic point of similarity between the tree and the king, and the greatness of each. This is explicit in the parallels between vv. 17 and 19. The tree's height 'reached to heaven' (v. 17, ימטא לשמיא), and the king's greatness reaches to heaven' (v. 19, מטת לשמיא). The tree's appearance is 'to all the earth' (v. 17, לכל־ארעא), while the king's rule is 'to the end of the earth' (v. 19, לסוף ארעא). That one point is expanded on as the king's greatness suffers the same fate as the tree's greatness. Both are cut down, both share a life with the beasts, and the sentence of both is for a limited period until the stump sends forth new shoots and the king is restored. The dream and its interpretation, the tree and the king, are in close correspondence but they are also

---

Because the date of the Messiah is foretold in it.' This passage, incidentally, is used when discussing the authorship of θ. See P. Grelot, 'Les versions grecques de Daniel', *Bib* 47 (1966), p. 395.

51. Berlin, *Poetics*, p. 51.

52. J.E. Goldingay, *Daniel* (Dallas: Word Books, 1989), p. 92, and P.W. Coxon, 'The Great Tree of Daniel 4', in J.D. Martin and P.R. Davies (eds.), *A Word in Season* (Sheffield: JSOT Press, 1986), pp. 94-96.

distinct.[53] In one sense the dream of the tree transcends its immediate historical context and becomes a symbol of the sovereignty of God over kings. This transcending effect is achieved by bracketing the story of Nebuchadnezzar with confessions of the greatness of God over human kings (3.33 and 4.34). The concept recurs as a leitmotif in the body of the chapter at vv. 14, 22, 29 and 32.

In the hands of the LXX a series of one-to-one correspondences between the dream and the life of the king results in an allegory on the life of Nebuchadnezzar, rather than a transcendent statement on the sovereignty of kings.[54] The birds of heaven represent 'the might of the earth...' (v. 21, ἡ ἰσχὺς τῆς γῆς), namely the various political entities within the empire. The growth of the tree is like the king's heart growing 'in arrogance and might towards the Holy One and his angels' (v. 22, ὑπερηφανίᾳ καὶ ἰσχύι τὰ πρὸς τὸν ἅγιον καὶ τοὺς ἀγγέλους αὐτοῦ). This arrogance is given a specific instance in how the king 'desolated the house of the living God' (v. 22, ἐξερήμωσας τὸν οἶκον τοῦ θεοῦ τοῦ ζῶντος). Although the band of iron and bronze around the stump of the tree in MT does not appear in the LXX version, it is known to the compiler and is hinted at in the reference to his being 'in bronze fetters and handcuffs' (v. 17a, ἐν πέδαις καὶ ἐν χειροπέδαις χαλκαῖς) and 'bound' (v. 32, δήσουσί σε). This picture is graphically expanded in the interpretation to include the idea of imprisonment and exile as events in the life of the king. In these ways a symbol of the humiliation of greatness has become something different.

An example of the allegorizing tendencies of the LXX version may be seen by comparing the versions at the point in the account of the dream where the 'it' of the tree becomes the 'him' of the person of the king. The dream is told twice in the MT, excluding its implementation in vv. 28-30. Verses 12-13 and v. 20 are almost identical in their use of the masculine pronominal suffix, הִי- or ה-. The fact that 'tree' (אִילָנָא) is masculine in Aramaic means the reference of the pronouns is

---

53. Coxon, 'The Great Tree', p. 99, uses the word parable, but considers that elements of animal fable are introduced, and the king is first symbolized by the tree then by the animals sheltering under it.

54. J.E. Goldingay, 'The Stories in Daniel: A Narrative Politics', *JSOT* 37 (1987), p. 105. See also W.S. Towner, *Daniel* (Atlanta: John Knox Press, 1984), p. 66. For a further example of such one-to-one correspondence in the LXX, see the interpretation of Mordecai's dream in the additional LXX material at the end of Esther (Esth. 10.3c-3f LXX).

ambiguous. This allows a subtle movement from dream to interpretation, with maximum effect and a minimum of artifice and intrusion on the part of the narrator. The central moment in the process is the phrase 'with the beasts (of the field) will be his lot' (v. 12, עם־חיותא חלרה and v. 20, עם־חיות ברא חלקה). Until then the referent is the tree. The only other occurrence of חלק in biblical Aramaic is in Ezra 4.16, where it has a clear application to human affairs. In biblical Hebrew there are numerous witnesses to the word, and almost all speak of some sort of allotment or destiny for human beings. It is likely then that the first readers of this account would have sensed that 'his lot' (חלקה) could not refer to the tree.

This dawning awareness is confirmed differently in each of the two MT accounts, and between them a progression in understanding may be observed, as the first is less specific than the second. In v. 13 the humanity of the one whose lot is with the beasts is emphasized by the use of 'heart' (לבב). In v. 21 the same effect is achieved with the statement 'it is a decree...which has come upon my lord, the king' (גזרת...די מטת על־מרא מלכא). By implication, what came before ועם־חיות ברא חלקה can be read back as applicable to the king. The Greek of θ is able to exploit the same ambiguity of personal pronoun as the Aramaic. The result is an identification of the tree and its fate with the king and his fate without any explanation being necessary. Remembering that the account is autobiographical at the first telling, this technique enables Nebuchadnezzar to tell the dream and hint at its solution, while remaining distinct from the implied author.

The LXX goes about its task in quite a different way. There is not the same sense of metamorphosis as the tree gradually becomes the king in the mind of the reader.[55] Here the narrator takes no chances that the reader may miss the point. The change from tree to king takes place between vv. 15 and 16. In v. 14 the neuter accusative 'it' (αὐτό) can only apply to 'tree' (δένδρον). In v. 16 'his body' (το σῶμα αὐτοῦ) can only apply to a person.[56] There is no point at which readers are left

---

55. R.A. Anderson, *Daniel, Signs and Wonders* (Grand Rapids: Eerdmans; Edinburgh: Handsel, 1984), p. 43, also uses 'metamorphosis' to describe the process.

56. P.W. Coxon, 'Another Look at Nebuchadnezzar's Madness', in A.S. van der Woude (ed.), *The Book of Daniel* (Leuven: University Press/Uitgeverij Peeters, 1993), p. 215, suggests τὸ κύτος (vv. 11 and 20) can mean a human torso. If he is correct, the word has a double referent. Coxon's suggestion receives some support from LSJ.

to draw their own conclusions. This adds to the impression explored above of a more allegorical interpretation. It also relates to earlier comments about the person of the narrator. Here Nebuchadnezzar not only tells the dream but almost takes responsibility for its interpretation. It is not unprecedented for narrators to reveal more than they can know about themselves, nor for them to double as commentator. There is always a risk in doing so that dramatic tension will be lost, and such a loss is sustained at this point by the LXX account.

Symbol and Allegory: A Distinction

In the above section I have used several terms and implied distinctions that need to be clarified at this point. In particular I used the terms 'symbol' and 'allegory' and also suggested that one account is more 'transcendent' than the other. This distinction can be explicated by looking at a debate that occurred some years ago between Perrin and Collins. Perrin suggested that symbols may be understood either as 'steno-symbols' or 'tensive' symbols.[57] The former are not transcendent and may be reduced to the one-to-one correspondence of allegory. He argued that such symbols are the type used in apocalyptic literature. Collins, and later Lacocque, took issue with Perrin to say that apocalyptic symbolism is not merely allegory.[58] Such symbols may indeed refer to historical events but they function in such a way as to transcend those events. They are not tied to a single one-to-one formulation.[59] Another way of expressing this is to say that allegory moves from the mysterious to the revealed, while symbol is rooted in everyday realities yet takes on a wider significance.[60] In subsequent work Collins explores the subtleties

57. N. Perrin, 'Wisdom and Apocalyptic in the Message of Jesus', in L.C. McGaughey (ed.), *Proceedings 2* (Missoula, MT: Society of Biblical Literature, 1972), p. 553.

58. J.J. Collins, 'The Symbolism of Transcendence in Jewish Apocalyptic', *BR* 19 (1974), p. 15; and A. Lacocque, 'Apocalyptic Symbolism: A Ricoeurian Hermeneutical Approach', *BR* 26 (1981), p. 7.

59. Collins, 'Symbolism of Transcendence', p. 17. See also J.S. Croatto, *Biblical Hermeneutics* (trans. R.R. Barr; Maryknoll, NY: Orbis Books, 1987), p. 78, who says that symbols are 'natural things transparently referring to a second meaning which somehow transcends phenomenal experience'.

60. Lacocque, *Daniel in his Time*, p. 127. Note Lacocque, 'Apocalyptic Symbolism', on the influence of Ricoeur in this debate. P. Ricoeur, *Interpretation Theory* (Fort Worth: Texas Christian University Press, 1976), pp. 55-56, says that a symbol is transcendent in that it gives access to a 'surplus of meaning' which takes

of the difference between allegory and symbol. Allegory is not always necessarily naive, he says, and can be thought of as one kind of symbolic language.[61] Nevertheless symbolism does tend to move in a different direction from allegory.

Lacocque discusses this point in terms of the interpretation of dreams.[62] He suggests that dreams were normally interpreted analogically in ancient thought but the Israelite approach broke new ground in that the significance of the dream transcended the signifier. Others approach the topic through an exploration of Daniel as either pesher or midrash. However they couch their discussion, such critics also accept that the symbols of apocalyptic transcend their temporal context.[63] What we see in this comparison of two versions of Daniel 4 is that the LXX perhaps reflects a more analogical, or allegorical, approach while MT seeks to bring a transcendent significance to the dream and events arising from it. Another aspect of the same phenomenon arises particularly acutely in grappling with the link between Daniel's vision and its interpretation in ch. 7. There the LXX keeps the earthly and heavenly realms more distinct from one another than does the MT. There too we will have cause to discuss in more detail the nature of symbols as they function in the book of Daniel. Like the consideration of different types of wisdom, discussion of the use made of symbols will continue to be a feature of the comparison in subsequent chapters.

the reader beyond the language in which the symbolism is couched. See also D.R. McGaughey, 'Ricoeur's Metaphor and Narrative Theories as a Foundation for a Theory of Symbol', *RelS* 24 (1988), pp. 431-32, for a discussion of Ricoeur's theory of symbol.

61. Collins, *Apocalyptic Vision*, p. 111. More recently Collins, *Daniel*, p. 234, adopts slightly different terminology when he says that Dan. 4 is to be understood as a 'paradigm'. Note also the comments of G.B. Caird, *The Language and Imagery of the Bible* (London: Gerald Duckworth, 1980), p. 163, on parable and allegory.

62. Lacocque, *Daniel in his Time*, p. 130.

63. See, for example, the debate between L.H. Silberman, 'Unriddling the Riddle: A Study in the Structure and Language of the Habbakuk Pesher (1QpHab)', *RevQ* 3 (1961–62), pp. 329-33, and Seeligmann, *The Septuagint Version of Isaiah*, p. 83. The latter places Daniel in a contemporizing midrashic tradition, whereas Silberman says that it is pesher rather than midrash which does the contemporizing. This is part of a wider debate on the applicability of the category 'midrash' to Daniel. M.P. Horgan, *Pesharim: Qumran Interpretations of Biblical Books* (Washington, DC: The Catholic Biblical Association of America, 1979), p. 252, on the evidence from Qumran, says pesher is pre-70 and midrash is post-70. See also the cautionary comments of K. Koch, 'Is Daniel also among the Prophets?', *Int* 39 (1985), pp. 125-26.

Differences in Interpretation

In contrast to the economy with which the MT recounts the dream and interprets it, the Old Greek version contains elements not present in the MT. At one level these variations reflect a different type of symbolism and approach to the interpretation of dreams. At another level, however, they have less to do with the story at hand than with the polemical requirements of the LXX narrator. The hint of a usurper is a case in point.[64] The king's vision does not demand any explanation of events during the 'seven times' or 'years' (MT vv. 13, 20, 22, 29, שׁבעה עדנין, and LXX vv. 16, 32, 34, ἑπτὰ ἔτη) and none is offered by the MT, besides the hint that the king was 'confirmed in (his) kingdom' (v. 33, על־מלכותי התקנת), and the suggestion by the voice from heaven that God gives kingdoms 'to whomever he pleases' (v. 29, למן־די יצבא).[65] The LXX, however, speaks of the kingdom 'given to another, a man of no account in your house' (v. 31, ἑτέρῳ δίδοται ἐξουθενημένῳ ἀνθρώπῳ ἐν τῷ οἴκῳ σου) and expands on what exactly that would entail.

Clearly the narrator of the LXX has something in mind also when he specifies the evidence of King Nebuchadnezzar's arrogance, that he 'desolated the house of the living God because of the sins of the conse-crated people' (v. 22, ἐξερήμωσας τὸν οἶκον τοῦ θεοῦ τοῦ ζῶντος ἐπὶ ταῖς ἁμαρτίαις τοῦ λαοῦ τοῦ ἡγιασμένου).[66] The reference to the desolation and to the consecrated people has echoes of the Maccabean period, and particularly the struggle with Antiochus IV, but neither aspect is witnessed to anywhere in the first six chapters of Daniel MT.[67] A possible exception is the condemnation of Belshazzar in 5.23, as the θ translation of that verse uses the word ὑψώθης, the same word used by the LXX in 4.22 of Nebuchadnezzar. The manifestation of Belshazzar's arrogance was his misuse of the Temple vessels, but even

---

64. F.F. Bruce, 'The Oldest Greek Version of Daniel', *OTS* 20 (1976), p. 31.

65. Josephus, *Ant.* 10.217, goes further than the MT to note 'none venturing to seize the government during these seven years'. This represents a different tradition again from that in the LXX.

66. P.-M. Bogaert, 'Relecture et refonte historicisante du livre de Daniel attestés par la première version grecque (Papyrus 967)', in R. Kuntzmann and J. Schlosser (eds.), *Etudes sur le judaïsme hellénestique* (Paris: Cerf, 1984), p. 206, considers that Nebuchadnezzar's faults in the LXX are more like those of Antiochus IV.

67. Grelot, 'La Septante', p. 15.

then there is no reference to the sort of events envisaged in 4.22 LXX. Similarly, the word ἐξερήμωσας has no presence in Daniel 1–6 MT, but is a familiar theme in the second half of the book. In 8.13, 9.27 and 11.31 ἐρημώσεως, or some other form of the same root, occurs in the context of violence against the Temple or the system of sacrifices or the covenant. 'The consecrated people' (τοῦ λαοῦ τοῦ ἡγιασμένου) likewise suggests the latter chapters of Daniel where the expression 'the holy ones' (οἱ ἅγιοι) features often.

Still in 4.22 LXX, the phrase ἐπὶ ταῖς ἁμαρτίαις is a puzzle. The ἐπί could carry a causal sense, so that the desolation has come about because of the sins of the people, who need refining and punishing. That appears to be the understanding in 3.37 LXX where Azariah laments the troubles of Israel brought about 'because of our sins' (3.37, διὰ τὰς ἁμαρτίας ἡμῶν). On the other hand ἐπί could be a preposition of agency in that the sinful ones themselves played a part in bringing about the desolation. Both senses may be found supported in 11.30-32, where there is talk of those who violated the covenant. It is this that perhaps lies behind the oblique reference to 'the sins of the consecrated people' and introduces a theme from a later period into the much earlier provenance of Nebuchadnezzar and his relations with exilic Jews.

There is only one exceptional reference to sacrifices and burnt offerings (2.46) in the Persian or Babylonian setting of chs. 2–6 MT. Yet the LXX version of ch. 4 introduces the concept with 'I will bring sacrifices for the sake of my soul to the Most High...' (v. 37a, περὶ τῆς ψυχῆς μου τῷ ὑψίστῳ θυσίας προσοίσω). Again this suggests the setting of chs. 7–12 where the MT is interested in matters relating to the Temple cult. Apart from the incidental allusion to the time of the evening sacrifice' (9.21, מנחת־ערב), there are two other important readings in 9.27 and 11.31, which speak of the end of the sacrifices. In both, the context is the destruction of the sanctuary, another theme from the visions that ch. 4 LXX shows to be a concern of the earlier chapters of the LXX.

Differences in the Account of the Dream

Dreams in the Old Testament are often clear in their meaning and non-specific in details. A dream-like sense of clarity with generality is preserved by the MT narrative. Phrases such as 'seven seasons' (vv. 13, 20, 29, שבעה עדנין) add to the effect. This tone is not present in the LXX narrative. On two occasions it includes details that reflect its more allegorical approach and seem inappropriate to the dream setting as evoked by the MT. The first is the description of the tree as 'thirty stadia in length' (v. 12, μήκει ὡς σταδίων τριάκοντα). The second is the use of the more specific ἔτη (vv. 33a, 34, 'year') instead of the undefined καιροί (θ) or עדנין (MT), which are best translated as 'times' or 'seasons'. Both of these examples are almost banal in the context of the dream of the great tree, and do not bring the same transcendent quality to the vision as MT. The 'thirty stadia' detracts from the sense of greatness that it is attempting to explicate. The 'years' attempts to define a period of time that is deliberately left ambiguous in the MT. The lack of definition as an expression of the sovereignty of God over kings is an effect not present in the LXX.

A similar example is found in v. 11 LXX where the cosmic tree acquires the quality of light-giver: 'The sun and moon dwelt in it, and it lit all the earth'. This element of the description is not inappropriate in the way I have suggested for the other extra details above, but it is an element that plays no further part in ch. 4 and contributes nothing to the subsequent allegorical interpretation of the dream. The fruitfulness, the height and bulk, the provision of shelter, and the greatness of the tree are all included in the interpretation, but there is no application to the king of its light-giving qualities.

Literary Merit in the Septuagint

If I have conveyed some dissatisfaction with the literary qualities of the LXX version, that is not to say it is without any merit. The section just referred to succeeds in applying the imagery of light and shade in contrasting ways to the tree. On the one hand it 'cast a shadow' (v. 12, ἐσκίαζον) over all those under it. On the other it becomes the source of light to all those living in its shadow (v. 11). It sustains by lighting and by protecting from light.

The style of the Old Greek is fulsome rather than economical but there are times when a neat turn of phrase arrests the reader. An example is the last part of v. 27: 'Accept these words for my word is accurate, and your time is fulfilled' (τούτους τοὺς λόγους ἀγάπησον ἀκριβὴς γάρ μου ὁ λόγος καὶ πλήρης ὁ χρόνος σου). The balance of the sentence encapsulates the contrast between God and King Nebuchadnezzar essential to the story. As God addresses the king his μου confronts Nebuchadnezzar's σου, his λόγος controls the king's χρόνος, and the certainty (ἀκριβής) of that word ensures its fulfillment (πλήρης). Similarly, the humiliation of being usurped and the gall of the usurper are captured in the phrase 'Until sunrise another king will make merry in your house...' (v. 31, ἕως δὲ ἡλίου ἀνατολῆς βασιλεὺς ἕτερος εὐφρανθήσεται ἐν τῷ οἴκῳ σου).[68]

Conclusion

The MT tells about a king's dream of a great tree and applies it to the issue of human rulers under the control of divine sovereignty. This issue is explored in the form of a letter from Nebuchadnezzar to his subjects, with allowance made for the divine viewpoint as well as the perspective that Daniel brings to the story. The dream is interpreted and applied as a symbol of the subjection of human greatness, with little reference to events in the king's life beyond the episode of madness or exile. In that respect the storyteller does not appear to have an axe to grind against Nebuchadnezzar personally. As a participant in the court contest, Daniel's point of view is also present in the story and he is the vehicle through whom the judgment of God is conveyed to Nebuchadnezzar. As a literary composition the MT is largely consistent in its use of the epistolary form and its manipulation of narrative person, dialogue and point of view within that form.[69] The result is a well-told story that fits the context given it by the MT in a series of accounts of Jews in the court at Babylon.

The LXX is not so concerned with narrative consistency or with setting the story in the context of other court stories. Consequently the placing of the epistolary material and the role of Nebuchadnezzar as narrator are problematic. Daniel exists only incidentally in the telling. The version's attitude towards the king is more adversarial, perhaps reflecting the setting behind chs. 7–12. In addition, the description of the tree is more detailed and its interpretation is more allegorical than symbolic. The LXX version, for all its similarity, is markedly different in both form and content from the story told in MT ch. 4.

As a by-product of this comparison of the MT and LXX versions of

68. Bruce, 'Oldest Greek Version', p. 30, translates the phrase somewhat differently but with similar results: 'By sunrise another king will make merry in your house...'

69. There is some unevenness, such as in v. 6 MT where חזי seems out of place, and is a disputed reading.

Daniel 4 I have also summarized several issues which serve as a background to the wider study. In noting that the narrator of the MT is more covert and that of the LXX more overt, I delineated several terms that will be used in future discussion of the role of the narrator. In connection with the presentation of the person of Daniel, distinctions between different types of wisdom were made although no conclusions were drawn in the application of them. The function of symbols was also touched on. As well as the literary points made, this chapter hinted at a historical puzzle posed by the comparison. The LXX seems to be later than the MT in that it tells the story in a way that looks forward to the visions. At the same time, the less crafted form of the story in the LXX suggests that it could be an earlier version than the MT. All of these issues await further illustration and clarification in other stories of Daniel and his friends in the court of the Babylonian king.

Chapter 3

DANIEL 5

In Daniel 5 the story of Belshazzar and the handwriting on the wall is told. The effects of the variations between the MT and the LXX stories are similar to those in Daniel 4, but their nature is somewhat different. While the contrasting motives of the narrators of ch. 4 are shown up in a lengthy LXX plus, those differences appear in a significant MT plus in the story to which we now turn our attention. As it is a different type of story from the dream of the great tree, and as there are not the same issues as were raised by the epistolary form in the previous chapter, the approach to a literary comparison will vary a little.

The plot structure is almost identical in both versions of ch. 5 and I refer to this aspect only incidentally. There are other similarities which I do touch on, particularly in the setting of the story and the sin for which Belshazzar is being condemned. There are also important differences in the setting which bear on other aspects of the story. I detail these, and then explore other variations between the MT and LXX accounts. In particular I consider the king's motivation, portrayal of characters, operation of perspective and the relationship of narrator to reader. I then consider what effect these differences in the way the story is told have on the part played by the writing on the wall. This allows us to detect a differing purpose and theological viewpoint between the two versions. As part of that exploration other noteworthy literary devices are considered, and there is a brief excursus on the theme of words and vision.

The final section constitutes a look at the links between this story and ch. 4. It will be seen that the two chapters are almost inseparable in the MT and almost independent of each other in the LXX, a phenomenon that has much to do with the differing narrative purposes of each.

But before turning to the main text, the presence of a prologue to the LXX account, in the form of a brief abstract of the story, should be noted. This contains the information unattested elsewhere that the feast took place at 'the dedication of his kingdoms' (ἐγκαινισμοῦ τῶν βασιλειῶν) and that the number of guests was two thousand. The words of the writing on the wall are transcribed as they appear in Daniel's interpretation (vv. 26-28), just as they are in v. 25 θ. The explanation for these variations is an unfinished debate between those who see a late attempt to clarify an incomplete LXX text and those who see an early form of the tradition underlying ch. 5.[1]

Setting

In both versions the setting is a feast put on by King Belshazzar for members of his court. The occasion for the feast is not made explicit in either version. In both accounts wine is drunk and the sacred vessels deported from Jerusalem by Nebuchadnezzar are desecrated. This action evokes an immediate divine response, the writing on the wall. The immediacy expressed by שעה (v. 5, 'moment') is watered down a little by the LXX use of ὥρᾳ, a reading also adopted by θ.[2] After the appearance of the hand, the rest of the chapter is spent in explicating the significance of that hand and the events that gave rise to it.

Wine and the banquet setting play a significant part in both accounts. Although neither version condemns the excessive behaviour of the participants per se, both link it with the sin of Belshazzar and his guests. The presence of the king's companions is mentioned again in v. 23, where Daniel outlines the king's failings. It seems important to both narrators to repeat the guest list. This has the effect of evoking the banquet milieu at the same time that the king's sins are recalled. Although it is not specifically against the excesses of a Gentile court setting that God is complaining, perhaps there is an undercurrent of Jewish thought at work which expects bad things to happen in such scenes of dissipation, and sees them as images of human pride.[3] The result is that the opening phrase has an immediate foreshadowing effect, and the negative imagery of the banquet resonates through the chapter.

At the same time the chief concern of both versions is the pride of Belshazzar, not the excess. This is obvious in the LXX, which tells of the

---

1. For example, compare Montgomery, *Daniel*, p. 267, with Wills, *The Jew in the Court*, p. 122.
2. Dan. 3.6 supports the view that שעה in earlier Aramaic has the sense of immediacy and consequence.
3. Goldingay, 'The Stories in Daniel', p. 106.

king that he orders the vessels because 'his heart was lifted up' (v. 2, ἀνυψώθη ἡ καρδία αὐτοῦ). Contrary to the Theodotionic understanding implied by the participle πίνων (v. 1), this is not the same thing as being drunk. Rather it carries the idea of deliberate self-aggrandizement. The idiom ὑψώθη ἡ καρδία is not uncommon in Septuagintal Greek, although the usage here of the prefixed form of the verb is unique. When it occurs it almost always conveys pride or unhealthy ambition or a false sense of superiority. It usually translates רבה לב or גבה לב or רום לב as, for example, in Deut. 8.14 and 17.20, and Ezek. 28.5. This contrasts with Est. 1.10, another story of banquets, where the king's action definitely is as a result of the wine. The Hebrew כטוב לב־המלך ביין ('when the king's heart was merry with wine') becomes in the A-text ἐν τῷ εὐφρανθῆναι τὸν βασιλέα ἐν τῷ οἴνῳ (2.10).[4]

The same can be said for the MT although the best way to understand בטעם חמרא is contested. One approach is to translate it 'under the influence of wine'. In that case the king is seen acting at a late stage in the banquet when the wine has either impaired his judgment or bestowed on him an alcoholic courage.[5] His calling for the Temple vessels from Jerusalem thereby becomes the final expression of courtly excess. This is the more usual approach to translation and is probably how θ understood it with καὶ πίνων (v. 1, 'and having drunk...'). The other main approach is that suggested by BDB and taken up by others, that טעם in Dan. 5.2 means the 'tasting' of the wine.[6] On this reasoning, Belshazzar's action, at whatever point in the banquet it may have taken place, could be understood as a kind of libation, a calculated action the motivation for which will need to be considered later.

Both usages of טעם are problematic however. The word occurs in biblical Hebrew, where its primary meaning relates to physical taste in the sense of eating something in small quantities (for example, 1 Sam. 14.24; 2 Sam. 3.35). This leads to the idea of tasting something to test it, and from there to a more general concept of exercising discernment or judgment. The parallelism of Job 12.11, where בחן ('test, examine') and טעם explicate each other, neatly illustrates this broadened sense. By the time of biblical Aramaic the core meaning is still found in the verb form,

---

4. Clines, *The Esther Scroll*, p. 218. LXX ἡδέως γενόμενος is a little more coy.
5. That is how Hartman and DiLella, *Daniel*, p. 181, see it.
6. RSV, for example. A. Bentzen, *Daniel* (Tübingen: J.C.B. Mohr, 1937), p. 23, detects the 'antiker Sitte' of libation but offers no ancient sources in support. See Montgomery, *Daniel*, p. 251, for a discussion of this point.

where טעם is used to describe Nebuchadnezzar being fed like a domestic animal (4.22, 29; 5.21). But the noun form has left that sense long behind and usually means a command, decree or report, the issuing of some sort of formal document or utterance. The difference is illustrated by the play on both senses in Jon. 3.7, where the king and his nobles issue a 'decree' (מטעם) commanding the people, 'do not taste' (אל־יטעמו) food. The earlier nuance of taste as discretion can still be detected in the idiom שׂים...טעם על (Dan. 3.12; 6.14) meaning to 'have a proper regard for' or to 'pay attention to'. By the time of the Targums the verb form still refers to physical taste, but the noun has come simply to mean 'good sense, wisdom or reason'.

The upshot of all this is that the suggested translation, 'at the tasting of the wine', is unlikely as it entails an anachronistic understanding which would be the only example of such a usage in either biblical Aramaic or later Aramaic. On the other hand, the development of the meaning of טעם makes it unlikely that a complete loss of judgment on the part of Belshazzar is intended. I suggest an understanding that steers between the two extremes of courtly excess and formal libation. This can be done by retaining the translation 'under the influence of wine' as long as the dual connotation of the English wording is understood.[7] Whether or not טעם denotes a formal ceremony of some sort, it is unlikely that Belshazzar's action simply shows that he was drunk. טעם tells the reader that he was still exercising judgment, albeit faulty, and so retaining a measure of responsibility for his actions. This has consequences for how the nature of Belshazzar's sin should be understood. At the same time it serves as a further resonance of the negative banquet imagery in the background of the story. There is also an element of irony at work. As Nebuchadnezzar was fed grass, so Belshazzar his son is fed wine. As other kings issue commands and receive reports, this king's adviser is his wine. Herein lies an early hint that Belshazzar is being unfavourably compared with other monarchs.

But there are also differences in the banquet setting. The MT implies some sort of formal occasion, with the king presiding. That implication comes through in several ways. It is found in the description of the

---

7. That sense is captured by Rashi whom A.F. Gallé (trans.), *Daniel avec commentaires de R. Saadia, Aben-Ezra, Raschi, etc.* (Paris: Ernest Leroux, 1900), p. 53, translates with 'conseil'. A. Lacocque, *Le livre de Daniel* (Paris: Delachaux & Niestlé, 1976), p. 76, follows Rashi. See also Fewell, *Circle of Sovereignty*, p. 185 n. 1.

guests as 'his nobles' (v. 1, רברבנוהי), who are clearly official figures. The word does not occur in biblical Aramaic outside Daniel, and within Daniel it is principally in this chapter. It is also applied to the officials who accompanied Darius to the mouth of the lion pit and with him affixed their seals to the stone (6.18).

As well as the nobles there are also women present, שגלתא and לחנתא, usually translated in English as 'wives and concubines' (vv. 2-3 and 23). The exact status of these women is unclear, but neither term has complimentary overtones. The difference between them is possibly one of degree rather than kind, and both groups would have been members of the royal harem.[8] The presence of women at official banquets in the Medo-Persian empire is well-attested, and 1 Esd. 4.25-32 contains a delightful sketch of their role on such occasions. The word that Esdras uses for 'concubine' there, παλλακή, is the same one that θ uses to translate שגל in v. 2. The other word that θ uses, παράκοιτοι, makes clear the limited functions of these women. Like the king's officials, the women are there because they belong to the king. The guests are all described in terms of their relationship to Belshazzar.[9]

The phrase 'before the thousand' (v. 1, לקבל אלפא) is also important. It provides a clue as to the possible layout of the banqueting hall. There are a group of women present in the hall, not included in that description, yet the account is clear that they participate in what follows. If the picture in 1 Esdras mentioned above is of any significance, such members of the harem who were present would have been seated near the king and, like him, facing the thousand guests. It also emphasizes the public nature of what is about to happen. The entire scene with its consequences for Belshazzar is enacted in front of the thousand.[10] What begins as a public exhibition of bravado ends in public humiliation. The word קבל has another important function in the story which I discuss later in connection with the double focus of the narration.

By describing the guests in terms of their functions, and the layout of the banquet in terms of the position of the king, the MT depicts an official and formal occasion. In the LXX the scene of the action is more in the nature of a private party. Rather than a group of royal officials, Belshazzar puts on a feast for an unspecified number of his friends or

---

8. Lacocque, *Daniel*, p. 76.

9. Fewell, *Circle of Sovereignty*, p. 135.

10. See N.W. Porteous, *Daniel* (London: SCM Press, 1965), p. 78, on the layout of the banquet hall.

compatriots or associates (v. 2, ἑταίροις).[11] There are no women present apart from the queen, who plays an important role in both stories. It
is a private gathering of friends, and the formality hinted at in the
description of the king facing a crowded hall is not present. Moreover,
once the mysterious hand has done its dreadful work, the response of
those at the feast is much more that of equals. They 'clamoured round'
(v. 6, ἐκαυχῶντο) making a drunken noise in consternation at what is
happening to the king.[12] In v. 23 these intimates are referred to by
Daniel as 'your friends' (τοῖς φίλοις σου) in the same breath that he
calls them 'your nobles' (οἱ μεγιστᾶνές σου), a word which carries
similar literal connotations to the Aramaic רברבן. It is not surprising that
the companions of Belshazzar are the 'greats' of the land, but the
emphasis is not so much on their position as on their intimacy with the
king. It is in the context of that private drinking bout that the ensuing
events happen.

The Sin of Belshazzar

Before proceeding further in this exploration, it would be helpful to clarify what exactly the sin is for which Belshazzar is condemned. It is
almost the same in both stories, notwithstanding the differences in the
king's motivation and fate between versions. The sin begins in his pride.
In the MT this resulted in his misguided attempt to exercise טעם (v. 2), a
concept expanded on by Daniel who reminds him, 'you lifted yourself
up' (v. 23, התרוממת). The LXX narrator coincides with the Aramaic sense
earlier in his story with the phrase ἀνυψώθη ἡ καρδία αὐτοῦ (v. 2,
'his heart was lifted up'). At this point in both narratives the results of
his arrogance are judged in similar terms, but the sin does not lie in possession of the sacred vessels.[13]

Nebuchadnezzar himself, who has just been mentioned in approving
tones (vv. 20-21 MT), was condemned for his pride alone, not for
possessing the items out of the Jerusalem Temple. But the sin of his

11. Although note the number 2000 in the Septuagintal prologue.
12. The prefix on συνεταῖροι (v. 6) may imply an increased intimacy or concern, or it may be introduced by the translator for variety.
13. Both versions remind us of the propensity of Nabonidus to collect foreign
deities. See W.H. Shea, 'Further Literary Structures in Daniel 2–7: An Analysis of
Daniel 5 and the Broader Relationships within Chapters 2–7', *AUSS* 23 (1985),
p. 282.

successor's pride is twofold. In the first place he desecrates the vessels by using them at the banquet. In the second place he praises other gods and neglects the living God. It is unclear in both versions whether these two things are distinct in the mind of the narrator, or whether they represent one action. What is clear is that a deliberate act of defiance is taking place.

The King's Motivation and Fate

One result of the small differences in setting is that they suggest different motivations for the king's actions. In the LXX the events that take place are in a less official setting, appropriate to Belshazzar's personal rebellion against God. In the MT he appears to be engaging in a deliberate act of public rebellion. This ties in with the different fate suffered by the king in each version. The narrator of the MT remains content with the result that 'Belshazzar...was killed' (v. 30, קְטִיל בֵּלְאשַׁצַּר).[14] The stark ending of the MT is more muted in the LXX and the fate of the king is not so final. There the judgment that comes is that 'the kingdom was taken from the Chaldeans' (v. 30, τὸ βασίλειον ἐξῆρται ἀπὸ τῶν Χαλδαίων) and given to the Medes and Persians. The loss by Belshazzar of his kingdom is only implied. At this climactic point in the narrative the LXX storyteller is more interested in the fate of the kingdom, whereas the emphatic 'in that night' (v. 30, בַּה בלֵיליָא) of the MT indicates a concern to link the sin of the king with his personal fate. At first glance it may seem strange that the MT account of public rebellion emphasizes personal consequences, while the LXX account of personal rebellion emphasizes public outcome. This interest in the sin of the king as an issue of personal allegiance, and the fate of his kingdom as an outcome of his choices, is typical of the LXX's treatment of the monarchs in other Daniel stories. As we will see, the emphasis of the MT relates to the MT interest in the political motives of Belshazzar that lie behind the events of the banquet.

Fewell links Belshazzar's motivation in the MT to the absent presence

---

14. The historicity of this incident is much debated. In connection with his view of Belshazzar as chief officer of Nabonidus, W.H. Shea, 'Bel(te)shazzar Meets Belshazzar', *AUSS* 26 (1988), p. 68, applies the evidence in Herodotus 1.191, and Xenophon, *Cyropaedia* 7.5.26-27, of a feasting king killed by the Persians to the king in Dan. 5.

of Nebuchadnezzar.[15] She argues that the banquet was intended to demonstrate Belshazzar's independence of his father, Nebuchadnezzar. The appellation of the latter as the present king's father raises issues which merit a brief comment at this point. It is known that Belshazzar was in fact the son of Nabonidus, no blood relation of Nebuchadnezzar but his usurper. There is a tradition that Belshazzar was related to Nebuchadnezzar through his mother but it does not bear much weight.[16] One explanation may be that ch. 4 was originally about Nabonidus, and the references in ch. 5 to an earlier king were also once to Nabonidus.[17] In that case the king of ch. 5 is indeed the son of the king of ch. 4. Another possibility is that this chapter echoes a court fiction designed to emphasize the continuity of the regime and legitimate the introduction of outside blood. In those terms Nebuchadnezzar was Belshazzar's 'father'. It is not essential to my present purpose to declare on this matter, for the story works the same in any case. Belshazzar may be the son of a successful father attempting to declare his independence and to come out from under his father's shadow, or he could be an insecure member of a usurping regime seeking to demonstrate his legitimacy. In either case he is troubled by the memory of Nebuchadnezzar and this story as told in the MT may be partly understood in those terms.

The first hint of that is found early in the story in a variation within repetitive statements, a device beloved of biblical narrative.[18] In v. 2 Belshazzar orders the vessels to be brought which 'Nebuchadnezzar his father had taken from the temple which is in Jerusalem' (הנפק נבוכדנצר אבוהי מן־היכלא די בירושלם). In v. 3 the vessels brought in response to this order are those 'from the temple which is the house of the God who is in Jerusalem' (מן־היכלא די־בית אלהא די בירושלם), with no mention of the king's father. The careful reader is thus alerted to the fact that, at least as far as Belshazzar is concerned, Nebuchadnezzar has some importance to the ensuing narrative.

15. Fewell, *Circle of Sovereignty*, pp. 118-22.

16. Wiseman, *Nebuchadrezzar*, pp. 11-12, takes seriously the possibility of Belshazzar being the grandson of Nebuchadnezzar through his mother. His father Nabonidus would therefore have been the son-in-law of Nebuchadnezzar. A.R. Millard, 'Daniel 1–6 and History', *EvQ* 49 (1977), p. 72, warns that this 'remains speculation'.

17. See Goldingay, *Daniel*, p. 108, for a discussion of this point. The argument for Nabonidus being the earlier referent of ch. 4 also relates to the question of the four kingdoms.

18. Alter, *Biblical Narrative*, p. 66.

A further clue comes with the king's curious ignorance of Daniel's existence, and diffidence towards him once he learns of it. This is hinted at in several ways. His description of Daniel in v. 13 as one of the 'sons of the exile of Judah' (בני גלותא די יהוד) is beside the point and so perhaps slightly derogatory. Daniel's Judean origins did not feature in the queen's introduction of him, but Belshazzar chooses to emphasize them.[19] At the same time he does not use the Chaldean name, Belteshazzar, which had been conferred on Daniel by Nebuchadnezzar. This is a name that the queen uses and that Nebuchadnezzar used quite frequently when addressing Daniel. The present king, in contrast to the queen, prefers to remember Daniel's non-Babylonian origins rather than his function in his father's court, and his Judean name rather than the one given him by a predecessor.[20] To use that name would be to admit his Babylonian significance.

Belshazzar's implicit attitude becomes explicit in two other carefully turned phrases in his address to Daniel. He reminds Daniel that he was one whom his father 'brought from Judah' (v. 13, היתי...מן־יהוד). This contrasts with the queen's speech where King Nebuchadnezzar is said to have 'set him up' (v. 11, הקימה).[21] By so referring to Daniel, Belshazzar

19. It does not matter whether מלכתא, 'the queen', is the mother or wife of the king. Persian and Babylonian sources both know of powerful women playing a political role at court either as mother or wife of the monarch. This is a role distinct from that of chief consort. Her dominance, freedom of movement and knowledge of the past suggest that the queen of this story is such a political figure, more likely to be the mother than the spouse of Belshazzar. Compare the restrictions placed on Vashti and Esther. Lewy, 'Cult of the Moon', pp. 414-27, discusses the role of Sumnadamqa, the Assyro-Babylonian vice-queen in connection with Nabonidus and the cult of the moon god. See also Montgomery, *Daniel*, p. 258, and A.L. Oppenheim, *Ancient Mesopotamia* (Chicago: University of Chicago Press, 1977), p. 104. The Greek βασίλισσα, also used of Esther and Vashti by both the LXX and the A-text, is as ambiguous as the Aramaic. I use the term 'queen' to denote this figure of influence at the court without defining her exact relationship to the king. A. Brenner, *The Israelite Woman* (Sheffield: JSOT Press, 1985), pp. 18-19, discusses the rarer occurrences of such figures in Israelite culture. See also Delcor, *Daniel*, p. 128.

20. E.J. Young, *Daniel* (London: Banner of Truth Trust, 1972), p. 123. Shea, 'Belshazzar', p. 74, considers that the king avoids Daniel's Babylonian name because it is the same as his own. The LXX reflects this.

21. See Savran, *Telling and Retelling*, pp. 6-7 and 109-110, on repetition in dialogue. He notes that Daniel here contrasts with Esther and Jonah, other examples of later texts, which employ less repetition. See further M. Sternberg, 'Proteus in Quotation Land', *PT* 3 (1982), pp. 108-11, on quotation.

reduces him to a level with the Temple vessels, which had also been brought out of Judah (vv. 2-3). He also adds a rider, 'I have heard concerning you' (vv. 14, 16, שמעת עליך), to his remarks. This contrasts with Nebuchadnezzar's 'I know that...' (4.6, אנה ידעת די). Belshazzar does not accept anything about Daniel at face value other than that he was brought into exile, a fact that is mentioned before the rider.

Many commentators have wondered why the king should not have known about such a prominent sage as Daniel had become, particularly in the light of the knowledge that his aforementioned speech betrays.[22] Goldingay suggests it is not so surprising.[23] The historical argument that Daniel by this time would have been an old man and perhaps had not been active during the reign of Belshazzar stretches credibility, particularly in light of the role he proceeded to play in Darius's administration. The literary and psychological arguments are more convincing. In literary terms the story satisfies many of the requirements for a court contest. Daniel enters the scene last through the intervention of another person, in this case the queen. However, another requirement of the genre is that the hero be a previously unknown figure, yet the queen's words establish Daniel as someone with previously recognized credentials.[24] The story now looks more like a court conflict, although there is no punishment of conspirators.[25] In that respect a rigid genre distinction breaks down, and the explanation of Belshazzar's non-recognition of Daniel as a function of literary genre is thereby problematic. It could equally be understood in psychological terms. Belshazzar does not choose to remember Daniel for reasons that we have already considered. The narrator conveys this through the differences between what the queen has to say and what Belshazzar seems to know about Daniel. He would not have been part of this king's administration for political reasons and was only called in as a final desperate resort by Belshazzar, who was given no option by the queen.

The setting of the story in the LXX creates a different dynamic. Because it is a private occasion it remains essentially a private matter between God and the king. The other characters exist in order to facilitate that encounter and Nebuchadnezzar is not the dominating absentee

22. For example, Lacocque, *Daniel*, p. 82.
23. Goldingay, *Daniel*, p. 110.
24. Zerubbabel in 1 Esd. 3–4 exemplifies such an unknown figure.
25. See again Humphreys, 'Lifestyle', pp. 217-18, on the distinction between court conflict and court contest.

to the same extent, although the LXX does recognize the tradition that he was Belshazzar's father. In the two places where he is mentioned in the LXX account his significance in relation to Belshazzar is downplayed. In v. 2 the word order differs from the MT. The vessels are from the house of God firstly and the fact that they were taken by his father from Jerusalem is incidental. Because v. 3 does not have the repetition that the MT contains, there is no opportunity at this point in the LXX narrative to observe any ambivalence about his predecessor on the part of the king. The only MT occurrence of Daniel's Babylonian name, Belteshazzar, occurs in a plus (v. 12b), so does not feature at all in the LXX.

In vv. 11-12 the queen reminds the king of Daniel, who did his work in the days of Nebuchadnezzar. As with the first example given, the LXX handles the narrative differently. In the LXX Daniel's qualifications as a wise man are given greater prominence than the description of his activities in the court of the late king. In this case there is no counter speech from Belshazzar hinting that he demurs from that opinion of Daniel. His motivation is not given the same sort of political significance as that accorded it by the MT narrator.

Characters

The differences in Belshazzar's motivation portrayed by the two narrators is a crucial difference between the two accounts. This may be brought out more clearly by considering the differences in portrayal of two other characters in the story, Daniel and the queen, along with a further look at the character of Belshazzar.

In the court contest form the protagonist is usually introduced to the king by some sort of intermediary figure. On one level this is the function of the queen in bringing Daniel to Belshazzar's notice. Arioch in ch. 2 served the same purpose.[26] But unlike the intermediary Arioch, who approaches Nebuchadnezzar with great apprehension, the queen of the MT betrays no hint of fear as she strides in and takes centre stage. By allowing her to leave her role as a functionary, the narrator epitomizes Belshazzar's problem. He does not feel he is his own boss. After issuing her advice the queen simply commands, 'Now let Daniel be called' (v. 12, כען דניאל יתקרי).[27] To whom is this command

26. Milne, *Vladimir Propp*, p. 225. Compare also the role of the chief cupbearer in the story of Joseph (Gen. 41.9-13).

27. A jussive form. See F. Rosenthal, *A Grammar of Biblical Aramaic*

addressed? The king or those under the king's orders? The structure of
the narrative suggests that the queen has bypassed the king entirely and
issued orders to his subordinates herself. The use of באדין in v. 13
supports this view of the queen's role. The word is almost always used
in Aramaic Daniel immediately after direct speech or some particular
action of a character or characters, and introduces action directly consequent on what precedes it. It almost always occurs at the beginning of
the verse (See 2.14, 35, 46; 3.3, 13, 19, 21, 26; 4.4; 5.3, 17, 29; 6.13, 14,
16, 17, 20, 24, 26).[28]

Apart from her attitude towards the king, what the queen has to say
to him is important. The first time she speaks she reminds the insecure
regent of a man who distinguished himself 'in the days of your father'
(v. 11, ביומי אביך) and whom 'King Nebuchadnezzar your father set up'
(v. 11, מלכא נבכדנצר אבוך...הקימה).[29] To round the speech off, and just in
case Belshazzar has missed the references to Nebuchadnezzar, she adds
the syntactically redundant phrase 'your father the king' (אבוך מלכא) to
force the point home. The LXX does not include this phrase as it comes
at the end of a block of MT plus material (v. 11b). It is omitted in θ by a
translator who recognized its redundancy, and perhaps failed to appreciate its emphatic role in the direct speech of the MT. The placement of
הקימה at the end of the phrase, and in juxtaposition to the extra reference
to the king, reinforces the link between Daniel and Nebuchadnezzar.

Minor characters often seem to appear and disappear in Old Testament
narrative without any attempt on the part of the narrator to set them in
context or give them an identity, but they bring some twist or surprise
element into the story in support of the narrator's purposes.[30] The
queen is functioning in such a way here. In this case her unbidden entry
alerts the reader that there is something going on. Her defiance of

(Wiesbaden: Otto Harrassowitz, 1968), p. 44.

28. The distinction between באדין and אדין as narrative connectives is blurred but
the latter, as it is used in Daniel, possibly indicates a slightly less causal relationship
with what precedes it. See, for example, the instances in ch. 6 (vv. 4, 5, 6, 7, 12,
15, 19 and 22). But in commenting on 2.14, Charles, *Daniel*, p. 34, says the prefixed form marks a new section or paragraph. He draws the distinction too boldly.

29. 4QprEsthar[d] 2-4, also contains an account of a queen who enters Balthasar's
hall unannounced and tells of a Jew who might help. See the edition of J.T. Milik,
'Les modèles araméens du livre d'Esther dans la grotte 4 de Qumran', *RevQ* 15
(1991–92), pp. 336-37, 342 and 378.

30. U. Simon, 'Minor Characters in Biblical Narrative', *JSOT* 46 (1990), p. 13.

convention reinforces the picture of Belshazzar's insecurity.[31]

In literary terms the LXX queen does not function as an intermediary in the way that she does in the MT. She enters only when the king 'called' (v. 9, ἐκάλεσε) her. Moreover, when she speaks her attitude is a more conciliatory one. She merely 'reminded' (v. 10, ἐμνήσθη) Belshazzar of the presence of Daniel and does not herself command that he should be brought forward. Indeed the LXX narrative seems to jump at this point from the queen's speech to Daniel's entry (v. 13) with no record of him having been summoned, the only place in the chapter where a character makes an uninvited entry. This leap may be a feature of style, similar to the unsolicited entry of Daniel in 4.5 MT, or representative of some incompleteness in the tradition. Whichever is the case, it shows another MT plus in the queen's speech (v. 12b) containing material which knits the story of Belshazzar to that of Nebuchadnezzar. In the LXX, where the narrator is not so concerned with that relationship between the stories, the queen simply serves as a link in the narrative and a purveyor of information about Daniel the wise man.

There are several ways in which the MT and LXX differ in their portrayal and use of Daniel also. In the MT Daniel serves a twofold function vis-à-vis King Belshazzar. On the one hand he is a symbol of the regime of Nebuchadnezzar, and on the other he brings the judgment of God. In response to the king's request Daniel purports as God's messenger to draw an unfavourable comparison between Nebuchadnezzar's eventual humility and Belshazzar's pride. At a subliminal level the description of Nebuchadnezzar's temporal successes (vv. 18-19) reinforces the suspicion that some sort of political apologia for Nebuchadnezzar is going on. He reminds the king again of his links with Nebuchadnezzar by recounting the events from ch. 4 (vv. 18-22). Yet when it comes to spelling out Belshazzar's sin to him (v. 23) there is no mention of his predecessor. Instead of facing the representative of Nebuchadnezzar, Belshazzar is suddenly facing God, and at this point the narrator begins to apply Daniel's other function in the story.[32]

---

31. Simon, 'Minor Characters', p. 18: 'The minor character is... instrumental in the ironic reversal of social conventions'. P.D. Miscall, *The Workings of Old Testament Narrative* (Philadelphia: Fortress Press; Chico, CA: Scholars Press, 1983), p. 57, reminds us of the significance of the unusual in Old Testament narrative. But contrast Collins, *Daniel*, p. 248, for whom 'The MT properly allows this venerable figure to take the initiative...'

32. Fewell, *Circle of Sovereignty*, p. 135.

The LXX narrative is less ambivalent about the role played by Daniel. This is apparent in the different uses made by each version of the phrase גלותא די יהוד ('exiles of Judah') and its Greek equivalent, ἐκ τῆς αἰχμαλωσίας τῆς Ιουδαίαις. As we have already seen, in the MT the king uses it (v. 13) in his initial address to Daniel to try and bolster his own position. The phrase in the LXX occurs as a piece of description from the narrator, indeed the only piece of narrative description of Daniel (v. 10). The rest of Daniel's portrait is painted within direct speech. There is no suggestion of any ambivalence on the part of Belshazzar regarding Daniel's qualifications as a sage. The first time he speaks he merely asks if Daniel can interpret, and Daniel's response is to do just that.

Another subtle difference in emphasis regards the agency of Daniel. In the MT account it is only implied that Nebuchadnezzar was ever the beneficiary of Daniel's 'wisdom of the gods' (v. 11, חכמת־אלהין), but it is explicit that the king 'set him up' (v. 11, הקימה). He is clearly a figure identified with the court in the Aramaic version. In the LXX the opposite is the case. He exercised his gifts in the days of Nebuchadnezzar, who was the beneficiary of those gifts (v. 12), but there is no suggestion that he acted as an appointee of the king. His authority therefore remains intrinsic rather than extrinsic and so poses no threat to the temporal authority of Belshazzar. This different role is appropriate to a version that does not include contest or conflict material, and represents the issues facing the king in spiritual rather than temporal terms.

Consequently, while neither Belshazzar nor Daniel respond to the other with much grace in the MT, there is a less adversarial tone to the exchanges between wise man and king in the LXX.[33] There is no record of Daniel declining the gifts in the abrupt fashion that he does in v. 17 MT. His response is simply to stand before the writing and read it (v. 17). He does not refer to Nebuchadnezzar at all. Indeed vv. 18-22, which enumerate Nebuchadnezzar's achievements and link them explicitly with Belshazzar's failure, do not form part of the LXX narrative.

The third character in the story is Belshazzar. In the previous section I considered his motivation, and aspects of his character were brought out in connection with that. But there is more to add on the characterization of Belshazzar in each version. Because of the differing attitudes of the

---

33. Contrast Montgomery, *Daniel*, p. 249, who suggests 'The king graciously accosts (Daniel)', in the MT. Hartman and DiLella, *Daniel*, p. 189, and E.W. Heaton, *The Book of Daniel* (London: SCM Press, 1956), p. 160, agree.

queen and Daniel, the portrait of him in the LXX is a more sympathetic one. His influence over the queen, Daniel's polite and immediate response to his request for an interpretation, the absence of a number of allusions to the greatness of Nebuchadnezzar, and the more open-ended conclusion, at least as far as Belshazzar personally is concerned, are all cases in point.

The more negative view of the MT comes through particularly in the sense of fear exuded by the king. This is portrayed by the physical manifestations of his terror (v. 6), the repetition and intensification of that terror in the phrase 'greatly terrified' (v. 9, שֹגיא מתבהל), and the manner in which he calls for his wise men. He 'called loudly' (v. 7, קרא...בחיל).[34] These are all in contrast to the account in the LXX and also in contrast to Nebuchadnezzar in the previous chapter, who describes the summoning of his wise men in the authoritative terms of a royal decree (4.3, מני שים טעם). Enough has already been said in connection with other points to show that this contrast between the monarchs is generally true throughout the chapter.

The charge has been laid against this particular tale that the characters are one-dimensional. It may be true that, 'The narrative reveals little of the distinctive personalities of the characters in the story...',[35] but it should be clear by now that the subtlety of characterization helps to bring out more clearly the agenda of the MT narrator. The king's fear, the appropriation of his authority by the queen, and the ambivalence of Daniel's attitude towards Belshazzar all give life to this portrait of a courtly power struggle, which serves as a backdrop to the writing on the wall and its interpretation.

The LXX is not so interested in that backdrop but focuses instead more sharply on the handwriting and its interpretation. As a result the characters are less surprising and more functional. The queen simply comes when she is called for and reminds Belshazzar of a wise man from the previous regime. Belshazzar does not exhibit the same fear or loss of control, both moral and physical, and continues to issue orders. Daniel, like the queen, comes and does what he is asked to do. He makes no response at all to the promise of a reward.

---

34. S.R. Driver, *Daniel* (Cambridge: Cambridge University Press, 1900), p. 63.
35. Goldingay, *Daniel*, p. 104.

Perspective

In discussing the character and role of Daniel I have noted a double focus in the story as told by the MT narrator. The result is that there is also a story behind the story of the handwriting on the wall. This second strand of emphasis can be elucidated further by considering the operation of perspective in ch. 5.[36]

The twofold perspective becomes clear in an examination of the use made of the preposition קְבֵל (vv. 1, 5). Belshazzar, who drank wine 'before or in front of' (קְבֵל) them, thought he was performing his actions facing the guests in the opening sentence of the story. In fact what turned out to be facing (קְבֵל) him was the handwriting on the wall (v. 5). There is an irony immediately apparent that reflects badly on the king. But the word is also used by the narrator to direct the point of view of the reader, with similar effects to a change in camera angle. Such an effect was also achieved in ch. 4 by the shift in narrative person. The narrator first describes Belshazzar facing his nobles, whose attention in turn is directed back towards him. But on the opposite (קְבֵל) wall the fingers of God face Belshazzar. The result is a series of physical manifestations of terror which the nobles observe without being aware of the immediate cause of the terror, the handwriting going on behind them. The reader sees what the nobles see, the terrified king, but not the words that are causing the terror. The fact that the royal harem (v. 3, שֵׁגְלָתֵהּ וּלְחֵנָתֵהּ) disappears from the story at that point tends to support my earlier suggestion regarding the banquet layout. From their position in the hall they would not have witnessed the king's terror. In this way the focus moves away from the handwriting seen by Belshazzar to the frightened king as observed by his guests.[37]

The shift in viewpoint serves two purposes. It puts the handwriting into abeyance so that it is not even read, much less interpreted, until much later in the story. This heightens suspense and reflects the ignorance of the nobles, who probably had not read the writing. It also clears the stage for the other focus of the story, the king's psychological and

36. See again Stanzel, *A Theory of Narrative*, p. 9, on the functions of point of view. By 'perspective' here I mean primarily the physical standpoint from which the story is narrated, but this also is part of the way the outlooks of different characters and the narrator are conveyed.

37. See Porteous, *Daniel*, p. 78, in support of this view on the operation of perspective within the story.

political struggle against the memory of his predecessor and the conse-quences of that insecurity for his kingdom. The writing itself does not appear again until v. 26. The two points of view in evidence are God's and Belshazzar's. The king thinks he is proving himself in some way at the banquet but God has quite a different attitude towards his misdeeds. What Belshazzar thought he was doing is dealt with in the long, and purposefully repetitive, section in vv. 11-22. Daniel, as we have seen, addresses both points of view.

There are clues directing the careful reader to the viewpoint that the narrator himself is backing. We have already seen that the descriptions of the vessels, repeated in vv. 2 and 3, are significant. By varying the emphasis slightly the narrator puts his own stress on them as belonging to God rather than Nebuchadnezzar. Immediately the narrator acquires his own persona and gives an ironic aspect to the dismantling of Belshazzar's political ambitions by the queen and Daniel, while the pri-mary matter of the handwriting is put on hold. But the viewpoint of Daniel is identified with that of the narrator when the matter of the Temple vessels is returned to in v. 23. There Daniel refers to them as 'the vessels of his house' (v. 23, למאניא די ביתה), adopting the stress applied by the narrator himself in v. 3. In this manner the narrator betrays his point of view as close to, if not identical with, that of Daniel.

The more personal setting of the LXX feast does not give rise to the same subtleties of shifting perspective. The more stereotypical roles of the queen and the sage, and the absence of variation in describing the sacred objects means that the second focus is not present at all. As a result there is not the same suspense built up around the writing and its meaning, nor is the aspect of comparison with Nebuchadnezzar nearly as prominent.

Narrative and Narrator

This point becomes more obvious in a consideration of the unusually long piece of narration uninterrupted by dialogue at the beginning of the story in both the MT and LXX. The first 10 verses in the MT and the first 11 in the LXX are devoted to the events leading up to the entrance of the queen. In the MT this long piece of descriptive narrative is highly visual. Belshazzar is facing his nobles, while the hand that appears is opposite him. The vessels are made of gold and silver. The gods are of gold, silver, bronze, iron, wood and stone. The hand writes on the plaster and is opposite the lampstand.[38] The king 'saw' (v. 5, חזה) the hand at work. The effect on him is observable as physical changes in his body. The one element in that description that is not physical, 'his thoughts terrified him' (v. 6, רעינהי יבהלונה) is embedded in three other elements that are all physical. Even the promised rewards are the tangible purple robe, gold necklace and authority over a third part of the kingdom (v. 7).[39] Compare this to ch. 2 where Nebuchadnezzar promises the more abstract 'gifts and rewards and great honour' (2.6, מתנן ונבזבה ויקר שׂגיא). Yet in all of this there is one vital visual detail missing, the writing in the plaster of the palace wall, which the wise men of the kingdom 'were not able to read' (v. 8, לאכהלין...למקרא).

The block of introductory narrative in the LXX version is similarly visual, although its effect is not quite so marked. To start with, the colour and action achieved by repetition in the MT is not present to the same extent. The vessels are only described once in vv. 2-3 and the guests, ἑταίροις αὐτοῦ (v. 2), are also only mentioned once and after that are referred to by pronoun.

The evocative description of v. 6, Belshazzar's initial reaction to the sign on the wall, is also handled differently. The MT mentions the king's terror as one of four elements in a description of his physical response. The other elements are well-known involuntary manifestations of fear in the human body. The change of facial colour on its own could be interpreted in more than one way, but when allied with the knees knocking together and the humiliating loss of sphincter control can only mean one thing.[40] The watchers at the feast would have deduced the king's fear

---

38. This is the majority opinion on the meaning of נברשׁתא. A.R. Millard, 'The Etymology of *Nebrasta*, Daniel 5:5', *Maarav* 4 (1987), pp. 88-92, has no doubt about the meaning of the word. The uncertainty is over its etymology, which he argues to be Akkadian. See also the discussion in Montgomery, *Daniel*, p. 255.

39. תלתי במלכותא (v. 7) could be a reference to rank or it could be the offer of a specific administrative position. Shea, 'Belshazzar', p. 70, argues that the 'third' rank for Daniel was after Belshazzar and Nabonidus, for whom Belshazzar was chief officer. R.P. Dougherty, *Nabonidus and Belshazzar* (New Haven: Yale University Press, 1929), pp. 68-69, assigns the same rank to Belshazzar, but in the reign of Neriglissar. Compare also Goldingay, *Daniel*, p. 100, and Lacocque, *Daniel*, p. 77.

40. Fewell, *Circle of Sovereignty*, p. 120, offers this understanding of קטרי חרצה משׁתרין which I accept as likely. Research by A. Wolters, 'Untying the King's Knots: Physiology and Wordplay in Daniel 5', *JBL* 110 (1991), pp. 119-21, backs up her interpretation. Note also the phrase 'loins were loosened' in *1 En.* 60.3. See M.A. Knibb, *The Ethiopic Book of Enoch* (Oxford: Clarendon Press, 1978), p. 142.

for themselves, and the narrator intends the reader to do the same.

The narrator is more overt in the LXX with the editorially omniscient statement that 'fears and fancies dismayed him' (v. 6, φόβοι καὶ ὑπόνοιαι αὐτὸν κατέσπευδον). This is preceded by the difficult phrase ἡ ὅρασις αὐτοῦ ἠλλοιώθη (v. 6), which is probably an attempt at expressing the same phenomenon as זיוהי שׁגנוהי. Some sort of change in the cast of the face seems to be intended by the LXX, perhaps a heightening or loss of colour. The reader of the LXX needs the help of the narrator to understand this phrase, as well as the king's subsequent action in standing and looking at the writing (v. 6), as manifestations of fear rather than another emotion such as anger or aggression.

The more specific ἀνυψώθη ἡ καρδία αὐτοῦ (v. 2) of the LXX, as against בטעם חמרא of the MT, also has a bearing on our discussion of narratorial presence. The Septuagintal narrator reveals to the reader the extent of his knowledge by declaring on Belshazzar's motivation. The MT uses a more ambiguous term, leaving readers to make their own judgment on the course of action that Belshazzar is about to undertake.

The Writing on the Wall

I noted earlier that, despite all the visual detail, the writing itself is entirely missing in the MT. What the king sees is 'the palm of the hand writing' (v. 5, פס ידה די כתבה) and that is the occasion of his reaction, not the writing itself.[41] There is no mention of his actually reading the writing. When he calls for his mantic officials in v. 7 he desires them to 'read' (קרה) as well as 'interpret' (פשׁר). They are able to do neither (v. 8), which intensifies the king's fear. When Belshazzar finally calls Daniel he asks for a reading as well as an interpretation (v. 16), and that is exactly what Daniel offers to give (v. 17). The only time in the chapter when interpretation appears without reading is when the queen, who was not present when the writing appeared first, orders Daniel to be called (v. 12).[42]

---

41. According to Torrey, 'Notes', p. 276, the narrator uses פס to emphasize that only the hand appears, since יד may include the forearm as well.

42. In light of the consistency of juxtaposition of the two terms in the rest of ch. 5, it is interesting that 4QDan[a] appears to add at the end of v. 12 כתבא יקרא, 'and read the writing'. A 4QDan[b] fragment may agree with that lengthened reading. See E. Ulrich, 'Daniel Manuscripts from Qumran. Part 1: A Preliminary Edition of 4QDan[a]', *BASOR* 268 (1987), pp. 23 and 30-31; and *idem*, 'Daniel Manuscripts

The writing comes back into the story much earlier in the LXX version (at v. 17), but even before that it is taken as understood within the narrative of vv. 1-10. The mysterious hand is also a source of fear in the LXX, but instead of dissolving as he does almost literally in the MT, Belshazzar gets up with his companions to have a closer look at the writing (v. 6). It is what he sees at that point, the words rather than the phenomenon, that causes him to call for the mantic officials (v. 7, τοὺς ἐπαοιδοὺς καὶ φαρμακοὺς καὶ χαλδαίους καὶ γαζαρηνούς). They come 'to see the writing and...were not able to provide the interpretation' (v. 7, ἰδεῖν τὴν γραφήν καὶ...οὐκ ἐδύναντο συγκρῖναι). The implication is that they can read without difficulty but cannot or will not interpret. Through the rest of the chapter in the LXX all that the king requests is the interpretation. The lack of an interpretation is a source of concern rather than fear to Belshazzar. In the MT a new wave of terror hits him when his wise men are not able to perform (v. 9), and the suspense of the narrative increases. In the LXX his response to their failure is expressed in the more measured phrase, 'then the king called the queen' (v. 9, τότε ὁ βασιλεὺς ἐκάλεσε τὴν βασίλισσαν), and then he 'showed' (v. 9, ὑπέδειξεν) her the sign. Although the reader does not yet know what the writing is, its presence for the characters is presumed.

A major puzzle for commentators of the MT has been in the necessity for the words to be read as well as interpreted, and the failure of the Babylonian wise men to do even the first satisfactorily. By now it should be clear that the king's request to read as well as interpret makes sense when considered in the light of the narrator's craft. It is not the narrator's intention that anybody other than Belshazzar should have seen the writing. The moment it appears the reader's view of events is from where the nobles sit. His likely companions at the top table, the 'wives and concubines' (v. 3, שֵׁגְלָתֵהּ וּלְחֵנָתֵהּ), at this point disappear from the narrative. The nobles are focused on the king and his terror which seems to

from Qumran. Part 2: Preliminary Editions of 4QDan^b and 4QDan^c', *BASOR* 274 (1989), pp. 6-11. Ulrich is uncertain if this witnesses to a loss from or an addition to the MT tradition. Collins, *Daniel*, p. 3, declares it to be a scribal addition. The literary evidence suggests the authenticity of the Qumran evidence should be reconsidered. Notwithstanding this particular instance, the Qumran discoveries in Daniel generally 'provide powerful evidence of the antiquity of the textual tradition of MT' (Collins, *Daniel*, p. 3). For useful summaries of Daniel at Qumran, see Collins, *Daniel*, pp. 2-3, and, from a more partisan perspective, G.F. Hasel, 'New Light on the Book of Daniel from the Dead Sea Scrolls', *Ministry* (Jan 1992), pp. 11-13.

lie principally in the phenomenon of the hand which he saw. His desire to have the writing read and interpreted is no doubt in the hope that such an achievement would make the intent of the hand clear, in the same way that Nebuchadnezzar in ch. 2 needed to know both the dream and its interpretation. This is all part of the narrator manipulating the reader's perspective from within the narrative.

In contrast, the LXX narrator shares his omniscience with the reader, as far as his treatment of the writing on the wall goes. Because the writing is presumed in the Septuagintal account to be clear to all those present, there is no point in having it read. Indeed Daniel does not do so. He simply gives one understanding of the words with the third person singular passives, 'counted, reckoned, taken away' (v. 17, ἠρίθμηται, κατελογίσθη, ἐξῆρται). The LXX makes no attempt to transliterate the Semitic words as θ and the prologue do. The interpretation (vv. 26-28) is another matter, as the solution given seems to bear little verbal correspondence, except in the first element, to the original reading. Instead of unpointed roots being given a double meaning, the interpretation could only have come through mantic wisdom. This throws some light on the LXX interest only in the interpretation.[43] Anybody could, and probably had, read the words for themselves and taken Daniel's initial meaning (v. 17) from them.

As a further comment on the MT treatment of the writing on the wall, an assortment of suggestions have been made as to why the Babylonian astrologers could not have read the writing. Wiseman notes the lack of any exact parallel to this type of writing in other ancient Near Eastern sources and traces the astrologers' puzzlement to the fact that the writing does not follow any known models, in that it was not linked to a king or dynasty nor did it appear to be a series of number omens.[44] It is

43. The present discussion does not attempt to solve the riddle of why there are four words written in MT but only three interpreted. But we note the debate. Goldingay, *Daniel*, p. 102, sees the three words of the Old Greek as assimilation towards the interpretation. Lacocque, *Daniel*, p. 83, also accepts the MT as the *lectio difficilior*. Hartman and DiLella, *Daniel*, p. 183, take the opposite tack and say that מנא is doubled in the MT through dittography. Torrey, 'Notes', p. 276, likewise sees the extra element as not original. O. Eissfeldt, 'Die Menetekel-Inschrift und ihre Deutung', *ZAW* 63 (1951), pp. 112-13, minimizes the difficulty by noting that variation between message and interpretation is a stylistic feature in Daniel.

44. Wiseman, *Nebuchadrezzar*, p. 90, cites *The Annals of Sennacherib*, 94.64 and 103.27-29, and C.J. Gadd, 'Omens Expressed in Numbers', *JCS* 21 (1967), pp. 55-58.

also possible that Belshazzar had experienced some sort of vision to which only he was privy, or else he observed some sort of cryptogram which had to be unscrambled before being interpreted.[45] As a development of this idea Finkel puts Daniel's interpretation of the inscription in the context of the biblical and rabbinic tradition of 'pesher' (פּשׁר) as a mode of interpretation.[46] One aspect of this tradition was discernment of the double meaning of words as a clue to their interpretation. It was only the one to whom the פּשׁר was granted who could see the double meaning. Another biblical example is the play on שׁקֵד in Jer 1.11-12, where a nominal form receives an interpretation from the participial form of the triliteral root. Goldingay also reminds us that any piece of unpointed text needs to be understood before it can be read aloud.[47] In that sense the interpretation lies in the reading. Daniel is able to apply the consonants in different ways when he eventually does read them, because he understands their significance.[48]

Words and Vision

It is interesting that this story about words has such a strong visual element, particularly in the first part of the chapter. Once the meaning of the words begins to be tackled, there is a return to dialogue and words are used to interpret the written message. This is in contrast to the dream tales of chs. 2 and 4, where the divine message is conveyed in the visual experiential media of dreams and visions. Indeed, Nebuchadnezzar in ch. 4 speaks of what he 'saw' (חזה), yet the story is almost entirely conveyed in the form of dialogue. In ch. 5 the divine message is verbal, but conveyed by the narrator in the visual experiential terms that belonged to the messages themselves in those dream tales of other chapters.

---

45. Compare A. Alt, 'Zur Menetekel-Inschrift', *VT* (1954), pp. 304-305.

46. A. Finkel, 'The Pesher of Dreams and Scriptures', *RevQ* 4 (1964), p. 359. Horgan, *Pesharim*, p. 256, says of 5.26 that דנה פּשׁד־מלתא is a Qumran pesher formula. Eissfeldt, 'Die Menetekel-Inschrift', p. 108, notes the differentiation between reading and interpretation as a feature of pesher in 1QpHab.

47. Goldingay, *Daniel*, p. 109.

48. Note also the rabbinic tradition in *b. Sanh.* 22a that the words were to be read vertically. See also Saadia in Gallé, *Daniel*, p. 59, and J.J. Slotki, *Daniel, Ezra and Nehemiah* (London: Soncino, 1951), p. 45. Rembrandt's painting of Belshazzar's feast reflects that tradition.

Other Literary Features

There are several other differences between the versions, none large in themselves, but all adding to the picture of theological and literary differences between the MT and LXX. Fewell has drawn attention to the wordplay in the speech of the queen, who in v. 12 reminds Belshazzar that Daniel could 'loosen knots' (מֹשֵׁרא קטרין). This is a metaphorical use of the phrase of v. 6 which describes one of the physical symptoms of the king's fear, 'the knots of his loins were loosened' (קטרי חרצה מֹשתרין).[49] As well as adding to the king's humiliation, the phrase confirms Daniel's role in the story as a bringer of judgment. This play on words is absent in the LXX. In v. 6 the phrase is not represented at all and the equivalent in v. 12 is more abstract and less picturesque. θ retains the image in Greek with οἱ σύνδεσμοι τῆς ὀσφύος αὐτοῦ διελύοντο (v. 6), which also has an echo in v. 12.

The phrase זיוהי שׁנוהי (vv. 6, 9) brings another ironic twist at Belshazzar's expense.[50] As we have seen, this difficult expression has the sense in the present context of some sort of change in the king's countenance, but זיו carries the primary meaning of splendour or brightness. The change in facial colour thereby becomes a further symbol of the reduction of Belshazzar's royal splendour. It is no coincidence that the word also describes the greatness of Nebuchadnezzar (4.33), against whom the present king is being contrasted, as well as the splendour of the statue in 2.31.[51] The LXX has no equivalent in v. 9, and the translation ὅρασις in v. 6 focuses on the immediate meaning of the word and so does not include the irony. θ, by contrast, 'uses μορφή to render זיו both here and at 4.36 in an attempt to capture the wider range of meaning of the Aramaic word.

There is a small but possibly significant variation in the story as told by the MT. In v. 2 the Temple vessels are of 'gold and silver' (דהבא וכספא) but the gods that Belshazzar praises are of 'silver and gold' (v. 23, כספא־ודהבא). The linking of these two items in v. 23 at the

---

49. Fewell, *Circle of Sovereignty*, p. 122. A. Brenner, 'Who's Afraid of Feminist Criticism? Who's Afraid of Biblical Humour? The Case of the Obtuse Foreign Ruler in the Hebrew Bible', *JSOT* 63 (1994), p. 49, takes this wordplay on the lips of the queen a step further and links the king's humiliating incontinence with impotence from which the queen must rescue him.

50. Slotki, *Daniel*, p. 40.

51. Saadia in Gallé, *Daniel*, p. 54, picks up the pun.

beginning of a list with a *maqqeph* and the only ו in the series suggests
that the reversal of order is deliberate. The gold and silver is reminiscent
of the statue of ch. 2 and Daniel's identification of the gold head of the
statue with Nebuchadnezzar, with the implication that what was to come
after him would be increasingly inferior. By reversing the order and
placing silver at the head of the list, another chance is not passed up of
reminding Belshazzar that he is inferior to Nebuchadnezzar as silver is
inferior to gold.[52] This is reinforced by the reference in v. 3 to the
vessels of 'gold' (דהבא) which Nebuchadnezzar had brought out. The
different emphasis of the LXX is seen in its description of the idols as
'made by hands of men' (v. 23, χειροποίητα τῶν ἀνθρώπων).
Incidentally, θ in vv. 3 and 23 has either read a different *Vorlage* or
amended the MT to read 'gold and silver'.

Occasionally the LXX conveys a different theological emphasis from
MT, as for example in the above mentioned v. 23 where the Old Greek
says that it is 'idols' (εἴδωλα) being praised by Belshazzar and his
nobles. In the MT it is 'gods' (אלהי). The two versions agree substantially
in their description of the living God whom the king has failed to
acknowledge and whose sacred vessels he has desecrated. The MT is less
clear on, or at least less interested in, whether or not the other gods
exist. The LXX allows less room for argument with made by hands of
men' (v. 23, χειροποίητα τῶν ἀνθρώπων). This reflects the
monotheistic emphasis of the LXX as against the MT.

A second instance is that the LXX does not refer to Daniel as 'chief
(רב) of the magicians...' as he is in v. 11 MT. In fact the LXX account
has the effect of distancing Daniel from those officials so that he is in a
separate category altogether. When Daniel enters the story Belshazzar
makes no reference to the failure of the Babylonian wise men, so the
aspect of contest is almost entirely absent. This continues the trend
already seen in ch. 4, where the same Aramaic title, רב חרטמיא (4.6), is
given Daniel by the MT, and where the LXX in contrast calls him 'ruler
of the wise men' (4.18, ἄρχοντα τῶν σοφιστῶν), although the contrast
is not as marked here, as the LXX continues on to refer to Daniel as
'leader of the interpreters of dreams' (v. 18, τὸν ἡγούμενον τῶν
κρινόντων τὰ ἐνύπνια). In this manner the LXX portrays the uniqueness of the wisdom evident in the Jewish sage.

The order of events in vv. 7-8 MT has worried some commentators.[53]

52. Shea, 'Daniel 5', p. 283.
53. Charles, *Daniel*, p. 107, for example.

The problem lies in the fact that the wise men seem to come in twice. Belshazzar orders the officials to be brought in (v. 7, לְהַעֲלָה). The ensuing use of עֲנֵה as response implies that the order has been carried out and they are now assembled to hear the king's speech. At the beginning of v. 8 all the king's wise men come in again, which suggests there is some confusion in the text. Against this, אֱדַיִן may serve a 'resumptive' function here, in which case the first phrase of v. 8 could be translated, 'All the king's wise men having come into the hall...'[54] Such a usage may be detected in Ezra 4.23. Montgomery also notes that עָלֲלִין is a *peal* participle form implying continuous action.[55]

Having said all that, some ambiguity remains in the MT narrative at this point. There is a similar ambiguity witnessed to by the Old Greek, which also has the magicians coming in twice (vv. 7-8). In between the two entrances, however, there is a block of plus material in which the king sets forth an ordinance promising rewards to anybody who is able to interpret the writing. As it stands this has the effect of clarifying the order of events and justifying the second entrance of the purveyors of Babylonian wisdom. They come in first in response to the king's summons but fail in their mission. This elicits a more formal challenge from the king, which the same group also responds to and with the same result. However it should be acknowledged that, although the textual witnesses are in harmony with each other, there is a hint of conflation about the story at this point in the LXX. If that is the case, the same ambiguity as in the MT remains.

Links with Daniel 4

There are obvious links in the MT with ch. 4. I have argued above that the links drawn are central to one of the purposes of ch. 5, namely to compare Belshazzar unfavourably with Nebuchadnezzar. Thematic links such as the kingship of Nebuchadnezzar, the Temple vessels, the contest between types of wisdom, interpretation (פְּשַׁר), and the role of Daniel at court have already been dealt with.

There are also organic links that may be seen most clearly where verbal correspondences occur. An example is the list of magicians in v. 11 which may be compared with the list in 4.4. The series in v. 7 is

54. Goldingay, *Daniel*, p. 101: 'The phrase is resumptive after v. 7b, to lead into the statement of the sages' incomprehension...'
55. Montgomery, *Daniel*, p. 254.

different only in that the first item, חרטמין, is absent. Verse 11 has two other turns of phrase strongly reminiscent of ch. 4. The first is the title of Daniel as 'chief of the magicians' (רב חרטמין), the same title used for him in 4.6. The second is in the queen's description of the sage as one in whom is 'the wisdom of the gods' (חכמת־אלהין) and who has 'an extraordinary spirit' (רוח יתירה). Although the verbal correspondence is not exact, the two phrases together recall the expression 'spirit of the holy gods' (4.5-6, רוח אלהין קדישין). Belshazzar himself uses the term רוח אלהין in his address to Daniel (v. 14).

The relationship between chs. 4 and 5 is strongest and most explicit in the long stretch of MT plus material in vv. 18-22, an account of the events of ch. 4, which is almost word for word in places. In v. 18 the words 'the kingdom and greatness and glory and majesty' (מלכותא ורבותא ויקרא והדרא) echo Nebuchadnezzar's boast in 'Babylon the great' (4.27, בבל רבתא) and 'the glory of my majesty' (4.27, יקר הדרי). The expression 'peoples, nations and tongues' (v. 19, עממיא אמיא ולשניא) is identical with the group to whom Nebuchadnezzar's letter is addressed (3.31). Verse 21 is very close to 4.22 which summarizes Nebuchadnezzar's experience and its significance. Every phrase reflects the previous chapter and the key expressions, 'God Most High rules' (שליט אלהא עליא) and 'whomever he pleases he sets up over it' (למן־די יצבה יהקים עליה), are almost identical.

The LXX account of Belshazzar and the writing on the wall relates to the dream of the great tree in a different way. The evidence for some sort of organic link between the two chapters is indecisive. On the one hand the unusual phrase 'fancies dismayed him' (v. 6, ὑπόνοιαι αὐτὸν κατέσπευδον) also occurs in 4.19, although in that context Daniel rather than the king is the object. On its own ὑπόνοιαί occurs in 4.33b in a sense more akin to that in 5.6. The expression 'the sight of him (Daniel) changed' is employed at both 5.6 (ἡ ὅρασις αὐτοῦ ἠλλοιώθη) and 4.19 (ἀλλοιωθείσης τῆς ὁράσεως αὐτοῦ). The word ὑποδείκνυμι (vv. 7, 9, 12, 16, 'show') is also characteristic of the LXX as compared to θ, and is used twice in ch. 4 (vv. 18, 37c) as well. In both chapters it has as its object σύγκριμα or σύγκρισις ('interpretation'). The occurrence of πνεῦμα (v. 12) is immediately reminiscent of ch. 4, yet the phrase that it is part of, πνεῦμα ἅγιον ('holy spirit') is unique in the Greek versions of Daniel.

However, other factors offset this already tenuous evidence. As well as the four occurrences of ὑποδείκνυμι in ch. 5, the LXX uses ἀπαγγέλω ('announce') synonymously three times (vv. 7, 8, 9). In v. 7 the two words occur in parallel. In contrast to ὑποδείκνυμι, ἀπαγγέλω only occurs elsewhere in Daniel LXX in ch. 2. Moreover, ch. 5 uses σύγκριμα (vv. 7, 8, 9, 12, 16, 26, 30) where elsewhere the LXX tends to favour the same word preferred by θ, σύγκρισις (2.4, 5, 6, 9, 26; 4.18, 19). In the MT the verbal correspondences are most marked when the events of ch. 4 are being recalled. If the same phenomenon were evident in the LXX it would be in a comparison of 5.11-12, where the queen recalls the work of Daniel under a previous regime, with 4.18. Yet there is no such agreement here. The evidence immediately above is to the contrary. What all this adds up to is that it is impossible to detect the type of linguistic links between chs. 4 and 5 in the LXX that the MT displays.

There is a consistency about the content minuses as far as the LXX is concerned. As I have already noted, the court contest or conflict is not a factor in either LXX chapter. Although the magicians make an entrance early in the story, the absence of v. 15 in ch. 5 means that they are not placed in opposition to Daniel. The more judgmental attitude of the LXX towards Nebuchadnezzar is not altered by the events of ch. 5. In fact a link is drawn between the sin of Belshazzar and the sin of Nebuchadnezzar with the phrase ἀνυψώθη ἡ καρδία αὐτοῦ (5.2). This recalls the accusing words of Daniel to Belshazzar's predecessor, 'your heart was exalted' (4.22, ὑψώθη σου ἡ καρδία). Certainly Nebuchadnezzar's political greatness and later acknowledgment of the Most High are not recalled. This is in contrast to what we have already seen about the MT use of the person of King Nebuchadnezzar. Likewise, the Septuagintal attitude towards Daniel as a member of the court administration is the same in both chapters. Daniel's position within the court is hardly touched on and he is thought of as entirely outside the category occupied by the Babylonian magicians.

The ordering of the stories in 967 means that chs. 4 and 5 are separated from one another by the visions of chs. 7 and 8. If that does in fact represent an earlier arrangement, the literary effect of chs. 4 and 5 as the central point in a chiasm focused on Nebuchadnezzar is not present. It is not surprising then that the two chapters are more distinct from one another in the LXX.[56]

---

56. Note Bogaert, 'Relecture et Refonte', pp. 199-200, on the priority of the 967 arrangement. He surmises that the MT order is part of that version's interest in showing Daniel as a reliable prophet.

Conclusion

There is much that these two accounts of Belshazzar and the hand-writing on the wall have in common. They are both set against the unsettling background of a Near Eastern banquet. In both, the excesses of the banquet are not the primary concern of the narrator so much as the sin of rebellion against God by the desecration of his sacred objects. Both narrators show, more or less explicitly, the premeditated nature of the king's action in profaning the Temple vessels.

But there are differences in the manner in which the story is told. In his portrayal of characters, his manipulation of perspective, and the sensory nature of his narrative, the MT narrator allows the reader to enter into the ambiguity of his story. From within the story he draws the reader to an identification with Daniel and the queen in their perception of Belshazzar. The LXX also shares its point of view with the reader, but the more overt omniscience of the LXX narrator means that both he and the reader remain outside the events.

The handwriting in both stories is central, but in quite different ways as a result of the two types of narrator. In the MT the centrality of the writing on the wall is emphasized by its absence, and in the LXX by its presence. The gap created in the MT story, as well as providing suspense, allows the narrator to imply an extra dimension to Belshazzar's motivation. This is where the theme of Nebuchadnezzar's kingship is expounded at Belshazzar's expense, a theme that the LXX only touches on incidentally in the introduction of Daniel, the interpreter of the writing. As a result the LXX version has a less negative view of Belshazzar than the MT, and views his fate in more personal terms.

There are various literary links with the previous chapter in the MT, primarily in the references to King Nebuchadnezzar. In this regard the viewpoint of ch. 4 is not only preserved but also developed. The most that can be said for the LXX perspective in ch. 5 is that it does not contradict that of ch. 4. As a result the MT has carried on in ch. 5 the more complimentary view of Nebuchadnezzar that emerges in the story of the dream of the great tree. Daniel's prominence in the court of Nebuchadnezzar is also confirmed. The story of the handwriting on the wall does not stand alone in the LXX, as we will see when exploring chs. 2 and 3, but is largely independent of ch. 4. It does, however, show the same Jewish suspicion of Gentile monarchs, polytheism and mantic wisdom as ch. 4 LXX.

Chapter 4

DANIEL 6

Daniel 6 differs from both the chapters previously studied. These differences as far as the MT is concerned have been described in various ways. In structural terms, chs. 3 and 6 seem to form a distinctive bracket around chs. 4 and 5.[1] In terms of genre, the present chapter is a classical court conflict in contrast to the contests in the Nebuchadnezzar and Belshazzar stories.[2] In morphological terms, a distinction has been drawn between *Märchen* (fairy tale) and *Legende* (legend). According to Müller, chs. 4 and 5 are fairy tales while chs. 3 and 6 are later legends.[3] Each analysis recognizes in its own way that chs. 4 and 5 are different from chs. 3 and 6 in the role assigned to the hero and in the purpose and background of the stories, although, as we will see and as Müller warns, such distinctions are helpful but must not be applied rigidly.[4] The LXX also reflects a change in form, principally in that Daniel is now a member of the official hierarchy, and the aspect of contest, hitherto not present in the LXX, plays an important part in the present story.

These differences form a backdrop to the present comparison of the two accounts of Daniel in the lion pit. After an acknowledgment that the ordering of events and dialogue are roughly the same in both narrations, I will move on to consider some important differences in narrative technique. The profiles of the narrator within the story will be examined in terms of the linking between scenes, the way motive is conveyed, and the pace of the stories. Then the functioning of irony and suspense within the stories will be compared in some detail. At that point a brief excursus will be necessary to clarify some terms used in the discussion of irony.

1. Lenglet, 'Daniel 2–7', pp. 182-85.
2. Humphreys, 'Lifestyle', pp. 217-18.
3. Müller, 'Märchen, Legende', pp. 338-39 and 342-45. Milne, *Vladimir Propp*, pp. 241 and 254-62, also marshals the morphological evidence.
4. Müller, 'Märchen, Legende', p. 347.

I then turn from narrative technique to theological emphasis. This will be done first with a close look at the vocabulary used for prayer or petition in each version. The findings there will lead us into the words of the final encyclical, which not only demonstrate the varying points of emphasis between versions, but also point up quite different treatments of the person of King Darius. In the process, a small difference in the portrayal of Daniel will be noted. The questions of narrative technique and theological emphasis are artificial distinctions, and each aspect necessarily intrudes into and helps to clarify discussion of the other. The study will demonstrate that the LXX version of the story is not an unsatisfactory one, and a brief section towards the end will exemplify that.

As with other stories in Daniel, there are historical problems around the person of the king, about which little scholarly consensus has emerged. The situation is not helped by the presence of Artaxerxes in v. 1 of the LXX.[5] There are also textual questions within and between the versions. It is uncertain how many conspirators there are, how many are finally punished, what the verb רגש means, or how Bel and the Dragon relates to the versions of Daniel 6.[6] In the LXX especially there are occasional signs of incomplete redaction that require acknowledgment. I treat these and other questions only at points in the study where they relate to the literary comparison being undertaken. I also include a section on the nature of Daniel's trial, where a discussion of the *Sitz im Leben* of the chapter brings out and clarifies certain differences between the MT and LXX as well as drawing attention to a parallel difference between the two accounts of ch. 4.

---

5.   See the differing treatments in J.C. Whitcomb, *Darius the Mede* (Grand Rapids: Eerdmans, 1959); and H.H. Rowley, *Darius the Mede and the Four World Empires in the Book of Daniel* (Cardiff: University of Wales Press Board, 1959). Note also D.J. Wiseman, 'Some Historical Problems in the Book of Daniel', in D.J. Wiseman *et al.*, *Notes on Some Problems in the Book of Daniel* (London: Tyndale Press, 1965), pp. 15-16; and W.H. Shea, 'Darius the Mede', *AUSS* 29 (1991), pp. 239 and 256. B.E. Colless, 'Cyrus the Persian as Darius the Mede in the Book of Daniel', *JSOT* 56 (1992), pp. 123-25, outlines a number of literary characteristics that support Wiseman's identification of Cyrus with Darius, and suggests that these features are a 'harmonizing solution' of a historical problem on the part of the author or redactor of Daniel MT.

6.   Wills, *The Jew in the Court*, pp. 129-38, argues for a close link between the stories in the Old Greek and Bel and the Dragon, but Collins, *Daniel*, p. 264, considers his evidence to be 'very fragile'.

Linking of Scenes

The story opens with Daniel's high position at court and the prospect of further advancement for him. At that point the conspirators hatch a plot to bring Daniel down, and manipulate the king to act in accordance with their designs. Daniel undergoes the trial of a night in the lions' pit, and the morning light brings his vindication. The punishment is then turned on the conspirators, and the king issues an encyclical commending the God of Daniel to his subjects. The ordering of dialogue and narration is almost identical in both accounts and in this highly episodic story the sequence of scenes is approximately the same.

Despite the similarity between the versions in the sequence of scenes, they do not relate to each other in the same way. In the MT the episodic nature of the story comes through in the frequency with which אדין or its prefixed form באדין is used. Of the 29 verses in ch. 6, no less than 15 begin with one of those two words, which is more than twice as often as they occur in any of the other Aramaic stories in Daniel.[7] A change of scene is always indicated by a form of אדין, except at v. 11 where the particle כדי is used.[8] There are also two occasions when the word introduces a change of speaker within a scene (vv. 14 and 22), although the latter case could be exceptional as the speakers are physically separated from each other. The emphasis in all of these short scenes is on the words and actions of the players. The narrator neither ascribes motives nor presumes any special knowledge. The only verbal links between scenes are found in the ubiquitous אדין, which does not give the reader many clues about the nature of the connections between events. Such connections must be deduced from the words and actions of the characters in the story. This brings a starkness as well as an ambivalence to the narrative.[9]

The delineation between the scenes is more blurred in the LXX. In the first place there is no uniformity in the way אדין is represented. The most likely translation would be τότε, which the LXX uses more than half the

---

7. Ch. 2, 9 times; ch. 3, 9 times; ch. 4, twice; ch. 5, 8 times; ch. 7, 3 times.

8. Contrast Goldingay, *Daniel*, p. 34, for whom אדין is equivalent to ו in biblical Hebrew.

9. Alter, *Biblical Narrative*, p. 158, expresses this phenomenon in biblical narrative thus: 'the biblical narrator knows all there is to know about the motives and feelings, the moral nature and spiritual condition of his characters, but... is highly selective about sharing his omniscience with his readers...'

time to translate אֱדַיִן in the other chapters noted above. In the present chapter this translation is only used six times (vv. 7, 13, 19, 22, 24, 26) while the somewhat weaker καί is used as often (vv. 6, 12, 14, 15, 16, 20), and ὅτε and δέ once each (vv. 5, 17). Once, the link is made by means of a participial clause (v. 4). θ also uses καί six times (vv. 4, 5, 6, 11, 19, 22) but uses τότε nine times (vv. 7, 12, 14, 15, 16, 17, 20, 24, 26). As often as not θ's choice does not correspond to that of the LXX. There is no discernible pattern in the translator's choice between καί and τότε in either the LXX or θ, and τότε is used less frequently here than elsewhere in Daniel.[10] τότε also occurs several times in the LXX where there is no equivalent in the MT (vv. 18, 21, 25). This suggests that the Greek versions do not display the particular stylistic feature that is signified by אֱדַיִן in the Aramaic.[11]

There are other ways also in which the delineation between scenes is blurred in the LXX. One is seen in the first two scene changes. At v. 4 the opening words, 'who had authority over all' (ὑπὲρ πάντας ἔχων ἐξουσίαν) is grammatically dependent on what has gone before. Consequently Daniel's appointment as one of three leaders is run together with his ascendancy over even his two peers. The two things are not discrete events as in the MT account. At the beginning of v. 5 also a grammatical link is drawn with the preceding scene. The information that 'the two young men' (v. 5, οἱ δυό νεανίσκοι) engage in a plot against Daniel is conveyed in a main clause preceded by the dependent clause, 'But when the king wished to set up Daniel...' (ὅτε δὲ ἐβουλεύσατο ὁ βασιλευς καταστῆσαι τὸν Δανιηλ). The narrator thus makes an explicit link between Daniel's promotion, detailed in v. 4, and the subsequent plot. A similar type of blurring also occurs at v. 11. Darius has just ratified his decree. Daniel then opens the window of his prayer chamber. Again the information is preceded by a participial clause, 'having found out about the injunction which he had set up against him...' (v. 11, ἐπιγνοὺς δὲ Δανιηλ τὸν ὁρισμόν ὅν ἔστησε κατ' αὐτοῦ). This has the effect of making explicit that Daniel recognizes the law as directed against him personally. Again the LXX narrator has made plain something that the MT requires readers to deduce for themselves.

---

10. Herein could be part of the evidence for a case that there is more than one LXX translator of Daniel, but the point is not crucial to the present discussion.

11. This is partly a function of translation out of a paratactic language into a hypotactic one. See Caird, *Language and Imagery*, p. 118.

If the preceding examples illustrate a deliberate stance adopted towards his material by the narrator, the MT plus material of v. 24 points up a certain clumsiness in the progress of the LXX narrative. At that point the conversation between the king and Daniel at the lion pit concludes. True to form the MT orders that Daniel be pulled up, the order is effected, and then the king directs that Daniel's enemies be cast into the now vacant lion pit.[12] The LXX never actually releases Daniel from the lion pit. The dialogue between Daniel and Darius begins in the same setting as in the MT, but all that happens next is that the powerful people who are gathered at the pit observe no harm on Daniel and are promptly thrown in. The release of Daniel is understood. While this may be irritating for one interested in the literary shape of the story, it points up the interest of the LXX in determining who is to blame, and then hurrying on to demonstrate the outworking of that judgment. The men who led the king astray are thrust into the lion pit without any further ceremony and Darius is then free to circulate his confession to the empire. This point is expanded in the section below on the role of Daniel in the story.

The transition from the court to the lion pit between vv. 16 and 17 is also a case in point although here the difference is not so clear cut. This arises because the two versions are at variance over the order of events, the only point in the story where such is the case. In the MT the king, having failed to gain a reprieve for his favourite, gives the order, Daniel is thrown into the pit, Darius speaks wishing him God's intervention, and finally the stone is put over the mouth and sealed in place (vv. 17-18). In the LXX the king speaks wishing Daniel well before he is thrown into the pit and the stone placed and sealed over the mouth. However, the order from the king that Daniel be thrown into the pit has occurred much earlier in the narrative at the start of v. 15. The result again is a blurring of the lines between scenes. The order of events in vv. 15-17 is ambiguous, and it is not clear whether the action of v. 17 takes place at the court or by the lion pit. The MT's use of אדין shown above gives a more straightforward progress through the narrative. Both these examples and the previous one must be treated with care however. They may illustrate the intent of the LXX narrative or its lack of literary craft, but they may also point up the composite nature of this version.[13]

12. According to Z. Stefanovic, 'Daniel: A Book of Significant Reversals', *AUSS* 30 (1992), pp. 141-46, at one level Daniel is 'a book of significant reversals', which emphasize main points. The fate of the conspirators is one such reversal.
13. See Montgomery, *Daniel*, p. 280, on this possibility.

Ascription of Motive

An important effect of the stance taken by the LXX narrator is that he habitually explicates the motives that lie behind the actions of the characters. The plotters plot because Daniel has been preferred to them (v. 5) and Daniel goes to prayer because he knows the king's edict is specifically directed against him (v. 11). But this effect is not only present in the way that the scenes are run together; there are other places in the story where it may be observed. The LXX plus material of v. 6 explains in full the line of reason sustaining the plotters. There is a reminder again in v. 9 that they were trying to catch Daniel out with his praying.[14] When Darius and his nobles seal the pit (v. 18), the LXX reader has no chance to miss the reason for their action, 'lest Daniel be carried away from them or the king draw him up out of the pit' (ὅπως μὴ ἀπ'αὐτῶν ἀρθῇ ὁ Δανιηλ ἤ ὁ βασιλεὺς αὐτὸν ἀνασπάσῃ ἐκ τοῦ λάκκου). This contrasts with the coy remark in the MT, די לא־תשנא צבו בדניאל (v. 18), roughly translated as 'so that Daniel's situation might not change'. It is left to the mind of the reader to suggest how the situation might change.

There is an ambivalence about motive running through the MT account. This can be seen at v. 15 where Darius discovers his courtiers' trick and 'it greatly grieved him' (שׁגיא באשׁ עלוהי).[15] It is not made clear what the referent of עלוהי is. Is he upset at himself, or the leaders and satraps, or Daniel?[16] The phrase 'concerning Daniel' (על דניאל) immediately following does not declare whether the sense is 'for Daniel's person' or 'about the Daniel situation'. Doubt is thereby cast on the king's subsequent motivation. Is it to rescue Daniel, is it to save his own reputation or is it simply revenge? The story leaves readers to witness the words and actions and settle the question for themselves. The LXX, by contrast, cannot be misunderstood. The phrase 'the king was greatly distressed concerning Daniel and strove...' (v. 15, ὁ βασιλεὺς σφόδρα ἐλυπήθη ἐπὶ τῷ Δανιηλ καὶ ἐβοήθει τοῦ ἐξελέσθαι αὐτόν) leaves less room for doubt about the king's motivation. There the king's grief is directly linked with the fact of Daniel being thrown to the lions, and

---

14. This is possibly a doublet with v. 6. See Montgomery, *Daniel*, p. 280, who argues that such doublets are evidence of the 'secondary character' of the LXX.

15. See Rosenthal, *Biblical Aramaic*, p. 36, on this construction.

16. Fewell, *Circle of Sovereignty*, pp. 149 and 191 n. 15.

his attempt at a rescue operation does not occur until after the order has been given. θ misinterprets both the idiom באש על and the phrase בל שׁם, so it is possible that part of the reason for the more explicit syntax of the LXX is a similar failure to recognize either expression.

The closest the MT narrator comes to ascribing motives to a character is with the hint that Daniel entered his prayer chamber 'when he heard about the writing of the edict' (v. 11, כדי ידע די־רשׁים כתבא). The MT is at this point more expansive than usual in ch. 6 with at least a hint of what is motivating Daniel, but is ambivalent about the level of Daniel's self-awareness in taking the action that he does. The LXX makes clear that he knows exactly what he is doing.

Narratorial Presence

One result of this attribution of motives, almost as editorial comment, is that the teller anticipates his story as the action unfolds. Similar examples of this narratorial presence in the LXX may be found at v. 19. In the MT account the king returns to his palace from the lion pit, 'then' (v. 19, אדין) he undergoes a sleepless night, 'then' (v. 20, באדין) he gets up early and hurries back to the lion pit. The reader remains with the king throughout this sequence. Suspense over what is happening to Daniel is achieved by keeping each scene distinct. The suspense is not relieved until the reader with Darius discovers the events of the night. This method of 'shaping space' is a characteristic of biblical narrative.[17] In the LXX account the narrator returns the king to his palace, and then takes the reader with him to the lion pit with the information that God was keeping the lions' mouths closed (v. 19). At that point the reader knows more than the king. Then Darius arises, receives his officials, and sets off to see what has happened to Daniel. The purpose is not to comment on inner motivation, as in other examples looked at, but the effect is similar in that the reader shares the omniscience and anticipatory perspective of the narrator whose understanding seems constantly to be running just ahead of events. As well as that, suspense over the fate of Daniel is not a factor in the story and the reader takes a less active role in perceiving the significance of the action.

Another difference between the versions in the same verse (v. 19) illustrates further this aspect of difference in narrative technique. In the

17. See Bar-Efrat, *Narrative Art*, pp. 184-85, who points out that 'only very rarely do we hear what is happening elsewhere through a messenger'.

MT all the verbs used to describe the king's sleepless night are objective. The king 'went' (אזל) and spent the night 'fasting' (טות) and no 'diversion' (דחון) was brought to him and sleep 'fled' (נדת) from) him.[18] As with Belshazzar's manifestations of fear (5.6) readers are left to observe the king and draw their own conclusions. The narrator poses simply as a reporter of facts waiting to be interpreted. In contrast to this the LXX narrator not only reports the king's movements but confides the inside knowledge that the king 'was distressed' (ἦν λυπούμενος), just as he showed the king's fear in ch. 5.

Pace

One of the by-products of the differences in narrative technique is a variation in pace between the two stories. We have noted the episodic nature of the MT, and will explore below the effects of a large group of spies moving from scene to scene undertaking an activity described by the verb רגש. The story proceeds briskly almost without a pause until Daniel is in the lion pit.[19] At that point there is a slowing which creates suspense. The story leaves Daniel out of sight and lingers over the tension in the king, the approach to the pit, and the king's speech which is too long for the circumstances (vv. 19-21).[20] The tension is broken with Daniel's reply and the story picks up speed again until another pause to hear Darius's final ordinance, after which it dismisses him without further ado.

The LXX progresses through the story with a little less haste. The linkages between scenes and the occasional pauses to describe a character's state of mind or heart have a slowing effect. Moreover the LXX narrator provides more background material at the start on Darius, and the events of v. 4 are incorporated into the story in such a way as to form part of the description of setting, rather than the first scene or

18. It is not crucial to the narrative to determine exactly what דחון means, whether it be food or concubines or musicians. The translation 'diversion', suggested by Montgomery, reflects the purpose of the noun without committing itself to the exact meaning. See Collins, *Daniel*, p. 271.

19. However compare Heaton, *Daniel*, p. 166, and Lacocque, *Daniel*, p. 92, who see built into the story a contrast between the tranquility of Daniel's roof top and the busyness of the spies.

20. See G. Genette, *Narrative Discourse* (trans. J.E. Lewin; Oxford: Basil Blackwell, 1980), p. 87, on the speed of narrative as a relationship between duration of time portrayed and length of narrative.

event as is the case with the MT. The final verse also is a slightly more leisurely completion of the framework of the story initially set up in the early verses. This narrative framework is discussed below in connection with the LXX's treatment of the person of Darius. One section where the pace does quicken is in vv. 18-26, where we have already noted a series of τότε sentences occurring in rapid succession.

Irony in Biblical Narrative

So far in my discussion of the differing narrative forms of the two versions I have dealt with matters that can be readily described. But in order to penetrate a little below the surface of the stories we turn our attention to the more subjective aspect of the tone behind the narrative. For this particular story the question is raised of irony inherent in the account. Any attempt to identify irony, comedy or absurdity in an ancient text should be undertaken with caution. Even within a contemporary cultural consensus humour or irony is an uncertain thing, let alone across the chasms of time, race and faith.[21] Good's approach is a help in crossing those chasms. According to him irony may be described as 'understatement or a method of suggestion rather than of plain statement'. It is also distinguished by what he calls 'its stance in truth'.[22] Therefore key characteristics of irony are a desire to portray the truth as discerned by the ironist without resorting to direct statement, and a reliance on the reader to discern that portrayal. Good distinguishes between comedy and irony in that, although both elicit laughter, ironic laughter is intended to sting. If it does not do so, it is merely funny.[23] Invective and sarcasm may also be ironic but tend not to be, as they generally make no attempt at ambiguity or narratorial neutrality.[24] When biblical narrative creates ironic situations the result is 'dramatic irony'.[25] Another useful term is 'parody', a form that ridicules by exaggeration.[26] 'Caricature' is a kind of parody and is a word that crops up in connection with parody from time to time. Although parody is not necessarily

---

21. See Brenner, 'Who's Afraid', p. 41.
22. E.M. Good, *Irony in the Old Testament* (Philadelphia: Westminster Press, 1965), p. 31.
23. Good, *Irony*, p. 26.
24. Good, *Irony*, pp. 26-27.
25. This is the term used by Bar-Efrat, *Narrative Art*, p. 125.
26. Good, *Irony*, pp. 27-28.

ironic and may be thought of as a type of sarcasm, we will see that part of the ironic tone of Daniel 6 is achieved through parody. I use the word 'humour' occasionally as a catch-all to cover the cluster of concepts just delineated.

'A Cheerful Haggadic Tone'

In light of the above distinctions and of the covert omniscience of the MT narrator, the term 'irony' is preferred to 'comedy' in describing one aspect of the narrative art in Daniel especially notable in chs. 6 and 3. The view that there is a measure of irony in the story of Daniel in the lion pit is not without precedent. Avalos makes a strong plea for a comedic function in Daniel. He uses slightly different terminology from Good but his concept of the comedic is close to what Good calls ironic. Deriving his views from Henri Bergson, Avalos defines comedy as a 'mode of discourse which provides social critique, exposes weaknesses in its target, and elicits laughter in the process'.[27] Within that framework he suggests that the repetition of the lists of ch. 3, both administrative and musical, have an important comedic function.[28] The movement of the large group of plotters has a similar effect in the chapter presently under discussion. Indeed, the list that the officials provide at their audience with the king (v. 8, סגניא ואחשדרפניא הדבריא ופחותא) is close enough to the list of ch. 3 (3.2, 3, 27) to recall the effects of those lists. The four elements are the first four in each of the ch. 3 lists, albeit with the order of the first two reversed. The item הדבריא also occurs once in ch. 3 (v. 27), and it is possible that it is a variant of גדבריא.

Whether or not a reader is able to go as far as Avalos, in general terms the 'cheerful haggadic tone' of this MT story has long been felt.[29] The point is important because the presence or otherwise of such a tone has a bearing on textual as well as literary conclusions. Take, for example, the question of how many plotters there are: two leaders as in the LXX, or 120 satraps and two leaders as in the MT? The answer

27. H.I. Avalos, 'The Comedic Function of the Enumerations of the Officials and Instruments in Daniel 3', *CBQ* 53 (1991), p. 582.

28. For Avalos the views of such as Lacocque, *Daniel*, p. 88, who sees a liturgical effect in the lists, do not go far enough.

29. J.D.M. Derrett, 'Daniel and Salvation History', in *Studies in the New Testament* (Leiden: Brill, 1986), IV, p. 133. Delcor, *Daniel*, p. 133, uses the expression 'un récit haggadique'.

arrived at is to some extent determined by the critic's reading of the tone of the MT. To illustrate the point, a summary of the different arguments is in order.

There is little room for manoeuvre in this question as far as the MT is concerned. The early part of the story is explicit. The aggrieved group at the start seems to include both leaders and satraps. In v. 4 we read that Daniel 'overshadowed the leaders and satraps' (מתנצח על־סרכיא ואחשדרפניא), the implied reason for Darius's intention to promote him. Immediately 'the leaders and satraps' (v. 5, סרכיא ואחשדרפניא), the same group overshadowed by Daniel, begin to look for grounds of complaint (עלה) against Daniel. It is the same group again who go to the king in v. 7, and the referent of 'these men' (v. 6, גבריא אלך) is clearly סרכיא ואחשדרפניא. The list of conspirators in v. 8 is slightly different, with a particular literary function that I have noted above, but again it must include the expanded group. For the rest of the account the conspirators who spy on Daniel and approach Darius are simply גבריא אלך ('these men', vv. 12, 16), which recalls the reference in v. 6 and the group that it is describing. To round off the story, the same group are pitched into the pit (v. 25) along with their families. It is inescapable that those plotting against Daniel in the MT are the larger group, and nowhere do the two leaders have any sort of identity in contradistinction to the satraps.

The situation is not so clear cut in the LXX. The account is different in that the two others appointed with Daniel are distinguished by the LXX narrator throughout. It is not clear who is intended by πάντας in the phrase ὑπὲρ πάντας ἔχων ἐξουσίαν (v. 4, 'having authority over all') but it seems likely to include the 127 satraps (v. 2) as well the men set over them (v. 3). Later in the verse Daniel is said to be over both groups, but both groups are enunciated separately. This prepares the way for v. 5 which shows a plot motivated by Darius's favouritism of Daniel. But nere it is clear that the plotters are 'the two young men' (οἱ δύο νεανίσκοι). In that context the following οἱ ἄνθρωποι ἐκεῖνοι ('these men', vv. 7, 13), as well as the use of the third person plural throughout, probably refers to these two conspirators even though the Aramaic equivalent, גבריא אלך, has a wider group in mind. The LXX is quite specific also at the end of the story that there are only two victims of the revenge punishment, 'these two men' (v. 25, οἱ δύο ἄνθρωποι ἐκεῖνοι).

Commentators have largely failed to notice, however, that the king strives to rescue Daniel not from the two men but 'from the hands of the satraps' (v. 15, ἀπὸ τῶν χειρῶν τῶν σατραπῶν). They are the same group who went with the king to the lions pit in the morning (v. 20) and at least a section of the group represented as 'all the powers' (v. 24, πᾶσαι αἱ δυνάμεις). The situation is further confused by a still different group, 'his nobles' (v. 18, τῶν μεγιστάνων αὐτοῦ), called in to witness the sealing of the pit. Cassin, as we see below, has made a useful distinction between the functions of the courtly officials as against the administrators of regions of the empire, and suggests that it is the former who exercise a legal function when Daniel is cast into the pit.[30] Yet it is the latter who are plotting against their colleague. This does not clarify why the satraps are implicated in the later stages of the story, nor who the 'two young men' of v. 4 might be. Montgomery sees in this confusion a variety of sources while Schmidt does not acknowledge a problem.[31] It is also possible that this phenomenon partly reflects the fact that a later redactor or translator has lost the distinctions between terms that would have applied in the earlier eastern diaspora provenance of the story.[32]

Differing conclusions have been drawn from these variations between versions. As is often the case, Charles and Montgomery represent the two main views.[33] Montgomery considers that the LXX is merely confused, while Charles would see an earlier story of two plotters underlying the interpolated version that has been preserved.[34] The latter's feeling is that the MT story is unsatisfactory in its present form because so large a group could not possibly have spied on Daniel, or had repeated audiences with the king, or all been devoured by the lions

---

30. E. Cassin, 'Daniel dans la "fosse" aux lions', *RHR* 139 (1951), p. 141.

31. See the debate between J.A. Montgomery, 'The "Two Youths" in the LXX to Dan 6', *JAOS* 41 (1921), pp. 316-17, and N. Schmidt, 'Daniel and Androcles', *JAOS* 46 (1926), p. 6.

32. Compare Seeligmann, *The Septuagint Version of Isaiah*, p. 82, who detects the same phenomenon in Isaiah LXX. See Anderson, *Daniel*, p. 31, on Persian administrative terms. A.P.J. McCrystall, 'Studies in the Old Greek Translation of Daniel' (unpublished DPhil thesis, Oxford University, 1980), p. 201, notes that no such problem occurs with the terms for mantic officials, which suggests to him that they were better known in the world of the second century BCE.

33. The 1993 commentary by Collins is a welcome addition to Daniel studies, at least in part because he treats the Greek versions of Daniel with a thoroughness unusual in an English language commentary since Charles and Montgomery did their work.

34. Charles, *Daniel*, p. 152, and Montgomery, 'The "Two Youths"', p. 317.

before hitting the bottom of the pit. Therefore the seeds of a story with two conspirators detected in the LXX must be the *Ursprung*.[35] Such a viewpoint assumes that the story of Daniel in the lion pit ought to emit a tone of sober fact, and does not do it very well.[36] Text-historical conclusions are arrived at to fit that assumption.

Parody

If, however, as readers we are open to the ironic possibilities of a text, and are not committed to the view that a text with less plotters is necessarily more satisfactory than one with more, the presence of a number of conspirators can be seen as evidence of caricature or parody.[37] We are then in a position to appreciate the patent absurdity of this large group of officials crashing on and off stage expecting that nobody could know what they are up to. The absurdity lies in the knowledge of the reader, the ignorance of a king blinded by his pride, and the lack of awareness on the part of the plotters that Daniel and the law of his God still hold the upper hand, all compounded by the size of the group.

This effect is conveyed through the recurring use of the verb רגשׁ (vv. 7, 12, 16) to describe the officials' movements. This verb clearly troubled the Greek translators. The LXX renders it 'they approached' (v. 7, προσήλθοσαν) or 'watched' (v. 12, ἐτήρησαν). The variant account of v. 16 avoids translating it at all. θ is similarly uncertain as to its meaning. Its primary meaning seems to be the idea of 'thronging' or 'causing a tumult'. The word does not occur elsewhere in biblical Aramaic, but 'to throng' or 'to cause a tumult' is its most obvious meaning in biblical Hebrew (Pss. 2.1, 64.3 for example). Moreover that remains the predominant sense in targumic Aramaic. The translators were confronting the same problem worrying modern commentators,

---

35. Similar views are held by Schmidt, 'Daniel and Androcles', p. 7, and Wills, *The Jew in the Court*, p. 144. In contrast, but based on a similar reading of the tone of the story, Porteous, *Daniel*, p. 89, sees the LXX as a later attempt to cope with the 'fantastic' in the MT.

36. See, for example, Anderson, *Daniel*, p. 67.

37. Lest we think such an approach to Scripture is a modern one, note the career of Bar Kappara the humourist (*b. Ned.* 51a and *b. 'Erub.* 2b). See also the self-irony of the rabbis evident in their discussion on sweating (*b. Šab.* 40a). This humour surfaces in conjecture on the later careers of Hananiah and his companions (probably drowned in spittle!), and in the reasons suggested for Daniel's absence from ch. 3 (*b. Sanh.* 93a).

that such a meaning does not appear to fit all three contexts in which the teller of ch. 6 uses it: twice at court before the king and once in between as part of their spying on Daniel.[38] This does not seem sufficient warrant in itself to abandon the primary meaning of the word. On the contrary, it can be seen as deliberate artifice adding to the tone that is being created by the MT, and is an important element in the caricature of the officials. The parody is enhanced by the inappropriate use of רגש in v. 12.

A related example of this phenomenon is the genre known as the idol parody. Idol parodies are found particularly in Isaiah 40 and 44, Jeremiah 10, Habakkuk 2, and Psalms 115 and 135.[39] They work by building up a detailed picture of the physical limitations of idols, and so emphasizing the incongruity of those who make them actually worshipping the works of their own hands. Although the apparent subject is the idols themselves, the target of the parody is those who worship them. This genre is later actualized in the stories of Bel and the Dragon.[40] Despite the differences between the idol parodies and Daniel 6, the mockery of sycophantic behaviour and the encounter of false powers with the true God in both suggests that parody was a thought form available to those who produced the MT of Daniel.[41]

Dramatic Irony

There is also dramatic irony at work through the ignorance by the characters of certain facts that are plain to the reader.[42] This is most clearly at the expense of Darius. He hears the fawning words of his officials but has no idea of the motivation behind them. The conspiratorial officials, who do not foresee the fast approaching pit floor, also display a level of

38. For examples of the varying views of recent commentators, see Fewell, *Circle of Sovereignty*, p. 145. Goldingay, *Daniel*, pp. 121 and 125, senses a nuance of the mob and recognizes the appropriateness of 'thronging' as a translation.

39. See the treatment of Old Testament idol parodies by W.M.W. Roth, 'For Life he Appeals to Death (Wis. 13.18): A Study of Old Testament Idol Parodies', *CBQ* 37 (1975), pp. 21-47.

40. Roth, 'Idol Parodies', p. 21.

41. See Roth, 'Idol Parodies', p. 43, on the link between idol parody and encounter story.

42. For Caird, *Language and Imagery*, p. 134, that ignorance is a defining feature of dramatic irony. See further the discussion of Fewell, *Circle of Sovereignty*, p. 147, on the irony of ignorance.

ignorance. We have seen that the reader of the MT is even uncertain as to how aware Daniel is of the events unfolding around him. His faithfulness may as well represent the habit of a lifetime (v. 11, עבד די־הוא מן־קדמת דנה) as an awareness of being caught in a conflict.

This irony is explicated by the MT through the play on the word דת. The officials early recognized that the way to catch Daniel was 'by the law of his God' (v. 6, בדת אלהה). The irony is that they then turn to a lesser law, 'the law of the Medes and the Persians' (vv. 9, 13, 16, דת־מדי ופרס) to achieve their ends, and fail because of their ignorance of the greater law. In the period in question דת had two distinct yet overlapping senses. It was probably a Persian loan word used for the law of the state. When applied to laws of the Jewish religion its meaning by extension came to include simply 'religion'. The sense of religion or custom was prevailing in Jewish Palestinian Aramaic, but there was still considerable fluidity in late biblical Hebrew.[43] Est. 3.8 sets the laws of the state (דת) against the law or custom of the Jews (דת) in explicit contrast.[44] This ambiguity between law and religion is exploited by the MT narrator. The two laws are considered in further detail in the context of the person of Darius below.

Another way of looking at the matter is to suggest that the effect being sought by the MT is in fact something akin to a modern day situation comedy, with its cast of easily recognizable caricatures, a clear progression of the plot through small segments of action, and carefully timed entries and exits to comic effect. Misunderstandings arise because each member of the cast relates to some of the characters but never to them all. The characters remain ignorant whereas the reader or viewer is able to build a wider picture and sense possibilities still hidden from the actors. There is a level of suspense maintained because the narrator does not confirm those possibilities for the reader except through the action. Daniel 6 MT can be understood in those terms. I have already noted in some detail the progress of the action through a series of short distinct scenes. After the brief introduction each scene contains two of the three main character groups: Daniel, Darius and the conspirators. Even the penultimate scene is between Darius and Daniel only (vv. 20-24), in contrast to the LXX. Only in the final episode (v. 25) are the three brought together, but then Daniel's presence is only by implication. We have also

43. See Slotki, *Daniel*, p. 48. Anderson, *Daniel*, p. 67, understands דת only in terms of 'religion'.

44. See Clines, *The Esther Scroll*, pp. 16-17.

seen that the narrator allows the action to speak for itself. This produces a level of suspense, particularly when Daniel spends the night with the lions.

As with parody, this kind of dramatic irony is not unique to Daniel. An oft-treated incident is that involving David's affair with Bathsheba and his subsequent attempts to cover his tracks in 2 Samuel 11.[45] That story also depends for its effect on reader uncertainty about the motivation of different characters as well as on the limited viewpoint of each of the actors. There is no explicit input from the narrator apart from the ominous conclusion that 'the thing that David had done was displeasing in the eyes of the Lord' (2 Sam. 11.27, וירע הדבר אשר־עשה דוד בעיני יהוה). Irony, although not necessarily dramatic irony, has also been noted in the oracles of the nations of Amos 1–2 and the metaphorical language of Hos. 6.3-4.[46]

The MT contains a couple of neat examples of double entendre in its description of the conspirators' fate, which reinforce the ironic tone of the MT. The first is in the description of the plotters with the idiom for slander that translated literally speaks of those 'who had eaten pieces' (v. 25, די־אכלו קרצוהי) of Daniel. The second is the use of שלט to describe the lions' overpowering of the conspirators. This is a word for sovereignty throughout the Aramaic of Daniel and encapsulates the debate over where sovereignty lies.[47] The link here is with Darius's final decree, which uses the corresponding verbal noun to describe both the kingdom of Darius and that of God (v. 27). In a somewhat macabre way the proponents of the law of the Medes and Persians discover that law not only turned against them, but now, in the form of the lions, was an expression of the law of Daniel's God. The double referent is not present in the LXX, as the kingdom of God in v. 27 is only in MT plus material. Moreover, in v. 25 the LXX conveys a literal interpretation of the idioms. The lions do not 'rule over' (שלט) but simply 'kill' (ἀπέκτειναν). In contrast θ captures the imagery of the MT with ἐκυρίευσαν. In the LXX the men are not those who had 'eaten pieces' of Daniel but those who 'had born witness against' (καταμαρτυρήσαντες) him. Thus the irony is not present to the same degree as in the MT.

---

45. See the treatments in Sternberg, *Poetics*, pp. 193-205, Bar-Efrat, *Narrative Art*, pp. 126-27, and Good, *Irony*, pp. 35-36.

46. Good, *Irony*, pp. 34-35 and 41 n. 5. While Good also sees the book of Jonah as ironic he admits that he has not found any commentators to support his opinion.

47. Fewell, *Circle of Sovereignty*, p. 152.

The Building Blocks of Irony

The building blocks used to create this tone of subversion through irony
are absent in the LXX.[48] The story is less episodic and the distinctions
between scenes blurred, while the more overt narrator anticipates events
and motives for the reader. The play on the words דת and רגש is not present. We have already seen the LXX's difficulty with the latter term. The
motif of דת does not occur because the issue of the law of God is not
raised. The LXX equivalent to v. 6 MT is an expansionary explanation of
the upcoming plot. The interest is not so much in the 'law of his God'
(v. 6, דת אלהה) as in its outworking, Daniel 'prayed and pleaded with the
Lord his God three times a day' (v. 6, προσεύχεται καὶ δεῖται
κυρίου τοῦ θεοῦ αὐτοῦ τρὶς τῆς ἡμέρας). The sole occurrence of
'the law of the Medes and Persians' (v. 13a) cannot be offset against the
law of God. The hyperbole of the MT is not present in the LXX which, if
it is not certain how many plotters there are, only has two of them and
their families thrown to the lions. The result is less a story that depends
for its effect on subversive humour as a straightforward moral tale
where the narrator's designs are explicit.

Perspectives on Prayer

An examination of the vocabulary for prayer in each version throws further light on the differences in the nature of the narratives as well as
moving the discussion toward the theological concerns of the stories. It
is noticeable that both versions use two types of word to describe
prayer. One type is confessional while the other is more ambiguous and
less necessarily descriptive of religious activity.[49] The MT uses the term
בעא in vv. 8, 13 and 14 with the object בעו on two of those occasions.[50]
It also occurs in v. 12 but this time in tandem with חנן in the *hithpaal*
form. The other mention of prayer is in v. 11 and there the two words
used are the participial forms of צלא and ידא.

---

48. Good, 'Apocalyptic as Comedy', p. 55, sees the Darius story as one of subversion from the inside.

49. Müller, 'Märchen, Legende', p. 345, explicates this interplay between public
and confessional terminology in chs. 3 and 6.

50. The variation in spelling between בעה and בעא is part of the wider Aramaic
phenomenon of vacillation in spelling for roots originally ending in ʾ/h and א. See
Rosenthal, *Biblical Aramaic*, p. 51. I use בעא to refer to either variant.

A look at the context of the words suggests that this MT variation in vocabulary comes about by deliberate choice. On each occasion that בעא is used on its own (vv. 8, 13, 14) the speakers are the plotting officials. Verses 8 and 13 speak of the activities forbidden by the king's decree, while the third usage is a description to the king of what the officials saw Daniel doing. The position of the speakers with respect to the activity being described, prayer or petition, is of outsiders looking in. In biblical Aramaic בעא has the sense of petitioning the king (Dan. 2.16, 49), God (Dan. 2.23) or a heavenly being (Dan. 7.16). The rare biblical Hebrew equivalent בעה in its meaning of 'to seek, inquire' (Isa. 21.12) has a prophet as its object. In Jewish Palestinian Aramaic the verbal noun means 'prayer' whereas the verb usually has a human object. The Theodotionic translator reflects this with his consistent choice of αἰτέω, a word that the LXX most often uses to represent the Hebrew שאל. This simply means 'to ask' with no special connection with a prayer context. Hence the MT narrator has chosen vocabulary that is ambiguous. In the first place it does not specify that the king has to be divine to be the object of such petitions, but there is a hint that he could be. At the same time the satraps and leaders choose a word when they speak which falls short of being a witness to the fact that Daniel is in contact with his God, but the suggestion is clear.

This becomes more obvious in v. 11, a point in the story when the scene shifts and the perspective changes. No longer is the reader seeing things through the eyes of Darius and his pagan advisers, but is witnessing a scene directly mediated by the narrator, who tells us that Daniel goes into his upper chamber to pray. At this point the pair of verbs צלא and ידא in their participial forms (מצלא ומודא) are employed. In contrast to בעא both verbs are confessional, particularly the latter. Its other occurrence in the book of Daniel is in Daniel's hymn of praise in ch. 2 (2.20-23). Its Hebrew equivalent ידה is used in the *hiphil* more than 50 times in the Psalms, emphasizing that it had become a word of ritual worship. It is almost always translated by the LXX as ἐξομολογέω as indeed it is by θ at this point and by both Greek versions in ch. 2. It is also a *Leitwort* in the Hymn of the Three Young Men in ch. 3. The verb צלא is not quite so well attested. Its only other biblical Aramaic occurrence is in Ezra 6.10 where it also has the sense of prayer to God. There, as with θ here, it is translated προσεύχομαι. There is no Hebrew equivalent but its *pael* form means 'to pray' in Jewish Palestinian Aramaic, and the Jewish Palestinian Aramaic verbal noun צלו means 'prayer'.

It would appear that the narrator wants the reader to be clear on the religious nature of Daniel's activity, whereas the plotters in their speeches link it to the idea of petitioning a human king and leave it undefined as to whether this implies divinity in the sovereign. There is another scene that uses prayer vocabulary when the narrator describes the officials' spying on Daniel at prayer. Here the pairing בעא ומתחנן (v. 12) brings together the two perspectives already noted. We have already seen the sense of בעא but חנן is not quite so flexible in referent. This *hithpaal* participle is the only biblical Aramaic occurrence of that root, but its Hebrew equivalent in the *hithpael* theme has as its object God more often than humanity. Indeed, the *hithpael* with the sense of seeking favour from God is always translated by the LXX as δέομαι. The two verbs in tandem like this reflect the dual perspective in this central verse in the prayer theme. Daniel 'seeking favour before his God' (v. 12, מתחנן קדם אלהה) is an echo of the narrator's description of the previous verse, particularly with the repetition of קדם אלהה. At the same time the use of בעא reflects the way his enemies view him.

The LXX also has this divergence in vocabulary, although variations in the shape of the story make it difficult to chart direct correspondence with the MT. The difference is encapsulated in v. 6, which contains two pairs of verbs relating to prayer or petition. In the first part of the verse the words of the royal decree are formulated by the discontented leaders. There they employ the pair of verbs ἀξιόω and εὔχομαι probably as an expression equivalent to the Aramaic בעא בעו (vv. 8, 14 MT). Each member of the pair reflects the Semitic construction of a verb taking its cognate noun as object. The second part of v. 6, a LXX plus, is a narratorial description of the plotters' motivation, and a completely different pair of words is used to give the narrator's, rather than the plotters', view of Daniel's activity: προσεύχεται καὶ δεῖται. The first pair, with the same Semitic construction, is also to be found in vv. 8 and 13 although in reverse order.

While ἀξιόω can be used of a petition addressed to God, its object is often human. The LXX most often uses it to reflect the Hebrew נטש or even נשא. The latter word is ubiquitous while the former has the primary meaning of 'to leave or abandon'. One of its senses in the *niphal* can be that of permission being granted, but even then a context of dealings with the divine is not required. In Daniel LXX the object of ἀξιόω can be the king, as it is in v. 9 (see also, for example, 2.16, 49). As far as εὔχομαι is concerned the situation is not so clear. The LXX uses the

word in almost equal proportions to translate נצר or נדר, 'to make a
vow', and פלל or עתר, 'to pray'. The 'vow' meaning often takes εὐχήν
as its object, or at least understands it. The vow is most often made to
God. This type of understanding is well illustrated in 1 Esd. 4.43-46. It is
not possible to draw any firm conclusions about the combination of
verbs as this particular pairing only occurs in Septuagintal Greek in this
chapter. The combination seems to be intended to represent בעא, perhaps
even as a type of hendiadys. The two words together result in the same
sort of ambiguity as is contained in the Aramaic בעא. This is in contrast
to θ's use of αἰτέω (vv. 8, 13) already alluded to, which reduces the
ambiguity by using a word with a strongly human referent. In that
respect θ can be said to be interpretative at this point.

The second pair in v. 6, which is part of a narratorial description of
Daniel's religious activities, is προσεύχεται καὶ δεῖται. The first term
hardly needs exposition as it inevitably means prayer to God. It is most
common in Daniel in ch. 9 where both Greek versions use it or its
related noun to render פלל or the related noun תפלה. In Ezra 6.10 it
translates the Aramaic צלא, which is probably the verb reflected in this
context. θ demonstrates this understanding with its translation of צלא as
προσευχόμενος in v. 11. The verb δέομαι is usually but not inevitably
a translation of חנן. It usually has the divine as its object. That is certainly
the sense in which θ understands it in v. 12. The LXX of Daniel brings
the two terms together in 9.20 with the phrase δεόμενος ἐν ταῖς
προσευχαῖς. That suggests that in this pairing with προσεύχομαι,
δέομαι has the nuance of bringing petitions to God rather than to a
human figure.[51] The same pair occurs in v. 9. These verbs together
probably correspond to MT מצלא ומודא in v. 11.

As far as the argument so far is concerned, the words of the decree in
the LXX reflect the same sort of ambivalence as do those of the MT, and
the narrator shows the same certainty about the nature of Daniel's
prayer activity when that is described. However, to complete the picture,
the words for prayer in vv. 12 and 14 do not reflect so clearly the pattern discernible in the MT. In v. 12, where the plotters catch Daniel
praying, the participle εὐχόμενον is used on its own. In this instance the

---

51. Such is the usage detected by Seeligmann, *The Septuagint Version of Isaiah*,
p. 101, in Isaiah who says προσευχή and δέησις are 'used more or less promiscu-
ously'. The translator of LXX Daniel at this point reflects a Septuagintal tradition.
However, compare Lacocque, *Daniel*, p. 91, who points out that Antiochus used
δέομαι of intercessions to himself.

LXX is in direct parallel with the MT, and one word is used to represent two in Aramaic, בעא ומתחנן. We have seen that εὔχομαι can vary in meaning but usually has God as object either of a petition or a vow. In the context of this passage the sense is almost certainly prayer to God, although, unlike the MT and θ, the object is not stated. In v. 14 a different pairing again is used, εὐχόμενον καὶ δεόμενον. This is in sharp contrast to the MT which has the more neutral בעא translated as αἰτέω by θ.

The upshot is that the LXX recognizes the same kind of distinctions in the words for prayer or petition as the MT. However, apart from the consistency with which the words of the actual decree are reported, the vocabulary of prayer is not used to the same extent to distinguish the viewpoint of the narrator from that of the characters in the story. On the occasions when the praying of Daniel is reported, the actions and viewpoint of the conspirators are in evidence, yet the verbs chosen all represent to some degree the confessional stance of the narrator. This stance is reinforced by the grammatical indicators chosen to indicate the direction of prayer. In the decree the words for prayer always take ἀπό or παρά (vv. 6, 8, 13), whereas when Daniel's prayer activity is described its object is either denoted by the genitive (v. 6) or by the idiom τοῦ προσώπου (v. 14). Twice there is no object. These more confessional forms of expression clarify the narrator's own views on the nature of Daniel's praying. This is all part of the phenomenon noted earlier of a more visible narrator and is epitomized in the LXX plus of v. 6 as well as its repeated form in v. 9. There the narrator ascribes motives to the leaders while overriding their perspective with his own point of view.

The Divinity of the King

At the same time the evidence from this prayer vocabulary hints at a different theological perspective between the versions. The MT has chosen words with carefully nuanced meaning which, as well as portraying perspective, suggest a certain subtlety to the issues at stake. Appropriately for its Persian setting, the question of the divinity of the king is not paramount in the MT, although it is undeniable that such a possibility tantalizes the reader of the MT.[52] The ambiguity of the story on this

52. The contention of M. Stuart, *A Commentary on the Book of Daniel* (Boston: Crocker & Brewster, 1850), p. 171, that 'Parsism taught its votaries to reverence the king as the symbol or personification of Ormusd...' must be treated with caution as

point could just as well make it a more general commentary on the tendency for authority figures of every age to take upon themselves as much importance as people are willing to ascribe to them.[53] That tendency partly feeds the satire of this story, which is less an issue of divinity and more a question of where Daniel's loyalties lie.[54] In other terms, whose דח ('law') has the first claim? This is reflected in the wording of the king's decree, which does not outlaw prayer to 'any god' but to 'any god or man' (vv. 8, 13, כל־אלה ואנש).[55] The ואנש following as it does the verb בעא reinforces the point that it does not matter whether Darius is human or divine but it does matter who is being petitioned, whose law is being obeyed. The issue of whether or not the king was divine is certainly present but it functions as a backdrop to the story.

The matter is more clear cut in the LXX. Prayer is prohibited to 'any god' (vv. 6, 13, ἀπὸ/παρὰ παντὸς θεοῦ). There is no modifying ואנש in any of the accounts of the content of the decree (vv. 6, 8, 13), which immediately suggests that something else is at stake. The focus is on the status of the one petitioned rather than the motivation of the petitioner. The issue of whether or not the king is divine moves into the foreground. Verse 14 is a moment of decision in both stories, and the process is in evidence there. The MT uses the same word as the edict uses to depict Daniel's action, בעא. Thereby the matter at stake is the sage's obedience or otherwise to the decree. The MT does not even specify at this point the object of Daniel's petitions. In contrast to this, the LXX by

most of his sources are later Greeks. J.H. Walton, 'The Decree of Darius the Mede in Daniel 6', *JETS* 31 (1988), pp. 283-85, wonders if the decree was intended to install the king as sole mediator of his subjects' prayers. He speculates that the decree may reflect a wider struggle within Zoroastrianism between an orthodox monotheism and the more eclectic practices of the Magi. See the survey of I. Gershevitch, 'Zoroaster's Own Contribution', *JNES* 23 (1964), pp. 14-16.

53. For variations on this view see Fewell, *Circle of Sovereignty*, p. 147, Goldingay, 'The Stories in Daniel', p. 100, and Slotki, *Daniel*, p. 48. Contrast this with R. Hammer, *The Book of Daniel* (Cambridge: Cambridge University Press, 1976), p. 69; and Montgomery, *Daniel*, p. 270, who sees an anachronistic reference to the times of Antiochus Epiphanes. Josephus avoids the issue of kingly divinity by saying the decree forbade petitions 'either to him (the king) or to gods' (*Ant.*, 10.253, μήτ' αὐτῷ τις μήτε τοῖς θεοῖς).

54. T.A. Boogaart, 'Daniel 6: A Tale of Two Empires', *RR* 39 (1986), p. 109, detects a *Sitz im Leben* of a king demanding loyalty from his vassals.

55. Contrast Montgomery, *Daniel*, p. 270, who sees no further significance in this phrase than as an example of hyperbole such as that found in Jon. 3.8.

its choice of the pair εὐχόμενον καὶ δεόμενον portrays the issue as one related to divinity. The LXX even specifies that Daniel is praying and petitioning 'the face of his God' (τοῦ προσώπου τοῦ θεοῦ αὐτοῦ), although too much should not be made of that particular difference with the MT as there is no clear pattern in the way the LXX uses that or similar expressions in the present chapter. This relates to the paucity of reference to the law of the Medes and the Persians in the LXX, a point which is discussed more fully elsewhere.

As a footnote to this section, it must be acknowledged that the LXX, like the MT, employs an ambiguous word order to describe the decree: 'from any god for thirty days except from you, O King' (v. 13, παρὰ παντὸς θεοῦ ἕως ἡμερῶν τριάκοντα ἀλλὰ παρὰ σοῦ βασιλεῦ). It could be argued that the intervention of ἕως ἡμερῶν τριάκοντα between 'any god' and 'except from you' leaves it unclear whether the king is to be thought of primarily as a god or as one being petitioned. The equivalent phrase in v. 6 employs the third rather than the second person but has the same word order. However, the consistency with which the words of the king's edict in the LXX equates with those in the MT suggests that the word order here simply reflects the Old Greek's *Vorlage*, and that the real points of significance are to be found where the two versions differ, as they do over the object of the prayers and petitions.

Darius and his Encyclical

The goal of both versions, if not the denouement of the story, is Darius's encyclical at the end of the chapter. If it is true that the theological issues can be differentiated in the way just outlined, then we could expect this to show through in the treatment by each version of the figure of King Darius at the end of the chapter. The focus of his letter is similar on most points. Everybody is required to worship the God of Daniel. This God's general attributes are set out for the benefit of the populace and his particular activity in rescuing Daniel is mentioned.

A crucial difference is in the stance adopted by Darius himself towards these events. The LXX Darius makes a personal commitment to the God of Daniel at v. 28 (ἐγὼ Δαρεῖος ἔσομαι αὐτῷ προσκυνῶν...) Because the usurpation of divine functions by the human is more central for the LXX, the response from a chastened Darius must be an ascription of divinity in the right quarter. Darius provides such a response with his

promise to 'serve' God all his days. The distinction between the two
participles λατρεύοντες (v. 27) and δουλεύων (v. 28) both meaning
'serving' is not immediately clear. Darius calls his people to do the
former and promises to do the latter himself. λατρεύω is a word almost
exclusively used in the context of service of God or gods, while
δουλεύω, also used to translate עבד, has a wider range of meaning. The
MT and θ are not able to help distinguish the meanings here as their content is different from the LXX.

It could be a matter of style that the LXX translator has opted for
variety and chosen a pair of synonyms, but the tenor of the rest of this
confession makes it likely that a particular section of the semantic field
of δουλεύω is intended and that it has not been used randomly. That
assumption, if it is correct, puts us in touch with a tradition that uses
δουλεύω when the context is God's delegation of authority to a Gentile
king so that he might be 'served' by the people of Israel. The Hebrew
uses עבד in both contexts, but the LXX seems to distinguish between
issues of divine allegiance for the people and issues of authority for
kings.[56] The distinction is neatly illustrated by Judg. 3.7-8 where the
people 'served' (ויעבדו translated by ἐλάτρευσαν) Baal, and God punished them by giving them over to King Cushan-risathaim whom they
'served' (ויעבדו translated as ἐδούλευσαν). Earlier in the chapter
(vv. 17, 21) Darius speaks of the God whom Daniel serves and the word
used is λατρεύω. Both times it translates פלח, which describes in 3.17
and 28/95 the service of the three young men to their God. Here too the
translation is λατρεύω by both the LXX and θ in 3.28/95, although the
LXX prefers φοβέομαι in 3.17.

A further dimension to the distinction may be that λατρεύω is a
word particularly associated with cultic matters. When it occurs in conjunction with προσκυνέω, as it does in v. 27 and ch. 3 and frequently in
the Pentateuch (for example Exod. 20.5; 23.24; Deut. 4.19; 5.9; 8.19;
11.16; 17.3; 30.17), the context is cultic worship. This is supremely illustrated in Exod. 20.5 where veneration of images is prohibited. In Daniel
6 and 3 the word is used to describe the heroes' ritual activity. Even
when Nebuchadnezzar promises to 'serve' (4.37a, λατρεύω), it could
be argued that the context is cultic, as later in the same verse he speaks
of making sacrifices. On the other hand δουλεύω rarely occurs with

56. Another word used in Greek to render עבד is ἐργάζομαι, which is probably
closest to the full semantic range of עבד. See, for example, Jer. 22.13; 27/34.6;
30/37.8-9; 34/41.14 and 18.

προσκυνέω in Septuagintal Greek (Gen. 27.29; 3 Kgdms 9.6; Ps. 71.11; Jer. 13.10; 25.6), and when it does the context has more to do with allegiance of the heart than direction of cultic ritual.

Nebuchadnezzar was also one whom God had appointed to be served (Jer. 34.6, ἔδωκα τὴν γῆν...δουλεύειν αὐτῷ) by his people as well as by the earth.[57] This tradition lurks in the shadows of the tree in ch. 4 LXX. Part of Daniel's allegorical interpretation of the great tree was that the creatures sheltered by it represented the nations serving Nebuchadnezzar (4.21, αἱ χῶραι σοὶ δουλεύουσι). Later on the message of the angel to the king is that he should serve the God of heaven (4.34, δούλευσον τῷ θεῷ τοῦ οὐρανοῦ). The one being served had to become the servant. If Darius is being thought of in the light of such a tradition, this helps to explain the choice of δουλεύω and suggests at the very least that the LXX puts Darius in good company.

The LXX may also reflect the tradition found in 1 Esdras 4 about Zerubbabel and Darius. In this tradition Zerubbabel is the successor to Daniel at the Persian court and helps Darius to play a significant role in facilitating the return of the Jews to Jerusalem. A link in administrative terminology is seen at 1 Esdr. 4.47 when the king writes a letter to 'treasurers and governors and prefects and satraps' (οἰκονόμους καὶ τοπάρχας καὶ στρατηγοὺς καὶ σατράπας). The list is very close to that of v. 8 MT ('prefects and satraps, courtiers and governors') which θ translates στρατηγοὶ καὶ σατράπαι, ὕπατοι καὶ τοπάρχαι.

The Personalizing of Darius

The interest of the LXX in the person of Darius in vv. 26-29 is in contrast to the MT. This is further illustrated at v. 29. The MT switches the focus immediately back to Daniel and displays no further personal interest in the king, whereas the LXX in a highly suggestive phrase tells us that King Darius 'was gathered to his people' (v. 29, προσετέθη

---

57. Humphreys, 'Lifestyle', p. 212, notes the importance of the Jeremiah tradition of Nebuchadnezzar in the diaspora world. This phrase is a textual crux as the LXX does not represent exactly the MT עבדי. For a full discussion, see E. Tov, 'Exegetical Notes on the Hebrew Vorlage of the LXX of Jeremiah 27 (34)', *ZAW* 91 (1979), p. 84; W.E. Lemke, 'Nebuchadnezzar, my Servant', *CBQ* 28 (1966), p. 48; and W. McKane, 'Jeremiah 27.5-8, especially "Nebuchadnezzar, my Servant"', in V. Fritz, K.-F. Pohlmann and H.-C. Schmitt (eds.), *Prophet und Prophetenbuch* (Berlin: de Gruyter, 1989), p. 100.

πρὸς τὸ γένος αὐτοῦ). Any Jewish reader of these words must have been aware of the history of the phrase in the LXX. Used in the sense here the verb always translates אסף, and either γένος or λαός is used to represent עם, or πατήρ to represent the Hebrew variation in the formula. It is always used of one of the chosen people generally approved of by the biblical account. In the historical books the patriarchs (along with Ishmael), Moses and Josiah are all gathered to their people (for example Gen. 25.8; 35.29; 49.29; Deut. 32.50). In later tradition Judith's husband Manasses, Mattathias and Jonathan the high priest are gathered to their people (Jdt. 16.22; 1 Macc. 2.69; 14.30). A portmanteau phrase probably intended to reflect approval is used of Achior the Ammonite who is 'gathered into the house of Israel' (Jdt. 14.10, προσετέθη εἰς τὸν οἶκον Ισραηλ). This is the closest a Gentile comes to such a reward in the LXX tradition. Significantly a whole generation are gathered to their fathers in Judg. 2.10 because they 'served the Lord' (Judg. 2.7, ἐδούλευσεν...τῷ κυρίῳ). Darius too promised that he would be serving (v. 28, δουλεύων). It is not certain and not crucial to the point being made whether the LXX narrator envisaged Darius as an honorary Israelite or simply intended to convey a sense of high regard for the king. Either way a note of approval is struck and the epitaph suggests a comprehensive conversion to the God of Israel on the part of the monarch.

This approval is foreshadowed in the first verse of the LXX version of the story, as opposed to the MT, where another ancient formula is used to describe the Gentile king. The phrase 'full of days' (v. 1, πλήρης τῶν ἡμερῶν) elsewhere in the Greek Old Testament always represents the Hebrew שבע ימים. It describes Abraham, Isaac, David, Solomon, Jehoiada and Job and nobody else. In Genesis (25.8; 35.29) it is used in conjunction with 'gathered to his people', and twice (Gen. 25.8; 1 Chron. 29.28) the phrase ἐν γήρει is also nearby. By bracketing the story of Daniel in the lions' den with such evocative descriptions of Darius, the narrator places his conversion to the God of Israel as a central theme in the story.

In contrast to the LXX, the MT does not develop Darius as fully as it succeeds in doing with Belshazzar. He begins and ends the story in close relationship to Daniel and changes little during the course of the narrative. His ordinance at the end is an important development for the theme of the two laws, but he himself is little touched by events.[58] This

---

58. Slotki, *Daniel*, p. 55, considers that 'The narrative of the chapter is intended to teach a lesson not to the king, but to his heathen subjects'.

highlights another difference between the versions at vv. 27-28. The MT uses kingdom and law language that is not present in the LXX. The phrase 'I have set up an ordinance...' (v. 27, מן־קדמי שׁים טעם) recalls the decree that Darius set up earlier, although the vocabulary is not identical. At the same time, the idiom שׁים...טעם echoes the central moment in v. 14 where the crime of Daniel was that he 'did not pay regard to' (לא־שׂם...טעם) the king. The MT also speaks of 'his (God's) kingdom' (v. 27, מלכותה) in contrast to 'my (Darius's) kingdom' (v. 27, מלכותי).[59]

In fact the distinction between the versions occurs much earlier, when the plotters begin their work. In the LXX plus material of v. 6, where their motivation is revealed, the trap is to be found in the fact that Daniel prays to 'his God' three times a day. In the MT the satraps and leaders are explicit that their complaint against Daniel must be found 'in the law of his God' (בדת אלהה). The terms are set right at the beginning. The effect of all this is to see Darius's declaration in terms of the theme of the two laws (דת), God's law or the law of the Medes and the Persians. The final encyclical is less personal and more of an expression of submission by one kingdom to another.[60] There is a corresponding loss of interest in the person of the king.

The King and Daniel

The matter of the character of the king can be taken a little further. There is a strange difference between the versions over the description of Daniel in v. 14, which is central to the struggle for loyalty. As in previous chapters of Daniel, a reminder is given by the MT of the origins of Daniel as a Jewish exile (v. 14, ...מן בני גלותא). These are the terms in which his enemies describe him here. This highlights the struggle between the law represented by the Judean and the Law of the Medes and the Persians. Strangely the LXX narrative simply describes Daniel in the words of the conspirators as 'your friend' (v. 14, τὸν φίλον σου). With this terminology the aspect of a contest between rival דת is not present and the issue is a much more personal one.

---

59. For J. Levinger, 'Daniel in the Lion's Den—A Model of National Literature of Struggle', *Beth Mikra* 70 (1977), p. 394, this aspect of the MT makes the story of Daniel 6 'a model of a fighting national literature'.

60. Young, *Daniel*, p. 139, puts it another way when he detects that 'Darius does not rise above his polytheistic background'. Compare Towner, *Daniel*, p. 90, who speaks of the king's 'confession' in the MT.

The phrase φίλον σου functions at more than one level. It describes an existing relationship with Daniel thus reinforcing the positive view of Darius foreshadowed in the first verse and brought to fruition at the end. It also introduces a tone of irony into the narrative which reflects on both the motivation of the plotters and the quandary of Darius. As far as the two leaders are concerned the issue is a personal one and their choice of words reflects badly on them. In the process a gap is allowed into the LXX narrative, unusually for a narrator who normally leaves little to the imagination of the reader. After Darius has foolishly reiterated his commitment to do what his officials tell him (v. 13) the plotters simply state what they have found in Daniel. Their description of Daniel to the king as 'your friend' is an effective, although unintended, portrayal of their own feelings at this point.

The Character of Daniel

A marked feature of the narrative, especially in the MT, is the silence maintained by Daniel right up to the climactic conversation and events on the morning of his release. In forming a picture of Daniel the reader is entirely dependent on the information of the narrator, who focuses on his competence, honesty and his adherence to the law (דח) of his God. The first time he speaks, the suspense of Darius's sleepless night is broken as Daniel witnesses to the angel's work on his behalf and declares his innocence (v. 23). Yet despite his silence Daniel functions as the focal point for the question of the two laws against which others are judged.

The character of Daniel is treated in a similar manner by the LXX although as we have seen he functions more as the embodiment of the question facing Darius of service or disobedience to God. Perhaps because of that particular role the silence of Daniel is not so complete. He breaks into speech at the same point in the story, but when he does he carries on to point an accusing finger at Darius and those who led him astray. As well as illustrating his role as judge, another effect of this extra speech containing the singular 'you cast' (v. 23, ἔρριψας) is to implicate Darius in the crime against Daniel and his God. This makes the whole issue more personal and prepares the way for the king's subsequent confession.

Idols

A further clue to the interests of the LXX version is found in the problematic reference to 'idols made by hands' (v. 28, εἴδωλα τὰ χειροποίητα). There does not seem to be any need to refer to idols as they have not been an issue in this story. The connective γάρ does not follow from what immediately precedes it nor from the content of the story as a whole. The phrase has no equivalent in the MT, but what follows, 'like the God of Daniel has redeemed Daniel' (ὡς ἐλυτρώσατο...) probably equates to the MT. The note about idols seems to be an interpolation on the part of the translator. While the logical links may not be obvious, the connective ὡς provides a clue that in the mind of the translator the comparison is encapsulated in the words 'cannot save' (οὐ δύνανται σῶσαι) and 'like (God)...has redeemed' (ὡς ἐλυτρώσατο). The contrast is heightened by the word order which juxtaposes them. The translator betrays his continuing interest in the issue of idolatry with this insertion.[61] This is a more explicit manifestation of the concern for cultic purity discernible behind the LXX choice of vocabulary discussed above.[62]

The Trial of Daniel

Other differences in the two stories come to light in a comparison of the trial undergone by Daniel. In this connection the LXX clarifies some matters that remain unclear in the MT. In the Aramaic telling of events the behaviour of the king after the committal of Daniel to the lions' pit, and Daniel's first words to him in the morning are puzzling. Why was he so desperate to see the dawn? The MT hints at its importance with a double reference to 'first thing in the morning' (v. 20, בשפרפרא and בנגהא). What thoughts lay behind the king's first words uttered on arrival at the pit? To the modern reader it seems strange to carry on a conversation with a man in a lions' pit when we would have expected rescue to be the first priority. The king's subsequent actions make it clear that for some reason he is entitled to rescue Daniel at this point despite the law of the Medes and the Persians. Daniel's reply is also strange, particularly

---

61. Seeligmann, *The Septuagint Version of Isaiah*, p. 100, notes a similar polemic against idol worship in LXX Isaiah. The references in Isa. 1.29, 27.9, 37.19, 41.28 and 57.5 are all interpretations rather than literal translations of MT.

62. See the discussion on 'idol parodies' in Wills, *The Jew in the Court*, p. 132.

his concern to claim innocence before the king (v. 23, ...‏ואף קדמיך...‏זו). He seems to draw a deliberate link not only between his rescue from the lions and his innocence before God but also between his rescue and the fact that he has done no 'harm' (v. 23, ‏חבולה‎) to the king. This latter aspect is left hanging by the MT, the significance of which we come to later. The thought occurs that some type of trial by ordeal of specific duration is taking place.[63]

There is little in the way of contemporary source material against which to check this notion, and certainly nothing that links a night in the lion pit to a legal procedure. Even the plentiful evidence for a river ordeal in Babylonian and Assyrian inscriptions is mostly prior to 1200 BCE.[64] There is, however, one set of late Babylonian inscriptions published and translated by Lambert and which he takes to be from Nebuchadnezzar.[65] Although there is nothing about lions, on one column there is talk of a river ordeal in terms strongly reminiscent of this chapter.[66] There is the same interest in time as it is a 'judgment by night'; there is the same collection of important figures in the early morning seen in the words, 'When dawn shone prince, regent and troops, gathering as the king had commanded...'; and there is the same concern for proof of innocence as the gathered dignitaries are there 'to behold justice...' There is some ambiguity in that, despite the phrase 'judgment by night', the actual ordeal seems to take place in the morning. It must also be granted that a river ordeal is quite another thing from a lion pit. Nevertheless, similar procedures and expectations seem

---

63. Cassin, 'Daniel', p. 142, refers to an 'ordalie' as part of her thesis on Dan. 6, but does not develop the idea. See also the allusion of Schmidt, 'Daniel and Androcles', p. 2, to 'The ordeal has been successful...' Boogaart, 'Daniel 6', p. 110, also sees a test of God's sovereignty 'according to the condition of the trial by ordeal'.

64. G.R. Driver and J.C. Miles, *The Assyrian Laws* (Oxford: Clarendon Press, 1935), pp. 87-99 and 390-93, for example, note the use of the ordeal for sexual and other unproved matters. See also the discussion of G. Cardascia, 'L'ordalie par le fleuve dans les "lois assyriennes"', in G. Wiessner (ed.), *Festschrift für Wilhelm Eilers* (Wiesbaden: Otto Harrassowitz, 1967), pp. 25-32, on the river ordeal in Assyrian law.

65. W.G. Lambert, 'Nebuchadnezzar King of Justice', *Iraq* 27 (1965), p. 2.

66. Lambert, 'Nebuchadnezzar', p. 9. Wiseman, *Nebuchadrezzar*, p. 100, links Daniel's ordeal with the late Babylonian river ordeal.

to surround them and suggest that there is something of the ordeal, in the technical sense, behind our story.

That such is the case is made more likely by an examination of some details in the LXX account. First there is the group who go with the king to seal the lion pit against any outside interference. They are the same group at the feast of Belshazzar, the μεγιστάνες (v. 18, רברבין MT). These 'nobles' do not appear at any other point in ch. 6. The groups that Darius deals with elsewhere are either the satraps or Daniel's fellow leaders. In the LXX, as we have seen, it tends to be the two leaders, while in the MT the satraps and their leaders work together. In neither version is there any other reference to the group of officials in v. 18. Cassin believes this to be a defined group distinct from the others in the story. She sees them as members of the king's entourage who are called in as legal witnesses at this point to take part in 'un acte de formalisme juridique'.[67] Such a view fits in with the link to ch. 5 that this group provides. The group at Belshazzar's feast would have been members of the central court as here, rather than those responsible for the administration of outlying areas appointed by Darius.

Both versions include the detail that the king strove 'until the setting of the sun' (v. 15, עד מעלי שמשא and ἕως δυσμῶν ἡλίου) implying that that was the time when the trial should begin. The LXX adds two notes that are not in the Aramaic. The first is the parting shot from the king that Daniel should 'Have courage till morning' (v. 17, ἕως πρωὶ θάρρει). This makes explicit that the trial has a time limit and is an absurd remark unless the king has some sort of expectation that Daniel could survive until morning.[68] It may just have been a hope of last resort that if he survived by some miracle he could be released, but the remark seems more definite than that. The second difference in the LXX is the detail that Darius after his sleepless night arose and 'received the satraps' (v. 20, παρέλαβε μεθ' ἑαυτοῦ τοὺς σατράπας) before they all went together to the lion pit (v. 20). It seems that the satraps fulfill some sort of legal function, equivalent to that of the group who applied their signet rings to the stone the night before. Perhaps they are witnesses to the end of the trial or ordeal of Daniel. A problem with this latter detail is that it is not the same group who witnessed the sealing of

---

67. Cassin, 'Daniel', p. 141.

68. See again Müller, 'Märchen, Legende', p. 345, who senses in the MT also an interaction between a human event and divine intervention. He speaks of an event 'übernatürliche und zugleich handfest-dingliche'.

the pit. If there is any weight to the argument that the witnesses are a different group of court officials, it is strange that the account reverts to the protagonists, the satraps, at this point. It could of course simply illustrate the uncertainty of the translator over Persian administrative terms, as I suggested above in another context.

In general terms, the possibility that an identifiable legal procedure lies behind the story of Daniel in the lions' pit is a helpful one. It may well tell us something about the *Sitz im Leben* behind the tradition of Daniel in the lion pit without necessarily clarifying questions of the priority of versions. Chapter 4 provides a parallel to this situation in that each version gives a different picture of the period spent in exile by Nebuchadnezzar, but the two accounts together suggest some sort of common source for the stories.

Literary Merit in the Septuagint

A different form of narrative and different concerns from the MT on the part of the LXX does not imply that this chapter is without literary merit. The same sort of storytelling touches that were noticeable in ch. 4 are here also.[69] Where problems in the narrative form do occur, the reasons are as likely to be compositional as literary. An example of the storyteller at work is the trace of irony about Darius's bold declaration that 'the word is accurate and the injunction remains' (v. 13, ’Ακριβὴς ὁ λόγος καὶ μενεῖ ὁ ὁρισμός). The words and syntax strike a resonance with the declaration by the angel to Nebuchadnezzar that 'my word is accurate and your time is fulfilled' (4.27, ἀκριβὴς γάρ μου ὁ λόγος καὶ πλήρης ὁ χρόνος σου), and reflect badly on Darius's bravado at this moment. It also explicates the issue of sovereignty which we saw earlier is not entirely absent from ch. 6 LXX.

The penultimate sentence of the LXX account contains a piece of parallelism that provides a nice summary of the concerns of the story: 'And King Darius was gathered to his people, and Daniel was set up in the kingdom of Darius'. Apart from the coincidence of syntax, the effectiveness of the summary is heightened by the assonance of the two verbs προσετέθη and κατεστάθη balanced against each other.

---

69. Montgomery, *Daniel*, p. 280, acknowledges 'some lively touches, which are characteristic of LXX's genius...'

Narrative Links with Daniel 4 and 5

A number of links with chapters previously studied have been alluded to in the course of the present discussion. However, there are still further links to be drawn out. This is undertaken with the proviso that the discussion is incomplete at this stage because, on most analyses, the story with the closest relationship to Daniel in the lion pit is the story of the three young men in ch. 3. A discussion of the connections between chs. 3 and 6 will take place after my treatment of ch. 3.

Several of the differences in narrative technique in Daniel 6 have already been identified in Daniel 4 and 5. The MT narrator seldom admits the reader into his counsel but leaves him to discern the significance of the action or words of the characters. Manipulation of perspective is undertaken to good effect. We have seen all this in the story of Darius and Daniel in the lion pit as well. However, the present chapter does not display the same concern for character development as do the previous two. This is a function of the difference between a conflict and a contest. In a court conflict the main character begins and ends in a position of prominence, and relationships between characters remain static.

In contrast, the LXX narrator in chs. 4 and 5 as well as here guides the reader by sharing his omniscience rather than by manipulation of perspective and repetition. A prominent result of that narratorial stance in ch. 6 is the attribution of motive to the different characters. That same effect, concerning the monarchs, was observable in the previous chapters studied, but it is applied here on a wider scale, right down to the explanation of why the stone over the pit has to be sealed.

Thematic Links with Daniel 4 and 5

A comparison of the LXX with the MT in ch. 6 reveals several themes that were also detected in earlier chapters. The issues are presented in terms of personal choices facing the monarch. Belshazzar is condemned for his personal sin rather than a public stance. Nebuchadnezzar's dream of the tree is understood as an allegory of that king's reign rather than a parable on the sovereignty of kings. Darius's final acknowledgement of God is couched in terms of a personal confession rather than a choice between two kingdoms. The translator of ch. 6 continues the polemic against idol worship that was a central theme in both versions of ch. 5,

despite the fact that the choice facing Darius had nothing to do with
idols. This theme is the obverse side of the concern for cultic purity that
may be detected in ch. 4 where Nebuchadnezzar is condemned for his
desecration of the Israelite cult. Just as Nebuchadnezzar responded in
cultic terms by promising to make sacrifices, so Darius makes a more
personal confession in the LXX than he does in the MT. Belshazzar never
gets the chance to make any sort of confession. The result for both chs.
4 and 6 is that the LXX emerges as less universalist in its attitude
towards the monarchs and more concerned for the purity of the God of
Israel. That theme is present strongly in both accounts of ch. 5, so the
difference between the versions is not manifest in that chapter.

Inherent in the different suggestions about Daniel's position at court
are different links to the preceding chapters. The MT story, as a court
conflict, opens with the hero already in a position of influence and
moves on to develop a threat to that position from within the court. In
v. 3 Daniel is one of three leaders already in power. The king 'set up'
(v. 2, הקים) the 120 satraps, but the leaders may already have been in
existence. This is suggested by the wording 'and over them were three
leaders' (v. 3, ועלא מנהון סרכין תלתא), of whom Daniel was one.[70] The
conclusion to the story is that Daniel 'prospered' (v. 29, הצלח) during the
reigns of Darius and Cyrus. The *haphel* form in Aramaic does not
require the sense of being promoted or caused to prosper, and the participle suggests continuity.[71] The picture of Daniel is that he continues in
a position already attained in previously charted contests. Chapters 4 and
5 are at ease with the picture of a Daniel moving in the secular life of the
court.

The LXX does not contain those contests in chs. 4 and 5. As we have
seen, ch. 5 LXX avoids the question of Daniel's courtly position while
ch. 4 plays down its significance. In ch. 6 Daniel is clearly a figure at
court. The story depends on him holding that position, but it is not
assumed from the beginning. When Darius promotes his 127 satraps he
also sets aside (v. 3) three men including Daniel, and subsequently in a
section of plus material decides 'to set up' (v. 4, καταστῆσαι) or
promote the sage further. The summary in v. 29 states that Daniel 'was

---

70. Delcor, *Daniel*, p. 135, describes him as 'super-satrape', a neat solution to
the problem of how exactly to translate סרך.

71. See Rosenthal, *Biblical Aramaic*, p. 55, on the participle. He considers
(p. 42) that the *haphel* is usually causative, but consultation of BDB and Jastrow
suggests that is not a necessary or usual sense for the *haphel* of צלח.

set up' (v. 29, κατεστάθη), the same word used of the 127 satraps in v. 2.[72] This is a word more appropriate to the conclusion of a contest than the successful outcome of a conflict depicted by צלח in the MT. It is the same word used to describe God's promotion of Nebuchadnezzar's usurper (4.31). The resulting introduction of a contest is appropriate to a story which has not recognized the contests that the MT assumes.

Literary Links with Daniel 4 and 5

We noted previously that the MT version of ch. 5 relied for its effect strongly on the preceding story of Nebuchadnezzar's tree and the positive traditions about his reign. On the other hand, a court contest was not one of the LXX's concerns and there was little in the way of linking between chs. 4 and 5. Despite that independence, the present story in the LXX shows traces of some literary links with both stories or at least with the tradition that produced their translation. The circular letter containing the king's confession in vv. 26-28 is a case in point. Darius's letter is addressed 'to the nations and regions and tongues' (v. 26, τοῖς ἔθνεσι καὶ χώραις καὶ γλώσσαις) just as is Nebuchadnezzar's in 4.37b LXX. This contrasts with the Theodotionic rendering of the Aramaic as λαοῖς, φυλαῖς, γλώσσαις both here and at 3.31/4.1, the MT equivalent of one of Nebuchadnezzar's confessions in the LXX. Similarly, Darius in the LXX acknowledges the God who endures 'from generation to generation' (v. 27, εἰς γενεὰς γενεῶν) while Nebuchadnezzar uses almost the same phrase (4.37c, ἀπο γενεῶν εἰς γενεάς). This is distinct from the θ translation of עם־דר ודר (3.33 MT) as εἰς γενεὰν καὶ γενεὰν (4.3 θ).[73] Darius also speaks of the God who 'has redeemed' Daniel (v. 28, ἐλυτρώσατο), which places the LXX reader in mind of Nebuchadnezzar's 'time of redemption' (4.34, ἀπολυτρώσεως). Neither instance is represented in the MT. Further links with ch. 4 LXX have already been explored in the section that considers the servanthood of Darius.

As far as ch. 5 goes, the additional polemic against idols in the LXX has already been noted. There is also a common vocabulary for court figures that seems to operate between the chapters. We have seen that Daniel is referred to as the king's 'friend' (φίλον) in 6.14 by his fellow

---

72. Charles, *Daniel*, p. 151, recognizes this distinction between the versions.

73. θ shows a more literal rendering in that it preserves the sequence of elements found in Aramaic. See Barr, *Typology of Literalism*, p. 296.

courtiers. In the previous chapter the same word is used, this time by Daniel, as a synonym for 'nobles' (5.23). In neither place is there an equivalent to this usage in the MT. It seems to represent those who occupy some sort of position in the central administration and are close to the king.[74] It signifies the distinction in stance between the two stories in the LXX that in one Daniel condemns the king's friends and in the other he is described as such himself. The word seems to be equivalent to μεγιστᾶνές (5.23 and 6.18) or its Aramaic equivalent in both places, רברבין, and is common to both chapters.

The significance of these echoes should not be overdrawn, however. There are signs that the links between the LXX chapters are not clear cut. There are aspects of Nebuchadnezzar's confession that are not present in the shorter statement of Darius. For example, the earlier king spoke of 'trembling from fear of him' (4.37a, ἀπὸ τοῦ φόβου αὐτοῦ τρόμος) in a block of LXX plus material. That concept has not been included in the LXX confession by Darius, but it is a phrase picked up in the MT, where the king orders that his subjects will 'tremble and be afraid' (v. 27, זאעין ודחלין translated by θ as τρέμοντας καὶ φοβουμένος). The same phrase also occurs at 5.19 MT, this time in MT plus material identically phrased in Aramaic and almost identically in Greek by θ. In neither place is it represented in the LXX. Likewise the 'signs and wonders' of both the MT and LXX in ch. 4 also occur in v. 28 MT (אתין ותמהין) but are not present in the LXX. It seems that there was some cross-fertilization going on between the traditions, and lines cannot be drawn too firmly.[75] It needs to be acknowledged that there are themes and interests running between the stories, and probably an awareness of one by the other, yet the sort of clear literary dependence that can be discerned between the MT stories is more difficult to chart in the LXX.

Conclusion

As with the previous two chapters studied, there is much that these two accounts of Darius and Daniel in the lion pit have in common. Both stories depict a Near Eastern monarch who is fooled into taking to himself functions that belong to God alone. In both, this results in a test of faith for Daniel, whose God delivers him from the power of the lions,

74. See again Cassin, 'Daniel', p. 141.
75. Bruce, 'Oldest Greek Version', p. 37.

and by implication from the hand of the king and those conspiring against him. This results in judgment on those who sought to bring Daniel down, while Darius is preserved to acknowledge publicly the sovereignty of Daniel's God.

As also in Daniel 4 and 5, there are differences in the manner in which the story is told. The narrator provides more clues of his intention in the LXX, where the MT requires his reader to draw conclusions from the words and actions. This is seen in the way perspective is manipulated, motives of characters dealt with, and the story anticipated by the respective storytellers. Irony and suspense are central to the functioning of the MT narrative, where the LXX is a more straightforward moral tale, although not without its ironic aspects. The LXX takes a closer interest in the person of Darius. Daniel remains largely a silent, aloof figure perceived through the eyes of others in both versions, although when he finally does speak, his role as a representative of judgment is more explicit in the LXX.

The differences in the way the story is told reflect different concerns on the part of the versions. The MT centres the conflict on the two laws, so the climax of the story is a further ordinance, which admits the superiority of the law of God over the law of the Medes and the Persians. The LXX centres the conflict more around the arrogation of divine powers to himself by Darius. Consequently the climax of the LXX's story is a confession of submission by Darius to the God whom he had been tricked into trying to usurp.

These differences in both narrative technique and theological concern broadly continue the differences that have already been discerned in chs. 4 and 5, and in that respect neither version of the story can be said to stand alone. As exceptions to that, Daniel plays a more positive courtly role in this chapter than the LXX has previously allowed him, and the attitude towards the king is more positive than was the case with Nebuchadnezzar and Belshazzar. Both these exceptions reflect an admission of the court contest on the part of the LXX that has previously been absent. There is a greater interplay in the LXX between this story and those of chs. 4 and 5, than we saw between chs. 4 and 5. However, the confessional material reveals an interplay across versions as well as between chapters.

Chapter 5

DANIEL 3

The MT and LXX versions of Daniel 3 are both more alike and more different from one another than in chs. 4–6. The Additions excepted, the LXX appears to spring from a *Vorlage* closer to the MT than has been the case so far, and as a result the story is almost the same in the ordering of events and characters. Shadrach, Meshach and Abednego defy the king's order to worship a golden image, and are thrust into the fiery furnace as punishment after some Chaldeans draw the king's attention to their defiance. In the process those deputed to carry out the execution are themselves killed by the flames. Nebuchadnezzar witnesses their deliverance by some sort of heavenly intervention and responds in acknowledgment of the God of Shadrach, Meshach and Abednego by issuing a second decree. This time he commands his subjects to worship the God of his Jewish subjects.

The major difference between the two accounts lies in the Additions, and an examination of them is my first priority in a literary comparison of the Aramaic and Greek versions of Daniel 3.[1] Although the main focus is on the MT and LXX versions, a feature of the present chapter is that θ also includes the Additions and has a little more in common with the LXX of ch. 3 than elsewhere in Daniel. Consequently ch. 3 θ receives fuller treatment in the survey in Appendix 1, the contents of which should be noted in conjunction with the discussion that follows. In treating the Prayer of Azariah, the Song of the Three and the narrative material linked to them, I do not propose to deal with them as discrete literary units.[2] Their survival in religious tradition speaks for the quality

---

1. The Greek material between vv. 23 and 24 MT is conventionally called the Additions. I use that term for convenience, although I will show in the course of my argument that the material is probably 'inserted' and so it is not inappropriate to speak of it as additional.

2. For examples of such treatments, see C.A. Moore, *Daniel, Esther, and*

of the compositions. Instead I will consider whether the material is inserted in or original to the context in which we now find it, before looking at its effect on the narrative of ch. 3 and on its theological or polemical concerns.

It will be seen that the issues so raised also pertain to other smaller narrative differences between the MT and the LXX. A discussion of differences in narrative shape and perspective leads into a look at the repetition of lists and phrases particularly by the MT, and the effect on the narrative when the LXX summarizes lists or abbreviates formulae. The resultant difference means that the versions use different means to convey narrative perspective. It is also a contributing factor to a significantly different setting for each version of the story. A brief note on two literary devices used by the Aramaic will constitute the final part of the consideration of the narrative. This will lead into an examination of theological differences, which again links back to the earlier discussion of the Additions and focuses primarily on the problematical vv. 16-18. The major issues of monotheism, idolatry, the nature of kingship, wisdom and angelology all recur, and the LXX's polemical concerns on these matters are consistent with what has already been seen.

The final section will examine the links between this chapter and the previous ones studied, chs. 4–6. This builds particularly on the work done for ch. 6 and discovers that genre is not the only aspect that chs. 3 and 6 have in common in the MT. While there are links with chs. 4 and 5 also, the strongest ties are with the story of Daniel in the lion pit. In contrast, ch. 3 LXX seems to form a pair with ch. 4 in a manner appropriate to the chapter order witnessed in 967 (1–4, 7–8, 5–6, 9–12). This has interesting connotations for the way the versions diverge in their treatment of Nebuchadnezzar, especially when other royal confessions in Daniel are taken into account.

The Additions: Narrative Insertions?

Most of the issues of this chapter are brought to the surface in a discussion of the Greek Additions. In particular the question of whether or not they may be properly described as insertions in the MT provides us with

Jeremiah: The Additions (Garden City, NY: Doubleday, 1977); W.H. Daubney, *The Three Additions of Daniel* (London: G. Bell & Sons, 1906); or M.P. Gilbert, 'La prière d'Azarias', *NRT* 6 (1974), pp. 561-82. Collins, *Daniel*, pp. 195-207, also devotes a section of commentary to the Additions.

a useful starting point. It has been suggested that there is a problem with the flow of the MT narrative in vv. 23-24. Verse 23 seems to be redundant to the action and v. 24 follows on too quickly from what has preceded it. It appears that there is something missing in the story between vv. 23 and 24.[3] Still others go on to wonder if perhaps the prose interlude between the Prayer of Azariah and the Song of the Three (vv. 46-51) represents that missing part of the Semitic narrative.[4]

The first question to be asked is whether or not 3.46-51 is a likely continuation of the narrative in the MT. A comparison of the depiction of characters in the two sections suggests that it is not. The LXX v. 24 refers to 'Hananiah and Azariah and Mishael' (Ανανιας καὶ Αζαριας καὶ Μισαηλ), although the focus shifts in v. 25 to Azariah as the central figure and the other two are 'his companions' (τοῖς συνεταίροις αὐτοῦ). This nomenclature is maintained in v. 49 where reference is made to 'those with Azariah' (τοῖς περὶ τὸν Αζαριαν) without naming his companions, and later simply to 'the three' (v. 51, οἱ τρεῖς). The MT never uses the Semitic names of the heroes, nor does it focus on one of them in particular. When they are named (vv. 13-14, 16, 19-20, 22, 26, 28-30) all three are listed in exactly the same order each time. Apart from early references to them as Judeans (v. 8, די יהודיא, v. 12, גברין יהודאין), the men are almost always referred to as 'these men' (vv. 12, 21, 27, גבריא אלך). The MT never speaks of 'the three' as a collective noun in the way that the LXX Addition does. The reference to 'three men' (v. 24, גברין תלתא) and 'these three men' (v. 23, גבריא אלך תלתהון) is not equivalent, since the emphasis in these particular instances is on the number 'three' as contrasted with the four figures that Nebuchadnezzar sees in the furnace.

The Additions also contain a different description of the functional characters who bind and despatch Shadrach, Meshach and Abednego to the flames and then are themselves consumed. The LXX appears to render the idiomatic Aramaic phrase for warriors (v. 20, גברי־חיל) literally into ἄνδρας ἰσχυροτάτους. The implication in both languages is of members of an elite group. Other biblical examples of this type of correspondence may be found. In 1 Chron. 8.40 the sons of Ulam are spoken

3. For example Delcor, *Daniel*, p. 105.
4. For example Hartman and DiLella, *Daniel*, pp. 159-60, and W. Rothstein, 'Die Zusätze zu Daniel', in E. Kautzsch (ed.), *Die Apokryphen und Pseudepigraphen des Alten Testaments* (Tübingen: J.C.B. Mohr, 1900), p. 175. See also other references in Moore, *Daniel*, p. 41.

of with approval as גברי־חיל in the MT and ἰσχυροὶ ἄνδρες in the LXX.
Prov. 30.30 uses the expression as an image of the lion. The Hebrew
refers to it as גבור 'among the beasts' (בבהמה), while the Greek describes
the lion as ἰσχυρότερος. Although the syntax is different, these
examples confirm the general sense evoked by the words used to
describe the executioners in both languages of Daniel 3. This impression
of an elite group is reinforced in v. 22 LXX where those same men are
described literally as 'hand-picked' (προχειρισθέντες). The prose interlude in the Greek Additions, however, describes them simply as
'labourers of the king' (v. 46, ὑπηρέται τοῦ βασιλέως). Normally the
word in Septuagintal Greek denotes the ordinary (Wis. 13.11) or sub-
servient (Wis. 19.6). Its only biblical occurrence with an attested Semitic
equivalent is in Isa. 32.5 where its Hebrew equivalent is כילי, the sense of
which is perhaps best captured by the Old English word 'knave'. It is
also in parallel with μῶρος. In sum, the executioners of v. 46 are from
quite a different class of functionary than those described in v. 20.

As well as Shadrach, Meshach and Abednego, and the executioners,
another 'character' that appears in the prose segments of the Additional
material is the furnace. Mostly the furnace is described along similar lines
to the Aramaic with fairly consistent use of the phrase τὴν κάμινον
τοῦ πυρὸς τὴν καιομένην (vv. 6, 11, 15, 20). The consistency lies
more in the vocabulary used than in the exact reproduction of the whole
phrase. Throughout the chapter κάμινος depicts the 'furnace'. In the
parts that coincide with the Aramaic tradition, the whole expression is
not always used but there is no variation in the vocabulary (vv. 17, 20).
In the Additional material there is different vocabulary and the same
vocabulary used differently. Specifically the word φλόξ is introduced
(vv. 23, 47, 49, 88), and participles are intensified with prefixes (v. 23,
ἐνεπύρισε, and v. 25, ὑποκαιομένης).

An examination of the flow of the narrative sheds further light on the
question. Both versions are in substantial agreement up until v. 22. They
state that the furnace was heated to excess and even agree in their
description of the king's decree as 'pressing' (v. 22 MT, מחצפה; LXX,
ἤπειγεν). Up to this point they appear to be following a common tradition. From v. 22b, however, there are differences. The MT has the
flames kill those bearing Shadrach, Meshach and Abednego and then
they fall bound into the furnace (v. 23). In the LXX the men bind them
and throw them into the furnace again, and in v. 23 the furnace kills the
executioners but the heroes are watched over. The LXX does not

mention the young men by name at all except to refer to one of them by his Hebrew name, Azariah (v. 23, Αζαριαν). This is in marked contrast to the MT which mentions the three in full twice in the equivalent verses. In light of the earlier discussion on names, this suggests that from v. 22b onwards the present form of the LXX reflects the same tradition behind the prose narrative of the Additions. Therefore the relationship of Additional prose material to vv. 21-23 needs to be considered in two parts. The first stage is to examine the flow of the prose narrative in the LXX version when the song and the prayer are removed, so that vv. 46-50 follow immediately on v. 23 and precede v. 24/91. The second is to insert vv. 46-50 LXX into the same place in the MT, between vv. 23 and 24, and to look at the effect on the narrative as we have it in the MT.

Problems become immediately apparent when the narrative flow of vv. 21-23, 46-50, 91 is considered in the LXX. The men are thrown into the furnace twice (vv. 21-22) and each time the same root verb, βάλλω, is used, although the second time it is prefixed by the translator or writer. Then the executioners are killed twice (vv. 23, 48), and the stoking of the furnace is described twice (vv. 22, 46-47). On the second mention, the work of the firemen and the resulting flames are described in some detail. As well as the apparent repetition, there is a difference in narrative detail on the second time of telling. In the prose section of the Additions, apart from the fact already noted that the executioners are of lower status, the same group who throw Azariah and his companions into the fire are responsible for maintaining its heat. This is made quite explicit with the participial expression 'who threw them in' (v. 46, οἱ...ἐμβάλλοντες αὐτούς). It is not at all clear that these are the same ones who are killed by the flames in v. 48. They are described there simply as those of the Chaldeans found near the 'furnace' (οὓς εὗρε περὶ τὴν κάμινον τῶν Χαλδαίων). Incidentally it is unlikely that any identification is intended of these Chaldeans and those who earlier had slandered the young Judeans (v. 8). Moreover, the question of what made Nebuchadnezzar stand up for a closer look remains unclear. The LXX suggests first that it was because he heard the singing (v. 91, ἐν τῷ ἀκοῦσαι τὸν βασιλέα ὑμνούντων αὐτῶν). However, in the following verse, in agreement with the MT, the king's direct speech centres on the fact that the men are no longer bound and that there are four of them (v. 25/92, ἄνδρας τέσσαρας λελυμένους). Nebuchadnezzar's speech does not seem to follow from what precedes it and is incomprehensible if divorced from the Prayer of Azariah and the Song of the Three.

Another possibility is that the tradition behind the MT narrative once included the material contained in vv. 46-50 LXX. One way to test that idea is to place vv. 46-50 LXX between vv. 21-23 MT and v. 24 MT. Similar problems in the shape of the narrative as above arise when this is done. The executioners are killed, and Shadrach, Meshach and Abednego fall bound into the fire (vv. 22-23). Immediately following this is the statement that those 'who threw them in' (v. 46) carried on stoking the furnace. On those grounds the material in vv. 46-50 does not seem to fit easily with the MT narrative. Against that however there is a less forced progression on to v. 24/91 MT than the LXX of that verse. The king's reaction 'in trepidation' (בהתבהלה) is more readily understood as a response to the action of the angel of the Lord in vv. 49-50. The implication of the king's concerns in v. 24/91 MT is that he sees the results of the angel's activities, namely that the three prisoners are now loose and unharmed in the flames and a fourth figure is with them. However, the problem of the names of the three heroes and the description of the executioners remains.

On balance it seems unlikely that the present form of vv. 46-50 LXX ever existed in the immediate precursor to the present MT. If the Additional narrative material was ever part of the MT tradition, it has left no trace in the present form of the text.[5] On the other hand, the way

---

5. The debate over the existence or otherwise of a Semitic original of the Additions is not germane to the present discussion. Bruce, 'Oldest Greek Version', p. 36, and Daubney, *The Three Additions*, p. 46, point to the close coincidence of LXX and θ in the poetic material in support of a Semitic original. Schmitt, 'Die griechischen Danieltexte', p. 29, favours the view that θ's *Vorlage* in the Additions was the Old Greek. M. Gaster, 'The Unknown Aramaic Original of Theodotion's Additions to the Book of Daniel', *PSBA* 16 (1894) and *PSBA* 17 (1895), p. 75; and M. Gaster (ed.), *The Chronicles of Jerahmeel* (London: Royal Asiatic Society, 1899), p. lv, is convinced that Jerahmeel's Aramaic version of the Song of the Three was original, and he has recently received some support from K. Koch, *Deuterokanonische Zusätze zum Danielbuch* (Neukirchen–Vluyn: Butzon & Bercker, 1987), p. 38. Collins, *Daniel*, p. 202, suggests the Prayer of Azariah was 'a traditional Hebrew composition' of which an Aramaic version was produced. With Koch he also takes seriously the Jerahmeel evidence concerning the Song of the Three. D.J. Harrington (ed.), *The Hebrew Fragments of Pseudo-Philo* (Missoula, MT: Society of Biblical Literature, 1974), pp. 3-4, says the Jerahmeel material is a

characters are perceived and the narrative shaped by the LXX in the
material where the two versions diverge (vv. 22b-24/91) indicates that
this particular representation of the tradition is closely tied to the poetic
material. As a discussion of the contents of the Additional material will
show, the Greek Additions are probably a later insertion into the story
of Shadrach, Meshach and Abednego.[6] In this instance, in contrast to
chs. 4 and 6, it is unlikely that the LXX draws us closer to an *Ursprung*
containing a more expansive account of angelic activity in the furnace.[7]

The Additions as Part of the Narrative

Insertion of the Additions into the tradition represented by the MT also
affects the wider narrative of the LXX. The first thing to note is that the
portrayal of time is distorted by the insertion. There is now too long a
period between when the three young men are pitched into the furnace
and the king's discovery that they are alive and well and have a companion with them.[8] The difference in pace between objective time and
literary time has become too great.[9] In order not to have credulity

---

retroversion from the Greek, while E. Schurer, *The History of the Jewish People in
the Age of Jesus Christ* (ed. G. Vermes, F. Miller and M. Goodman; Edinburgh: T.
& T. Clark, 1986), III, pp. 326 and 330, sees it as a retranslation from the Latin.
W.H. Bennett, 'The Prayer of Azariah and the Song of the Three Children', in R.H.
Charles (ed.), *Apocrypha and Pseudepigrapha of the Old Testament* (Oxford:
Clarendon Press, 1913), I, p. 627, summarizes the position neatly: 'there is not
much that could not have been written in Hellenistic Greek, and nothing that cannot
have been translated from Hebrew'.

6.   P.-M. Bogaert, 'Daniel 3 LXX et son supplément grec', in A.S. van der
Woude (ed.), *The Book of Daniel* (Leuven: University Press/Uitgeverij Peeters,
1993), pp. 19 and 34-36, considers the supplements were inserted by a Maccabean
translator. In the view of Collins, *Daniel*, p. 203, the Prayer of Azariah originates
from the same period as the visions of chs. 7–12. In this regard see the comment of
Rothstein, 'Die Zusätze zu Daniel', p. 174, that v. 88 was probably an insertion into
an older song designed to make it fit the present context.

7.   The suggestion of B.G. Sanders, 'The Burning Fiery Furnace', *Theology* 58
(1955), p. 343, that fire-walking in an ecstatic state lies behind our story is highly
unlikely as it ignores too many other details in the story. But see also E. Bickerman,
Four Strange Books of the Bible (New York: Schocken Books, 1967), p. 89.

8.   Wills, *The Jew in the Court*, p. 86, notes they are in the furnace 'for what
seems to be an eternity'.

9.   See Bar-Efrat, *Narrative Art*, pp. 143-65, on the distinction between
'objective time' and 'literary time'.

strained too far, the reader must concentrate on the prayer and song for their own sakes and put to one side the existence of the wider narrative of which they form a part.[10] There are occasions when difference in pace can be exploited to create suspense, but such is not the case here because the narrator has already anticipated events with the editorial aside, 'but they were kept' (v. 23, αὐτοὶ δὲ συνετηρήθησαν).

The second major literary effect of the insertion of the Additions is that it shifts the centre of the narrative. As we will see below, vv. 16-18 of the MT function effectively as the central point in the story, the moment at which the issues crystallize. The language of the LXX works to similar effect as the two versions are extremely close at this point. Yet vv. 16-18 seem off centre in the LXX, particularly as the tension created by the conditional clause in v. 17 is soon dissipated by the anticipation of events in v. 23. The positioning of the Additions and their length relative to the rest of ch. 3 means that the centre shifts to the prayer and song, even though their links with the story of the fiery furnace are at best tenuous.

Differing Interests of the Additions

The most obvious incongruity of the Additions with the story surrounding them is in the concerns that motivate them. The penitential tone of the Prayer of Azariah is notable in this regard. The entire prayer is a collective and vicarious expression of national guilt before God, with hardly a trace of Azariah's own dilemma. At least the comparable instance of the prayer of Jonah (Jon. 2.2-9) is couched in personal terms with a veiled reference by Jonah to his own crisis.[11] Reference to being made 'the smallest of all the nations' (v. 37, ἐσμικρύνθημεν παρὰ πάντα τὰ ἔθνη) and to the absence of 'ruler and prophet nor leader' (v. 38, ἄρχων καὶ προφήτης οὐδὲ ἡγούμενος) makes clear that the heroes speak on behalf of the nation. Just punishment has come upon a sinful people (v. 31) in the form of oppression by a king 'unrighteous and the most evil in all the earth' (v. 32, ἀδίκιῳ καὶ πονηροτάτῳ παρὰ πᾶσαν τὴν γήν). The guilt of God's people is not a concern of the MT and the test facing Shadrach, Meshach and Abednego is more one of personal faithfulness in a foreign land than of national crisis.[12] The

10. Rothstein, 'Die Zusätze zu Daniel', p. 173.
11. Daubney, *The Three Additions*, p. 39.
12. Young, *Daniel*, p. 91, notes that the Jews' reply in MT vv. 17-18 is at a

aspect of national guilt is more a feature of the later chapters of Daniel in the MT, as witnessed in the confession of Daniel in 9.4-20, a prayer similar to Azariah's.[13]

At v. 39 the prayer does become personal with talk of a 'shattered soul and humbled spirit' (ψυχῇ συντετριμμένῃ καὶ πνεύματι τεταπεινωμένῳ), and the lament for the lost cultic sacrifice (v. 38) is linked to the three companions' own self-sacrifice in the fire (v. 40).[14] It thereby becomes a kind of atonement. The interest in patriarchal history (v. 35) and the well-being of Jerusalem (v. 28) relate to this concern for the political and cultic life of the nation (v. 38). Indeed it has been pointed out that whenever the patriarchs are listed in this unusual way the context is cultic (Exod. 32.13; 1 Kgs 18.36; 1 Chron. 29.18; 2 Chron. 30.6).[15] Even in the more universalist Song of the Three, the Temple theme may be detected early on with τῷ ναῷ (v. 53) and χερουβιμ (v. 55). The song is directed towards Israel (v. 83) and its cultic officials (v. 84, ἱερεῖς, and v. 85, δοῦλοι), and ultimately towards the Hebraically named Hananiah, Azariah and Mishael (v. 88). The use of Hebrew names perhaps emphasizes their Palestinian Jewish concerns, in contrast to the courtly figures of Shadrach, Meshach and Abednego in the Babylonian or Persian diaspora. This difference in content adds further weight to the argument that the Additions in their entirety may fairly be described as insertions.[16]

Narrative Shape

If that is indeed the case, the MT story should function satisfactorily in its present form. The section that has been the object of most discussion about the MT narrative is vv. 23-24. The implication of v. 21 is that Shadrach, Meshach and Abednego have been thrown into the furnace and the information follows that those who bound them and threw them in were killed in the process. Then comes v. 23 which seems only to repeat what was conveyed two verses earlier. With hardly a pause for

---

considerable remove from Maccabean nationalism. But Collins, *Daniel*, p. 188, disagrees.

13. Daubney, *The Three Additions*, p. 58. See also Gilbert, 'La prière d'Azarias', p. 563, for a detailed comparison.

14. Gilbert, 'La prière d'Azarias', p. 579.

15. Gilbert, 'La prière d'Azarias', p. 569.

16. Moore, *Daniel*, p. 24, describes them as intrusive and secondary.

the reader to register what has happened to the three young men, the focus shifts to Nebuchadnezzar whom we are told 'was startled and stood up in trepidation' (v. 24, תוה וקם בהתבהלה). All this is conveyed with no hint as to what has caused such a response on the part of the king. There is an apparent flaw in the depiction of time as it does not seem possible that Nebuchadnezzar has had time to see, let alone respond to, anything.

Yet the functioning of these two verses in the narrative as it is now found in the MT, while surprising, displays several of the characteristics that we have come to expect from the teller of the Aramaic stories in Daniel. Instead of being redundant, v. 23 can be thought of as serving a resumptive purpose that leads into the next stage of the narrative.[17] The result is a necessary pause that contains, but does not describe, the passage of time leading up to the king's reactions in v. 24. The MT fills the time while the three are languishing in the furnace by reinforcing two important facts about what has just happened to Shadrach, Meshach and Abednego. The first one is that there were three of them who fell into the furnace. This is the only time in ch. 3 MT where Shadrach, Meshach and Abednego are referred to as 'these three men' (v. 23, גבריא אלך תלתהין). Elsewhere, as I have noted above, they are either named or referred to as 'these men'. The result of this change in formula is a particular emphasis on the number. The second key item in the description is that they were 'bound' (מכפתין). The participle is particularly emphasized by being disentangled from the formulaic phrase '(they) fell into the midst of the furnace of burning fire' (נפלו לגא־אתון־נורא יקדתא) and placed at the end of the sentence. This description foreshadows Nebuchadnezzar's question in the following verse, 'Did we not throw three men (גברין תלתא) into the midst of the fire bound (מכפתין)?' Again the adjective 'bound' is placed emphatically.

Another effect of v. 23 is that it builds suspense by shifting the focus of the narrative away from the protagonists at a crucial moment. At the end of v. 22 we are told that the heat killed 'these men who took up' (גבריא אלך די הסקו) Shadrach, Meshach and Abednego. The obvious question arising from that—what happened to the intended victims?—is not addressed. Instead we get an intrusive reminder of things we already know. The suspense continues into v. 24 when Nebuchadnezzar starts

---

17. Goldingay, *Daniel*, p. 66. Compare Charles, *Daniel*, p. 72, who brackets out v. 23 entirely.

up from where he was seated and questions his officials.[18] The camera remains focused on the person of the king and not his victims, while the reader's curiosity is whetted by the king's line of questioning. We only find out what has happened in the furnace when the king lets us in on what he has already seen, that the men are alive and unbound and there are now four of them. As when Daniel was in the lion pit (ch. 6), the reader does not find out what happened in the hour of danger until it is revealed from the point of view of the king. There is a difference, though, in that the king knows before the reader, whereas in 6.21 reader and king find out at the same time. Yet the same covert narratorial manipulation of perspective to build and maintain suspense operates in both stories. This contrasts with the LXX account which answers the obvious question that the MT leaves tantalizingly unanswered: 'But they were kept' (v. 23, αὐτοὶ δὲ συνετηρήθησαν). The result is the same anticipation of the story by the narrator observable in ch. 6.

The usage of the words אדין and ענה in v. 24 is also typical of the MT narrative in the Daniel stories. The former normally indicates a change of scene and almost always occurs at the beginning of a verse. This was seen in ch. 6 where it marks a series of rapid scene changes. It may also denote that what follows is in some measure dependent on what has gone before, without always defining exactly how. This lack of a range of connectives, such as is available in English, at times brings about a hiatus in the narrative that the storyteller is able to exploit. We have already seen an example of this at 5.13 where Daniel enters the banqueting hall after the queen advises Belshazzar to call him. The use of באדין leaves it unclear whether or not the queen had issued an order over the authority of the king. In the present context also a gap is created in the narrative by אדין, signalling an abrupt change in focus and an uncertainty as to what exactly has upset Nebuchadnezzar. The same sort of surprise shift in the narrative also occurred earlier between vv. 7 and 8. Just as the Chaldeans began to 'eat pieces of' the three heroes before the reader knows why, so here Nebuchadnezzar is 'startled and stood up in trepidation' (v. 24, תוה וקם בהתבהלה) before the reason for his surprise is clear. Thus the suspense already noted in this section of narrative is heightened. At the same time the untranslatable ענה precedes the king's speech to his officials. The word is used to indicate a response or reaction to what immediately precedes it and is not necessarily an 'answer' to

---

18. An example of variation in psychological time within a narrative to heighten tension. See Bar-Efrat, *Narrative Art*, p. 161, on this aspect of biblical narrative.

another character's speech. The result is a strong hint that what the king is about to say relates directly to what he saw in the furnace. But still the reader waits to know what that is.

Another much discussed section of ch. 3 is vv. 15-18. Earlier I suggested that this is a central moment in the development of the conflict. It is the moment when Nebuchadnezzar betrays his deepest motives: 'what god is there who will rescue you from my hand?' (v. 15, מן־הוא אלה די ישׁיזבנכון מן־ידי). And it is the time when Shadrach, Meshach and Abednego reach the point of no return with 'we will not serve your gods' (v. 18, לאלהיך לא־איתנא פלחין). In a curious twist this central point of the narrative becomes an anticlimax because the test that the list of musical instruments has been building towards is never actually put to the three heroes.[19] What we get instead is the famous unresolved protasis containing again the list of musical instruments followed by the statement from Shadrach, Meshach and Abednego that there is nothing to discuss (vv. 15-16).[20] It is that action and not their failure to respond to the music that is the final straw for Nebuchadnezzar. It is as though the sound and fury of the idol's dedication is trivialized by the tranquility of the moment when the choice between masters is recognized (vv. 16-18). The MT expresses this in terms of service. Setting aside for the moment the complexities of v. 17a, in the speech of the Jewish rebels, allegiance to the God whom they 'serve' (v. 17, פלחין) entails their refusal to 'serve' (v. 18, פלחין) the gods of Nebuchadnezzar. Once the moment has passed and its significance sunk in, the emotional and physical temperature of the narrative rises again as Nebuchadnezzar is 'filled with fury' (v. 19, התמלי חמא). As a result of the king's failure to put the test of the music to the Judeans, the furnace becomes the test itself rather than the consequence of failure.

The same twist in the tale is present in the LXX. The difference is that with the absence of the full orchestra at this point the build up is muted and so the twist to the tale is less startling. Likewise the issue of service is not carried forward with the same repetition of key words as is the case with the MT use of פלח. θ reflects this with its consistent choice of λατρεύω. Despite the use of λατρεύω in vv. 14 and 18, the LXX chooses φοβέω instead in v. 17. Both of these points will be treated in

19. Good, 'Apocalyptic as Comedy', p. 51.

20. Some suggest a facial expression or gesture on the part of the Jews as a reason for the aposiopesis. See, for example, Stuart, *Daniel*, p. 87, and Charles, *Daniel*, p. 68.

greater depth when the use of repetition is compared and the differing theological emphases examined.

While one possible response to vv. 23-24 in the MT is that there is a gap in the narrative because something is missing, another is to see the gap as a deliberate piece of narrative technique. The result is that, at least in literary terms, the MT can be seen as a coherent piece of narrative in its present form.[21] The importance of the young men's meeting with King Nebuchadnezzar (vv. 15-18) as a key episode in the story is also reinforced by the shape of the MT narrative.

Narrative Perspective

These central verses also provide a starting point in an examination of the manipulation of perspective by the storyteller. It is an astonishing feature of the MT narrative that Shadrach, Meshach and Abednego hardly utter a word.[22] They say nothing in the build up to the central meeting with the king (vv. 16-18) and nothing after they emerge from the furnace. Like Daniel in ch. 6, they refrain from any condemnation of the king. Even their short affirmation of faith is ambiguous in content if not in courage. The storyteller leaves the reader to decide that the Judean heroes' attitude is also the narrator's, because Nebuchadnezzar himself comes to recognize it.

As in the other stories examined, the MT narrator is covert in that he does not anticipate the story. This may be further illustrated by the progress of the action from v. 8. Up until that point Shadrach, Meshach and Abednego have not entered the story and their presence at the plain of Dura is only by implication. The narrator does not let us see their act of defiance. Instead he brings them into the story through the agency of the Chaldeans whom we are told 'ate pieces of the Judeans' (v. 8 אכלו קרציהון די יהודיא) in an audience with the king. Even then the reason for the slander is not told. They are not mentioned by name until the end of the sycophantic speech and then only with the preface, 'men of Judah' (v. 12, גברין יהודאין) and the reminder to the king that he had appointed them. Finally, through the agency of the Chaldeans, the reader hears the crime of which they are accused. Only then does the focus shift to King Nebuchadnezzar as his reaction to this new knowledge is documented

---

21. Of vv. 21-25, Torrey, 'Notes', p. 264, says, 'I see no reason for doubting that its original author wrote it in just this way.'

22. Fewell, *Circle of Sovereignty*, p. 82.

(vv. 13-15). Events in the furnace are also seen through the eyes of the king. The reader is only allowed to see what the king can see. The person of King Nebuchadnezzar is central to the operation of perspective as every scene either observes him or is observed by him, and the action unfolds as he sees it. This incidentally is a literary argument to add to the others above in favour of the integrity of the MT as it stands.

There is less opportunity for a covert narrator to project his point of view in the present chapter. There is still a significant amount of direct speech but less varied repetition between speakers and between speaker and narrator. Such variation is an important means for manipulation of perspective, but is not employed in the story of the three young men. Instead the narrator uses the repetition of identical formulae. When such phrases or lists or formulae occur both in narrative sections and in the mouths of characters, they become a vehicle for irony. The narrator of this chapter is dependent on that irony being understood in the portrayal of his point of view, as we will see in the sections on irony and repetition below.

The account in the LXX is substantially the same as the MT except at key points that we have examined. The balance between narrative and dialogue is similar, so perspective is conveyed in the same way. The major difference, apart from ones relating to the Additions, is found in the summarizing tendency of the LXX. The resulting difference in the degree of irony present could have meant some ambiguity in perspective. In fact the Additions ensure that such is not the case. In the first place the narrator becomes more visible in the LXX once the traditions begin to diverge at v. 22. The contrast between the people of Nebuchadnezzar and the people of God, implicit in the MT, is explicit in v. 23 with the information that, unlike the executioners, Azariah and his friends 'were kept' (συνετηρήθησαν). Not only does this comment direct the sympathies of the reader, it also anticipates the safety of the three men. The more editorially omniscient LXX narrator also takes us right into the furnace in the Additional interlude for a physical description of the angelic activity (vv. 49-50). As well as bringing the reader on side with the narrator, this section renders mundane an episode that remains inscrutable in the MT story. A similar effect was noted in ch. 4 when the dimensions of the tree are expressed by the LXX in terms of stadia (4.12).

At the point where the LXX and MT begin to converge again on each other (v. 24/91) there is a further anticipation of the narrative. Unlike the

MT, the LXX tells the reader that the king started up from his seat 'when (he) heard them singing praises' (ἐν τῷ ἀκοῦσαι τὸν βασιλέα ὑμνούντων αὐτῶν). Immediately we are granted the information that he 'saw them living' (ἐθεώρει αὐτοὺς ζῶντας). Only then does he address his question to his companions (v. 25/92). The MT reader must wait till the king begins to speak (v. 25) to know the reason for his 'trepidation' (התבהלה).

In the meantime the three have a great deal to say once they are in the fire, in contrast to their counterparts in the MT. In the context in which the prayer is made, the description of 'a king unrighteous and the most evil in all the earth' (v. 32, βασιλεῖ ἀδίκιῳ καὶ πονηροτάτῳ παρὰ πᾶσαν τὴν γῆν) is an explicit condemnation of Nebuchadnezzar, although the original *Sitz im Leben* may well have had a different monarch in mind. Such condemnation as the MT contains is implicit in the attitude adopted by Shadrach, Meshach and Abednego, and is reliant on the narrator's skill at winning the reader's sympathy for that attitude. The LXX focuses on God's ability to act rather than on the young men's courage. This point relates to the LXX's treatment of the difficult vv. 17-18, to which I return below. Suffice to say for now that the characters in the LXX are little more than vehicles for the narrator's monotheistic confession. To some extent they play the same sort of passive role as Daniel in ch. 4 LXX, where Nebuchadnezzar's viewpoint dominates the story. In the MT, because God's willingness to intervene still hangs in the balance, the focus is more on the courage of Shadrach, Meshach and Abednego. In a way the narrator, as so often in the LXX, anticipates the narrative in that there is little room for doubt that God will act and that Nebuchadnezzar will capitulate.

The Repeated Lists

No discussion of the story of the fiery furnace is complete without reference to the amount of repetitive material in ch. 3. Nowhere in Daniel is the Semitic narrative habit of making lists used to such marked effect as in the present story. But the effect comes not so much in the lists themselves as in the way they are repeated several times. It is hardly possible to read Daniel 3 without being struck by the importance of the two major lists to the narrative, nor to read a commentary on Daniel without encountering a detailed treatment of those lists item by item. Repetition as literary device is also used for certain words and phrases other than

the lists. The practice of Septuagintal narrators of summarizing repetition
is a notable feature of the LXX in this chapter, and results in significant
differences in the narrative of the two versions.

The first list is of imperial officials summoned to the 'image of gold'
(v. 1, צלם די־דהב, MT, εἰκόνα χρυσῆν, LXX). It appears in v. 2 and is
repeated by the MT in its entirety in v. 3 and in part in v. 27. The form
of the list of officials in the Aramaic is reproduced exactly each time,
including the ו before the third item (vv. 2-3, and 'governors', ופחותא).
Most commentators agree that this suggests a group of different status
comprising the 'satraps, prefects and governors' (אחשדרפניא סגניא ופחותא).[23]
That possibility is rendered the more likely when the same group
appears in v. 27 to witness the miraculous deliverance. At the same time
the earlier and fuller enumerations of officials are recalled.

The LXX omits the second full list of officials entirely, being content to
refer the reader back to 'the aforementioned' (v. 3, οἱ προγεγραμμένοι).
The aforementioned in question are not quite the same people as those
spoken of in the MT. To begin with there are only five items noted
before the summarizing phrase, 'all those in authority over...' (v. 2,
τοὺς ἐπ' ἐξουσιῶν κατά), although the first three are agreed upon by
each version. At first glance the use of καί appears to be indiscriminate,
but closer examination suggests that the different distribution of καί
results in different groupings. It looks as if 'governors and courtiers'
(τοπάρχας καὶ ὑπάτους) is a single grouping, and so is 'administrators
and all those in authority...' (διοικητὰς καὶ τοὺς ἐπ' ἐξουσιῶν). This
puts satraps and prefects on their own as separate items at the head of
the list in contrast to the trio of the MT. Also in contrast to the MT they
do not appear at all in v. 94 LXX. Instead, one of the other groupings
from v. 2, 'courtiers, governors' (ὕπατοι τοπάρχαι), is mentioned
again, and then two other categories otherwise absent from the story
arrive on stage. They are the 'hereditary leaders and friends of the king'
(ἀρχιπατριῶται καὶ οἱ φίλοι τοῦ βασιλέως). The first term has
only one other occurrence in the Greek Old Testament (Josh. 21.1).
'Friends' of the king also feature in 5.23 as those who shared with
Belshazzar in the events of the banquet, and Daniel is described by his
enemies as a 'friend' of the king (6.14 LXX). Some courtly role is probably in mind for those so described. Beyond that general statement, no
pattern seems to emerge in the way the LXX translator handles titles. As

23. See, for example, Hartman and DiLella, *Daniel*, pp. 156-57, on Persian
administrative terms.

in ch. 6, it is possible that he is working from a different *Vorlage*, but more likely that he has no clear idea of what distinctions there may have been between such titles.

The second list is of musical instruments, which first appears in v. 5 MT and is repeated almost exactly in vv. 7, 10 and 15. Inexplicably there is one item missing in the text of v. 7. θ either assumes it should be there or testifies to a *Vorlage* before its mistaken omission. There are other textual problems with this particular item (סומפניה). In vv. 10 and 15 there is a *kethib/qere* issue and a ו is appended.[24] It would seem that even in the early stages of the tradition the meaning of the word was unclear. It certainly was for the versions. The omission in v. 7 MT will be treated as accidental in the present literary comparison, and the textual problems surrounding the ו will be assumed to be a product of this confusion over meaning.[25] In the LXX the series of musical instruments is only cited in full at the first appearance (v. 5). Subsequent mentions are all in the summary form, 'the sound of the horn and all the sounding of music' (vv. 7, 10, τῆς φωνῆς τῆς σάλπιγγος καὶ παντὸς ἤχου μουσικῶν), in much the same way the officials are summarized in v. 3. There is one small variation in that φωνῆς is not present in v. 15. Apart from discrepancies in the distribution of καί, the list is an exact copy of that in both the MT and θ. There is not enough evidence to suppose that the use of καί in the LXX denotes an attempt to group the musical instruments. Unlike the case with the list of officials, the LXX translator seems clear about the meaning of each of the terms in his *Vorlage* with the possible exception of the final item.

---

24. This suggests a case could be made for סומפניה as a collective musical term. See T.C. Mitchell and R. Joyce, 'Musical Instruments in Nebuchadnezzar's Orchestra', in D.J. Wiseman *et al.*, *Notes on Some Problems in the Book of Daniel* (London: Tyndale Press, 1965), pp. 25-26. Against this the biblical Greek cognate verb συμφωνέω is a political one and is never used in a musical context (Gen. 14.3, 4 Kgdms 12.9, Isa. 7.2, *4 Macc.* 14.6). It is also difficult to see why two collective terms would occur next to each other. On balance, I assume a particular musical instrument as the meaning of סומפניא/συμφωνή, and translate it as 'bagpipes' in the absence of a better idea. The suggestion made by Mitchell and Joyce of a percussion instrument seems not to have won much support.

25. The variation between ס and שׂ in the spelling of the fourth instrument was a common vacillation in biblical Aramaic, where the movement from שׂ to ס was in process, and for our purposes only needs to be noted. See Rosenthal, *Biblical Aramaic*, p. 16. Mitchell and Joyce, 'Musical Instruments', p. 24, consider this vacillation indicates a word of foreign origin.

As a result, the difference between versions in the literary effects of the list is limited. Each list or a summary of it appears at identical points in the narrative and is mentioned by the same speakers in both the LXX and MT. The chief point of comparison comes in a consideration of the effectiveness or otherwise of the word-for-word repetition in the MT. Any effect thereby noted will necessarily be absent in the summarizing LXX story. This type of repetition is exceptional in late biblical Hebrew, and is different from others that we have looked at elsewhere in Daniel.[26] Apart from matters that point to text transmission issues, there is little variation in the tellings.

Most obviously, each repetition of a series emphasizes the point being made the first time the list is produced. It becomes unforgettable in this story that all officialdom was to be present for the dedication of the statue without exception (v. 1), and that the command was obeyed without exception (v. 2). The presence of a summary item at the end of both lists ensures that this is so. Immediately the scene is set for the conflict, and suspense begins to build as the list is repeated. Similarly, on the first occasion on which the music list is enunciated, the herald is the speaker and those in the foregoing list are the listeners. The message requires from them instant obedience (v. 5, בעדנא), and the sound of the instruments is both the signal for and test of that obedience. Moreover, cultic overtones foreshadow the exact test to which they are being put, as the repetition of the series of instruments emphasizes the ritual setting within which the conflict of loyalties will be resolved.[27] After that every sounding of the music is protracted by the recital of the complete ensemble. Each one reminds the reader of the choice facing the worshippers and increases the sense of anticipation. Finally, on the fourth and last occasion (v. 15) the moment of truth arrives.

There is also an expression of immediacy present in the LXX. The Aramaic בעדנה of v. 5 is not quite so strongly expressed with the Greek ὅταν, meaning 'when' or 'whenever'. 'At that time' (v. 7, ἐν τῷ καιρῷ ἐκείνῳ) is if anything more emphatic than the MT's בה־זמנא (v. 7), and the difference at v. 5 may well be understood as LXX's attempt to express in translation the difference between Aramaic עדנא (v. 5) and זמנא (v. 7). In other respects, however, the summarizing of the lists means that the LXX story is told in more muted tones than is its

---

26. Savran, *Telling and Retelling*, p. 110.

27. P.W. Coxon, 'The "List" Genre and Narrative Style in the Court Tales of Daniel', *JSOT* 35 (1986), p. 103.

Aramaic counterpart. The result is a different kind of story, as will become clearer when we look at the tone and setting of each in more detail.

Repetition of the Lists as Comedy

Another important effect of the repetition of ch. 3 is that it brings an element of parody into the story, and in so doing becomes a vehicle for the covert narrator's point of view. Diverse commentators agree on its presence and have described it in different ways.[28] The comedic effect noted in ch. 6 is different in that it is achieved more by the movements of characters and the narrative description of those movements. Here the humour rests in words rather than action and is found primarily in the repetition of long lists of officials and musical instruments. In this case, the deployment of the lists emphasizes the absurdity of what is going on.[29] The picture painted is of an unquestioning mechanistic acceptance of the commands issued.[30] Because the repetition of lists is so exact, compared to the subtle variations we have detected elsewhere, the story becomes a parody on Nebuchadnezzar and his administrators.[31] An impression of order is conveyed, the better to expose the false basis of that order.[32]

The frequency of expressions for immediacy, by reinforcing the mechanistic response that is expected and given, also reinforces the parody.[33] The Aramaic organizes its three words for time in a significant

28. Lacocque, *Daniel*, p. 55: 'la partie haggadique'. Porteous, *Daniel*, p. 60, sees 'an element of caricature'. Wills, *The Jew in the Court*, p. 80, speaks of the story's 'essentially comic nature'. Baldwin, *Daniel*, p. 102, uses the term 'satire'. However, contrast Goldingay, *Daniel*, p. 68. In his study of 'idol parodies', Roth, 'Idol Parodies', pp. 21-43, does not include Dan. 3 and 6 directly, but he does link them with Bel and the Dragon, which he says is an actualization of the genre.

29. Avalos, 'The Comedic Function', p. 585.

30. Alter, *Biblical Narrative*, p. 106, also recognizes 'the mechanical in human affairs' as 'a primary source of comedy' in biblical narrative. His point is made with the story of Balaam's ass in Num. 22.

31. Good, 'Apocalyptic as Comedy', p. 52, cites Frye's concept of 'unincremental repetition'.

32. But contrast Coxon, 'The "List" Genre', p. 107, who sees no irony, but rather an expression of 'the writer's sense of immanent cosmic order despite the turbulence and chaos of the contemporary scene'.

33. Avalos, 'The Comedic Function', p. 585.

manner. The herald (vv. 5-6) tells the assembly to fall and worship 'at the appointed time' (בעדנא). He then follows up with the threat to any who do not do so 'in that moment' (v. 6, בה־שעתא). This time the word used is a more general one indicating an immediate response to the pre-arranged signal understood by עדנא. The narrator takes over in vv. 7-8, and uses another word to express immediate consequence, זמנא. This word also has the sense of an appointed moment and expresses not only the response of the officials to the music but also the reaction of 'the Chaldean men' (v. 8, גברין כשדאין) to Shadrach, Meshach and Abednego's non-compliance. The use of כל־קבל דנה at the beginning of vv. 7 and 8 links the response of both the officials and the Chaldeans as the subject of parody.[34] On the next two occasions that immediate action is called for (v. 15) the speaker is the king. In an echo of the message previously stated by his herald, the speaker reverts to the time words already used by that herald, עדנא and שעתא. This differentiation, as well as emphasizing the mindless response to an order given, distinguishes the narrator from his speakers. The similarity in vocabulary of the official speeches heightens the irony.

The LXX is not so consistent in its use of time vocabulary. The references in vv. 7-8 echo those of the MT with the use of ἐν τῷ καιρῷ ἐκείνῳ. However, the other four occurrences are all much less emphatic expressions. Verse 6 does not contain any temporal particle at all. Verse 5 uses ὅταν, while v. 15 has ἅμα and αὐθωρί. A consequence of this is that the parody is not reinforced in the same way, and temporal expressions are not used as part of the distinction between the narrator and his speakers. The abbreviated lists also mean that a satirical edge is not present to the same extent as in the MT. The effect on the ear of repeated lists should not be underestimated as part of this process, and that effect is simply not present in the LXX.[35] The point of view of the LXX narrator is conveyed instead by the greater editorial involvement already noted in the story.

---

34. But note that Goldingay, *Daniel*, p. 66, believes on the grounds of 'poor sense' that the second occurrence arises from dittography. In this he concurs with *BHS*.

35. Coxon, 'The "List" Genre', p. 107.

Repetition of Phrases

The MT liking for repeated sounds is also seen in the repetition of formulae, often in tripartite phrases. As elsewhere in Daniel (5.7, 11 for example), there are several obvious examples in this chapter.[36] Of the 22 occasions on which the Jewish heroes feature in the narrative, 13 indicate them by naming all three (שׁדרך מישׁך ועבד נגו). One is never mentioned without the other two, and they appear in exactly the same order and with the ו in the same place each time. The impression of a formula is heightened when the names occur as direct or indirect object or with a possessive sense. On each of these seven occasions the grammatical indicators are organically connected only to the first name in the list. This is not only true for the preposition ל (vv. 13, 20, 22, 30), but also for על (v. 19) and די (vv. 28-29), each of which is connected to the first element by a *maqqeph*. This feature is also illustrated in the list of officials (v. 2, לאחשׁדרפניא), and on other occasions in Aramaic Daniel when the mantic officials appear (for example 5.7, לאשׁפיא). Another tripartite phrase which is used with the same sort of precision is 'peoples, nations and tongues' (vv. 4, 7, 29, עממיא אמיא ולשׁניא). Even when each item in the series is in the singular (v. 29), the shape of the formula is not disturbed.

In the nature of the languages, the connection of grammatical indicators to the lead item in a list is a feature of Aramaic that is not able to be reproduced by the Greek except in the most rigidly literal translations. The LXX uses the names of the young Jews in a similar way to the MT and represents most occurrences of the list of names in the MT. Apart from the detail that there is never a καί in the series, the three are always named together and in the same order. Against the MT they do not appear by name in vv. 19, 23 and 26/93. The difference in v. 23 may be accounted for by the tradition behind the Additions which uses the Hebrew names. In v. 26/93 the propensity of the LXX to reduce repetition is a probable explanation, as the list has already occurred once in each verse.

The situation is less clear-cut with the other Aramaic tripartite phrase as represented by the LXX. The herald addresses 'nations and regions, peoples and tongues' (v. 4, ἔθνη καὶ χῶραι λαοὶ καὶ γλῶσσαι), where θ represents the MT exactly apart from the absence of a καί. Later the narrator refers to 'all the nations, tribes and tongues' (v. 7,

---

36. Coxon, 'The "List" Genre', p. 106.

πάντα τὰ ἔθνη φυλαὶ καὶ γλῶσσαι) and on that occasion the phrasing is a replica of the Aramaic including even the πᾶς. However, v. 96 is different again. Nebuchadnezzar's declaration is applied to 'every nation and all tribes and all tongues' (πᾶν ἔθνος καὶ πᾶσαι φυλαὶ καὶ πᾶσαι γλῶσσαι), so the formula is fragmented by the insertion of a qualifying πᾶς before each item. This becomes another example of the less formulaic nature of the Septuagintal Greek.

There are a number of other repeated phrases which serve to emphasize a particular point in the story. The 'image' is usually described as that 'which King Nebuchadnezzar set up' (v. 2, די הקים נבוכדנצר מלכא). That exact wording is used again in vv. 3 and 7. On other occasions, such as when the king is being addressed directly or is himself speaking, there are variations, but the verb קום is always present (vv. 3, 14, 18). In the process the human origins of the statue are hammered home and the repetition of this has an ironic effect. The 'furnace of blazing fire' (v. 11, אתון נורא יקדתא) is repeated again and again as if it were a technical term (vv. 15, 17, 20, 23, 26).[37] Often the expression is attached by a *maqqeph* to 'in the midst of' (לגוא־). Unlike the above examples, though, it is a formula that is subject to change. In v. 19 'the furnace' (אתונא) occurs on its own, and vv. 24-25 only uses נורא.

The ironic emphasis of the descriptive phrase 'which King Nebuchadnezzar set up' is not nearly as prominent in the LXX. The MT's opening sentence sets the tone: 'King Nebuchadnezzar made an image' (v. 1, נבוכדנצר מלכא עבד צלם). There follows a description of its dimensions and the statement that 'he set it up' (אקימה). The LXX includes the same material, but the effect is more diffuse as it is intertwined with the date and summary of the king's achievements. Verses 2, 14 and 18 are identical to Aramaic in their use of the descriptive phrase. However, there is no description of the 'image' (εἰκόνος) at all in v. 3, again with less emphatic results. The term 'furnace of blazing fire' receives similar treatment in the LXX and MT, where there is the same variation not in vocabulary but in the number of key words used each time. The Greek consistently uses the phrase τὴν κάμινον τοῦ πυρὸς τὴν καιομένην (vv. 11, 15, 20, 93) or a shortened form (vv. 17, 21). However, in the problematical v. 23, with its divergent tradition, the term ἐνεπύρισε is introduced. This relates to issues surrounding the insertion of the Greek Additions explored earlier.

Of a slightly different order, each time the defiance of Shadrach,

37. Baldwin, *Daniel*, p. 103.

Meshach and Abednego is spoken of (vv. 12, 14, 18, 28/95) the two verbs פלח and סגד are used in tandem. They would not 'serve' other gods nor 'worship' the image set up by the king. That these words are heard in the mouths of the Chaldean plotters, the king, and the heroes themselves, highlights the exact nature of the choice being put before the three as well as clarifying the particular cultic use being made of פלח in the present context. The terms 'serve' (λατρεύω) and 'worship' (προσκυνέω) also form a pair in the same verses in the LXX. This is an exception to the overall picture of the MT as a version that uses repetition consistently to underline important points and signpost the perspective of the storyteller, and of the LXX as a version that achieves this end by more overt means.

Setting of the Story

A number of the characteristics of the respective narratives so far highlighted also combine to give the stories slightly different settings. The Nebuchadnezzar of the MT is a Babylonian figure who must be confronted by Jews of the Babylonian diaspora. He sets up a statue of some sort on the plain of Dura 'in the province of Babylon' (v. 1, במדינת בבל). It is unclear exactly where or what 'the plain of Dura' (v. 1, בקעת דורא) was. θ does not provide us with any clues as he simply transliterates the word. Cook makes a convincing case that the noun דור should be taken to mean 'wall', and the large open area between the outer ramparts of the city and its inner wall, 'the plain of the wall', is where the scene took place.[38] Such could well be the understanding lying behind LXX's choice of περιβόλου in the phrase 'around the region of Babylon' (v. 1, τοῦ περιβόλου χώρας βαβυλωνίας).[39] This places the MT story in a definite local setting. The summarizing phrase at the end of the officials list, 'all the high officials of the province' (vv. 2-3, כל שלטני מדינתא), denotes by the recurrence of מדינתא that the preceding list relates also to this particular place.

The point of conflict when it arrives is also expressed in local terms. The slanderous informers are Chaldeans (v. 8). They tell the king about

38. E.M. Cook, '"In the Plain of the Wall" (Dan 3.1)', *JBL* 108 (1989), p. 116. This point had also earlier been made by Montgomery, *Daniel*, p. 197. But Collins, *Daniel*, p. 182, demurs in favour of Dura as a place name.

39. McCrystall, 'Daniel', pp. 74-75, sees in the use of περίβολος by LXX a deliberate etymological rendering.

'men of Judah' (v. 12, גברין יהודאין) who are supposed to be in 'the service of the province of Babylon' (v. 12, עבידת מדינת בבל), which puts the tension of being Jewish and being in the pay of the Babylonian king in a nutshell. The rehabilitation of Shadrach, Meshach and Abednego when it comes is also expressed in terms of their position 'in the province of Babylon' (v. 30/97).

Moreover, the salutation of the herald, 'O peoples, nations and tongues' (v. 4, עממיא אמיא ולשניא), does not include the hyperbolic כל, almost always included with this phrase (3.31 and 6.26, for example). The result is that here the formula is subsumed under the categories previously mentioned in the list of officials. It functions more as another way of describing the diverse group assembled before the king and less as the catch-all expression of universal sovereignty that we see in other contexts. With that in mind, the order from the king at v. 29 to 'any people, nation and tongue who...' (כל-עם אמה ולשן די-) is to be understood as the group assembled earlier in the chapter. It is true that the formula כל עממיא אמיא ולשניא appears in v. 7, apparently in contradiction of the point being made above. However, by this stage in the narrative the repeated use of the list of imperial functionaries ensures that this all-embracing formula is given a more particular content.

The setting of the LXX story is somewhat different. The first group mentioned by the LXX is 'all those inhabiting the earth' (v. 1, πάντας τοὺς κατοικοῦντας ἐπὶ τῆς γῆς) from India to Ethiopia. King Nebuchadnezzar, ruler of 'the whole inhabited world' (v. 2, τῆς οἰκουμένης ὅλης) does not call together a large group of officials but 'all the peoples and tribes and tongues' (πάντα τὰ ἔθνη καὶ φυλὰς καὶ γλώσσας). Only then does the list of dignitaries come into the account. They become a representative group of the universal reign of Babylon, and it is in that light that the address of the herald is understood. The herald in the MT (v. 4) addresses the same comprehensive group, but the structure of the narrative is such that the expression is understood in terms of the more limited reality of the province of Babylon.

This argument is dependent to some extent on the meaning of the words χώρα and מדינה ('province' or 'region' or 'city') as they are understood in this chapter, and the point merits some discussion. The Greek word is considerably more common than the Hebrew/Aramaic. The former often also translates מקום or ארץ, and occasionally אדמה. When used to represent מדינה, it can either refer in general terms to the countryside or environs or to a specific administrative unit. The more specific usage is most prevalent where a Persian provenance is possible as in 2 Esdras (5.8 and 7.16, for example) or Esther (2.3 and 3.12-13, for example). We have already noted a differentiation in Daniel 5 and 6 between governing officials of the outlying provincial units (מדינה) and the central court officials. This distinction is explicitly stated in 2.49. Most of the time in the Aramaic of Daniel 3 the Persian sense seems to be intended of Babylon as a province within the empire.[40] Hence the 'high officials of the province' (vv. 2 etc., שלטני מדינתא) can be seen as a group of centralized officials distinct from earlier leaders in the list. The phrase is more than simply a summary of the preceding functionaries.

If the LXX understands χώρα in the same sense, the argument for a more universalized story in the LXX is weakened. The usage in v. 2 is identical to the Aramaic (τοὺς ἐπ' ἐξουσιῶν κατὰ χώραν) and implies a specific province. The same can be said of its first appearance in v. 1. This is also the probable meaning in most of the translations of מדינה in the Persian settings indicated above. Yet in v. 4 the term has become part of the general phrase 'nations and regions, peoples and tongues' (ἔθνη καὶ χῶραι λαοὶ καὶ γλῶσσαι). Moreover, the second usage in v. 1, although in the singular, is confused by its attachment to τοῦ περιβόλου. Perhaps this reflects the 'plain of the wall' idea mentioned earlier, or else introduces yet another sense of χώρα, 'city'. In neither case does it seem to carry a technical sense. On balance, the same uncertainty about administrative terminology may be seen here as elsewhere noted in the Old Greek, and the LXX's use of χώρα in the present chapter is not consistent enough to deny the notion of Nebuchadnezzar's universal sovereignty being portrayed.

The repetition in v. 2 of οἰκουμένην after the list of officials emphasizes that point. The word occurs frequently in the Psalms and Isaiah, no less than 15 and 12 times respectively. It usually translates the Hebrew noun תבל, but also on occasions ארץ. In the Psalms תבל/οἰκουμένη is often in parallel with ארץ/γῆ (Pss. 19.5; 24.1; 33.8, for example) or עמים/λαός (Ps. 9.8). The context is generally an expression of God's universal sovereignty, rather than particular appeals to the God of Israel. The use of οἰκουμένη in the present context, then, has the backing not

40. D.C.T. Sherriffs, '"A Tale of Two Cities"—Nationalism in Zion and Babylon', *TynBul* 39 (1988), p. 32, argues that Babylonian nationalism was centred on the city. Perhaps, then, the distinction between province and city was a later Persian understanding.

only of a tradition of worship but also of a universalist referent. This is reinforced by its use in prophetic sayings. Of the occurrences in Isaiah, one of particular interest is Isa. 14.17. The context is an oracle against Babylon, who desired to become like God (Isa. 14.13-14). An expression of that was that he made 'the world' (חבל/οἰκούμενην) a desert. Another example from the prophetic traditions about Babylon is to be found in Jer. 51/28.15, and we have seen in other places the significance of the Jeremiah traditions about Nebuchadnezzar for Daniel. There the Lord declares his power in universal terms. Because the Lord has made 'the world' (חבל/οἰκούμενη) as well as 'the earth' and 'the heavens', the claims of Nebuchadnezzar to the inhabited world (οἰκούμενη) will one day be shattered (Jer. 51/28.24-26). The double use of οἰκούμενη by the LXX in v. 2 strengthens the notion of universal sovereignty being promoted by Nebuchadnezzar.

The summarizing tendency of the LXX also affects the setting of the stories. As Coxon has shown, the list was a feature of Babylonian decrees and this included lists of musical instruments.[41] Such lists of musical instruments are known to have had ritual associations in Akkadian. Apart from their other effects in the narrative outlined above, the lists in the MT enhance the Babylonian setting and reinforce the ritual context of the challenge facing Shadrach, Meshach and Abednego.[42] The effect of the summaries in the LXX, intentional or not, is to distance the story from its specific ritual setting in Babylon.

Other Literary Devices

The Aramaic of Daniel contains two further literary devices that are part of the narrative effects discussed above. The first is the suggestive use of the word צלם in v. 19 where in Nebuchadnezzar's anger 'the image of his face was changed' (צלם אנפוהי אשתנו).[43] This word in biblical Hebrew has a primary sense of some sort of physical representation, either of humans (Ezek. 23.14) or of false gods (2 Kgs 11.18; Ezek. 7.20). Even when Seth is described as 'according to his (Adam's) image' (Gen. 5.3, כצלמו), the fact that the phrase is in apposition with 'in his likeness' (בדמותו) suggests that physical likeness is intended. There are two obscure

---

41. Coxon, 'The "List" Genre', p. 103.
42. Coxon, 'The "List" Genre', p. 102, considers that this is a conscious use of 'the literary *Gattung* of the list' by the MT writer.
43. Fewell, *Circle of Sovereignty*, p. 76.

references in the Psalms (39.7; 73.20) which seem to intend a shadow of the whole human person. It is not certain whether the phrase צלם אלהים (Gen. 1.27, 'image of God') extends beyond the physical likeness of God. What is clear is that nowhere does צלם have the particular facial referent of v. 19. Even elsewhere in Daniel its use is always in connection with idols or statues (2.31-35). The expected Aramaic word would have been זיו, which occurs commonly enough elsewhere in Daniel (4.33; 5.6, 9-10; 7.15).

The result of this unexpected usage is a link between Nebuchadnezzar and the image that he set up. Without suggesting that the image is necessarily in his likeness or that he is claiming divinity, the thought is sown by the narrator that the king himself is the one before whom they are really being asked to fall and worship. Perhaps at the same time he will turn out to be as powerless as the statue of ch. 2 that is smashed by the rock quarried out of the mountain but not with human hands. Darius learned a similar lesson. The LXX recognizes this unique usage with μορφή (v. 19), a word that is used elsewhere to translate other words that more definitely mean 'face' or 'visage' (Judg. 8.18; Job 4.16; Isa. 44.13). However the LXX does not proceed to draw a direct verbal link between the king and his statue because the statue, צלם, is always called εἰκών.

There is another play on words in v. 7 that is peculiar to the Aramaic. When 'all' (כל) the people hear 'all' (כל) kinds of music, 'all' (כל) the people fall and worship. The emphasis of this repetition is reinforced by the sound associations in the idiom כל קבל דנה at the beginning of the verse, as well as by the homonym קל ('sound'). This strengthens the parody on the mechanistic response of the gathered worshippers. While the LXX also has 'all' three times, it is not able to represent the beginning phrase of the MT or the play on words with קל.

Theological Differences

The above note about the cultic setting of the story leads us into a consideration of the theological or polemical differences between the MT and LXX. These differences are not so marked as in chs. 4–6, but the same emphasis is suggested by them as in those chapters. Just as our discussion of narrative shape was tied to a consideration of the effect of the Additions on narrative flow, so the present discussion relates to what has already been noted about the concerns of the Additions.

As good a place as any to begin is at the famous textual crux in v. 17.

The problem, centred on the difficult Aramaic phrase, הֵן אִיתַי אֱלָהַנָא,
דִי־אֲנַחְנָא פָלְחִין יָכִל has a double focus. Semantically the possible meanings
of הֵן and אִיתַי are at issue, and syntactically the separation of יָכִל from אִיתַי
is a problem. This phrase can be understood as, 'If there is a God whom
we serve, he is able...' or 'If the God whom we serve is able...'[44] Either
the existence or the competence of God is at stake. Various attempts
have been made to skirt round the apparent theological problem inherent in the grammatical problem. Charles resorts to textual emendation to
get a text which reads אִיתַי דִי.[45] Less subjective solutions have included
placing אִיתַי with הֵן and reading the emphatic 'if it be so', or taking the
participle יָכִל together with the copula אִיתַי as a single construction giving
'if our God is able'.[46] The problem with the latter solution is that there is
seldom that sort of separation of participle from copula and the copula
normally has a suffix attached.[47] The problem with understanding הֵן אִיתַי
as 'if it be so' is that it strains the natural sense of the phrase. Coxon has
shown that אִיתַי denotes existence in biblical Aramaic on two thirds of its
15 occurrences in Daniel (as, for example, at 2.28; 3.29; 5.11).[48] Yet his
own argument that הֵן אִיתַי bears an emphatic sense contradicts that evidence, and is dependent on unusual usages both of the Aramaic and of
the Akkadian cognate *basu* ('to be, exist') that he summons in support
of the suggestion.[49] It becomes a syntactical argument addressed to a
theological problem and as such is not finally compelling.

The most convincing interpretation of 3.17a MT is still the plainest, 'if
our God exists...' But such an interpretation raises questions of sense
when vv. 17 and 18 are considered together. First, it is strange that the
young men express doubt in the existence of a god described as the one
'whom we serve' (דִי־אֲנַחְנָא פָלְחִין), a phrase which does not appear to

44. Few would disagree with Montgomery, *Daniel*, p. 206, that הֵן can only be
translated 'if'.

45. Charles, *Daniel*, p. 69, claims to follow the Versions in so doing.

46. See Torrey, 'Notes', p. 241, for 'if it be so...' See Porteous, *Daniel*, p. 59,
Delcor, *Daniel*, p. 94, and J. Wharton, 'Daniel 3.16-18', *Int* 39 (1985), p. 173, for
'if he is able...'

47. The unusual argument of J.W. Wesselius, 'Language and Style in Biblical
Aramaic: Observations on the Unity of Daniel 2–6', *VT* 38 (1988), p. 206, that v. 16
is the apodosis of v. 17 is of the same type, but fails because it does not treat אִיתַי
adequately.

48. P.W. Coxon, 'Daniel III 17: A Linguistic and Theological Problem', *VT* 26
(1976), p. 407.

49. Coxon, 'Daniel III 17', p. 406.

admit of the possibility of non-existence. Secondly, the logic of their reply is such that God's deliverance of his followers becomes a necessary consequence of his existence (v. 17). It is not possible to determine from ch. 3 whether or not a certainty of rescue partly motivates their faithfulness, but it seems unlikely. After all, in the companion story of ch. 6 Daniel clearly acts in defiance of the king's command because that is the right thing to do, and the only one in the story who expresses any hope of rescue from the lions for him is Darius. Thirdly, if the הן in v. 17 applies to the existence of God, the הן לא of v. 18 must apply to the consequence of his non-existence. It seems strange that Shadrach, Meshach and Abednego's defiance is founded solely on a desire to thwart the king, when there is no indication either here or in ch. 6 that the Jewish courtiers are anything other than committed to their service as officials of the king. In short, there is an impasse when meaning and syntax confront each other.

The best way out of this impasse is to accept the text as it is without assuming the presence of exceptional syntax, and at the same time to take the prevailing direction of thought in vv. 17-18 in the context of the thinking of chs. 3 and 6. In that case איתי is most likely to denote existence, as Coxon has demonstrated, but the precursor of והן לא (v. 18) is most likely to be ישיזב rather than איתי. Hence the young men are expressing their determination in the face of God's potential inactivity, not his inability.[50] Montgomery's objection that to doubt God's willingness is to doubt his ability flies in the face of much Old Testament thinking where God is upbraided for his inactivity.[51] It would seem then that the first part of v. 17 represents an *ad hominem* argument by Shadrach, Meshach and Abednego without them considering for a moment the possibility of God's non-existence. The rest of the speech is based on the assumption that God is there and on the common enough attitude that loyalty to him is not dependent on whether or not he acts on their behalf.

Translations from antiquity onwards have struggled with the ambiguity of this text that is arguing two different things at once. θ interprets

---

50. This was the interpretation of Jephet Ibn Ali, *A Commentary on the Book of Daniel* (ed. D.S. Margoliouth; Oxford: Clarendon Press, 1889), p. 17, who says v. 18 means 'if he should not deliver us; for he will not leave us in thy hand out of inability'. See also Ibn-Ezra in Gallé, *Daniel*, p. 35.

51. Montgomery, *Daniel*, p. 206. See, for example, Ps. 88 where the existence of God is never in doubt.

the beginning of v. 17 by omitting entirely the 'if...' section while preserving the 'if not...' of v. 18. The result is a simple affirmation that 'there is a God' (v. 17, ἔστιν γὰρ θεός). The thought behind the LXX is even more different from the MT in several ways. The speech of Shadrach, Meshach and Abednego becomes a confession of faith, and the basic 'if...if not' sense progression of the MT is not present. The question of existence, absent in θ but present in the MT, is still there but without the 'if'. Instead, the LXX affirms that 'there is (a) God in the heavens' (ἔστι γὰρ θεὸς ἐν οὐρανοῖς). Moreover, there is only 'one' (εἷς) such God who is also described confessionally as 'our Lord' (κύριος ἡμῶν). The LXX also asserts that he is able to rescue, so there is no shadow of doubt either that God is or that God is able.[52] Without the heroes saying explicitly that he would rescue them, their phrase 'And then it will be plain to you' (v. 18, καὶ τότε φανερόν σοι ἔσται) suggests that his doing so will be a vindication of their stand.

As a literary aside, although the Greek of v. 17 reflects the word order of the Aramaic, the result is a felicitously balanced sentence that focuses the issues of the story quite sharply. After the first phrase, whose problems we have examined, the heroes express confidence in a God who is able 'to rescue us out of the furnace of fire and out of your hand, O King, he will rescue us' (ἐξελέσθαι ἡμᾶς ἐκ τῆς καμίνου τοῦ πυρός καὶ ἐκ τῶν χειρῶν σου, βασιλεῦ, ἐξελεῖται ἡμᾶς). The juxtaposition of the furnace with the hand of the king and the bracketing of both by the verb ἐξαιρέω reinforce the point that the issue centres on the person of the king. In rescuing them from the furnace, God rescues them from the hand of Nebuchadnezzar who thought there was no god able to do so (v. 15).

This interpretative translation on the part of the LXX demonstrates once again the version's monotheistic emphasis and its concern to promote the cause of the God of Israel. The inclusion of the word κύριος at vv. 28-29/95-96 is typical of the LXX and reinforces the uniqueness rather than the primacy of God. The expression 'Most High God of gods' (v. 26/93, τοῦ θεοῦ τῶν θεῶν τοῦ ὑψίστου) in Rahlfs cannot be taken as an exception to that trend as 967 does not include τῶν θεῶν. This theme is made explicit by the Additional declaration at v. 45 that

---

52. In a similar way the 'secularity' of the Esther story in MT contrasts with the A-text, which brings God much more into the foreground. See the discussion in Fox, *Esther*, pp. 129-33.

'you alone are the Lord God...' (σὺ εἶ μόνος κύριος ὁ θεός).[53]
κύριος occurs as a *Leitwort* in the prayer and song. The universal
sovereignty of the God of Israel in particular, as emphasized here by the
LXX, is a theme noted in the other LXX chapters studied so far.

Here, as elsewhere, the theme of sovereignty is closely related to that
of idolatry. The difference between the versions is not as marked
because the theme of the 'image' (צלם) is already crucial to the Aramaic
story. Nevertheless the Septuagintal concern over idolatry is hinted at
again in vv. 12 and 18 when the three young men refuse to worship the
king's 'idols' (εἴδωλον) instead of his 'gods' as in the MT. It is difficult
to say whether the question of the divinization of kings lurks behind the
LXX of ch. 3, as it undoubtedly does in ch. 6.[54] It is a matter for debate
whether or not the statue was the representation of a figure or not, and
if it was, whether that figure was the king or one of his gods.[55]
Hippolytus connects the figure with the head of gold in the preceding
chapter.[56] Even so, that does not require a representation of
Nebuchadnezzar himself and the contents of vv. 12-14 MT render it
unlikely. The LXX at v. 12 hints at the possibility that the idol was of the
king himself with 'your idol they did not serve, and your golden
image...they did not worship' (τῷ εἰδώλῳ σου οὐκ ἐλάτρευσαν καὶ
τῇ εἰκόνι σου τῇ χρυσῇ...οὐ προσεκύνησαν). But the evidence is
tenuous and hangs on the extra σου, so too much cannot be made of
the issue in this particular chapter.[57]

Another difference in outlook is possibly present in the LXX's use of
φοβέω in v. 17, a matter that has been touched on above. Out of the
several hundred uses of φοβέω in the LXX most are a translation of ירא,
so the Greek word normally shows the same breadth of semantic range.
It is not used elsewhere to translate either עבד or פלח. A broad generalization could be made that the word does not often occur in a cultic

---

53. Daubney, *The Three Additions*, p. 63.

54. But compare M. Delcor, 'Un cas de traduction "targumique" de la LXX à
propos de la statue en or de Dan III', *Textus* 7 (1969), p. 33.

55. See, for example, Delcor, *Daniel*, pp. 91-92, Goldingay, *Daniel*, p. 69, and
Montgomery, *Daniel*, p. 195.

56. Hippolytus, I.3.1.

57. *ANEP*, pl. 537 depicts 'a procession of gods mounted on animals, between
two figures of the Assyrian king'. Some of the gods bear a remarkable resemblance
to the king, suggesting that identification of the king with the gods does not require a
direct representation of him in the statue. See Roth, 'Idol Parodies', p. 29.

setting, and expresses fear either of God or humans. A comparison of the usage of φοβέω may be brought a little closer to the present context if we look at its occurrences in apocryphal Greek books, particularly Sirach and Maccabees. We find 29 uses in Sirach, only one of which has a cultic referent (Sir. 7.31). It is overwhelmingly used as a wisdom term to describe an attitude of heart and mind toward God encapsulated in Sir. 1.14 and 15.1. Only in Sir. 26.5 does φοβέω speak of the fear of humans. By contrast the books of the Maccabees use the word mostly in terms of the fear of human enemies. Despite the Maccabean concern for the desecration of the Temple, the word is not used in those books in connection with cultic worship. To continue the comparison with two prophets, Isaiah seems representative of the rest of the Old Testament in using φοβέω indifferently with God or humans as its object. Of the 22 uses in Septuagintal Jeremiah, the same can be said. The expression 'another heart to fear me' (καρδίαν ἑτέραν φοβηθῆναί με) in Jer. 32/39.39 reflects the same sort of usage as in Sirach. The only time when 'fearing the Lord' has a possible cultic significance is at Jer. 3.8, where the setting is a condemnation of involvement in the fertility cult.

Against this, as we saw in the context of Darius's confession (6.27-28), λατρεύω is a word that probably has connotations of service in worship and as such reflects a portion of the semantic range of the Aramaic פלח.[58] In fact, by the time of Official Aramaic, and on into Middle and Late Aramaic, although there is still considerable crossover between the meanings of the two words, פלח is more likely than עבד to be used in a worship context.[59] Typical of the biblical Aramaic usage of עבד is 5.1 where Belshazzar 'makes' a feast, 6.28 where God 'does' signs and wonders, or Ezra 6.12 where Darius commands a decree to be 'carried out'. In short almost all the vocabulary indicators of both the Aramaic and Greek in v. 17 (פלח and λατρεύω) suggest a cultic context and raise the question of whether or not any significance may be detected in the unexpected use of φοβέω by the LXX at this point.

It could be simply an attempt at variety on the part of a translator who did not make such distinctions.[60] Another possibility is that the

---

58. Coxon, 'Daniel III 17', p. 403.

59. See the chronology of Aramaic outlined by Z. Stefanovic, *The Aramaic of Daniel in the Light of Old Aramaic* (Sheffield: JSOT Press, 1992), p. 17. Coxon, 'Daniel III 17', p. 403, with Ibn Ezra does not consider the possibility of historical development.

60. I am conscious of the caution from J. Barr, *The Semantics of Biblical*

creator of the LXX version is hinting at the fact that the question of cultic service is part of the much wider question, 'whom shall we fear?' In its attempt to understand the Aramaic idiom שׂים...שׂם in v. 12, the LXX has already hinted at this sort of understanding with 'did not fear your commandment' (οὐκ ἐφοβήθησάν σου τὴν ἐντολήν). This is consistent with the less mantic view of wisdom that the LXX also demonstrates in chs. 4–6 by its concern to distance Daniel from other wisdom officials.

Narrative Links with Daniel 4–6

A discussion of the links between this and other chapters in Daniel is necessarily incomplete, as was the case after ch. 6, as there are a number of points of contact between chs. 3 and 2. These will feature as part of the work on ch. 2. It is, however, now possible to return to the analysis begun in the context of Daniel 6 where the closeness of the relationship between chs. 3 and 6 was noted. There are also some features in common with chs. 4 and 5. Some of these have been touched on in the course of the foregoing discussion, but others warrant more detailed treatment. Several aspects of narrative technique show the same differences between the versions as can be detected in the previous chapters treated. The omniscience of the LXX narrator is more editorial and that of the MT more neutral. The LXX signposts perspective in more overt ways such as its anticipation of events in the story, whereas the MT relies on the story and the words of the characters.

In particular, in chs. 3 and 6 MT the heroes remain largely silent throughout their ordeal.[61] Before being thrown into the furnace Shadrach, Meshach and Abednego assert that their God can save them and they are determined to follow him. After being lifted out of the lion pit, Daniel says that his God has delivered him. In neither case do the Jews condemn the king for his actions nor do they use the events as a vindication of themselves or their God. Each time the king himself recognizes and speaks that vindication. On both occasions the LXX portrays

---

Language (London: Oxford University Press, 1961), p. 120, for care to be taken in etymological matters. In this instance, however, there does seem to be evidence of historical development of meaning in the directions I have indicated.

61. Bickerman, *Four Strange Books*, pp. 81 and 89, thinks of their casting into the fire as an 'ordeal' in the judicial sense. If both the fire and the lions' pit are ordeals, the ordeal procedure serves as a further narrative link between chs. 3 and 6.

its point of view by placing an explicit condemnation of the sovereign in the mouths of the heroes.

As was particularly the case in ch. 6, the MT is reliant on the reader picking up the irony inherent in the story to deduce the point of view of the narrator himself. For the various reasons noted this is not so prominent a feature of the LXX. On the subject of irony, though, it should be noted that there is a different type of comedic effect at work in the MT than was the case in ch. 6. There the effect was achieved through what we called the irony of ignorance. Here the effect is achieved primarily through incremental repetition. In both cases the LXX narrative does not contain the same degree of irony, not through any deliberate policy on the part of the translator but by the natural outworking of some aspect of his technique. In ch. 6 this comes about because of the more overt narratorial stance, whereas in ch. 3 it is a result of the summarizing tendencies of the LXX.

Despite the differences in genre, a number of similarities between the opening verses of chs. 3 and 5 in the MT have been noted.[62] The dating of ch. 3 by the LXX and its inclusion of other plus material in the first verse means that this parallelism is not as marked in the LXX.

Literary Links with Daniel 4–6

The relationship between chs. 3 and 6 in the MT can also be demonstrated in literary terms.[63] There is the same play on the theme of the 'law' (vv. 10, 29, טעם). The uses of שׁיזב ('deliver', 3.15, 17, 28; 6.15, 21, 28), שׁלו ('blasphemy' or 'incompetence', 3.29; 6.5), and צלח ('to succeed', 3.30; 6.29) are all particular in Daniel to these two chapters.[64] בהתבהלה ('in trepidation', 3.24; 6.20) is also an unusual expression in both, although it also appears at 2.25. There are two idiomatic expressions that are shared by chs. 3 and 6. The heroes' opponents 'eat pieces of' (3.8; 6.25, אכל קרציהון) their Jewish counterparts in both chapters.

---

62. See Fewell, *Circle of Sovereignty*, pp. 114-15, for a detailed exposition of this narrative parallelism.

63. Goldingay, *Daniel*, p. 126.

64. See *BHS* on the *kethib/qere* variants of שׁלו in 3.29. Most accept the *qere* reading, but see S. Paul, 'Daniel 3.29—A Case Study of "Neglected" Blasphemy', *JNES* 42 (1983), pp. 292-93, who prefers the *kethib*. His accompanying attempt to read שׁלה in 6.5 is not convincing.

The idiom 'to take notice of' (3.12; 6.14, שׂים טעם על) is also a common feature.[65]

The LXX represents שׁיזב with either ἐξέρχομαι or σώζω. ἐξέρχομαι is also used to translate נפק (5.5). שׁלו is translated differently on each occasion, once with βλάσφημος (3.29/96) and once with ἄγνοια (6.5). The latter word also appears in 4.34 and is used at 6.23 to represent חבולה ('harm'). It is uncertain what the exact equivalent of the ch. 3 occurrence of צלח is, but it is translated with καθίστημι in ch. 6. Again this is a word in common use elsewhere in Daniel, translating variously קום (2.21; 6.2), מנה (2.24, 49), and שׁלט (2.48). The expression בהתבהלה is unrepresented in the Greek on both occasions while שׂים...טעם is unrepresented once and interpreted as 'fear' at 3.12. The LXX gives a straightforward non-idiomatic translation of אכל קרציהון each time, but not the same one. Dan. 3.8 has διαβάλλω while 6.25 has καταμαρτυρέω. This variety of translation is a further indication that the pairing of chs. 3 and 6 that seems likely in the MT is not a feature of the Septuagintal version of these two stories. Exceptionally, the LXX draws a link between the fire of ch. 3 and the lions of ch. 6 in that neither 'troubled' (3.50, παρηνώχλησεν, and 6.19, παρηνώχλησαν) those who were subjected to their rigours. Neither reference is represented in the MT.

Thematic Links with Daniel 4–6

Chapters 4–6 in the LXX all displayed a greater polemic against idolatry than their MT counterparts. Because a major theme of the Aramaic story of ch. 3 is already idolatry there is not the same marked thematic variation. But allied to this is a concern in the LXX to assert the uniqueness of God and to rediscover the purity of an Israelite cult corrupted by an evil monarch because of the sins of the chosen people. The more monotheist outlook of the LXX is a feature of all the chapters studied so far, while the sins of the people and the desecration of the cult appears in ch. 4 LXX. The Additions bring out these concerns strongly and they are reinforced by small differences between the versions in the main part of the chapter.

This chapter raises problems for anybody seeking to find a development in Jewish angelology between the two versions. A feature of ch. 6 was the difference in agency in the lion pit. The LXX attributes Daniel's

---

65. Lacocque, *Daniel*, p. 88, has a comprehensive list of the similarities in vocabulary between chs. 3 and 6.

deliverance to the direct intervention of God, whereas the MT says God
sent an angel to close the lions' mouths. In contrast, ch. 3 LXX features
an angel as the agent of salvation in the furnace. The MT remains
ambiguous about the fourth figure in the fire, but the Additions dispel
the ambiguity and enter into some physical detail about the angel's work
(3.49-50, 25/92).[66] Both versions of ch. 4 speak of the work of a heavenly being. So it looks as though there is no consistent evidence pointing
to different views on angels between versions. What can been said is that
the LXX tends to be more specific about their activities while the MT
surrounds them with an air of mystery.

Septuagint Links with Daniel 4

The dating of the story by the LXX creates a significant link not present
in MT. There is no date on the story of the fiery furnace in the MT but
the LXX puts it in the 'eighteenth year of Nebuchadnezzar the king'.
This is the same date given to ch. 4 which is also undated in the MT, and
seems like a conscious attempt by the LXX to link both stories with each
other and with the events described in Jeremiah 52.[67] They concern the
attack on the sovereignty of Israel and the integrity of Jerusalem and the
Temple cult. Those are the same concerns, but from a different era, that
the LXX is worried about. This does not contradict the earlier observation that the LXX setting is more general than the MT setting. Both highlight in different ways the distance of the LXX from the setting in the
Babylonian or Persian diaspora. The diaspora is concerned with the
accommodation of individual Jews to the empire while the second Temple
concerns of the LXX are to do with the struggle for survival of the
Jewish nation. The dating of chs. 3 and 4 highlight the nationalist concerns,
while the universalizing of Nebuchadnezzar's sovereignty supports the
monotheistic idea that the God of Israel is the God of the nations.

---

66. Saadia, in Gallé, *Daniel*, pp. 38-39, interprets בר־אלהין as מלאך ('angel'). He
identifies the angel who cools the furnace as Gabriel. See the discussion of
S.P. Brock, 'To Revise or not to Revise: Attitudes to Jewish Biblical Translation', in
G.J. Brooke and B. Lindars (eds.), *Septuagint, Scrolls and Cognate Writings*
(Atlanta: Scholars Press, 1992), pp. 318-19; and P. Walters (ed. D.W. Gooding),
The Text of the Septuagint (Cambridge: University Press, 1973), pp. 254-55, on the
rendering of בני־האלהים in Gen. 6.2.

67. Porteous, *Daniel*, p. 60. Others suggest a further tie-up with Jeremiah in the
burning of the prophets described at Jer. 29/36.21-23. See J.P. Peters, 'Notes on the
Old Testament', *JBL* 15 (1896), p. 109.

One result of this is that the LXX picture of Nebuchadnezzar with respect to the nation of Israel is quite different from the one it draws of Darius in ch. 6. We saw that the LXX, although condemning Darius, at the same time seems to view him in terms reminiscent of the patriarchs and other heroes of the nation. In ch. 3 the LXX, by dating the story, consciously sets Nebuchadnezzar as a threat to the nation. Although he ultimately submits in cultic terms to the God of Israel at the end of ch. 4, he is never accorded the honours that are implicitly given Darius. This is the opposite of what is happening in the MT. Darius's capitulation is only partial and the condemnation of Belshazzar is total. Nebuchadnezzar, however, is projected in a more favourable light. At least he is no worse than Darius and is considerably better than Belshazzar. He capitulates to the God of the Jews in terms appropriate to the exilic setting, and certainly poses no long-term threat to the nation. As we have seen, his portrayal in the MT story is in one sense a development of the theme 'Nebuchadnezzar my servant' (Jer. 27/34.6). Such can certainly not be said for the LXX, where the more explicit conversion is a vindication of the God and nation of Israel rather than an endorsement of Nebuchadnezzar.

In 967 chs. 7 and 8 intervene between 4 and 5 in what many see as the older order.[68] Certainly the effect is to place chs. 3 and 4 as a pair in a way that they are not in the MT, and their common dating is part of that. The confessional material in ch. 4 LXX also contains strong echoes of the Song of the Three. Nebuchadnezzar's acknowledgment of the creator of 'heaven and earth and the sea and the rivers and all that are in them' (4.37, τὸν οὐρανὸν καὶ τὴν γῆν καὶ τὰς θαλάσσας καὶ τοὺς ποταμοὺς καὶ πάντα τὰ ἐν αὐτοῖς) appears to be a summary of vv. 59-81. The expression 'God of gods' (4.37, θεὸς τῶν θεῶν) reflects v. 90.[69] The king's praise of 'all his holy ones' (4.37a, πάντας τοὺς ἁγίους αὐτοῦ) appears as a reminder of vv. 85-87. As a result of the pairing of these two chapters, Nebuchadnezzar's confession in the LXX plus material of ch. 4 becomes partly a response to what he has seen and heard of Hananiah, Mishael and Azariah.

---

68. See again Bogaert, 'Relecture et refonte', pp. 198-200, who regards this order as original. J. Lust, 'The Septuagint Version of Daniel 4–5', in A.S. van der Woude (ed.), *The Book of Daniel* (Leuven: University Press/Uitgeverij Peeters, 1993), p. 46, agrees.

69. 967 has this reading despite the fact that at v. 26/93 it differs from Syh-88 by not having τῶν θεῶν.

In further support of this suggestion is the king's statement that he is overcome by 'trembling from fear of him (God)' (4.37a, ἀπὸ τοῦ φόβου αὐτοῦ τρόμος). This picks up on the unusual usage that we noted of φοβέω by the LXX in v. 17. Just as Nebuchadnezzar is moved in ch. 4 to praise the God whom the young men praise in ch. 3, so he adopts the same 'fear' of God in ch. 4 that they show in ch. 3. The pairing of chs. 3 and 4 also explains why the final speech of Nebuchadnezzar in ch. 3 is not as confessional as its counterparts in chs. 4 and 6. If chs. 3 and 4 reflect a process of development in the king, the confession of ch. 4 becomes the completion of the partial acknowledgment in ch. 3. The corollary of this is that chs. 5 and 6 are also a pairing culminating in the same sort of confession by Darius.

Conclusion

The major difference between the two accounts of ch. 3 lies in the insertion of Additional material between vv. 23 and 24. In narrative terms it shifts the centre of the story away from the moment of defiance described in vv. 16-18 MT and on to the contents of the Prayer of Azariah and Song of the Three. The divergence of traditions immediately before and after the insertion, as well as the piece of narrative between the prayer and song, results in similar differences between the narrative art of the MT and LXX as have been observed in chs. 4–6. There are also other smaller differences between the MT and LXX in the commonly held material that reinforce the narrative effects of the Additions. The LXX narrator is more overt and less neutral than his MT counterpart. One result of this is an anticipation of the narrative by the LXX and more explicit guidance to the reader on matters of perspective. The MT is more dependent on the inherent development of the story to portray perspective. In this particular instance the perception of irony is crucial to an understanding of the MT where such is not the case in the LXX. The same was true of ch. 6 although the differences came about there by different means. In another parallel with ch. 6, the heroes of the fiery furnace maintain a pregnant silence in the MT except at the moment of declaring God's faithfulness, and it is left to the king to declare the vindication of their God. In both instances the LXX has Shadrach, Meshach and Abednego and Daniel explicitly condemn the king. The LXX habit seen particularly in ch. 4 of explicating the mysterious is also present in ch. 3.

The particular concerns of the Additions are borne out by a comparison of the rest of the chapter with the MT. The interest in the Jewish nation and the integrity of its major institutions is reinforced by the slightly different setting of the LXX story which places Nebuchadnezzar in a position of explicit opposition to those institutions. The MT account is a more local story of courage in the diaspora. Moreover, the emphasis by the LXX on the uniqueness of the God of Israel with its accompanying suspicion of idolatry or the divinization of the monarch are also features of a comparison with the MT in Daniel 3. The difference is less marked on the subject of idolatry as that is an explicit concern of the Aramaic version anyway. There is also a hint at the different view of wisdom held by the LXX in other chapters, although the evidence is not conclusive.

It is generally true that the structural and literary links between chs. 3 and 6 are much stronger in the MT. In the LXX a stronger relationship between chs. 3 and 4 may be detected. This is seen first in the paired dating of the chapters by the LXX, which alerts the reader to the part played by Nebuchadnezzar in the destruction of Jewish national life and links him with the evil king of the Additions. It is then noticeable that the royal confession of ch. 4 echoes the Song of the Three and completes the partial capitulation of Nebuchadnezzar in ch. 3. This pairing of chs. 3 and 4 fits in with the 967 ordering of the book of Daniel. By contrast, the MT displays strong organic links with ch. 6 in the way that ch. 5 assumed ch. 4. One result of this difference is that the positive picture of Nebuchadnezzar displayed in chs. 4–5 MT is not present in the LXX to the same extent. This pairing does not preclude a relationship with other MT stories and the similarity of the opening with ch. 5 was noted. But there is more to be said on the subject once the story of the statue in ch. 2 has been examined.

Chapter 6

DANIEL 2

Daniel 2 is different from each of the stories so far considered in chs. 3–6 in two important respects. First, the LXX and the MT are closer to each other than is the case in chs. 3–6. Secondly, the redaction history of the text of the MT is more visible than in the other Aramaic stories about Babylonian or Persian kings. As a result of these differences my approach to Daniel 2 will diverge from the pattern that has informed our discussion of the other stories. The relative closeness of the two versions to each other means that the literary focus is less on matters of structure and literary craftsmanship and more on questions of content, although the two aspects interconnect. The visibility of the process of redaction means that ch. 2 MT does not yield as readily to a narrative-critical approach that assumes the literary unity of the story. Before a literary comparison can be made I must therefore deal with the fact that there is more than one level of tradition evident in the MT.

The two particular sections that have a bearing on the present discussion are vv. 13-23 and vv. 40-43. There is evidence of some corruption or emendation of the tradition in vv. 40-43. Because they do not have a direct bearing on the narrative criticism of the chapter as a whole, I do not analyse those verses explicitly in source-critical terms. However, I note the problems they pose where it is appropriate to do so. Verses 13-23 bear more directly on the ensuing discussion. Accordingly, this treatment begins with a detailed examination of the case both for vv. 13-23 being a later insertion and for the song of praise in vv. 20-23 being an independent unit. I then proceed to a comparison of the MT with the LXX on the basis that material in vv. 13-23 is not original to the proto-type of the MT, and that vv. 20-23 have probably been introduced.

This comparison is made with respect to the narrative structures, the presence or otherwise of irony and ambiguity, and the narrator's stance and manipulation of point of view. Certain literary devices within the versions will also be noted. There are some significant variations in these areas despite the closeness of the versions to each other. In turning from there to the more substantial matters of content, I will compare the interpretation of the dream, and note some evidence for differences in theological outlook. In the process differences are detected in the backdrop to each story and in the way the protagonists, Daniel and Nebuchadnezzar, are portrayed.

In the nature of this approach to Daniel 2, links with other chapters form an integral part of the discussion and so are not treated separately at the end, except as part of the conclusion. There I suggest that the trends evident in chs. 3–6 are also present in ch. 2, although they have been obscured by the transmission history of the MT.

Verses 13-23: Inserted Material?

Up until now I have worked with the premise, particularly where the MT is concerned, that, notwithstanding the historical process of composition discernible behind the stories, each of them functions in their received form as a literary unit. The composition of Daniel 2 forces an exception to that practice, as the possibility that vv. 13-23 have been inserted cannot be ignored in a literary discussion of the texts. I treat vv. 13-23 as a whole first and then turn the focus onto Daniel's song of praise within that material (vv. 20-23). Although they differ over where exactly the interpolated material begins, most commentators see these verses as a subsequent insertion.[1] Generally they do so in order to solve the problem of Daniel's two audiences with Arioch (vv. 15, 24) and also with the king (vv. 16, 25-26).[2] It seems strange that Daniel needs an introduction by Arioch when he has already been to see the king on his own. Moreover, Daniel's ignorance of the king's actions is difficult to explain in the light of v. 13 and also of his promotion at the end of ch. 1.

In fact, the evidence for vv. 13-23 having been inserted into the MT is indecisive. The above argument as an objection to the literary unity of ch. 2 assumes that narrative time always corresponds to real chronological time. While the use of flashback and anticipation in biblical narrative

---

1. P.R. Davies, *Daniel* (Sheffield: JSOT Press, 1985), p. 46; and Hartman and DiLella, *Daniel*, p. 139, see the inserted material beginning at v. 13. Lacocque, *Daniel*, p. 46, Porteous, *Daniel*, p. 42, and Heaton, *Daniel*, p. 128, prefer v. 14.

2. See, for example, Wills, *The Jew in the Court*, p. 82, who follows Hartman and DiLella, *Daniel*, p. 139.

is rare, it is not unheard of, and chronological and narrative time should not always be strictly equated.[3] For example, the reference in 1.21 to Daniel's service until the days of Cyrus is a narratorial intrusion in that it moves outside the time frame of the story to provide a panoramic introduction to the career of Daniel. If 1.20 is also part of that anticipation, it is not necessary for Daniel to be a prominent figure in the court when the present story opens. Furthermore, the doubling of action in itself is not necessarily a marker of secondary material, as we saw in the discussion on 3.23. It can serve a resumptive or anticipatory function, although admittedly it is difficult to see what purpose would be served in this particular instance.[4] The functioning of time within the narrative on its own does not demand the conclusion that vv. 13-23 are secondary.

Moreover, much the same use of revelation and interpretation terminology may be discerned in this section as in the rest of the chapter. That aspect is explored in more detail in the section on point of view within the narrative. Suffice to say at this stage that when Daniel makes a play for extra time from the king, he offers 'to declare' (v. 16, להחויה) the interpretation to the king. The object of that verb is פשרא just as it usually is elsewhere in ch. 2. He uses words appropriate to his function as a human intermediary of wisdom, which would have been how he perceived himself and how he was perceived by Nebuchadnezzar. Yet when the activity of God in revelation is described (vv. 19, 22), the verb גלא is used in the same specialized sense as elsewhere in the chapter. In the first instance the usual object, רז (v. 19), is also present.

A comparison of other vocabulary used in these verses likewise fails to yield a consistent pattern in favour of the distinction. There are several words or phrases that are unique to this part of Daniel, namely עטא וטעם (v. 14, 'wisdom and discretion'), על־מה (v. 15, 'why?') and רחם (v. 18, 'mercy'). But that fact on its own does not function as an argument for a different source. Most of the key words also occur in ch. 2 outside vv. 13-19. There are a few that do not, but they do not provide a large enough sample from which to draw conclusions. Indeed, the instances in question are normally well represented elsewhere in Daniel 2–7. Examples are בית (v. 17, 'house', also in 3.29; 4.1, 27; 5.23;

<hr />

3. Bar-Efrat, *Narrative Art*, p. 179.
4. Contrast the reading of Fewell, *Circle of Sovereignty*, p. 52, who integrates vv. 13-23 by her interpretation of the function of Arioch in the story. Contrast also Goldingay, *Daniel*, p. 42, whose opinion that this section heightens suspense is treated below.

6.11), בעה (v. 18, 'seek', also in 4.33; 6.8, 13; 7.16), שאר (v. 18, 'the rest', also in 7.12, 19), and ברך (v. 19, 'blessed', also in 4.31; 6.11). The one statement that could tentatively be made is that the choice of words in vv. 13-19 MT shows some resemblance to ch. 7. שאר above is one example as is the form of the phrase 'vision of the night' (v. 19, חזוא די־ליליא, also in 7.2, 7, 13). Despite that, there is little in the vocabulary used that distinguishes vv. 13-19 from the rest of ch. 2.

However, a more compelling argument for vv. 13-23 as an insertion emerges in an examination of the balance between narrative and dialogue in the structure of the chapter. The predominance of direct speech is a notable feature of Daniel 2. There are two verses of narrative at the beginning and end of the story. Excluding the problematical vv. 13-23 for the moment, 32 of the remaining 34 verses consist of direct speech or narrative indicators of direct speech. The exceptions are vv. 12 and 46. In fact there is more direct speech than in any of the other chapters so far studied. Such is not the case in vv. 14-19, however. Daniel asks a direct question of Arioch in v. 15, but apart from that all the interchanges between characters are reported indirectly. To begin with, at v. 14 there is an unusual form of expression when Daniel is said to have 'responded with counsel and discretion' (התיב עטא וטעם) to Arioch. תוב is a word more specifically connected with the conduct of dialogue than the wide-ranging ענה, but is never so used in Daniel except here. The occurrence in 3.16 is a different type of usage. It seems therefore to be more of a descriptive term than a narrative marker and so not in character with the rest of the narrative surrounding these verses. This becomes even more clear in the next few verses. Arioch 'made known' (v. 15, הודע) the state of affairs to Daniel, who thereupon goes in and 'asks of the king' (v. 16, בעה מן־מלכא) for more time. Having done that, he goes home and 'made known' (v. 17, הודע) the matter to his companions. Despite all this communication between characters, their words are never reported directly. As a result the action is filtered through the narrator to the reader, who is not permitted the first-hand view that direct speech allows.

In terms of narrative structure, then, a case could perhaps be made that the material in vv. 13-19 is different in kind from that surrounding it. A consideration of the subject matter of those verses leads in the same direction since the presumption by the MT of Daniel's qualifications as a wise man lies entirely within the verses under discussion.[5] Outside that

5. Davies, *Daniel*, p. 46. Jephet, *Daniel*, p. 8, suggests that Daniel does not

material the MT is a pure court contest.[6] The rank outsider, whose only achievement so far has been to graduate with honours from the king's training programme, inquires about the harsh decree and proves himself as a wise man by solving the problem set the wise men by the king. Daniel's petition on behalf of Shadrach, Meshach and Abednego at the end of the chapter thereby links back to the events of ch. 1 rather than to their role as his confidants in the present story.

In corroboration note that the only time the Aramaic section calls Daniel's three friends by their Semitic names is in v. 17. They are called Hananiah, Mishael and Azariah elsewhere only in the Hebrew ch. 1 or in the Additional Greek material of ch. 3. This fact may not be grounds on its own to identify and draw firm lines between traditions, but it does suggest that this material comes from a different source, albeit one that has a great deal still in common with the material surrounding it.

The main argument against this view is found in vv. 36 and 47 where plural forms seem to include Daniel's compatriots in the narrative. In v. 36 Daniel tells the king that 'we will tell' (נאמר) his dream and give its interpretation, while in v. 47 Nebuchadnezzar uses the plural suffix in 'your God' (אלהכון).[7] In the canonical context the most obvious referent of the first person plural prefix is Daniel with his three friends. Both the LXX and θ take that to be the case with their use of ἐροῦμεν. But this has for long been recognized as an unsatisfactory aspect of the MT narrative.[8] If the point is accepted that vv. 13-23 are later additions in the Aramaic, the plurals in vv. 36 and 47 are inexplicable as meaning the four young Jews, because three of them are not even present. Various explanations have been attempted. The direct approach is to say that the MT rendering is itself a result of amendment to bring it into line with the earlier inclusion of the companions of Daniel. The difficulty with this argument is that the process is curiously incomplete in light of the craftsmanship demonstrated elsewhere in the MT, and it is unsupported by any Aramaic textual tradition. The only support comes from several

appear when the Babylonian wise men are first called because he does not see himself in the same category as the Chaldeans.

6. Collins, *Apocalyptic Vision*, p. 36, notes that the rivalry is not a hostile one.

7. Young, *Daniel*, p. 81.

8. J. Ziegler, *Septuaginta: Susanna, Daniel, Bel et Draco* (Göttingen: Vandenhoeck & Ruprecht, 1954), p. 108. Ethiopic and Arabic traditions follow the Peshitta in preferring the first person with *dicam*. Similarly Bohairic presents *annuntiabo tibi et dicam*.

late translations alluded to by Ziegler. In narrative terms, Montgomery summarizes the several commonly offered explanations.[9] The plural could be understood as an expression of deference or humility.[10] It could also be understood along the lines taken by the medieval Jewish commentators as 'I and His Wisdom'.[11] This is similar to the notion of a divine council lying behind the expression.[12] All these suggestions have their attractions and all can be supported by other biblical examples.

Their greatest weakness is that they do not explain away the plural אלהכון of v. 47. Furthermore they have no parallel in Daniel's other encounters with kings. When Daniel offers messages and interpretations as from the Lord, he normally preserves the distinction between the messenger and the message. This is well illustrated at 4.24 where Daniel breaks off his interpretation of the dream to plead with the king to amend his ways. The Jewish protagonists' use of the phrase '(if) there is a God' (v. 28, איתי אלה; 3.17, הן איתי אלהנא) functions in the same way to separate the words from the speaker. This is different from the earlier prophetic tradition embodied in phrases such as נאם־יהוה, where the speaker and his words are not differentiated. As a result, it is unlikely that Daniel identifies his words as coterminous with God's words, and therefore also unlikely that he suddenly speaks as a member of the heavenly council.[13] It is equally unlikely that the first person plural represents a conventional form of address before the king. Were that the case, we would expect the convention to occur as frequently as others do in Daniel. The use of קדם in the context of approaching the king, and the hope expressed of long life for the king are two such conventions consistently observed in the book of Daniel.

Until more evidence comes to hand, a satisfactory explanation of the plurals in vv. 36 and 47 is not available. There is no convincing alternative to the obvious answer that they refer to Shadrach, Meshach and Abednego, but this does not alter the fact that Daniel on his own is clearly the protagonist. Even in the two verses in question, there are also singular pronouns on either side of the plurals. The narrative seems to nod

---

9. Montgomery, *Daniel*, pp. 71-72.
10. Delcor, *Daniel*, p. 179, thinks of it as a 'royal we' by the intermediary.
11. Ibn-Ezra in Gallé, *Daniel*, p. 24.
12. Heaton, *Daniel*, p. 130.
13. Koch, 'Is Daniel also among the Prophets?', pp. 125-26, attributes this to a growing sense of transcendence, as a result of which the bearer of revelation could only be an intermediary.

politely in the direction of the three, who remain silent bystanders. Therefore the plurals of vv. 36 and 47 alone do not serve as a counter-argument to the view that vv. 13-23 MT has been interpolated in the Aramaic.

Even in the possibly interpolated material, the presence of Hananiah, Mishael and Azariah is problematic as nowhere are the three companions seen as the equals of Daniel. The song of praise itself is in the first person singular. It could be objected that Daniel in v. 23 includes his compatriots in the phrases 'which we asked...' (די־בעינא) and 'you made known to us...' (הודעתנא). But הודעתנא sits uncomfortably in the same verse with the singular suffix on הודעתני. There are no Aramaic textual witnesses to a singular suffix on the final ידע of v. 23, although there is a singular in θ's translation. This reflects either a singular in θ's *Vorlage* or the translator's unease on narrative grounds with the the variation in person in v. 23.[14] However, in agreement with the MT, he allows for the plural with 'which we asked...' (ἄ ἠξιώσαμεν). The LXX translation is not a close equivalent of the existing Aramaic, but does contain the singular form ἠξιώσα in contrast to θ.[15] Even if v. 23 is not an insertion, the textual doubt surrounding the persons of the verbs and their suffixes makes it uncertain whether or not the plural was intended. θ best reflects the sense of the rest of the chapter, in that the friends of Daniel joined in asking for revelation, but Daniel alone received it.

The Song of Praise as Insert

These verses also contain the much-discussed song of praise of Daniel. Many commentators recognize in the material of vv. 20-23 a song that was probably composed for the present purpose.[16] They also recognize it as a distinct and self-contained unit within ch. 2.[17] The revelation

14. Scribal confusion between the sounds of י and א suggests itself as an explanation of a different *Vorlage*, or the eye of the copyist may have been confused by the ending on בעינא and appropriated that suffix for the final word in the verse. See R.W. Klein, *Textual Criticism of the Old Testament* (Philadelphia: Fortress Press, 1974), pp. 76-77, for examples of words which sound alike.

15. Ziegler, *Septuaginta*, p. 104, cites two witnesses from the Lucianic recension as well as the Bohairic and Ethiopic in support of the singular ἠξιώσα in θ.

16. Montgomery, *Daniel*, p. 157, says, 'it is an original composition, entirely to the point of the story'. This view is agreeable to many. See, for example, Goldingay, *Daniel*, p. 38, and Lacocque, *Daniel*, p. 45.

17. Baldwin, *Daniel*, p. 90, exemplifies this with her analysis of the literary qualities of the song.

granted to Daniel (v. 19) brings forth a hymn of praise to the God who reveals (v. 22). The hymn proceeds from a description of the characteristics of God's wisdom, to thanksgiving for the gift of wisdom to Daniel, to the specific 'for you have made known to us the matter of the king' (v. 23, דִּי־מִלַּח מַלְכָּא הוֹדַעְתֶּנָא).

Comparisons are inevitable with the song and prayer that are part of ch. 3 in the Greek, and there are certain superficial similarities.[18] They are both uttered by the Jewish heroes in moments of extreme danger. In each case their deliverance has been assured but not yet implemented. There is the same progression in thought from the general concerns of a wider audience towards the particular circumstances of those uttering the praise, Daniel in ch. 2 and Hananiah, Mishael and Azariah in ch. 3. Despite the particular mention of the heroes, their predicament is not central to the subject matter, but is alluded to. There are two different kinds of grammatical structure in each song. In ch. 3 the first few verses (vv. 52-56) are addressed by the three directly to God in the second person singular. There is then a switch into a series of imperatives directed at various recipients. God is no longer addressed directly (vv. 57-90), but becomes the subject of the commands. Daniel's hymn in ch. 2 also has the same two types of sections although they are in reverse order from the Song of the Three. Verses 20-22 is set in the framework of an imperative or jussive sense, 'Blessed be the name of God' (v. 20, לֶהֱוֵא שְׁמֵהּ דִּי־אֱלָהָא מְבָרַךְ). Daniel switches into the first person at v. 23 and addresses God directly. Notwithstanding the problematic command to Hananiah and Mishael in 3.88, whereby the singers are suddenly introduced into the song itself, the persona of the singer remains outside the song in both cases. In 3.88 the switch in direction of the song to Hananiah and Mishael has come about in the attempt to contextualize the material.[19] This, along with the change into the first person, indicates the assumption that Azariah was the singer of the song just as Daniel is in ch. 2.

Despite the similarities in context and form, however, there are some marked differences in content and syntax. A particular syntactical difference is the way the singer conveys the attributes of the God being praised. In ch. 3 the tendency is to portray God through a series of adjectival phrases, particularly in vv. 52-56. Only at the end of the song

---

18. See the treatment by W.S. Towner, 'Poetic Passages of Daniel 1–6', *CBQ* 31 (1969), p. 326.

19. See Rothstein, 'Die Zusätze zu Daniel', p. 174, and Moore, *Daniel*, p. 74.

is there specific mention of God's actions on behalf of the singer. The song in ch. 2 conveys its information about God through a series of indicative statements all dependent on the ד of v. 20b, explaining why God's name is blessed.[20]

More significant than the syntactical variations are the differences in which aspects of God are highlighted by the hymns. We have seen in an earlier treatment that the sentiments of the Song of the Three are expressed in terms of the created order and of the cult. From v. 57 there is a movement through creation to Israel (v. 83) to priests and servants and the holy ones (vv. 84-87). Hananiah and Mishael (v. 88) are thereby set in company with the people of God. The second section (vv. 57-90) is a long hymn to the created order, both seen and unseen. The first part is filled with cultic imagery. The 'God of our fathers' (v. 52, ὁ θεὸς τῶν πατέρων ἡμῶν) is depicted in his 'Temple' (v. 53, τῷ ναῷ) with the 'cherubim' (v. 55, χερουβιμ) and 'on the throne' (v. 54, ἐπὶ θρόνου). In contrast, the God of 2.20-23 is primarily the one who is the source of secret knowledge, not the one who is revealed in the cult and in creation. He is blessed because he possesses 'wisdom and might' (v. 20, חכמתא וגבורתא) and conveys it 'to the wise...and to those who know' (v. 21, לחכימין...לידעי).[21] The vocabulary of v. 22, to which I return later, intensifies this effect.

There also seem to be different motivations behind the songs. The Prayer of the Three is at least partly penitential in character, so that the ordeal by fire in the Greek versions becomes an act of atonement. Such a motive for praise does not appear in ch. 2.[22] Daniel and his companions go to God for help because they are in a corner (v. 18). There is no

20. Stefanovic, *The Aramaic of Daniel*, p. 41, likens the structure of this 'hymn-prayer' to the Tell Fekherye inscription (J.C. Greenfield and A. Shaffer, 'Notes on the Akkadian–Aramaic Bilingual Statue from Tell Fekherye', *Iraq* 45 [1983], pp. 112-13) partly on the grounds of its use of participles. His comparison ignores the fact that the participles in vv. 21-22 belong with the הוא at the beginning of each verse and so are used indicatively. There is no equivalent in the Tell Fekherye inscription to הוא, or to ד. See Rosenthal, *Biblical Aramaic*, p. 55, on this use of the participle as a narrative tense.

21. Bentzen, *Daniel*, pp. 9-10, and Porteous, *Daniel*, p. 43. This chapter can be viewed as illustrating the assertion of Y. Kaufmann, *The Religion of Israel* (trans. M. Greenberg; London: George Allen & Unwin, 1961), p. 79, that 'The contrast between YHWH and the magician is... between divine and human wisdom'.

22. J.G. Gammie, 'On the Intention and Sources of Daniel I–VI', *VT* 31 (1981), p. 290, notes that the aspect of vicarious suffering is missing.

suggestion of penitence in their tone. On balance the LXX plus in v. 18, where Daniel, as well as going to prayer, 'declared a fast' (v. 18, παρήγγειλε νηστείαν), probably does not imply penitence either. Certainly there is a strong Old Testament tradition linking fasting to repentance, and paralleling it with the donning of sackcloth and ashes (Neh. 9.1; Ps. 68.11/69.10; Isa. 58.5, for example). But there are other occasions where fasting is part of the plea for help in difficult circumstances. Sometimes the context hints that fasting is part of repentance in acknowledgment that the trouble has come about through sin (2 Sam. 12.16; Zech. 7.5). At other times the context is clearly not penitential, and the fast is only part of a cry for help. The clearest examples of this come from later biblical and apocryphal material (2 Chron. 20.3; 1 Esd. 8.50; 2 Macc. 13.12). So fasting in the LXX of v. 18 need not imply the same sort of motivation as lies behind the Song and Prayer of the Three. This contrasts with ch. 9 where Daniel's fast (9.3) is obviously penitential on behalf of the nation, and is accompanied by 'sackcloth and ashes' (9.3, שׂק ואפר).

It should not be thought that these substantial differences between the songs necessarily mean that Daniel's song is any more at home in its context than were the Additions of ch. 3.[23] The apparently successful integration of 2.20-23 is not as watertight as it might seem. Apart from the final reference to מלת־מלכא there is nothing that specifically relates to the predicament that Daniel and his friends find themselves in. At the point where the hymn is applied to the current setting there is a change of note. In particular the grammatical persons and moods change. God is spoken about in vv. 20-22 and addressed directly in v. 23, and the jussive mood at the beginning of the song becomes indicative at v. 23 where Daniel adopts the first person. This is reminiscent of what happens in 3.88 where the Song of the Three is probably adjusted to fit its new context.

In terms of vocabulary, the appearance in v. 22 of the deep things and the hidden things (עמיקתא ומסתרתא) is unique in biblical Aramaic. It comes in the midst of a string of references to 'interpretation' (פשר) and 'secrets' (רזין), which are consistently used except at this point. The two words also occur together in Isa. 29.15, the only instance in biblical Hebrew where such is the case. That verse contains the only example of מסתר, whereas מעמיקים is relatively common. However, it often has a geographical (Isa. 22.7, for example) or physical (Ezek. 23.32, for

---

23. See Rothstein, 'Die Zusätze zu Daniel', p. 174.

example) referent. Where the sense is metaphorical, it usually refers to the depths of Sheol (Job 11.8) or the human mind (Ps. 64.7), and even in later Aramaic does not normally carry the apocalyptic sense of a divine secret which the context of v. 22 gives it. The word was a puzzle to the θ and LXX translators, who both render it literally with βαθέα. As with the Hebrew equivalent usually so translated, עמיק (for example in Prov. 18.4; 25.3; Isa. 31.6), the adjective modifies the human mind or human action, or is used as part of an image of the same. There did not seem to be a different Greek word available to the translators with which to convey the precise sense of the word in this context. This is a further hint that the present setting for the song is unlikely to have been its original one. The rare מסתרתא also supports that argument. It occurs occasionally in later Aramaic meaning 'secret', but even then human secrets are usually intended. Again the present meaning is unique to this context and suggestive of a different original setting.

The imagery of dark and light in v. 22 is not used in the same way anywhere else in chs. 2–6, not even in the Greek Additions of ch. 3, where God is lord of both light and dark (3.71-72). It is part of a biblical tradition represented in Job 12.22 and Isa. 29.15, where interestingly enough 'the deep things' (עמקות in Job, המעמיקים in Isaiah) also feature, but is not at all common.[24] Such a dualistic use of the imagery is more akin to the Community Rule found at Qumran (1QS 3), a document from the first or even late second century BCE.[25] Dating the sources is beyond the scope of this discussion, but the use of imagery and the unusual aspects of vocabulary suggest a different provenance for the Song of ch. 2, and so support the view that the hymnic material has been imported into the story.

Despite the attempts at integration, the contents of the Song also echo quite different, and probably later, sentiments. Reference to the God who 'changes the seasons and the times' (v. 21, מהשנא עדניא וזמניא) res-onates of the little horn, the arrogant king who sought 'to change sea-sons' (7.25, להשניה זמנין) as well as the law. A similar reference is also to be found in the LXX plus material of 4.37, where the God who 'changes seasons and times' (ἀλλοιοῖ καιροὺς καὶ χρόνους) is acknowledged

---

24. Charles, *Daniel*, p. 37.

25. M. Knibb, *The Qumran Community* (Cambridge: Cambridge University Press, 1987), pp. 78 and 94. Hartman and DiLella, *Daniel*, p. 140, also draw attention to a link with the War Scroll of Qumran as well as parts of the New Testament, particularly the Johannine writings.

by Nebuchadnezzar. Both θ and the LXX translate v. 21 with the identical phrase. The power to remove (עדה) and set up kings (v. 21) also reminds the reader of the fate of the arrogant king represented by the little horn in 7.26, whose power is taken away (עדה). This is a slightly different tradition from that of ch. 4 in Aramaic, where the negative power to remove kings is not mentioned alongside the power to set them up (4.14, 22, 29). However in 4.37 LXX God removes as well as sets up (ἀφαιρῶν...καὶ καθιστῶν) kings in terms similar to those of the Greek of v. 21 (μεθιστῶν...καὶ καθιστῶν). All of this suggests that the Song of Praise in ch. 2 has a closer literary relationship with the tradition behind ch. 7 and the LXX of ch. 4 than with its immediate context.

Although there is some ambiguity in the source-critical evidence relating to vv. 13-23 as outlined above, it seems likely that the material in question has been inserted into an earlier original of the story of Nebuchadnezzar and his dream statue.[26] Whether or not the song in vv. 20-23 is an integrated part of that unit, it is inescapable that the song is not original within the chapter as a whole. The indications are that both the LXX and θ translated a *Vorlage* that already contained vv. 13-23. These are the assumptions about Dan. 2.13-23 that will inform the remainder of this literary comparison of the LXX and MT versions of ch. 2.

A literary objection to this conclusion might be that these verses are part of a long build-up to the revelation of the interpretation of the dream and the dream itself. The length of the build-up is a deliberate artifice intended to create suspense, and vv. 13-23 are integral to that effect.[27] It could be argued that this is the same phenomenon present in the MT version of ch. 5, where the writing on the wall is central by its absence. There are two possible replies to that argument. One is that it is not of sufficient weight on its own to counter contrary evidence. The other is to note that there is still considerable suspense built into the story without vv. 13-23. Daniel does not begin to tell the dream until v. 31, which is well over half way through the postulated older version of the story. The reader has to wait through the exchange between Nebuchadnezzar and his officials (vv. 1-12), Arioch's mediation (vv. 24-26), and Daniel's disclaimer (vv. 27-30).[28] Because the dream is not yet

---

26. Davies, *Daniel*, pp. 46-48, reaches this conclusion and sees the insertion as part of the process of refashioning a much older kernel to fit the Hellenistic period.

27. Goldingay, *Daniel*, p. 42.

28. Fewell, *Circle of Sovereignty*, p. 174.

known by anyone else, the repeated reference by Daniel in vv. 27-30 to the purpose of the dream heightens the suspense.

Narrative Structure

The type of narrative analysis that has been applied to chs. 3–6 is less applicable in the present case. In the nature of a closer translation on the part of the LXX, ch. 2 contains no variations between versions that affect the structure or narrative shape of the story. Apart from divergences that are explicable in technical terms, such differences as there are normally suggest either a different theology or provenance, or some discrepancy in the way point of view is perceived and manipulated within the narrative. A useful starting point for this discussion of narrative technique, then, is to note something that has already been touched on: the primacy of dialogue in both versions. Apart from the bare bones of the setting and what is needed to maintain the clarity of the narrative, no information is imparted directly to the reader in the older version of the story. In this respect the MT and LXX narrators of ch. 2 are both as covert and neutral as each other, and therefore potentially ambiguous. They do not anticipate plot developments nor do they attribute motives to the characters.

The characteristic use of a minor figure in furthering the plot is also in evidence in both versions.[29] In fact, the appearance of Arioch signals a pivotal shift in focus when vv. 13-23 are excluded. Until v. 12 the exchange between king and wise men sets the main tensions in place. From vv. 26 to the end, the conversation between Nebuchadnezzar and Daniel builds on that platform. Arioch, the executioner, is the vehicle by which the Babylonians are ushered off stage, and Arioch, the intermediary, is the one who then brings on Daniel in their place.[30]

Irony and Ambiguity

At a discourse level, the perception of point of view by the reader of this sort of narration is dependent on ironic suggestion and subtlety in variation. Even there the versions are in agreement with each other in many respects. One example of irony centres on the question of the source of

---

29. Simon, 'Minor Characters', p. 14. Arioch is a more functional character than his counterpart in ch. 5, the queen.

30. See Fewell, *Circle of Sovereignty*, p. 53, on the role of Arioch.

Aramaic Daniel and Greek Daniel

the wisdom required to know and interpret the king's dream. The Chaldeans unwittingly encapsulate the issue by declaring that no human could know the answer and only 'the gods' (v. 11 MT, אלהין) or 'an angel' (v. 11 LXX, ἄγγελος) could show it. Thereby the mantic officials not only betray their own sources of wisdom as less than divine, but they also set the stage for a subsequent revelation. So Daniel's statement that 'no wise men...are able to declare...but there is a God' (vv. 27-28, לא חכימין...יכלין להחויה...ברם איתי אלה) who can, is a counterpoint to the earlier incident.[31] The Babylonians' earlier statement is confirmed as true and the superiority of Daniel's God is confirmed.

Some have suspected a touch of gentle irony in other aspects of the story also. In the early stages of the chapter the king seems to hold the whip hand as he exposes his wise men's ignorance of true revelation. Yet it is the wise men who utter the truth of the matter (v. 11), albeit accidentally.[32] At the end of the story Nebuchadnezzar's exaggerated and inappropriate homage paid to Daniel's success indicates that he still has not understood fully. The irony remains, this time at the expense of the king.[33] Good goes even further with his suggestion that the story as a whole can be interpreted as the archetypically comic 'impossible task' set by the king and accomplished by Daniel.[34] These aspects are also present in the LXX version.

Whether or not we go as far as Good in viewing the story largely in comic terms, it is inescapable that there is some ambiguity about the whole episode. In particular, because of the primacy of dialogue, the narrator leaves a measure of inscrutability in the characters of both the king and Daniel. There is no external judgment on the king's behaviour when he worships Daniel at the end, and the message given to the reader is mixed. In v. 46 his worship is focused entirely on the sage, but then his speech of v. 47 about 'your God' (אלהכון) shifts from Daniel to his God. However, the consequence of his recognition of Daniel's God is completely secular and almost beside the point. The syntax of v. 48, which begins 'Then the king set up Daniel' (אדין מלכא לדניאל רבי), shifts the focus of the king's response back onto Daniel. The character of Daniel

31. Lacocque, *Daniel*, p. 46.

32. Towner, *Daniel*, p. 32.

33. Porteous, *Daniel*, p. 51. B.A. Mastin, 'Daniel 2.46 and the Hellenistic World', *ZAW* 85 (1973), p. 92, echoes Porteous's views.

34. Good, 'Apocalyptic as Comedy', p. 50. Montgomery, *Daniel*, p. 146, finds 'grim humour' in Nebuchadnezzar's setting of the task.

also contains some puzzles. The most obvious is Daniel's silence in the face of this worship, an aspect that is considered elsewhere. But this is only a reflection of a bigger problem that arises in Daniel's interpretation of the dream. The dream of the statue is primarily a vision of judgment on temporal power along with the eventual supremacy of divine power, and Daniel brings that out in his interpretation. In that light, his emphatic statement to Nebuchadnezzar, 'You are the head of gold' (v. 38, אנתה־הוא ראשה די דהבא), is a surprising one as it reduces the disturbing aspects of the vision to political terms.[35] I will return to this element in the story when considering theological differences between the versions. As with the ironic aspects, this ambiguity is also part of the LXX translation of this chapter.

Point of View

The above examples do not mean that the narrator is entirely neutral in ch. 2. Indeed the MT contains several examples of subtle variation in vocabulary which are designed to enhance the reader's perception of the different points of view present in the narrative.[36] It is here that some disparity between the MT and LXX may be detected. Such a variation is an important element in the early part of the narrative, where the wise men fail to understand the exact nature of the king's request. There is no talk of 'the interpretation' (פשרא) until v. 4. Before that the king calls in his functionaries and they are ordered 'to tell the king his dream' (v. 2, להגיד למלך חלמתיו). At this stage there is no distinction in the king's mind between dream and interpretation. This is reinforced by the king's next statement that he needs 'to know the dream' (v. 3, לדעת את־החלום).[37] The hapless Chaldeans are not to know that when the king uses ידע he is usually thinking of dream and interpretation as a package (vv. 5, 26). They are the first to separate the two when they ask for an account of

---

35. See Goldingay, *Daniel*, p. 147, on the distinction between 'eschatological' and 'political'. Fewell, *Circle of Sovereignty*, pp. 56-60, explores this ambiguity extensively and well, although her assessment of Daniel as 'one who tells the truth but not the whole truth' does not take sufficient account of developments between Daniel and the kings in subsequent chapters.

36. Niditch and Doran, 'The Success Story', p. 188, identify this as a characteristic of Dan. 2. Other stories in what they have identified as the literary type of Dan. 2 tend to have extended repetition instead. Gen. 41 and *Ahiqar* 5–7 are their other cases in point.

37. Lacocque, *Daniel*, p. 41.

the dream so that they might interpret (v. 4). Only then does Nebuchadnezzar emphasize that he wants to hear both 'the dream and its interpretation' (v. 5, חלמא ופשרה). The wise men's dawning awareness is marked by a repetition of the request for an account of the king's dream (v. 7), weakened this time by the use of a jussive instead of the self-confident imperative of v. 4.[38] Both parties are talking at cross purposes, and the contrast between the wise men's abilities and what is required of them is heightened by this ambiguity of usage on the part of the king.

The ambiguity is not as consistently portrayed by the LXX, probably as a result of an attempt to clarify its MT-like *Vorlage*. One reason for the Babylonians' misunderstanding of Nebuchadnezzar is that dream and interpretation function as a double object of the same verb in the early speeches of the king. The verb in question is either ידע (vv. 5, 9, 'to make known') or חוה (v. 6 twice, 'to declare'). This characteristic form of expression does not occur when the mantic officials are speaking. Their habit of making dream and interpretation each objects of their own verb (vv. 4, 7) betrays the mind set that keeps them in separate categories. The distinction between the point of view of the king and that of his advisers is not present in the LXX, because in each of the above instances of speech by the king (vv. 5, 6, 9) 'dream' and 'interpretation' are distinguished by being the objects of their own verb. Moreover, the difference in mood between vv. 4 and 7, as portrayed in the MT, is not inherent in the verb forms chosen by the LXX.

Closely related to the use of 'dream' and 'interpretation' words is the narrator's deployment of the different declaratory verbs that govern them. They too are varied in order to manipulate viewpoint from within the narrative. To make this clear, it is necessary to examine in some detail the way these verbs operate in Daniel 2. We have seen that King Nebuchadnezzar apparently does not distinguish between ידע and חוה in describing the process of telling and interpreting the dream, nor does he distinguish initially between the functions of telling and interpreting. He begins to do so in the second half of v. 9, by which time the Chaldeans have worked out exactly what the king is asking of them and ambiguity is no longer required by the narrative. On that occasion he uses the same term as the wise men, חוה, when speaking of the dream's interpretation.

The verb ידע has an extremely wide semantic range in both biblical

38. Goldingay, *Daniel*, p. 32.

Hebrew and biblical Aramaic. The sense of revealing what is known by God or the gods is only one part of that range, and does not occur commonly in Hebrew. The *hiphil* is more likely to carry that sense (see Dan. 8.19) but not inevitably. The Aramaic of Daniel frequently uses ידע to portray the idea of revelation (for example 4.3; 5.8; 7.16), but it also contains the more usual everyday usage (for example 5.22; 6.11). The second verb most commonly used with פשר as its object is חוה. In biblical Aramaic it is almost exclusively a term of mantic practice, whereas there is a strand of the biblical Hebrew tradition in which it functions as a term of aphoristic wisdom, used in declaring opinions or knowledge about God (see Ps. 19.3; Job 32.10, 17; 36.2). A third verb of revelation in ch. 2 is גלא.[39] Apart from its several occurrences in this chapter (vv. 19, 22, 28, 29, 30, 47), its only other uses in biblical Aramaic are in Ezra 4.10 and 5.12. There it simply means 'to be taken into exile'. The word is much more common in biblical Hebrew where, although the idea of being removed into exile occurs from time to time, the primary sense is of uncovering something previously hidden, whether that be a person's nakedness or the secrets of God. It is nowhere associated with divination, but particularly in the prophets and writings has been used to talk about God's self-revelation.[40] Examples may be seen at Isa. 22.14, 40.5 and 53.1, and Ps. 98.2.

Using that information as background, it is possible to discern an emerging pattern in the way the various words are used in Daniel 2. We have already seen the variegated use of terms employed by Nebuchadnezzar. When the wise men speak, however, it is clear that they use חוה as a technical term which is never applied to the dream itself. Twice it takes 'interpretation' as its object in the mouths of the wise men (vv. 4, 7). Once it governs the general term מלת (v. 10, 'matter') which clearly includes the interpretation now that the Chaldeans recognize the double focus of Nebuchadnezzar's request. The other occasion is in v. 11 when they tell the king that there is nobody who can 'declare it' (יחונה), referring back to the 'matter'.[41]

---

39. This spelling is used to include the alternative גלה also. See Rosenthal, *Biblical Aramaic*, p. 51.

40. When used in that sense it sometimes takes סוד as its object (see Amos 3.7 and Prov. 20.19). See R.E. Brown, 'The Pre-Christian Semitic Concept of "Mystery"', *CBQ* 20 (1958), p. 421, who links סוד with the Aramaic רז, which is also the usual object of גלא in Daniel.

41. According to *BHS* some manuscripts witness to יחונה. That tradition would

So far in the MT account the vocabulary used in this regard is consistent with the point of view and understanding of the heathen king and his advisers. Daniel has a different outlook, and his choice of verbs when talking about interpretation and revelation reflects that outlook. At first he uses חוה in common with the other protagonists (vv. 16, 24, 27). We set aside the instance of v. 16 for the time being as that is part of the larger question of how to deal with literary differences in vv. 13-23. In v. 24 Daniel is speaking to Arioch and reflects that functionary's perspective on Daniel as one of a kind with all the others he has been ordered to kill. In v. 27 he is speaking to Nebuchadnezzar and uses חוה to describe in their own terms the activities of the Babylonians. Daniel's speech to the king continues in v. 28 but now he is explaining the role of God in revealing mysteries.

It is then (v. 28) that he uses גלא, the word used uniquely in this chapter in connection with God's revelation. This is also true of vv. 19 and 22 in the inserted material. Several times (vv. 28, 29, 30) the verb occurs in conjunction with ידע. On each occasion the object of גלא is 'secret(s)' (רז or רזין), whereas the phrase containing ידע describes the consequence of the uncovered secret. By this stage in the story it is clear that only God can reveal (גלא) the particular secret which no human agent, not even Daniel on his own, can reveal (חוה). In the light of all this, the verb chosen by Nebuchadnezzar in v. 47 is significant. By using גלא to describe the revelatory actions of both God and Daniel, he recognizes the unique actions of God and the distinctiveness of the role that Daniel has played compared to the other wise men. At the same time, his application of the word demonstrates further Nebuchadnezzar's inability to differentiate between Daniel and his God, a point to which I shall return in a later section.

The process whereby points of view are distinguished by the MT is further illustrated by examining the various objects of the verbs just discussed: 'interpretation' (פשר), 'dream' (חלם), and 'secret' (רז). Once the smoke screen created by Nebuchadnezzar's deliberately obscure use of חלם has begun to clear, the distinction between 'dream' and 'interpretation' is respected, but at the same time a third concept holding dream and interpretation together begins to emerge. At first the dream and interpretation together is referred to by the Chaldeans with the neutral 'matter' (vv. 10-11, מלתא). After that the content intended by מלתא is conveyed into the wisdom term רז ('secret', vv. 27-29).

strengthen the impression of חוה as a technical term in the mouths of the wise men.

Gradually it becomes clear to the reader that the matter of the king is a dream and an interpretation, which together constitute a secret that God must reveal.[42] There is a further development in thought as Daniel spells out to the king that the particular secret in question is what will take place (v. 29) 'at the end of the days' (v. 28, באחרית יומיא) or 'after this' (v. 45, אחרי דנה). In that context Daniel's use of רז as the object of חוה in v. 27 is surprising but effective. By noting that the other wise men have not been able to 'declare' (v. 27, חוה) the 'secret' (v. 27, רז) he recalls and encapsulates the irony of the early exchanges between Nebuchadnezzar and his officials, whose skills only ran to interpretation (פשר) when it was secrets (רזין) that really needed uncovering.[43] After this pivotal verse the vocabulary particular to the revelation of God's secrets through his agent is used exclusively.

Identification of points of view within the narrative by choice of vocabulary does not occur to the same extent within the LXX. It is true that the distinction between פשר and רז of the MT is largely preserved. פשר is normally translated as σύγκρισις or κρίσις (vv. 4, 5, 6, 9, 26, 36, 45), although πάντα (v. 16) and ἕκαστα (vv. 24-25) are exceptions that probably both represent כל in the Aramaic. רז is always translated with μυστήριον. So the pattern of the objects of interpretation verbs in the MT is also discernible in the LXX, but this is not backed up by the choice of verbs governing them. As well as the interpretative practice of the LXX in vv. 5-6 already alluded to, the LXX uses no less than nine verbs to represent the three Aramaic ones just discussed. Taking into account the speaker, his listener and the subject of the conversation, there is no consistent pattern of usage evident. Even the patterns visible in θ contain an unusual number of exceptions. For example ידע is usually rendered in θ by γινώσκω or γνωρίζω (vv. 3, 5, 23, 29, 30, 45) but sometimes ἀναγγέλλω is used (vv. 9, 25, 26). Yet that word, or its cousin ἀπαγγέλλω, is also the usual translation of חוה (vv. 4, 6, 7, 9, 11, 16, 24, 27). θ is most consistent in its representation of גלא by ἀποκαλύπτω.

ἀποκαλύπτω is the one Greek word for telling or revealing in Daniel 2 that has particular mantic connotations, and is thereby the most appropriate translation of גלא. However, even here the LXX is surprisingly

42. See G.K. Beale, *The Use of Daniel in Jewish Apocalyptic Literature and in the Revelation of St John* (Lanham, MD: University Press of America, 1984), pp. 13-14, on the fact that רז includes content and interpretation.

43. Compare Horgan, *Pesharim*, p. 237, who says that פשר corresponds to רז at Qumran.

loose in its choice of words. The LXX usually translates נלא with ἀνακαλύπτω (vv. 22, 28, 29) or ἐκφαίνω (vv. 19, 30, 47), two words which it seems to treat as synonyms. Once it also uses δηλόω (v. 47), even though that word has already been used extensively to represent both ידע and חוה. The result is that the distinction between divine revelation and the type on offer from the Chaldeans is not as clearly drawn in the LXX, nor is the impact of Nebuchadnezzar's confession heightened to the same extent. It is true that ἐκφαίνω in v. 47 may have particular revelatory connotations, but δηλόω (also v. 47) does not carry a specialized sense.

A further variation between the MT and LXX is in their observation of the distinction between 'dreams' and 'visions'. The two words used in the Aramaic section of Daniel are חזו ('vision') and חלם ('dream'), and their usage there suggests a distinction in meaning. Although any type of dream or vision in the night is regarded as communication from outside, חזו is used to denote visions that are explicitly from the God of Daniel as opposed to the 'dreams' the Babylonians have.[44] Daniel is the recipient of visions while Nebuchadnezzar has dreams. θ invariably translates חזו with ὅραμα and חלם with ἐνύπνιον, which suggests that a distinction between the two words was recognized and preserved in translation.[45]

The situation in the Hebrew chapters is not so clear cut. In biblical Hebrew the infrequently occurring מחזה carries the same sort of meaning as its Aramaic equivalent (Gen. 15.1; Job 7.14). Another word, משא, is peculiar to Isaiah and speaks of divine revelation through a prophetic utterance or oracle (Isa. 15.1; 21.11; 22.1; 23.1). The most common word is מראה which can denote a divine vision (Gen. 46.2, for example), but it can simply refer to a sight of some significance (for example, Deut. 28.67). Although חלם often carries the general meaning of its Aramaic counterpart, it is also used in parallel with מחזה in Job 7.14. Moreover, it is sometimes used on its own with the sense of divine revelation as is the case in Gen. 37.5-10. In the Hebrew of Daniel, חלם is not used in this way. In fact, in chs. 8–12 the only visions or dreams spoken of are the revelatory ones experienced by Daniel. Two words, מחזה (8.1, 2, 17, 26; 9.21, 24; 10.14) and מראה (8.16, 26, 27; 9.23; 10.7, 8, 16) are used in these chapters more or less synonymously. It would seem likely

---

44. According to Slotki, *Daniel*, p. 12, a vision is a revelation from God 'superior to that by a "dream"'.

45. Despite the observation by McCrystall, 'Daniel', p. 152, that ὅραμα and ἐνύπνιον are not wholly exclusive, they seem to be treated as distinctive terms by θ.

then that the same more secular understanding of חלם is preserved in the Hebrew section of Daniel.

The distinction between חלם and חזו becomes another means by which the MT portrays point of view in ch. 2. The conversation between Nebuchadnezzar and the wise men in the first nine verses is couched entirely in terms of the 'dream' (חלם, vv. 1-7, 9). Later on, when Daniel and Nebuchadnezzar discuss the latter's dream, they also speak of חלם (vv. 26, 36). Even at the end of the chapter when Daniel's intervention has turned the dream into a message from God, it is still only a 'dream' (v. 45). Daniel, on the other hand, perceived the dream and its interpretation through a 'vision' (v. 19, חזו). By his choice of the same vocabulary used predominantly in ch. 7 (7.1, 7, 13, 15) to denote Daniel's visions, the narrator reinforces the message that this vision comes from God.

Normally the LXX observes the same sort of differentiation in meaning. In ch. 4, at least where the LXX seems to represent the same material as the MT, the Aramaic חלם always has ἐνύπνιον (4.2/5, 15/18, 16/19) as its Greek counterpart. In ch. 7 'vision' (חזו) is always translated by ὅραμα. It may be no more than an inconsistency on the part of the translator, but in ch. 2 the LXX uses ἐνύπνιον and ὅραμα almost synonymously. As a result the LXX narrative does not deploy the words like its MT counterpart to distinguish point of view. The translator usually represents חלם with ἐνύπνιον, but not inevitably. In vv. 7, 26, 36 and 45 he uses ὅραμα, and in v. 1 the 'dreams' (חלמות) of the MT are 'visions and dreams' (ὁράματα καὶ ἐνύπνια) according to the LXX.

Narratorial Stance

A more obvious difference in the narrative technique of the versions occurs at v. 12. The Aramaic tells the reader that Nebuchadnezzar 'was angry and very furious' (בנס וקצף שׂגיא).[46] This is further confirmed by the ensuing extreme command issued by the king. While both verbs are rare in biblical Aramaic, their meanings are well attested in the Targums, and קצף is also a common word in biblical Hebrew. θ represents the hendiadys in the expected way with ἐν θυμῷ καὶ ὀργῇ πολλῇ. It could be argued that this is an overt statement on the part of the narrator,

---

46. One of several cases of hendiadys in ch. 2. Others may be found in vv. 9, 22 and 23. See Goldingay, *Daniel*, p. 43, for a comprehensive look at stylistic features of ch. 2.

although such emotion is normally clearly visible to the observer. However, the LXX suggests that the king 'became sad and in great sorrow...' (στυγνὸς γενόμενος καὶ περίλυπος). Although στυγνός can contain a sense of hostility in certain contexts, it also means 'sorrowful/gloomy'. The likelihood that it should be so understood here is heightened by its proximity to περίλυπος, which can only mean 'sorrow'. It is difficult to see how this interpretation by the LXX could be solely due to a misunderstanding of the MT.[47] Whatever its source, this depiction of the king's emotional state is something that owes more to the editorial omniscience of the narrator than to the observations of the reader. It is difficult also to see how sorrow gives rise to an order to massacre a whole raft of officialdom, unless it were at the thought of the resultant administrative chaos. But this is an exceptional case within ch. 2 and may well be a textual rather than a translational issue. It is nevertheless a further indication that within the same narrative structure as the MT, the LXX account does not exhibit the same degree of ambiguity and irony normally associated with covert narration in Daniel.

Literary Devices

One particular play on words in the MT is not available to the Greek versions. We have already seen the importance of the verb גלא (vv. 19, 22, 28, 30, 47) in the manipulation of point of view. In the *haphel* form it means to 'deport' just as its Hebrew equivalent does in the *hiphil*. The noun arising from this in the Aramaic is גלו, which means 'exile'. Daniel is himself identified by Arioch as one 'from the sons of the exile of Judah' (v. 25, מן־בני גלותא די יהוד). A verbal link is thereby made between God the revealer and Daniel the exile, through whom God is able to reveal. Despite a literal translation by the LXX (ἐκ τῆς αἰχμαλωσίας τῶν υἱῶν τῆς Ἰουδαίας), the link cannot be drawn in the Greek.

The LXX is also coy about the fate Nebuchadnezzar promises the wise men in the event of their failure. In the MT the king provides a vivid incentive for them with the promise that they will be 'made into limbs' (v. 5, הדמין תתעבדון) and their 'houses made a dung heap' (ובתיכון נולי יתשמון). The LXX holds out hope of a slightly longer future for them with the suggestion that in the event of failure 'you will be made an example of

---

47. Montgomery, *Daniel*, p. 153, wonders if the first element, בנס, has been read by LXX as נסס ('be sick, grieve'), but does not attempt to explain the presence of περίλυπος.

and your possessions will be taken into the king's treasury' (παραδειγματισθήσεσθε καὶ ἀναληφθήσεται ὑμῶν τὰ ὑπάρ-χοντα εἰς τὸ βασιλικόν). The imagery is not unique in the Aramaic of Daniel (see 3.29/96). θ translates it in ch. 3 almost exactly as he does in this verse, so the *Vorlage* was likely on both occasions to be what we now find in the MT. In ch. 3 the LXX translates 'dismembered' literally (διαμελισθήσεται) but shifts the fate of the property from destruction to confiscation. The evidence of ch. 3 indicates that the difference came about in the process of translation. Montgomery suggests that 'to be made an example of' came about through a reading of הדמין as a form of the verb דמה, while 'dunghill' was understood as 'booty' under the influence of an Arabic cognate.[48] Whatever the reasons for this interpretative translation, the evocative imagery of the MT is not a feature of the LXX at this point.

This is not to deny the art of the LXX translator, which shows in the occasional felicitously balanced phrasing that serves to emphasize and summarize the key issues. Such is the case with the contention that 'the vision is accurate and this interpretation trustworthy' (v. 45, ἀκριβὲς τὸ ὅραμα καὶ πιστὴ ἡ τούτου κρίσις). The same balance is evident in 4.27 and 6.13. A further link with those verses is also drawn through the use of ἀκριβής at the start of each of the phrases.

Interpretation of the Dream

Just as there are differences in literary effect between the MT and LXX, so there are variations in content. These could signify nothing more than a latitude in translation technique, but cumulatively they hint at significant differences between the versions. A close look at the dream and its interpretation provides some instances. Two small differences are most likely to be technical questions of translation or transmission. The rock not quarried by human hands struck the statue and then in the MT 'filled' (v. 35, מלה) all the earth. In the LXX, as well as striking the statue, it 'struck' (v. 35, ἐπάταξε) all the earth. This meaning does not seem to fit with the development of thought in Daniel's interpretation of the dream. That argument on its own is not compelling, as logic is not a reliable criterion by which to judge dreams, but it also denies the interpretation of the dream in both the MT and LXX. In the interpretation there is a distinction between the sovereignty represented by the image and

48. Montgomery, *Daniel*, pp. 148-49.

the subject of its rule, the earth. The rock not hewn by human hands has a double function, firstly to dethrone the image by striking it on its feet, and then to exercise its own sovereignty over the earth by filling it. The contest is not with the earth but with the image. This is confirmed by both versions in v. 44. To describe the stone as smashing both the statue and its subjects works against such use of the imagery. The possibilities of a different Aramaic *Vorlage* or a misreading of the MT remain speculative. It is more likely either that the earlier verb in v. 35 has been misapplied by the translator in the last part of the verse, or that the LXX has read מחת (v. 34) for מלת.[49]

Another difference of the same type is the inclusion by the MT of 'and toes' (v. 41, ואצבעתא) where the LXX makes no mention of them. Both versions devote v. 42 to the significance of the 'toes of the feet' (אצבעת רגליא in the MT, οἱ δάκτυλοι τῶν ποδῶν in the LXX). It has been suggested that v. 42 has been interpolated, perhaps to bring the vision into line with the ten horns of ch. 7 by reference to ten toes. Verse 41 has therefore been amended by the addition of ואצבעתא, so the argument goes, and its absence in the LXX is evidence of that process.[50] If the LXX is a translation of a *Vorlage* that contains the toes and their significance, this argument breaks down. And such seems to be the case in that v. 42 in Greek is syntactically close to the Aramaic. This is strikingly the case in that the construct relationship between the toes and the feet in the MT is also represented in the LXX, despite the fact that they are simply linked by ו in the previous verse. It is therefore possible that the LXX was translating a *Vorlage* which did not include ואצבעתא in v. 41, and that the variation has arisen in the transmission of the MT. There need not be a problem with extra detail inserted into the interpretation that was not included in the original revelation. The same phenomenon is observable in ch. 5 as well as the interpretation of Daniel's vision in ch. 7.[51]

A more extensive variation is found in v. 40, but again the difference does not have literary consequences. At one level it could be seen as an attempt to tidy up what is generally reckoned to be a corrupt verse in

49. Montgomery, *Daniel*, p. 171, prefers the latter explanation.

50. This argument is epitomized by Hartman and DiLella, *Daniel*, p. 141. Stuart, *Daniel*, p. 65, in a much earlier commentary, also connects the ten toes with the ten horns of ch. 7.

51. See again Eissfeldt, 'Die Menetekel-Inschrift', p. 112, who calls this a feature of style.

the MT. This, however, does not account for the appearance from nowhere of the phrase 'hews down every tree' (v. 40, πᾶν δένδρον ἐκκόπτων). The explanation offered by Charles is that כל־אלין in the MT has been misread by either the translator of the LXX or the producer of his *Vorlage* as כל־אילן.[52] Again the difference probably has a technical explanation.

It is tempting to cite the LXX rendering of v. 29 as evidence of an extended interpretation of the dream in the mind of the translator. Where the MT speaks of 'what will happen after this' (v. 29, מה די להוא אחרי דנה) the LXX has what appears to be the somewhat stronger expression, 'which must happen at the last days' (v. 29, ὅσα δεῖ γενέσθαι ἐπ' ἐσχάτων τῶν ἡμερῶν).[53] Is this evidence of a more eschatological focus on the part of the LXX, which sees the statue struck by the rock as a series of kingdoms rather than a single entity? Do the differences between the versions therefore represent the same opinions that have divided commentators ever since?[54] Any answer must include an exploration of the uses of δεῖ and ἔσχατος. The former could introduce a suggestion of a predetermined course of action into the text, but in fact its use in the LXX is not always particularly deterministic. There is no syntactical equivalent of the impersonal δεῖ in Hebrew or Aramaic and its appearance is often an attempt to translate the Hebrew construction of ל plus the infinitive as an expression of necessity (for example, Est. 1.15). It is possible that the sight of the irregular Aramaic form להוא has brought forth that sort of translation.

The use of ἔσχατος in Greek tends to have a more absolute than relative sense, in that it refers to the last rather than the latter things. That is certainly the sense conveyed in the New Testament and appropriated by Christian usage. However, that can be misleading when it comes to discerning meaning in the LXX. Its numerous appearances in

52. Charles, *Daniel*, p. 48.
53. Bruce, 'Oldest Greek Version', p. 24, maintains that δεῖ here implies necessity.
54. See Montgomery, *Daniel*, pp. 185-92, for an extended treatment. Goldingay, *Daniel*, pp. 57-61, considers that 'The statue represents the empire led by Nebuchadnezzar. It is a single statue, a single empire...' Many modern commentators agree. Lacocque, *Daniel*, p. 51, however, considers that 'les perspectives dernières' are not entirely absent. Jephet, *Daniel*, p. 13, as well as Young, *Daniel*, p. 78, represent a more eschatological interpretation. More recently E.C. Lucas, 'The Origin of Daniel's Four Empires Schemes Re-Examined', *TynBul* 40 (1989), p. 194, speaks of a 'Jewish perception of history' in Daniel 2 and 7.

Septuagintal Greek usually represent some form of the Hebrew or Aramaic אחר. This root has a wider range of meaning than ἔσχατος, and can take both ultimate and relative senses. The LXX tends to use a form of ἔσχατος in both senses, and so the word in the LXX has come to reflect the same range of meaning as אחר.[55] By and large it appears in Aramaic either as a feminine noun in the construct state (אחרית), which normally carries an absolute meaning, or as the prepositional אחרי, which simply means 'after'. In Hebrew the grammatical range is wider, including adjectival, adverbial and various nominal forms, sometimes with an eschatological and sometimes with a temporal sense. For example, the good wife of Proverbs 31 looks ahead in a purely secular sense 'to the days to come' (Prov. 31.25, ליום אחרין), whereas the song of Moses in Deuteronomy 32 looks ahead to 'the end' (Deut. 32.20, אחריתם). The LXX uses ἔσχατος in both contexts. It was the most appropriate option available to both the LXX and θ when they encountered the preposition אחרי, as they have done in vv. 29 and 45. They could have used μετά but that would not have quite captured the forward-looking nature of אחרי, or its significance as a word used on important occasions. In the Hebrew sections of Daniel, אחר appears in the form of the feminine noun and reflects a sense of finality (8.19, 23; 10.14; 11.29; 12.8).

Daniel 2 MT is not clear whether the events of the vision represent the end or the next stage. Whereas v. 28 speaks with some finality of 'the end of the days' (באחרית יומיא), vv. 29 and 45 in the MT simply speak of what will be 'after these things' (אחרי דנה).[56] The LXX or its *Vorlage* is identical to the MT at v. 28 with ἐπ' ἐσχάτων τῶν ἡμερῶν. However, it retains that reading for the rest of the chapter where the MT has the weaker sense. This comes about partly because the LXX has followed the lead provided by Septuagintal Greek in using ἔσχατος to translate אחרי. The continuing inclusion of τῶν ἡμερῶν as a plus, however, at least suggests a predilection on the part of the LXX for seeing the vision in terms of the last days rather than the next days.[57] It seems to be something more than a careless lapse into an expression encountered earlier in the chapter. While it is certain that ἔσχατος can bear eschatological implications in the LXX, as it clearly does in Sir. 48.24 for example, to

55. See Walters, *The Text of the Septuagint*, pp. 143ff., on this phenomenon.
56. Collins, *Apocalyptic Vision*, p. 41, notes the tension and explains it as a Babylonian oracle glorifying Nebuchadnezzar modified by Jewish redaction.
57. Collins, *Daniel*, p. 8, normally cautious on the degree of *Tendenz* discernible in the Old Greek, countenances the possibility.

suggest that it does so particularly in the LXX pluses in question remains only a possibility. This possibility is further explored in the context of possible differences in theology and provenance.

Differences in Theological Outlook

Because the LXX story is closer to the MT in ch. 2 than in chs. 3–6, there is not the same opportunity for the LXX to exhibit an independent point of view. There are, however, several differences that together reflect the same ideology that has been observed elsewhere. First of all, 'the gods' (v. 11, אלהין) become 'an angel' (ἄγγελος) in the LXX. Apart from that, the two versions of v. 11 are in substantial agreement with one another. Even the unusual phrase in the MT, 'whose dwelling is not with flesh' (די מדרהון עם־בשרא לא איתוהי) is only slightly different in the LXX (οὗ οὐκ ἔστι κατοικητήριον μετὰ πάσης σαρκός). This makes it likely that the change occurred at the point of translation. It is a surprising one because the speakers are the Chaldeans, and there can hardly be an objection to their espousal of a polytheistic perspective. It would seem that the LXX is so alert to departures in the text from strict monotheism that it amends אלהין wherever it is encountered, even when it is spoken by pagans. The same thing happens to the words of King Nebuchadnezzar at 3.25/92, where he says in the LXX that the fourth figure in the furnace was like 'an angel of God' (ἀγγέλου θεοῦ). The MT equivalent is 'a son of the gods' (בר־אלהין). The more monotheistic stance of the LXX is similarly demonstrated at 3.28/95 and 6.28.

This stance also appears in the LXX's ascription of titles to God.[58] We have already noted a tendency on the part of the LXX to use κύριος when talking of or to God (3.28/95, for example).[59] The same tendency is noticeable in ch. 2 at vv. 18 and 37.[60] In both cases the MT reads 'God of heaven' (אלה שמיא), probably a term used in the Persian diaspora, while the LXX has the variant equivalent 'the Lord Most High' (v. 18, τοῦ κυρίου τοῦ ὑψίστου) or 'the Lord of heaven' (v. 37, ὁ κύριος

---

58. The reading by M.J. Davidson, *Angels at Qumran: A Comparative Study of 1 Enoch 1–36, 72–108, and Sectarian Writings from Qumran* (Sheffield: JSOT Press, 1992), p. 86 n. 3, of vv. 27-28 MT as a monotheistic statement is unconvincing.

59. Schmitt, 'Die griechischen Danieltexte', p. 20.

60. See the discussion of Jeansonne, *Daniel 7–12*, pp. 63-64. She notes the LXX rendering in 2.28 as an exception to this tendency.

τοῦ οὐρανοῦ).[61] In vv. 20 and 23 also the LXX substitutes κύριος for אלה.

In that connection another expression that merits attention is the title 'king of kings' (v. 37, מלך מלכיא) ascribed by Daniel to King Nebuchadnezzar.[62] Given the LXX's suspicion of any divinity being attributed to the king, particularly as demonstrated in chs. 3 and 6, it is surprising that this expression also occurs in the Old Greek.[63] The argument that it is merely a conventional Persian form of address is a convincing one as far as the Aramaic is concerned.[64] It is a title assumed by Artaxerxes in Ezra 7.12, and it is given to Nebuchadrezzar by God himself in Ezek. 26.7, so it is likely that Daniel was using it as nothing more than a polite form.[65] In both places it is witnessed to in the LXX translation, although the syntax surrounding the Ezekiel reference indicates a parenthetical function for the title.[66] In the light of this rather scarce evidence it would appear that the LXX accepts the Aramaic terminology in the spirit with which it was offered by Daniel.

The LXX's acceptance of Nebuchadnezzar's extravagant response to Daniel's success is even more of a puzzle. Not only does the king fall on his face and 'worship' (v. 46, סגד) the sage, but he calls on those present to perform cultic rites in Daniel's honour. סגד is the same word used throughout ch. 3 (vv. 5-7, 10-12, 14, 15, 18, 28) to describe the homage paid to the statue. While the exact object of their worship remains an open question in ch. 3 MT, the dominant sense of the word in later Aramaic as well as biblical Hebrew has to do with worship, and the same is likely to be true of the Aramaic in Daniel.[67] It is inescapable here that the king is offering the kind of homage due to divinity while

---

61. See Stefanovic, *The Aramaic of Daniel*, p. 49, on the parallel from Tell Fekherye. See also Montgomery, *Daniel*, p. 159, Lacocque, *Daniel*, p. 44, Hartman and DiLella, *Daniel*, p. 139, and Bevan, *Daniel*, p. 72. Hanhart, 'The Translation of the Septuagint', p. 348, explains the LXX variation as a response to the syncretistic possibilities of a more literal translation (such as that of θ) in a Hellenist environment.

62. Montgomery, *Daniel*, p. 171.

63. Slotki, *Daniel*, p. 37, records the rabbinic reinterpretation of this verse: 'the king of kings who is the God of heaven'.

64. Lacocque, *Daniel*, p. 44. Wiseman, *Nebuchadrezzar*, p. 41, deems it not unlikely that Nebuchadnezzar described himself thus.

65. Heaton, *Daniel*, p. 131.

66. Rahlfs's brackets around the phrase indicate the same.

67. See Mastin, 'Daniel 2.46', p. 82, and Lacocque, *Daniel*, p. 52.

Daniel remains unperturbed about this state of affairs.[68] The LXX makes no attempt to modify the king's extravagance in so doing. The translation of v. 46 is close to the Aramaic in the MT, including the use of προσκυνέω to represent סגד. The Greek even more firmly demands a divine object for the verb. It is the word used throughout ch. 3 as equivalent to סגד, and almost without exception in the Old Greek translation of biblical Hebrew it translates the *hithpael* השתחוה with its strong connotations of bowing down in worship of divinity. This usage of προσκυνέω is well illustrated in both versions of Bel and the Dragon (v. 4) where the worship of Bel by the king and God by Daniel is couched in the same terms.

The problem is not so much that Daniel is worshipped by Nebuchadnezzar, as that he does not demur on finding himself the object of such homage. The usual explanation is that in his limited pagan understanding Nebuchadnezzar perceives Daniel's God through Daniel, and so worships Daniel as the human representative.[69] This is understood by Daniel to be the case hence no objection is made. The argument goes that the king's subsequent words to Daniel, 'your God is the God of gods' (v. 47, אלהכון הוא אלה אלהין) makes clear his line of thought.[70] He offers homage to Daniel because Daniel's God is worthy of it. According to Josephus a parallel incident took place in the career of Alexander when he entered Jerusalem.[71] On first entering the city he 'prostrated himself before the Name' (προσεκύνησε τὸ ὄνομα) on the high priest's mitre. He then explained that it was not the high priest he worshipped but the God he represented. That the LXX also witnesses to a text very close to the MT in v. 47 suggests that the LXX follows this line of thought.

It is also possible that the LXX merely reflects the ambiguity of Daniel's response to royal rewards that is seen in other stories. In ch. 5 Daniel scorns Belshazzar's promise of a reward, yet later accepts the same despite his message that the kingdom is essentially finished (5.29). In this instance Daniel identifies Nebuchadnezzar as the head of gold while ignoring, deliberately or not, the irony that at another level the interpretation dooms the entity of which the king is the present head. He

---

68. The medieval commentators all struggled with the problem. Rashi, in Gallé, *Daniel*, p. 28, solves it by believing that Daniel did not accept the king's worship.
69. For example Montgomery, *Daniel*, p. 181.
70. Goldingay, *Daniel*, p. 52.
71. Josephus, *Ant*. 11.331-35.

then accepts promotion in that entity. In both of these cases the LXX also accepts the stance adopted by Daniel towards the Gentile sovereign.

Differing Traditions about Daniel and Nebuchadnezzar

My comparison of the interpretation of the dream above hinted that the LXX understands Nebuchadnezzar's dream in more eschatological terms, as compared to the MT's more political outlook. The possibility becomes more likely when the greater differences in provenance are examined.[72] Earlier in the present chapter I argued that the LXX plus reference to fasting (v. 18) does not imply a different function for the song of praise in the LXX. It does, however, provide a starting point for a discussion on provenance, as it hints at a different view on the role of Daniel lurking behind the LXX translation. Fasting in the Old Testament is only occasionally an individual activity. Such is the case when David manifests grief for his dead child (2 Sam. 12.16) and in the Psalms (Pss. 34/35.13; 68.11/69.10; 108/109.24). Usually a fast is something that the leader of a community calls and the implementation of the order is a communal activity. This is certainly so in the late biblical and apocryphal instances cited in our earlier discussion (2 Chron. 20.3; 1 Esd. 8.50; 2 Macc. 13.12). When the fasting is an expression of repentance at Neh. 9.1 it is also something called by the leadership of Israel. This aspect of the calling of the fast is not so apparent in the prophetic references, but the later prophetic traditions in particular mention fasting as if it were a communal or national activity (Zech. 7.5; 8.19; Isa. 58, for example).

Daniel's calling of a fast implies an audience much wider than the three companions, and suggests that the architect of the LXX envisages him already in a position of leadership within the exilic community of Jews. There are further hints in the comparison of the MT and LXX in ch. 2 that this might be the case. The ones in danger in the MT are 'Daniel and his companions' (v. 18, דניאל וחברוהי). Following as it does the description of Hananiah, Azariah and Mishael as 'his companions' (v. 17, חברוהי), this reference can only apply to the three young men.

---

72. The difference between ארמית ('Aramaic') and Συριστί ('Syriac') in v. 4 is of no significance. This is the standard LXX translation (see 4 Kgdms 18.26, Ezra 4.7 and Isa. 36.11). Indeed ארם is often translated with Σύρια, and ארמי usually with σύρος in the Septuagint. Josephus, *Ant.* 1.144, tells us of 'Αραμαίους...οὕς "Ελληνες Σύρους προσαγορεύουσιν ('Arameans...whom the Greeks term Syrians').

However, in the LXX the targets of Nebuchadnezzar's wrath are 'Daniel and those with him' (v. 18, Δανιηλ καὶ οἱ μετ' αὐτοῦ). They are described in similar terms in v. 13. There is no evidence within the story that the three companions are the same ones as those who are with Daniel. Indeed the LXX concurs with the MT in describing the three as Daniel's 'companions' (v. 17, συνεταίροις), as distinct from οἱ μετ' αὐτοῦ. The link then between vv. 17 and 18 is that after sharing the problem with his three companions, Daniel declares a fast for the whole threatened community. This is quite different from the link in the MT necessitated by the repetition of חברוהי. It is also different from the reference in 3.49 to 'those with Azariah' (τοῖς περὶ τὸν Ἀζαριαν). The choice of preposition is not the same and the referent is clearly the companions who entered the fire with Azariah.

The picture of Daniel as an established leader amongst the exiles is reinforced by Arioch's description of Daniel to the king in the LXX. There Arioch tells the king that he has found among the exiles of Judah 'a wise man' (v. 25, ἄνθρωπον σοφόν). In the MT he merely finds a man among the exiles. Therefore the promotion of Daniel in the LXX is from a leader of the exiles to leader of the wise men in Babylon, whereas his promotion in the MT is from one of the exiles to a leader in the empire. One consequence of this view is that the contest element is played down in the LXX, just as it is entirely absent in chs. 4 and 5 in comparison to the MT.

It cannot be denied that this strand of Daniel as an already established member of the group labeled 'wise men' (חכים) is also present in the MT. The law goes out to kill the wise men of Babylon (v. 12), the killing commences (v. 13a) 'and' (ו) Daniel and his companions are recognized as part of the target group for the king's assassins (v. 13b). Verse 18 is more explicit with its reference to 'with the rest of the wise men of Babylon' (עם־שאר חכימי בבל). However all of those references are from the inserted vv. 13-23. The LXX translation of those verses brings no change to the view of Daniel's position, but highlights it further in the remainder of the chapter.

The same process was discernible in previous chapters studied where issues of individual Jewish conduct in exile are reinterpreted in terms of the Jewish nation. The tradition of leadership of the exiles occurs in θ at the end of ch. 3 where the three young men are promoted with special responsibility for the Jews in the kingdom (3.30/97). The Greek Additions show a concern for the fate of the nation and contain images related to the cult, as well as showing a tendency to Hebraize the characters of the three companions. The Daniel of ch. 6 LXX has been noted as a precursor to the tradition of Zerubbabel as leader of the exilic community (1 Esd. 4.47-63). Daniel's qualities as a wise man are similarly emphasized by the LXX in 5.11-12. In short, the Daniel of the LXX is the one who began his career among the Jews in the story of Susanna, which sets the scene for all these other stories in the canonical tradition of the LXX.[73]

The MT and the LXX also diverge in their treatment of Nebuchadnezzar. In v. 38 MT the function of the opening phrase ובכל־די דארין is not entirely clear. It could be the object of יהב, with the subsequent list in apposition. However, in that case the ב in בכל is a problem as it does not normally indicate the object of יהב. It could express 'amongst all that live, he has given...' as a way of emphasizing God's choice of Nebuchadnezzar. The latter emphasis also results when the phrase is read with the first item in the list, 'sons of men' (בני־אנשא), to give an opening 'Out of all the sons of men who live...' While none of these solutions are flawless, they all view Nebuchadnezzar's dominion over creation on a level with his sovereignty over his human subjects. Grammatically, apart from its placing at the head of the list, 'sons of men' (בני־אנשא) is in the same category as 'beasts of the field' (חיות ברא) and 'birds of heaven' (עוף שמיא). In contrast the LXX does not represent the ו at the beginning of the verse and so connects the first phrase with what has preceded it in v. 37. The effect of this syntactical difference is to distinguish the sovereignty exercised by Nebuchadnezzar over his human subjects from his dominion over nature, and to make the MT more interested than the LXX in his role in creation as a whole.

This may seem a far-fetched suggestion in the face of such a small difference. However, it does tally with more definite variations in the Nebuchadnezzar tradition elsewhere. In an MT plus at Jer. 28/35.14 God promises that 'even the beasts of the field have I given to him (Nebuchadnezzar)' (וגם את־חית השדה נתתי לו). The LXX stops at 'all the nations' (πάντων τῶν ἐθνῶν). In the previous chapter the MT has another plus phrase, 'the people and the animals who are upon the face of the earth' (Jer. 27/34.5, את־האדם ואת־הבהמה אשר על־פני הארץ). The placing of את makes it clear that the phrase is in the same grammatical relationship to the verb as הארץ and so is an expansion of הארץ. The LXX

---

73. It is the view of Müller, 'Mantische Weisheit', p. 290, that the wisdom of Daniel in Susanna is different in kind from that conveyed by the MT.

does not have this phrase which makes explicit that Nebuchadnezzar's dominion will also be over nature. It is closer to the MT in the next verse, but even there the syntax of the LXX preserves the distinction between human and animal subjects. The MT gives 'all these lands' (Jer. 27/34.6, כל־הארצות האלה) to Nebuchadnezzar as well as 'the beasts of the field' (חית השדה), all of whom together are 'to serve him' (לעבדו). Both beasts and lands function as the subject of the infinitive.[74] In contrast the LXX maintains a distinction by assigning separate verbs to each of 'the earth' and 'the beasts of the field'. The earth is 'to serve him' (δουλεύειν αὐτῷ) while the beasts are 'to work for him' (ἐργάζεσθαι αὐτῷ). The LXX approaches the issue in less universalistic and more nationalistic terms than is the case in the MT. This same difference in tradition may well be hinted at in Dan. 2.38.

Differing Historical Backgrounds

Another variation likely to reflect a difference in historical traditions may be found in v. 43.[75] In question is the significance of iron mixed with clay and the resultant fragility. According to the MT this fore-shadows a kingdom which will be mixed 'by the seed of men' (בזרע אנשא) and the two parts will not 'cleave' (דבק) to one another. θ preserves equivalence of elements in his translation of these phrases with ἐν σπέρματι ἀνθρώπων and a participial form of προσκολλάω. The picture is most likely to be one of mixed marriage.[76] That is clearly what is meant by the mixing of seed in Ezra 9.2. The verb דבק, although unique here in biblical Aramaic, is commonly used in biblical Hebrew of

---

74. See the discussions of Jer. 27/34 by Tov, 'Exegetical Notes', pp. 84-93, and McKane, 'Jeremiah 27.5-8', pp. 98-110.

75. The dating of chs. 3 and 4 by the LXX provided some clues as to the translator's intentions. In ch. 2 the dates are identical so no help is forthcoming from that quarter. Even if the 967 reading of δωδεκάτω (v. 11, 'twelfth') instead of δευτέρῳ ('second') is correct, that in itself does not provide a clue, although it does create a parallel with the dating in Jdt. 1.1 and 2.1 which would be worth further investigation. The δωδεκάτω reading provides a nice progression in chs. 2–4, but does not tie events to a significant part of Nebuchadnezzar's reign in the way that 'the eighteenth year' (3.1; 4.4 LXX) does. Hamm, *Daniel Kap 1–2*, pp. 140-42, con-siders the 88-Syh reading is a correction towards the MT. See also Hartman and DiLella, *Daniel*, p. 138, on the 967 dating.

76. Goldingay, *Daniel*, p. 36, says the phrase 'more naturally denotes intermarriage'.

marriage or loyalty within a binding relationship (for example, Gen. 2.24; Ruth 1.14). Commentators are divided over whether the use of דבק in v. 43 reflects a particular historical relationship or a general policy of the mingling of nationalities within an empire.[77] θ's translation indicates that he read it as a reference to a particular alliance through marriage. The LXX, however, renders the verse in less relational language. The mixture of iron and earthenware signifies the mingling of 'races of men' (γένεσιν ἀνθρώπων). The consequent weakness arises because they are not 'in harmony nor well-disposed to one another' (ὁμονοοῦντες οὔτε εὐνοοῦτες ἀλλήλοις). This phrase is more descriptive of relations between groups of people than of marriage.

The majority opinion is that the MT represents political marriages between the Seleucids and Ptolemies, which of course were notably unsuccessful in bringing about harmony.[78] If that is the case, the events envisaged would have taken place in either 250 or 193 BCE.[79] Another view is that it refers to Alexander's policy of intermarriage with the Persians as a way of encouraging the conglomeration of races within the empire. This latter view allows for a late Persian provenance, although the choice of relational vocabulary by the MT makes this possible rather than probable. The former view reflects more accurately the spirit of disharmony within the empire that is crucial to Daniel's interpretation of the dream of the statue. At the same time it is a more likely explanation of the marriage imagery implied by the MT.

The question then arises as to what particular situation may be behind the interpretative translation on the part of the LXX. Disharmony between races of people can be found in any era, and the most that can be said is that the LXX version of this chapter arose in a period when intermarriage was not a particular feature of troubled relationships between races. In that case the problems the Seleucids had with Egypt and the Jews around the time of the Maccabean revolt could form the backdrop to the LXX. Such a view is consistent with the Jewish reinterpretation of Nebuchadnezzar, possibly as a product of the struggles with Antiochus IV already noted. It must be emphasized that the text of the

---

77. Porteous, *Daniel*, pp. 49-50, takes issue with the interpretation of Montgomery, *Daniel*, p. 190, that the phrase represents Alexander's policy of 'the fusion of races and cultures'.

78. See, for example, Delcor, *Daniel*, p. 86.

79. Torrey, 'Notes', p. 248. But compare J.J. Collins, *The Apocalyptic Imagination* (New York: Crossroad, 1984), p. 77.

LXX allows for this sort of provenance, but by no means requires it. It is, however, consistent with trends that have been noted in chs. 3–6, and with the slightly more absolute understanding of what happens 'after these things' in the LXX.

At the same time, whatever is chosen as the historical referent of בזרע אנשא, it almost certainly refers to events much earlier than the mid-second century BCE, even if vv. 40-43 are taken to have been subject to later amendment.[80] In its canonical setting it is part of an unmistakably Persian context, as a comparison of the use of administrative terms in the MT and LXX shows. In my discussion of ch. 3 I suggested that the phrase 'high officials of the province' (3.2, שלטני מדינתא), rather than being a summary of the preceding items in the list, is a group of centralized officials, and that מדינתא is in fact a province within the wider Persian empire. The other officials function in the outlying provincial units. This terminology seems to be present also at the end of ch. 2. Daniel becomes 'ruler over the whole province of Babylon' (v. 48, השלפה על כל־מדינת בבל) as well as a 'chief prefect' (רב־סגנין) over the wise men. Both of these are terms reminiscent of chs. 3 and 6 in particular. Shadrach, Meshach and Abednego have a slightly different function, probably in a provincial unit of the empire.[81]

The LXX does not make these distinctions. It gives no particular title to the promoted Daniel, but instead makes the descriptive statement that Nebuchadnezzar 'set him up over the affairs of Babylon' (v. 48, κατέστησεν ἐπὶ τῶν πραγμάτων τῆς Βαβυλωνίας). Similarly, his function with respect to the wise men is described in general terms as 'ruler and leader' (ἄρχοντα καὶ ἡγούμενον), the same terms used of him in 4.18 LXX. Moreover, no distinction is made between Daniel whom the king 'set up over the affairs of Babylon' (v. 48, κατέστησεν ἐπὶ τῶν πραγμάτων Βαβυλωνίας), and his three companions who also 'were set up over the affairs of Babylon' (v. 49, κατασταθῶσιν ἐπὶ τῶν πραγμάτων τῆς Βαβυλωνίας). θ shows the same lack of awareness of the technical terms as the LXX. This is apparent in v. 48 where θ calls Daniel a 'ruler of the satraps' (ἄρχοντα σατραπῶν), while the MT terms him 'chief of the prefects' (רב־סגנין).

---

80. For his part Torrey, 'Notes', p. 246, opines that the Aramaic vv. 40-43 show no acquaintance with the Seleucids or Maccabees. But compare again Collins, *Apocalyptic Imagination*, p. 77.

81. Jephet, *Daniel*, p. 15, says the promotion of Daniel's companions is an 'introduction to the sequel'.

Conclusion: Links with Daniel 3–6

It is generally recognized that ch. 2 is in some measure different from the other Aramaic stories about Daniel's relationships with his sovereigns. Often this is expressed as a consequence of its obvious links with the only vision of Daniel conveyed in Aramaic, ch. 7. Lenglet's analysis of these two chapters as the outer pair in a chiasm has won widespread acceptance.[82] However, he also notes that they are in a contrast as much as in parallel.[83] The parallels with ch. 7 will become apparent in the next chapter. The contrasts may be seen in that, as well as being set apart from chs. 3–6, ch. 2 has much in common with them and in some respects is in continuity with them. Much of the discussion of this chapter has pointed up that continuity in imagery, narrative technique, provenance and theology.

The nature of this relationship between ch. 2 and chs. 3–6 is debatable. Goldingay encapsulates the debate with the comment, 'it might be that these chapters depend on chap. 2, but it is simpler to assume that chap. 2 was written in the light of those other chapters...'[84] In fact, outside vv. 13-23 and 40-43, there is little support for that assumption. Even regarding vv. 40-43 opinions are divided over the type of date required by the application of the iron and earthenware imagery. The bulk of the chapter demonstrates a Persian setting which makes it contemporary with chs. 3–6.[85] In literary terms, we have also seen how the ambiguities resident in the responses of Daniel and Nebuchadnezzar to the dream of the statue look forward to subsequent stories for their resolution. The assumption that ch. 2 is later perhaps partly arises because it is a different genre from chs. 3–6. It explores the difference between

82. The idiosyncratic structure offered by D.W. Gooding, 'The Literary Structure of the Book of Daniel and its Implications', *TynBul* 32 (1981), pp. 60-62, agrees with Lenglet on no other point than that chs. 2 and 7 belong together.

83. Lenglet, 'Daniel 2–7', p. 180. See also Collins, *Apocalyptic Vision*, pp. 13-19, and Davies, *Daniel*, p. 44.

84. Goldingay, *Daniel*, p. 38. Collins, *Daniel*, p. 174, posits an early Hellenist date for ch. 2, whereas he sets the basis of chs. 4–6 in Persian times. On ch. 3 he is not so sure.

85. Davies, *Daniel*, p. 48, dates the original from the early years of Cyrus. M. McNamara, 'Nabonidus and the Book of Daniel', *ITQ* 137 (1970), p. 149, notes the 'intense oriental colouring' of the traditions enshrined in Dan. 2–6 MT, which he attributes to its 'eastern origin'. See also Millard, 'Daniel 1–6', p. 73, on the 'high proportion of correct detail' in the court scenes in Daniel.

human and divine wisdom, whereas the succeeding chapters focus more on the temporal relationships between the king and his subjects who belong also to the Jewish faithful.[86] That does not mean that it has to belong to a different era.

However, there is evidence that vv. 13-23 do belong to a period closer to, although probably not concurrent with, the times reflected in ch. 7 and the Septuagintal translations of chs. 3–6.[87] As a result, the probable *Vorlage* of the LXX had already been partly adjusted towards a Hellenistic setting, and the process of redefining the exilic Daniel stories to fit the later Jewish interest in cult and nation had begun.[88] That the adjustment is only partial is illustrated by the difference in focus between the song of vv. 20-23 and the song of praise in the Greek Additions in ch. 3. Even so, it is not surprising that the result is a translation closer to the Aramaic in ch. 2 than in chs. 3–6. This means that many of the literary aspects of the Aramaic are also present in the Old Greek. At times the nature of such a translation even results in a relaxation of LXX's vigilance in promoting monotheism and denying the divinity of kings. Nevertheless, it is still possible to detect in its translation of the older material of ch. 2, characteristics in LXX that are much more obvious in chs. 3–6. The LXX's inability to translate the Persian Babylonian backdrop is a case in point, as is its preference for κύριος and suspicion of the plural אלהין. The concern about a distinct Jewish community in hostile surroundings and the more nationalistic interpretation of Nebuchadnezzar also relates to the interest of the LXX in the Jewish cult and nation.

86. J.J. Collins, 'The Court-Tales in Daniel and the Development of Apocalyptic', *JBL* 94 (1975), p. 222.

87. Anderson, *Daniel*, p. 16.

88. Goldingay, *Daniel*, p. 48, speaks of a shift from 'empirical... knowledge' to 'supernatural insight' brought about by the insertion of vv. 20-23. Hammer, *Daniel*, p. 26, notes the beginnings of 'the transcendent character of wisdom' characteristic of later wisdom. Gammie, 'Intention and Sources', p. 292, in the context of his discussion on the influence of Deutero-Isaiah on Daniel, sees in Daniel a link between wisdom and apocalyptic.

Chapter 7

DANIEL 7

There is a marked shift in genre between chs. 6 and 7 in the MT of Daniel. The interpreter becomes the dreamer, stories give way to visions, and the political concerns of earlier chapters are overtaken by the future orientation of apocalyptic.[1] It is also clear that ch. 7 occupies a 'pivotal position' in the received form of the book of Daniel.[2] As well as looking forward to chs. 8–12 in its introduction of the vision genre, it is also linked back to the stories of Jewish heroes in foreign courts. This is most obvious in its use of the Aramaic language, but there are a number of literary and thematic links with the stories that go far beyond the sharing of a common language. The focus of this chapter on Daniel 7 will be more on what has gone before that pivotal position than what is yet to come in the visions.

The first sight that meets the eye in that look backwards is Daniel 2, and my approach to Daniel 7 takes up where the discussion of Daniel 2 left off. We have seen that an adjustment towards a more Hellenistic setting and a shift in emphasis is evident in ch. 2, particularly in vv. 13-23. The process of redefining the exilic Daniel in terms of Jewish cult and nation has begun. The result in ch. 2 was a LXX translation that reflected a *Vorlage* much closer to the Aramaic of the MT than was the case in the other narratives. I suggested that at least vv. 13-23 of Daniel 2 reflected a period closer to that behind Daniel 7 and the Septuagintal translations of chs. 3–6 than the Persian setting evident elsewhere in the stories. Once we come to ch. 7, with the exception of the transitional v. 1 which sets Daniel's vision in the reign of Belshazzar, the Persian

---

1.   Heaton, *Daniel*, p. 186.

2.   Davies, *Daniel*, p. 58. See also P.R. Raabe, 'Daniel 7: Its Structure and Role in the Book', *HAR* 9 (1985), p. 271, and Rowley, 'The Unity of the Book of Daniel', p. 250. David, 'Composition and Structure', p. 97 treats ch. 7 as the 'literary hinge' on which the book swings.

diaspora is not a factor. Interest is much more in the identity of the Jewish people as a nation and the threat to their nationhood and cult (v. 24). The seer is most concerned about the fourth beast and particularly the extra horn, because he locates therein the immediate threat to the holy ones. These are concerns that I have also attributed to the Old Greek translator in chs. 2–6, so it is not surprising that the LXX and the MT are even closer to one another than was the case with Daniel 2.

As a result, the bulk of the variations between the MT and LXX can be explained on technical grounds and do not entail a change in meaning between the versions. There are, however, still some differences that are noteworthy. To demonstrate this I compare the narrative structures of the two versions and especially their handling of the hidden personae behind the autobiographical account. In connection with that, a literary device linking the vision and its interpretation is also explored, and a possible difference in the way the two narrators view Daniel is noted. The greater part of this treatment of ch. 7, though, deals with issues of content and meaning. Variations that are best accounted for on technical grounds and do not entail a change in meaning between versions are enumerated first. I then centre the comparative work on the key figures of the son of man, the holy ones, and the four beasts, and on how the elements of vision and interpretation relate to one another. This leads in to the final part of the chapter, where I draw out the main literary and thematic links between ch. 7 and the other Aramaic narratives. One area where there is a substantial difference between the MT and LXX is in the way the versions give an overall structure to Daniel 2–7, and that forms the final part of the discussion on links.

The vast secondary literature on this particular chapter of the Bible witnesses to the number and complexity of exegetical issues it presents. Many of them do not admit of easy solutions, as the literature amply demonstrates. The primary aim of this treatment of Daniel 7 is not to solve all the exegetical problems. A full attempt to do so would swamp the main purpose, which is to explore the interaction between the Aramaic and Greek from a narrative perspective. However, a necessary backdrop to that is a summary of the issues surrounding the Ancient of Days, the son of man, the holy ones of the Most High, and the unity or otherwise of the chapter.[3] The last of those entails a close look at the

---

3.   Since I follow the practice of capitalizing names for the deity, I shall capitalize Ancient of Days in line with my view that he is a divine figure. I leave son of man uncapitalized because I argue that the figure in Dan. 7.13 is primarily human.

place of vv. 21-22 in the chapter. As v. 13 is central to several of the questions, I am also compelled to consider the most likely Old Greek form of that verse in light of the evidence in 967. I state the position I take regarding these matters for the purpose of the ensuing discussion, but other issues are treated in detail only to the extent that they are germane to the particular perspective of this study.

The Ancient of Days in the Masoretic Text

A discussion of the Ancient of Days figure in Daniel 7 inevitably revolves around the source of the imagery in this puzzling chapter.[4] Whether or not the Ancient of Days can be identified with El or the Father of Years of Ugaritic literature, an aged deity is almost certainly in question here.[5] I adopt the view that, in whatever terms he may be described, the Ancient of Days is a figure representative of the God of Israel, and to be identified with the Most High who appears elsewhere in ch. 7.[6] As will become clearer later in this discussion, the relationship of

---

4. See, for example, J.A. Emerton, 'The Origins of the Son of Man Imagery', *JTS* 9 (1958), pp. 225-42, and Collins, *Apocalyptic Vision*, pp. 100-106, on the Canaanite origins. A. Bentzen, *King and Messiah* (London: Lutterworth Press, 1955), p. 74, has been influential with his view that an enthronement ritual along the lines of Ps. 2 is a source. S.B. Reid, *Enoch and Daniel: A Form Critical and Sociological Study of Historical Apocalypses* (Berkeley: BIBAL Press, 1989), p. 87, who sees an amalgam of sources, backs several horses. He alerts us to the danger of putting Canaanite and Old Testament background in opposition to one another. E.C. Lucas, 'The Source of Daniel's Animal Imagery', *TynBul* 41 (1990), p. 184, tends to do so and is in danger of caricaturing Emerton's position. P.G. Mosca, 'Ugarit and Daniel 7: A Missing Link', *Bib* 67 (1986), pp. 500-502, argues that biblical material is the 'missing link' between Ugarit and Dan. 7. But see also the sceptical note on Canaanite origins sounded by A.J. Ferch, 'Daniel 7 and Ugarit: A Reconsideration', *JBL* 99 (1980), pp. 79-86.

5. Emerton, 'Son of Man Imagery', p. 230. M. Delcor, 'Les sources du chapitre VII de Daniel', *VT* 18 (1968), p. 302, considers the Ancient of Days equates with the 'father of years' in Ugaritic. See also M.H. Pope, *El in the Ugaritic Texts* (Leiden: Brill, 1955), p. 32, who is not so sure. U. Oldenburg, *The Conflict between El and Baal in Canaanite Religion* (Leiden: Brill, 1969), pp. 17-19, and N. Wyatt, 'The Story of Dinah and Shechem', *UF* 22 (1990), p. 447, dissent.

6. G.F. Keil, *Commentary on the Book of Daniel* (trans. M.G. Easton; Edinburgh: T. & T. Clark, 1872), p. 230, expresses it thus: Daniel sees 'an old man, or a man of grey hairs, in whose majestic form God makes Himself visible'. See also

the Ancient of Days to the son of man is therefore analogous to the relationship between the Most High and the holy ones.

The Son of Man in the Masoretic Text

It is more difficult to describe any sort of consensus on the figure of the son of man (v. 13). What is generally agreed is that the indefinite Aramaic expression, בר אנש, normally speaks of a human being.[7] Even in biblical Hebrew this is the case where God commonly addresses Ezekiel as 'son of man' (בן־אדם, Ezek. 2.1; 37.11; 38.2, 14; 39.1, 17). Some would also argue that Ps. 80.18 reflects a tradition that uses the son of man as a collective term for Israel.[8] However, a human likeness is sometimes used in Ezekiel to depict a different sort of presence, although the exact expression is slightly different. The prophet saw one with 'an appearance like the form of a man' (Ezek. 1.26, דמות כמראה אדם). The vocabulary chosen explicitly links this personage with 'the form of the appearance of the glory of the Lord' (Ezek. 1.28, מראה דמות כבוד־יהוה). Some would argue that the prefix כ before בר אנש alerts us to the possibility that such is the case in Daniel 7 also.[9] The equation is not quite so clear in Ezekiel 8. There it seems more as though the one with 'the appearance like the form of a man' (Ezek. 8.2, דמות כמראה־אש) is a heavenly

---

Slotki, *Daniel*, p. 58, and Driver, *Daniel*, p. 85, although Emerton, 'Son of Man Imagery', p. 230, takes issue with Driver's use of *1 En.* 14.18-22. But note the view of Jephet, *Daniel*, p. 35, that the Ancient of Days is a judging angel. Other medieval Jewish commentators were divided. For Rashi he was God but for Ibn-Ezra he was Michael. See Gallé, *Daniel*, p. 74.

7.   See G. Vermes, 'Appendix E: The Use of בר נשא/בר נש in Jewish Aramaic', in M. Black, *An Aramaic Approach to the Gospels* (Oxford: Clarendon Press, 1967), p. 327. Usages in earlier and later non-biblical Aramaic are expounded by J. Fitzmyer in *The Aramaic Inscriptions of Sefîre* (Rome: Pontifical Biblical Institute, 1967), p. 99, and *Genesis Apocryphon*, p. 60. An example of the indefinite use from Ugarit is found in ll . 14f of RIH 78/20.14-15 where *l'adam* is in parallel with *lbn 'adam*. See J.C. de Moor, 'An Incantation against Evil Spirits (Ras Ibn Hani 78/20)', *UF* 12 (1980), p. 430.

8.   D.S. Russell, *The Method and Message of Jewish Apocalyptic* (London: SCM Press, 1964), p. 340. M.D. Hooker, *The Son of Man in Mark* (London: SPCK, 1967), p. 13, also asserts that that is the case.

9.   For example A. Feuillet, 'Le fils de l'homme de Daniel et la tradition biblique', *RB* 60 (1953), p. 184, and E.J. Young, *Daniel's Vision of the Son of Man* (London: Tyndale Press, 1958), p. 20.

messenger sent to bring Ezekiel into the presence of God. The information that his bodily parts only take the form of bodily parts (Ezek. 8.2-3) emphasizes that the figure only looks like a man. In the Hebrew portions of Daniel a similar form of expression appears in 10.16 and 18. Somebody with 'the form of sons of men' (10.16, כדמות בני אדם) approaches Daniel and somebody with 'the appearance of a man' (10.18, כמראה אדם) touches him.

The ambiguous use of the expression within Ezekiel and the Psalms sums up in broad outline the views that have been taken on the son of man in Daniel 7.[10] He is either a human figure who functions as a symbol for the saints, or he is an angelic or ancient mythical figure, or he is divine or messianic.[11] After a lengthy review of the options, Montgomery opts for the son of man as symbol and in doing so cites 'the Semitic genius to personify the people'.[12] When it comes to a comparison of the versions, I see the son of man in the MT as symbolic of a temporal reality.

Following from there, v. 14 seems to depict a process whereby the son of man acquires a divine authority.[13] While his authority is derived (יהיב), the service offered him is the same sort that is due to divinity. This

10. Note within *1 Enoch* a similar variation between chs. 46-47, where the son of man appears to be a heavenly or angelic figure, and ch. 60, where Enoch himself is addressed as Son of Man.

11. See the summaries of Feuillet, 'Le fils de l'homme', p. 191, and Montgomery, *Daniel*, p. 317, and the excursus in Collins, *Daniel*, pp. 304-10. Collins, *Apocalyptic Vision*, pp. 142-46, sees Dan. 7 entirely in terms of a heavenly battle where the son of man is the archangel Michael and the holy ones have angelic counterparts. See also J. Coppens and L. Dequeker, *Le fils de l'homme et les saints du très-haut en Daniel VII* (Bruges: Publications Universitaires de Louvain, 1961), pp. 50 and 67. Z. Zevit, 'The Structure and Individual Elements of Daniel 7', *ZAW* 80 (1968), p. 395, prefers Gabriel. For Davies, *Daniel*, pp. 102 and 104-105, the holy ones are Israel while the son of man is a collective referent. Delcor, 'Sources', p. 312, sees the son of man as symbol. See also Hooker, *Son of Man*, p. 28, and P.M. Casey, *Son of Man* (London: SPCK, 1979), p. 25. Goldingay, *Daniel*, p. 177, steers a middle course with the comment that the ambiguity is perhaps deliberate.

12. Montgomery, *Daniel*, p. 323. As long ago as the third century CE Porphyry, as cited in P.M. Casey, 'Porphyry and the Book of Daniel', *JTS* 27 (1976), p. 21, saw the son of man in this light.

13. Lacocque, *Daniel*, p. 111, and Delcor, *Daniel*, p. 156. This process may also be thought of in the Canaanite terms of enthronement by the aged deity. See Emerton, 'Son of Man Imagery', p. 242.

is portrayed by פלח, the same word used in the confrontation between the king and the young men of ch. 3 over whose God should be served (3.12, 14, 17, 18, 28).[14] In 6.17 and 21 Darius describes Daniel's relationship with God in terms of פלח. The process has perhaps been duplicated in *4 Ezra* 13, where a human figure (*4 Ezra* 13.3, 'this man', *ille homo*) comes out of the depths of the sea 'with the clouds of heaven' (*4 Ezra* 13.3, *cum nubibus caeli*).[15] That figure is later described as a man whom the Most High 'had kept' (*4 Ezra* 13.25-26, *conseruat*) for the work of deliverance. At this stage he is implicitly identified with the creator God by the phrase 'his creation' (*creaturam suam*), yet is still distinct from the Most High.[16] Since the Most High is speaking the interpretation, *suam* can only refer to the being who has arrived with the clouds of heaven. Later still he is revealed to be the son of the Most High (*4 Ezra* 13.52, *filium meum*).[17] But in both Daniel 7 and *4 Ezra* 13 it remains an open question whether or not the son of man's authority becomes intrinsic or remains derived.

The Holy Ones of the Most High in the Masoretic Text

There are complex textual and translational issues linked to the question of who the holy ones might be. As was the case for the son of man, commentators opt broadly for three types of understanding. These holy ones can be angelic figures, or the earthly people of Israel.[18] A third intermediate possibility is that they are an earthly people who somehow become heavenly beings. The 'wise' (12.3, משכלים) are perhaps considered in those terms when Dan. 12.3 states that they 'will shine...like the stars for ever and ever' (יזהרי...ככוכבים לעולם ועד). An

---

14. Despite the comments of Driver, *Daniel*, p. 88.

15. Beale, *The Use of Daniel*, p. 141, considers the picture to be an amalgam of the imagery in Dan. 7.2-3 and 13a.

16. R.L. Bensly (ed.), 'The Fourth Book of Ezra', in J.A. Robinson (ed.), *Texts and Studies* (Cambridge: Cambridge University Press, 1895), III.2.

17. Delcor, 'Sources', p. 305, notes that the clouds in *4 Ezra* 13 seem to provide transport from earth to heaven for a terrestrial being. He uses this as an argument that the son of man is a human figure. Contrast Feuillet, 'Le fils de l'homme', p. 188, who argues for a messiah figure prefigured in the Old Testament.

18. For a helpfully brief summary of the arguments each way, see V.S. Poythress, 'The Holy Ones of the Most High in Daniel VII', *VT* 26 (1976), p. 209.

important proponent of the angelic view has been Noth, who understands the עם in the phrase, 'people of the holy ones of the most high'
(v. 27, עם קדישי עליונין) as 'host'.[19] While his understanding of עם has not
prevailed, there remains a substantial body of opinion who see the holy
ones as heavenly figures.[20] Others, sometimes using the same data as
their opponents, are equally insistent that a group of humans is
intended.[21] Collins provides an example of one variety of the
intermediate view, whereby the referent of the holy ones is human, but
in the context of v. 27 they are represented by angelic counterparts in a
heavenly battle.[22] I accept Brekelmans's argument that the understanding of קדישין must be decided by context. In 4.11 the 'holy one' is
in apposition to 'the watcher' (עיר), whereas in ch. 7 'the holy ones' are
best understood in temporal terms.[23]

19. 'Schar', according to M. Noth, 'Die heiligen des Höchsten', in *Gesammelte
Studien zum Alten Testament* (Munich: Chr. Kaiser Verlag, 1966), pp. 285 and 287.
That view depends on vv. 20-22 being secondary. See the counter-argument of
C.H.W. Brekelmans, 'The Saints of the Most High and their Kingdom', *OTS* 14
(1965), p. 329.

20. Dequeker, '"Saints of the Most High"', pp. 135-73, argues exhaustively
from the Qumran texts that the holy ones are angelic. See also Reid, *Enoch and
Daniel*, p. 89. For example, 11QMelch 9 explicitly interprets קדושי אל as gods, and
עמים at 11-12 are said to refer to Satan and the spirits of 'his lot' (גורלו). See
J.T. Milik, 'Milkî-ṣedeq et milki-rešaᶜ', *JJS* 23 (1972), pp. 98-99, and G. Vermes,
The Dead Sea Scrolls in English (London: Penguin Books, 1987), p. 301.
P.R. Davies, *1QM, the War Scroll from Qumran* (Rome: Biblical Institute Press,
1977), p. 102, reads the same term in 1QM 12.9 and says it means 'angels', but
Goldingay, *Daniel*, p. 177, would not agree.

21. See Brekelmans, 'Saints of the Most High', pp. 319-26, who differs from
Dequeker in his handling of the Qumran material. He says the issue must be decided
on context, and the present context requires a human referent. See also Davies,
Daniel, p. 104, Casey, *Son of Man*, p. 44, and G.F. Hasel, 'The Identity of "The
Saints of the Most High" in Daniel 7', *Bib* 56 (1975), pp. 186-88. For Saadia and
Rashi, in Gallé, *Daniel*, p. 81, Israel is represented in v. 18. G.R. Beasley-Murray,
'The Interpretation of Daniel 7', *CBQ* 45 (1983), pp. 52-53, points to עם־קדשים in
8.24 where he says the referent is also human.

22. Collins, *Apocalyptic Vision*, pp. 126 and 142-47. See also a more recent
treatment by Collins in *Daniel*, pp. 313-17.

23. See G. Vermes, 'Qumran Forum Miscellanea I', *JJS* 43 (1992), pp. 302-
303, for his translation and comment on Qumran fragment 4Q246. There 'the people
of God' (4, עם אל) receive an 'eternal kingdom' (5, מלכות עלם) and their dominion is
an 'eternal dominion' (9, שלטן עלם). Vermes says this 'may constitute the earliest

However, the view of Collins and others who wish to see the whole chapter as the enactment of a heavenly battle, raises an important point about the function of symbolism in the vision of Daniel 7.[24] For Collins 'angels are not symbols but real beings' so 'it is unthinkable that humans would be symbolized by angels, or depicted in language which is normally understood to refer to heavenly beings'.[25] Therefore visions are not so much interpretations of ongoing temporal events as a transformation of the present existence. According to Davies, this approach does not tally with the interpretation of the visionary beasts and horns and so does not work for an understanding either of the son of man or of the holy ones of the Most High.[26] Rather, visions provide a glimpse into the interaction of the human and the divine, the temporal and the eternal.[27] The interpretation therefore must be to some extent about temporal realities, while also transcending them.[28] Such was the case in both chs. 2 and 4, and to a lesser extent may be applied to the interaction between 'mystery' (רז) and 'interpretation' (פשר) in ch. 5. That understanding of the link between vision and interpretation, as a meeting of the divine with the temporal and human, is presupposed in my comparison of the MT and LXX in ch. 7.

non-biblical evidence for the collective understanding of "one like a son of man"'.

24. Note also the thesis of M. Barker, *The Great Angel* (London: SPCK, 1987), pp. 29 and 38, that the holy ones are angel figures and the deity in the Aramaic chapters is Elyon, the ancient High God. The unnamed son of man is in fact the Holy One, Yahweh.

25. Collins, *Apocalyptic Vision*, pp. 140-41.

26. Davies, *Daniel*, pp. 103-104. He disagrees with Collins's position, which he says is that 'visions... portray both earthly and heavenly realities as two dimensions of the same reality'.

27. For Goldingay, *Daniel*, p. 177, the ambiguity of the holy ones contributes to this effect. Lacocque, *Daniel in his Time*, pp. 145-47, speaks of the tension between chaos and cosmos. For him the genius of the son of man image is that it combines eschatological vision with mythical time. Caird, *Language and Imagery*, p. 264, speaks of the fluctuation between temporal and transcendental in apocalyptic.

28. See the discussion of Sheriffs, '"A Tale of Two Cities"', p. 39, on hermeneutical approaches to eschatology. In the context of a comparison of Zionist and Babylonian nationalism, he calls this approach 'contextualist' and prefers it over 'reductionist' and 'literalist' understandings.

Daniel 7: Coherent and Consistent?

The above-mentioned link between vision and interpretation is part of the wider question of whether or not Daniel 7 in its present form is a 'coherent and consistent account', in terms of both narrative structure and deployment of symbolism.[29] The chief stumbling block for those who see a literary and logical unity in Daniel 7 lies in the relationship between interpretation and vision, and in particular the problematic vv. 21-22. These verses provide a challenge to most attempts at a commentary on Daniel 7, and the present one is no exception. The problem is easier to deal with for those who discern the overlapping of several visions in Daniel 7. The material in vv. 21-22 is then simply evidence of a seam in the process of redaction.[30]

Problems with vv. 21-22 are particularly acute for those who perceive the chapter's unity to be partly in some sort of equivalence, however that may be defined, between the son of man in the vision and the holy ones in the interpretation. Because Daniel is the speaker, the reader expects to hear about the vision already outlined. The conventional 'I looked' (v. 21, חזה הוית) reminds the reader of Daniel's earlier speech which interspersed the telling of the vision with such expressions.[31] It is then a surprise to hear from his mouth new details of the vision. In the original account of the vision there is no mention of war being made on God's people before the court of the Ancient of Days convenes. The only objects of the final horn's aggression are the horns that it uproots (v. 8), which are probably themselves either pagan kingdoms or kings of the same kingdom from which the boastful horn springs. Verse 22 also makes a more explicit link between the judgment scene and the handing over of eternal sovereignty to the holy ones of the Most High, than does the first telling of the vision. In the earlier account the result of judgment seems to be condemnation of the fourth beast, a stay of execution for its three predecessors (vv. 11-12), and the eventual granting of eternal

---

29. Casey, *Son of Man*, p. 29.

30. In addition to Noth, the view that vv. 21-22 are secondary is found in a variety of commentators. See, for example, Porteous, *Daniel*, p. 113, O. Plöger, *Das Buch Daniel* (Gütersloh: Gütersloher Verlagshaus/Gerd Mohn, 1965), p. 115, Dequeker, '"Saints of the Most High"', p. 127, and Bickerman, *Four Strange Books*, p. 108. Hartman and DiLella, *Daniel*, p. 210, consider as additional all material relating to the eleventh horn.

31. Raabe, 'Daniel 7', p. 268.

sovereignty to the son of man (v. 14). The holy ones of the Most High do not feature as beneficiaries at all. If the holy ones are in the vision of Daniel prior to the advent of the son of man, how can they also be an interpretation of the son of man?

At the same time, Daniel's speech seems to contain the beginnings of interpretation. The final phrase of v. 22, 'and the holy ones took possession of the kingdom' (ומלכותא החסנו קדישין), recalls the words of interpretation in v. 18. The choice of חסן here and in v. 18 is slightly at odds with the emphasis elsewhere in ch. 7. The suggestion is of aggressive military action by the holy ones in gaining the kingdom.[32] Otherwise the choice of vocabulary makes it clear that the holy ones as well as the son of man receive what is given them.[33] Each time a phrase containing חסן appears, it is linked to some sort of reference to the heavenly origins of their possession. Perhaps then the use of חסן implies a look forward to the means by which celestial intent is to be implemented. At the same time, v. 22 anticipates the expansion in vv. 25-27. This is the one time in ch. 7 when the distinction between vision and interpretation, or seer and interpreter, is blurred.

For all that, there is a strong body of opinion arguing for the integrity of the chapter.[34] Without denying a possible redactional history, ch. 7 may substantially be understood as a coherent narrative about a vision and the interpretation that is given to Daniel. With particular reference to vv. 21-22, Daniel's later expansion of the vision can be appreciated in literary terms.[35] The technique of leaving lacunae in the accounts that are only later filled in is one we have seen before.[36] In effect, the gap between the accession of the final horn and its final destruction

32. Casey, *Son of Man*, p. 45, notes that military action is not ruled out.

33. This supposes the most likely meaning of דינא יהב לקדישי to be 'he gave judgment for/in favour of the holy ones...' See Driver, *Daniel*, p. 91.

34. Casey, *Son of Man*, p. 27, and Hooker, *Son of Man*, pp. 24-30, agree on the coherence but differ on other matters. See also Anderson, *Daniel*, p. 76, and Hasel, '"Saints of the Most High"', p. 189. Beasley-Murray, 'Interpretation of Daniel 7', p. 45, speaks of 'a vision in two acts'. S. Niditch, *The Symbolic Vision in Biblical Tradition* (Chico, CA: Scholars Press, 1983), p. 194, holds the integrity of the chapter together with its anthological nature, not altogether convincingly. Collins, *Apocalyptic Vision*, p. 129, and Delcor, 'Sources', p. 290, both link their views to the mythological background of ch. 7.

35. Casey, *Son of Man*, pp. 27-39, makes a particularly strong case for this.

36. Note again the comment of Eissfeldt, 'Die Menetekel-Inschrift', p. 112, on variation between message and interpretation as a stylistic feature.

(vv. 8-11) corresponds to the gap in the summary interpretation between the rise of the four kings and the reception of the kingdom by the holy ones (vv. 17-18). What occurred in the silence is eventually revealed at vv. 21-22 as a war on the holy ones and action taken by them which leads to their receiving eternal sovereignty. The verb חסן noted above is a further indication of this process.

The question of consistency may also be approached in terms of the nature of the relationship between the son of man and the holy ones of the Most High. Hooker and Casey both demonstrate this approach. While they differ over the exact nature of the link, for both of them the material in vv. 21-22 is an important part of their explanation of it.[37] Each in their own way needs vv. 21-22 to be at the point in the chapter where it is. I accept the argument that Daniel 7 is a coherent and consistence account, largely on the literary and symbolic grounds offered by Casey, and assume that to be the case in what follows. At the same time, the huge corpus of divergent secondary material on Daniel 7 indicates the caution required in handling such ambivalent texts.

Narrative Structure

The narrative structure of ch. 7 is more complex than it at first appears. It is more than a simple account by Daniel of a vision seen and an interpretation obtained. The narrative belongs to several personae. The third-person narrator of v. 1 quickly gives way to Daniel's recounting of his vision.[38] Then the bystander of whom Daniel requests an interpretation takes up the telling, briefly in vv. 17-18 and more fully in vv. 23-27. Finally, Daniel himself, speaking in the first person, closes the account. The bystander or interpreter exists only within the framework of Daniel's story.

Behind these personae are certain implied personalities. While he is recounting the initial vision (vv. 2-14), Daniel intersperses his speech with the formulae 'I looked and behold...' (vv. 2, 6, 7, 13, חזה הוית וארו), 'I looked until...' (vv. 4, 9, 11, חזה הוית עד די), or simply 'and behold...'

---

37. Casey, *Son of Man*, p. 39, insists that the son of man is 'a pure symbol'. For him this makes impossible the views of Hooker, *Son of Man*, pp. 13-17, on the suffering son of man as equivalent to the suffering holy ones.

38. Charles, *Daniel*, p. 173, notes a similar phenomenon in *1 En.* 1.1, 3, and 92.1.

(vv. 5, 8, ואֵרוּ).[39] As a variation, when he expands on the activities of the little horn he also breaks his narration with 'I looked' (v. 21, חָזֵה הֲוֵית).[40] These interjections ensure that the person of Daniel in the story is not eclipsed entirely by the vision itself. At the same time they point the reader outside his speech to an implied listener. It is not clear whether the listener is the narrator of v. 1, or an audience completely outside the narrative.

Furthermore, a feature of the Aramaic syntax of vv. 4-13 is the number of verbs in the *peil* conjugation and also in the causative *haphel* form, which gives rise to a sense that another presence is at work behind the scenes.[41] The wings of the first beast were 'plucked out' (v. 4, מְרִיטוּ), and it was 'raised up' (v. 4, נְטִילַת) and 'caused to stand' (v. 4, הֳקִימַת) like a person before a human heart 'was given' (v. 4, יְהִיב) to it. Rule 'was given' (v. 6, יְהִיב) to the third beast. Later in the vision, thrones 'were placed' (v. 9, רְמִיו) and books 'were opened' (v. 10, פְּתִיחוּ). The culmination of the judgment scene is that the fourth beast 'was killed' (v. 11, קְטִילַת) and its body 'destroyed' (v. 11, הוּבַד) and 'given' (v. 11, יְהִיבַת) over to burning. Finally, the sovereignty of the first three beasts 'was taken away' (v. 12, הֶעְדִּיו), although an extension of life 'was given' (v. 12, יְהִיבַת) them for a period of time. This cluster of *peils* and *haphels* to express the passive is a deliberate literary effect, intended to hint at a presence outside the scene but in some way responsible for it.[42] It foreshadows the revelation of divine activity in the interpretation of the vision.

Outside of Daniel the *peil* form is rarely found in extant Aramaic writings, and when it does occur it is normally employed in an impersonal rather than a passive sense.[43] Even in Daniel the passive is

---

39. Davies, *Daniel*, p. 59, considers v. 8 to be secondary partly because of the spelling of אֵלוּ. Casey, *Son of Man*, p. 13, argues that the spelling variation is insignificant.

40. See the parallels drawn by Delcor, *Daniel*, p. 143, with 2.31 and 4.7, 10.

41. In the expression used by Auerbach, *Mimesis*, p. 11, the narrative is 'fraught with background'.

42. Goldingay, *Daniel*, p. 164.

43. See Fitzmyer, *Genesis Apocryphon*, p. 190, and J.C.L. Gibson, *Textbook of Syrian Semitic Inscriptions* (Oxford: Clarendon Press, 1975), II, pp. 131 and 134, both of whose examples are of the impersonal use. Occurrences in Ezra (4.18, 23; 5.7, 14; 6.2) are also impersonal rather than passive. See H. Bauer and P. Leander, *Grammatik des Biblisch-Aramäischen* (Hildesheim: Georg Olms, 1962), pp. 93 and 104. Milik, 'Les modèles araméens', pp. 361-62, has recently identified a possible *peil* passive in 4QprEsthar[f] 2. G. Dalman, *Grammatik des Jüdisch-*

normally expressed either with the third person impersonal construction or by the *hithpaal*. The former is instanced in vv. 25 and 26 of the present chapter (יתיהבון and יהעדון) as well as on a number of occasions in the other stories of Daniel (2.13, 18; 3.21; 4.22, 29). The *hithpaal* is pressed into service as a passive at 7.8, 2.34, 3.6, 11, 15, 29, 4.30, 5.12, and 6.8 and 13. When the *peil* form features in the book of Daniel it does so in a setting of divine activity and appears to be a deliberate usage. Apart from vv. 4-13 there are two other occasions in Daniel where *peil*s occur in a cluster (2.19, 21, 30; 5.21-30), and there also it is clear that divine agency is intended to be understood behind the verb forms chosen. In ch. 5 the queen reminds her audience that Nebuchadnezzar 'was driven away' (5.21, טריד). Because of Belshazzar's ignorance of these things, a hand 'was sent' (5.24, שליח) and a message 'was inscribed' (5.25, רשים).[44] The theme of God's election of sovereigns is also reinforced by Daniel's interpretative statement that Belshazzar's kingdom 'was given' (5.28, יהיבת) to the Persians. Later, the mystery surrounding the fate of Belshazzar is heightened by the storyteller's choice of קטיל in 5.30. The use of the *peil* in ch. 2 involves the verb גלה, which was discussed at some length in the chapter on Daniel 2. The secret of the king's vision 'was revealed' (2.19, 30, גלי) to Daniel.

Daniel 7 is as much a story about a man who saw a vision and its interpretation, as a report of the vision and the interpretation given.[45] As well as the constant interaction with the reader already noted in Daniel's use of formulae, the links between episodes make the chapter a narrative rather than a simple report. These links are in vv. 15-16, 19-22, and 28. Their focus on the feelings and thoughts of the first-person narrator are characteristic of a story. Moreover, the culmination of the story is not so much that the kingdom of the Most High will last forever, as that Daniel has been frightened by what he saw to the extent that his 'colours changed' (v. 28, זיוי ישתנון).

Palästinischen Aramäisch (Leipzig: Hinrichs, 1894), p. 202, notes only two or three exceptional instances in Jewish Palestinian Aramaic literature. W.B. Stevenson, *Grammar of Palestinian Jewish Aramaic* (Oxford: Clarendon Press, 1924), pp. 44-45, says the passive in Jewish Palestinian Aramaic is almost always expressed by forms using the *ith-* prefix.

44. BDB lists שלח as a *peal* passive participle, and so the form is exceptional to the present discussion. Nevertheless it functions in the same way as the finite forms of the *peil* that we have been looking at.

45. Casey, *Son of Man*, p. 8.

Some have suggested that phrases in the first and last verses contain a formal title and conclusion for the narrative. 'The main point' (v. 1, ראש מלין) is an opening, and 'the end of the matter' (v. 28, סופא די־מלתא) is the corresponding close.[46] The principal problem with this suggestion is that the first verse contains the words of the narrator while the last verse is spoken by Daniel himself. It is more likely that v. 1 in the third person is simply a device to introduce the change of perspective in ch. 7.[47] Verse 28 is not so much a convention of the genre as part of the comparison of Daniel the visionary with his royal counterparts.[48] This becomes more obvious when links between ch. 7 and the stories are discussed.

Effectively the narrative belongs to Daniel, in the same way that the story of ch. 4 belongs to Nebuchadnezzar. The chief difference is that the block of third-person material in ch. 4 means that the narrator at least retains a foothold in that story, whereas he drops out entirely in ch. 7. That foothold is not necessary as the first person of Daniel in ch. 7 conveys the narrator's point of view, whereas the first person of Nebuchadnezzar in ch. 4 cannot be relied upon to do so. The form of autobiographical narration shared by chs. 4 and 7 also results in a similarity in the way the dialogue is managed, and unseen figures are hinted at. These aspects have been more fully discussed in relation to Daniel 4.

In broad outlines, the narrative takes the same shape in the LXX. The opening phrase in v. 23 is problematic in that it could be introducing indirect rather than direct speech. However, the probability is that the ὅτι is a ὅτι recitative preceded by a summarizing statement in anticipation of what is to follow. The LXX also uses ὅτι in this way in ch. 2 (vv. 5, 10, 25), whether or not there is an equivalent element in the Aramaic. The chief narrative difference is that the distinction between reflexive and passive that we have considered in some detail above is not available to the Greek translator. The passive form is much more readily used in Greek than Aramaic, and often represents the reflexive

---

46. For example Montgomery, *Daniel*, p. 284.

47. Miller, 'Redaction of Daniel', p. 116, sees 7.1 as a central clue to the redaction history of the book of Daniel. The fact that חלם is found only here in ch. 7 forms part of his argument. Lacocque, *Daniel in his Time*, p. 132, also notes the shift from 'dream' to 'vision' between 'Daniel A and B'.

48. But Hartman and DiLella, *Daniel*, p. 220, see the contents of v. 28 entirely in terms of genre.

forms in Aramaic.[49] This means that it cannot so easily distinguish the *peil* form when it occurs. In this section of narrative the *peil* is invariably represented in the Greek by an aorist passive. The same form is also often used to render a *haphel* (7.4) or a *hithpaal* (7.8; 2.9, 34; 5.23, for example). Often the LXX represents the impersonal third person literally, even though the passive is intended, but sometimes this construction is also translated with an aorist passive (3.21). As a result, the foreshadowing effect of the Aramaic passive is also present in vv. 4–13 LXX, but is not as striking. This is partly because the link with other *peil* clusters in chs. 2 and 5 as indicators of divine activity is not able to be made in the Greek.

In connection with that point, it is not clear who the speaker of the direct speech is in v. 5. In the MT the bear is commanded by the outside presence with the impersonal third person plural, אמרין. The LXX equivalent is 'it/he spoke thus:' (v. 5, οὕτως εἶπεν). This can possibly be explained as an attempt to represent the Aramaic impersonal. Against that, the LXX is normally accurate about the person of the verb in such a situation. See, for example, προσήγαγον (967, v. 13) and ἀποστελοῦσί (4.25). Moreover לה in the MT means that the bear-like creature is explicitly the object of the command. The absence of any object in the LXX suggests that 'it' is the subject of the verb in the Greek. Putting aside the problem of whom the LXX thinks that the second beast might be addressing, the Greek phrase οὕτως εἶπεν is a further dilution of the effect of the passives observable in Aramaic.

A Further Literary Note

There is an intriguing interplay of tense in this chapter, particularly relating to the son of man and the holy ones of the Most High. After the son of man approached the Ancient of Days, authority 'was given' (v. 14, יהיב) to him. The verb is in the perfect tense, in common with the rest of the preceding account of a vision. Yet the outworkings of this encounter are expressed in the imperfect (יפלחון, יעדה and תתחבל). At this point the vision transcends the narrative form of a vision account and begins to tell of events which are yet to be. Something different happens during the interpretation of the vision, which largely adopts the imperfect tense. Yet the perfect appears at the beginning of v. 27 where the kingdom

---

49. M. Black, *An Aramaic Approach to the Gospels and Acts* (Oxford: Clarendon Press, 1967), pp. 126-28.

'is/was given' (יהיבת) to the people.[50] The imperfect returns in a description of the resulting homage that will come to the saints.[51]

While the imperfect of v. 14b is exceptional in the telling of the vision, the perfect of v. 27 is exceptional in the interpretation. The literary effect is that the verbal structures of vv. 14 and 27 are in parallel to one another. This serves as a further literary indicator that the giving of the kingdom to the people of the saints is linked to its reception by the son of man in the vision. This parallel is also present in the LXX, although the passive יהיבת (v. 27) equates to an aorist active in the LXX (ἔδωκε).

The Character of Daniel

Related to the point of ch. 7 as narration is the portrayal of the character of Daniel in the narrative. There seems to be some difference in how the versions depict the effect of the vision on Daniel. The MT description is bipartite, referring to 'spirit' (v. 15, רוח) and 'sheath' (נדנה).[52] Daniel's spirit was 'troubled' (v. 15, אתכרית) and the visions 'frightened (me)' him (v. 15, יבהלני). This separation of the mental and the physical continues in v. 28 MT. The MT first records Daniel's mental state, that of intensified fear (v. 28, שׂניא), and then describes the physical manifestation: 'my colours changed upon me' (זיוי ישתנון עלי). Whatever effect is being described, it is the same one observable in the person of Belshazzar (5.9).

The LXX gathers both concepts into the phrase 'I Daniel' (v. 15, ἐγὼ Δανιηλ), and then translates in a manner that focuses on his mental and emotional state. Daniel in the LXX describes himself as ἀκηδιάσας.

---

50. The feminine singular form must be governed by מלכותה as the main subject, with the subsequent nouns in a type of parentheses formed by a ו explicative. Rosenthal, *Biblical Aramaic*, p. 56, cites יהיבת as an example of the perfect indicating the future, but gives no other examples of the phenomenon. His comment does not take account of the literary context.

51. This interplay between the perfect and the imperfect is a characteristic also of New Testament eschatology. See, for example, 1 Pet. 4.7, where a future orientation is expressed with the aorist ἤγγικεν, and in the Gospels see Mt. 10.7.

52. The problems raised by נדנה, 'sheath', in v. 15 are beyond the scope of the present discussion. But note the full comment of Fitzmyer, *Genesis Apocryphon*, p. 78, on the word as used in *Genesis Apocryphon* 2.10. See also Driver, *Daniel*, p. 89. The sheath seems to be a metaphor for the body as a receptacle for the soul or life force, and that is how I understand it in the present context. *B. Sanh.* 108a and *Gen. R.* 26.6 also use the word to mean the body as distinct from the soul.

This can hardly mean 'heedless/uncaring' in the present context, and is more likely to denote exhaustion. If the producer of the LXX is translating the MT's בהל at this point, he is doing so with some freedom. The same freedom is evident at v. 28 where Daniel, according to the LXX, confesses that σφόδρα ἐκστάσει περιειχόμην. Again, the exact meaning of the phrase is open to debate, but in general terms it denotes considerable mental turmoil. The following phrase, 'my state of mind altered me' (v. 28, ἡ ἕξις μου διήνεγκεν ἐμοί), is in apposition to, and clarifies what precedes it. This is different from the MT, where the physical effect is described as the result of Daniel's fear.

Particularly in v. 28, the divergence results in a more emphatic description by the LXX of Daniel as visionary. Several strong words in close proximity to one another alert the reader to this emphasis. Each one can sometimes carry the ordinary sense of its Aramaic equivalent, but taken together they have a cumulative effect. First, ἕως καταστροφῆς ('until the conclusion') is a possible rendering of סופא, but it is unusual. And σφόδρα ἐκστάσει ('great distraction') is not an exact rendering of the Aramaic, as we have noted above. The LXX nowhere else uses καταστροφή as a translation of סופא. This Aramaic word, like its Hebrew cognate, can have an eschatological sense with implications of divine activity, but it can be understood in purely physical or political terms. Both uses occur in Daniel. Its physical sense is in 4.8 and 19, where the tree could be seen 'to the end of the earth' (לסוף [כל-]ארעא). It is used in a more eschatological manner in 6.27 where God's rule is said by Darius to last 'until the end' (עד-סופא). This range is representative of the semantic range of the word in biblical Hebrew also. θ's choice of either τέλος (6.27) or πέρας (4.11, 22) roughly reflects that range. καταστροφή, however, is much more redolent of human consequences of divine activity. In Sirach the NEB translates it as 'fate' (Sir. 9.11; 18.12). In Job the LXX uses it to represent שדד (Job 15.21, 'destroyer') or איד (Job 21.17, 'calamity'). It is also used in Proverbs to denote איד (Prov. 1.27).

The eschatological nuances of καταστροφή are epitomized by the LXX's attempt to capture in Greek the sense of the metaphorical language of Hos. 8.7a MT, 'for they will sow the wind and reap the whirlwind'. The Old Greek makes no attempt to reproduce the imagery of the second half of the line, וסופתה יקצרו. Instead it gives the interpretation, ἡ καταστροφὴ αὐτῶν ἐκδέξεται. The word used there for 'whirlwind' (סופתה) is interpreted by the LXX with καταστροφή. The most literal sense of καταστροφή is 'turning against', and by extension that came to mean some sort of destructive event. By a further extension of meaning, that event could be thought of as the final end. It is not certain whether the two words סוף ('end') and סופה ('whirlwind') are etymologically related, but the translator perceives them to be so. Hence his assumption that the whirlwind has as its referent 'the end'. He chooses καταστροφή as a rendering of the image which captures the eschatological overtones of the Hebrew as he sees it. With such a tradition behind it, the word καταστροφή is used by the translator of Daniel 7 to interpret סופא in an eschatological direction.[53]

This effect is reinforced by the description of Daniel as subjected to σφόδρα ἐκστάσει. The LXX translates a number of different words with ἔκστασις, all of which denote some sort of turmoil or fear. Unlike its English derivative, it does not normally denote derangement. Nevertheless, despite the range of usage in translation, it is generally selected by the LXX in the context of fear or confusion or panic generated in response to the activity of the Lord. Examples may be cited from Deut. 28.28 (translating תמהון), 1 Kgs 11.7 (translating פחד), and 2 Chron. 29.8 (translating זוע). Also significant to its use as an indicator of divine involvement with humanity is the choice of ἔκστασις in Gen. 2.21 and 15.12 as the translation of תרדמה, the 'deep sleep' in which Adam and Abram both encountered God. Whatever its exact meaning, this word also is evocative of divine activity and judgment. The effect is intensified by σφόδρα.

The emphasis discernible in the LXX on Daniel as an eschatological visionary, subject to, as well as an intermediary of, the judgment of God, is further reinforced by another small variation between versions in v. 28. While the MT tells the reader that the source of Daniel's fear is '(his) thoughts' (רעיוני), the LXX pictures him as overcome by the external source of his vision, 'great distraction' (σφόδρα ἐκστάσει). This perspective on Daniel in the LXX has also been hinted at in chs. 2 and 4 of Daniel.

Vision and Interpretation: Insignificant Differences

In the light of the point made immediately above, the possibility that the versions may understand the vision differently bears examination. This

53. See Tov, 'Three Dimensions', pp. 540-41, on etymologizing renderings in the LXX.

will largely be done by looking at how the four beasts, the son of man, and the holy ones of the Most High are presented and then interpreted by each version. Before doing so, however, there are some apparent differences that need to be ruled out as insignificant. According to v. 2 MT, the four winds were 'churning up' (מגיחן) the sea. The LXX's view that the wind 'fell into' (ἐνέπεσον) the sea, like θ's προσέβαλλον, is more of an explanation of how the churning occurred. It may not be exactly literal, and may reflect an unfamiliarity with the mythological underpinnings of the vision, but it does not lose the essential elements. The four winds are still present. The sea as a source of chaos is not so evident, but the fact that the beasts emerge from the sea in both versions means that that aspect is also present in the LXX.[54] So the difference does not reflect any interpretation of the vision.

The large LXX plus in v. 8, 'and it made war against the holy ones' (καὶ ἐποίει πόλεμον πρὸς τοὺς ἁγίους), is probably introduced from v. 21. A likely Aramaic retroversion of the Greek ἐποίει πόλεμον (v. 8 LXX) would be עבדה קרב ('did battle'), which occurs subsequently in the MT at v. 21. This suggests that the plus represented in the LXX is more likely to have occurred in the *Vorlage*. That is the expression used by θ to translate the Aramaic in v. 21, where the LXX expresses the concept somewhat differently. The result of the plus is that the LXX anticipates a detail in Daniel's later recounting of his vision, so any literary effect that may have been intended by withholding that information in v. 8 MT is not present. However, it does not alter the position of the saints and the small horn with respect to each other. There is a similar plus in v. 9, this time in the MT, where the throne has 'its wheels blazing with fire' (גלגלוהי נור דלק). The most likely explanation of the difference is a different *Vorlage*, and again there is no significance for the understanding of the vision. In either case, the Ezekiel source of the imagery is evident.[55]

A similar case is the difference between versions in v. 23. According to the MT the fourth kingdom 'will be different from all the kingdoms

---

54. See Anderson, *Daniel*, p. 78, Collins, *Apocalyptic Vision*, pp. 97-98, and from a slightly different perspective, Young, *Daniel*, p. 142.

55. P. Grelot, 'Daniel VII,9-10 et le livre d'Henoch', *Semitica* 28 (1978), p. 82. J. Schaberg, 'Mark 14.62: Early Christian Merkabah Imagery?', in J. Marcus and M.L. Soards (eds.), *Apocalyptic and the New Testament* (Sheffield: JSOT Press, 1989), p. 77, demonstrates the strength of the link between Dan. 7 and Ezek. 1 in the frequency with which the two texts appear in combination in the midrashic history of each.

and will devour all the earth', whereas the fourth kingdom of the LXX 'will be different from all the earth'. This is most likely to be a case of omission by homoeoteleuton between the two instances of כל־. As a result מלכותא ותאכל is missing from the LXX's *Vorlage*. Even if that is not the correct explanation of the difference, the sense is not significantly altered.

The versions also differ in places over whether or not the beasts represent kings or kingdoms. The MT speaks of 'four kings' (v. 17, ארבעה מלכין) where the LXX has 'four kingdoms' (τέσσαρες βασιλεῖαι). At v. 23 the versions are in agreement on 'kingdoms'. Given the prevailing argument that the distinction in Aramaic and Hebrew between 'king' and 'kingdom' is a fluid one, the difference does not disturb the picture of four regimes, probably personalized as particular monarchs.[56] In this light, the displacing of 'of/from the kingdom' in v. 24 is interesting but does not alter the picture. Whether the phrase is used as indirect object of יקמון (MT) or as a modifier in the appositional clause καὶ τὰ δέκα κέρατα τῆς βασιλείας (LXX), the sense is of ten kings from one kingdom. Again, no variation in interpretation of the vision results.

Verses 26-27: Further Insignificant Differences

Verses 26-27 are difficult in both versions. The difficult LXX is probably a result of the translator trying to make sense of a problematic Aramaic *Vorlage*.[57] The sense of the Aramaic seems to run as follows: 'The court will sit in the future (יתב) and still in the future will take away the sovereignty (שלטנה) of the last king'. The possessive suffix refers back to the figure in v. 25. The verb יהעדון is a plural, although the singular court is doing the confiscating. It is therefore an impersonal usage, with the sense that something 'will be taken away', although the sitting court is still envisaged as the agent.

---

56. Lacocque, *Daniel*, p. 114, notes that the author uses king and kingdom indifferently. See also Goldingay, *Daniel*, p. 146. But contrast Montgomery, *Daniel*, p. 307, who regards βασιλεῖαι in LXX v. 17 as an interpretation.

57. J.H. Sailhamer, *The Translation Technique of the Greek Septuagint for the Hebrew Verbs and Participles in Psalms 3–41* (New York: Peter Lang, 1990), p. 194, notes a tendency on the part of the LXX translator, when confronted with difficult syntax, to rely on the most common equivalency even though the sense of the translation might suffer as a result.

Then come two problematic *haphel* infinitives, להשמדה and להובדה, and the awkwardly placed 'until the end' (עד־סופא). The two difficulties are related to one another. We return to the infinitives after considering the positioning of עד־סופא. It is not evident how that phrase could apply to the infinitives immediately preceding it, yet it seems a long way from the finite verb. Perhaps the writer has drawn on a formula also evident in 6.27 where God's 'rule is until the end' (6.27, שלטנה עד־סופא). If that sort of association lies behind v. 26, the point being made is that, unlike God, the eleventh king will not rule to the end. The placement of עד־סופא at the end of the sentence not only emphasizes the finite nature of this king's reign, but also enhances the contrast with the eternal kingdom of v. 27. Another effect of the formula being split is to form a bracket around the phrase יהעדון להשמדה ולהובדה, which suggests that the sense of the infinitives should be thought of as part of a unit with the immediately preceding finite verb. One way to make this link is to take the prefixed *lamedh*s as indicative of purpose, giving the idea that authority 'was taken away so that...'[58] In that case the infinitives also need to be thought of in a passive sense, even though they are active in form. From time to time the Aramaic of Daniel does require such an interpretation of the active infinitive.[59] Understanding יהעדון as an impersonal construction, we may translate the entire phrase, 'its rule until the end will be taken away so that it might be annihilated and destroyed'. In support of this interpretation, which makes the boastful horn recipient rather than provider of annihilation and destruction, it should be noted that the verb אבד also applies to the fate of the fourth beast in v. 11.

Then the singular יהיבת (v. 27, 'has been given') apparently treats the list of attributes, 'kingdom and rule and greatness' (מלכותה ושטנא ורבותא), as a collective noun. The exact referent of the third person singular לה (v. 27) remains ambiguous. It could either be the people (עם) or the one who originally granted the authority. I return to this point when discussing the holy ones of the Most High.

There are several difficulties evident in the LXX of vv. 26-27. The

---

58. Bauer and Leander, *Grammatik*, p. 302, cite להתקטלה in 2.13 as a similar example.

59. Apart from this instance, W.F. Stinespring, 'The Active Infinitive with Passive Meaning in Biblical Aramaic', *JBL* 81 (1962), pp. 392-93, identifies infinitives active in form but passive in sense in 2.12, 46; 3.2, 13, 19; 4.3; 5.2, 7; 6.9, 16, 24. He argues that they are an extension of the third person plural indefinite idiom, and so are implicitly third person plural.

confusion of persons is one instance. The court sits (καθίσεται, singular) and does away with (ἀπολοῦσι, plural) the king's authority. Next 'he gives' (v. 27, ἔδωκε, singular) 'their' (v. 27, αὐτῶν, plural) sovereignty to the holy ones of the Most High. It is clear neither who is giving authority nor whose authority is being given. The second instance is the LXX plus, 'they will plot' (v. 26, βουλεύσονται). Not only is the plural unexpected, but it is also unclear who is the subject of the verb, the court or a figure reintroduced from v. 25. In either case the plural number is inappropriate. Whatever option is chosen, the sense is puzzling. The infinitives that βουλεύσονται governs, μιᾶναι καὶ ἀπολέσαι, are also difficult in that their use to describe the activity of God is unusual.

The variation in person is largely explicable as an attempt to deal with the Aramaic third person plural impersonal constructions in v. 26. Often the LXX renders this construction by a grammatical equivalence with no ill effect on the sense. In this case a literal rendering of יהעדון with ἀπολοῦσι leaves the verb in search of an object. The Septuagintal solution is to read שלטנה as the accusative ἐξουσίαν. As a result the translator clearly views the court as the subject of both the subsequent verbs, 'will sit' and 'will take away', but allows the inconsistency of person between them to remain.

The same difficulty with person is evident in v. 27. Word order suggests that the LXX is attempting to translate the MT or something very like it. As noted earlier, the Aramaic has a singular *peil*, יהיבת. The Greek equivalent is ἔδωκε, which is similarly placed in the sentence. It is intended to refer to the action of the court despite the use of an aorist active as equivalent to the Aramaic *peil* form. The use of a third person singular is explicable in terms of the Aramaic equivalent, despite the normal LXX habit of employing an aorist passive to represent the *peil*. Either the translator wishes to clarify that the court is the active subject of the verb, or he has tried to represent the MT syntax exactly and in so doing erroneously employs an active aorist. In either case the sense is not affected, even if the nuance of the passive is not available. The court is still the donor and the saints are still the recipients of authority.

The additional verb βουλεύσονται is also problematical. It may be representative of a *Vorlage* variant from the one preserved in the MT. It is equally possible that it provides an explanatory note from the translator, possibly in an attempt to represent the force of the ל prefixes on שמד and אבד suggested above. Whatever the source of the verb, its form as a third person plural future indicative is in parallel with ἀπολοῦσι and derives also from the third person plural impersonal idiom of the Aramaic. Even if the translator fails to understand the Aramaic as equivalent to a Greek passive, as appears to be the case with ἀπολοῦσι, the same subject is implied by the LXX as by the MT. The sitting court is understood as the author of the action represented by both finite verbs. In the same vein the infinitives μιᾶναι καὶ ἀπολέσαι are literal translations of the active infinitives in the MT, even though they probably carry a passive sense in the Aramaic. The resultant Greek syntax leaves a question mark over who exactly does the polluting and destroying, but the likelihood is that the LXX translator understands the same subject as the MT, however badly he may have conveyed that in his translation.

One problem with the foregoing argument is that μιᾶναι is a surprising rendering of שמד to describe divine activity. It does not occur again in Daniel but is common elsewhere in the LXX. It almost invariably translates the Hebrew טמא with its strong connotations of ritual defilement or pollution. In later Aramaic the semantic range of שמד also came to include the concept of being forced into apostasy. If the LXX choice of vocabulary has been influenced by that, it could suggest that the infinitives are meant by the LXX to express the activity of the eleventh horn rather than that of the heavenly court. If that is the case, it could be a reflection of the cultic concerns of the Old Greek translation.[60] However, that point on its own does not explain the presence of βουλεύσονται adequately, and is not sufficient to overturn the previous argument. As with the difficulty over person in vv. 26-27, questions raised by the phrase beginning βουλεύσονται can substantially be understood to reflect the difficult syntax of the *Vorlage*.

The pronoun αὔτων, which is a plus in v. 27 LXX, is a further difficulty in translation. At one level it is no more than an attempt to clarify whose authority is being given to the holy ones. In that sense it is the same sort of plus as 'made war against the holy ones' (ἐποίει πόλεμον πρὸς τοὺς ἁγίους) noted in v. 8. The translator may also have been confused by the MT treatment of the expression מלכותה ושלטנא ורבותא... (v. 27, 'kingdom and rule and greatness...') as a

---

60. Note the parallel in Isa. 43.28 where LXX reads a cultic pollution in the Hebrew חלל. The LXX translates with μιᾶναι but reapplies the first person so that it is not God but the leaders who profane the sanctuary. See the discussion of K. Elliger, *Deuterojesaja. I. Jesaja 40,1–45,7* (Neukirchen–Vluyn: Neukirchener Verlag, 1978), p. 362, on this point.

collective singular. But it is also a further manifestation of the tension evident in vv. 26-27 between representing the syntax accurately and preserving the sense of the Aramaic idiom. Its occurrence in conjunction with the singular subject of ἔδωκε means that the plural of the pronoun is in grammatical agreement with ἀπολοῦσι καὶ βουλεύσονται in v. 26, even though it is intended to convey the sense of the Aramaic that the authority belongs to the one who gives (singular). Once again, a difficult *Vorlage*, rather than theological interpretation on the part of the LXX, has given rise to the divergence.

Differences in Understanding of the Four Beasts

Because the variations above probably stem from difficulties in translation or in the *Vorlage* of the LXX, they do not necessarily point to differences in understanding between the LXX and MT. But there are some more significant divergences. A look at the depictions of the four beasts, individually and in their relationships to one another, provides examples. The theme of speech creeps into the LXX portrayal of both the second and third creatures. This is implicit in the case of the bear-like creature. Instead of hearing a command the beast itself speaks: 'and he/it spoke thus...' (v. 5, καὶ οὕτως εἶπεν). This in itself may be no more than another Septuagintal attempt at the impersonal passive, but it forms an interesting link with the more explicit Greek description of the leopard. The MT gives the third beast 'rule' (v. 6, שִׁלְטָן), whereas it receives from the LXX 'speech' (γλῶσσα).[61] The resulting humanization of the earlier beasts is also evident in v. 7. The MT seems to view the fourth beast as qualitatively different from what has come before with the absolute statement 'It was different from all the beasts who were before it' (מְשַׁנְיָה מִן־כָּל־חֵיוָתָא דִּי קָדָמַיהּ).[62] The LXX, which has already humanized the second and third beasts, merely says that 'it behaved differently' (διαφόρως χρώμενον) from its predecessors. In the LXX view the fourth beast is an unpleasant continuation of what has gone before rather than an entirely different type.

A lessening of the distinction between beasts on the part of the LXX is observable elsewhere in ch. 7. The picture presented by the MT in

61. Jeansonne, *Daniel 7–12*, p. 119, cites Montgomery, *Daniel*, p. 295, in support of her point that γλῶσσα represents a misreading of שִׁלְטָן as לִשָׁן through metathesis of שׁ and ל. Neither Jeansonne nor Montgomery give other examples of the same type of misreading.

62. A. Caquot, 'Sur les quatre bêtes de Daniel VII', *Semitica* 5 (1955), p. 13.

vv. 11-12 is that judgment is passed on the boastful horn, who is then destroyed and given over to the burning. At that point the earlier beasts are also deprived of their influence, but their fate contrasts with that of the horn when they are given a 'prolongation of life' (v. 12, ארכה בחיין). The boastful horn is destroyed and burned in the LXX as well, but in v. 12 his authority over those round about him is also removed. There is no mention of 'the rest of the beasts' (v. 12 MT, שאר חיותא). As told by the LXX, they fade from the vision entirely. The other figures in v. 12 LXX are not the other beasts but 'those round about him' (τοὺς κύκλῳ αὐτοῦ). As a result, there is no contrast between the last king and the former powers. A further difference is that the syntax of the LXX draws a direct link between the little horn and the figures in v. 12, whereas there is no such link in the MT.

The differences are partly explicable in terms of translation issues. In particular, the change of person probably comes about in a rendering of the impersonal *haphel* העדיו. They can also partly be understood in his-torical terms. It remains an open question whether or not the vision of Daniel is intended to portray the earlier empires as still in existence at the time of the critical later events.[63] Verse 12 suggests that is so, but there is nothing in the interpretation of the vision to back up the notion. The LXX puts no such interpretation on the events foreshadowed by the vision. The earlier beasts are not required to be present in vv. 11-12. The best that can be said is that they may be included in 'those round about (the little horn)', to whom a 'time of life' (χρόνος ζωῆς) was given. However, that is far from clear in the LXX version of the vision, and even if it is the case, they exist as well as, rather than in contrast to, the boastful little horn.

This difference is further illustrated in vv. 19 and 24. The former verse displays again the same lack of distinction observable in vv. 11-12. The MT describes the fourth beast as 'different from all of them' (v. 19, שניה מן־כלהון), whereas the LXX omits that phrase and moves directly into a description of the beast.[64] In v. 24 also the last king is not different in

---

63. Caquot, 'Les quatre bêtes', pp. 40-41, explores the ambivalence of MT on that point. See the full discussion by Rowley, *Darius the Mede*, on the possible iden-tities of the four kingdoms.

64. In v. 19 Ziegler emends διαφθείροντος ('destroying') to διαφέροντος ('differing'), and Jeansonne, *Daniel 7–12*, p. 94, argues on the grounds of ortho-graphic corruption that Ziegler is a more likely reflection of the Old Greek. But 967 and 88-Syh agree on διαφθείροντος.

kind from his predecessors according to the LXX. He merely differs from 'the first (kings)' (v. 24, τοὺς πρώτους) in his 'evil deeds' (κακοῖς). The MT emphasizes rather that the king is different from 'the former ones' (קדמיא) themselves, not from their deeds.[65]

Both versions agree at v. 3 where it is said that the beasts are 'different one from the other' (διαφέροντα ἕν παρὰ τὸ ἕν, שנין דא מן־דא). However, from that point they disagree somewhat in the manner outlined above on the nature of that difference. The MT tends to place the fourth beast and then the eleventh king in a different category. The LXX rather sees them as the culmination of a process.

Differences in Understanding of the Son of Man

If these differences in the way the beasts are distinguished from one another are finely drawn and partly due to translation technique, variations in the way the figure like a son of man is treated are more clearly distinguishable. The first task in dealing with these variations is to establish the most likely text of the LXX at the crucial v. 13.

The phrase ὡς παλαιὸς ἡμερῶν ('one like an ancient of days') poses a problem. Montgomery has labelled this as an erroneous reading which attempts to render the MT's עד.[66] However, Lust points out that ὡς is the reading of 967, so there is no textual evidence available in support of its emendation to ἕως.[67] Moreover, the nominative form of παλαιός that follows is correct for the reading as it stands. If ἕως were correct, we would expect it to take a genitive, as happens in θ. Despite the inconvenience caused by the fact, the reading 'one like an ancient of days' must be allowed to stand in the LXX. Another textual problem concerns the final phrase of the Greek. The reading preferred by Rahlfs, following 88-Syh, is παρῆσαν αὐτῷ ('were by/with him'). 967, in contrast, witnesses to προσήγαγον αὐτῷ, but Lust this time considers the Cologne papyrus to be in error. His grounds are that it is

---

65. The MT tradition of the different fourth beast is also present in *Barn.* 4.5, where it is said to be 'wicked and powerful and fiercer than all the beasts of the sea' (translation by J. Reeves, 'An Enochic Citation in Barnabas 4:3 and the Oracles of Hystaspes' [IOUDAIOS Electronic Bulletin Board: November 1992], p. 2). Reeves (p. 4) sees in *Barnabas* several points of correspondence with the Oracle of Hystaspes.

66. Montgomery, *Daniel*, p. 304. He is supported by Collins, *Daniel*, p. 311.

67. J. Lust, 'Daniel 7.13 and the Septuagint', *ETL* 54 (1978), p. 65.

grammatically incorrect, and has come about as a corruption from θ/MT.[68] In fact, there does not need to be a grammatical problem with the 967 reading. The προσήγαγον form is the second aorist third person plural of προσάγω, used intransitively with αὐτῷ as its indirect object. Hence, 'they (the bystanders) drew close to him'. Other occurrences of this form in the LXX may be found in Num. 7.3 and 15.33 as well as Susanna 52. If there has been no cause to doubt the reliability of 967 for the rest of v. 13, there seem to be no grounds for rejecting it at this point. Indeed, the whole verse makes adequate grammatical sense as presented by 967.[69] The sense is as follows: 'on the clouds of heaven one like a son of man came and one like an ancient of days was nearby, and those standing by drew near to him'. That is the meaning presumed for the rest of this discussion.

The most obvious difference between the versions at v. 13 is the question of whether the son of man arrives 'with the clouds of heaven' (MT, עם־ענני שׁמיא) or 'on the clouds of heaven' (LXX, ἐπὶ τῶν νεφελῶν τοῦ οὐρανοῦ). Are the prepositions עם and ἐπί equivalent or not? The Greek rendering could represent על in its *Vorlage*, or it could be an interpretation of the preposition עם on the part of the translator. Some say that there is no significance in the difference.[70] Prepositions are extremely fluid, and it is possible that ἐπί possessed a shade of meaning appropriate to עם in the mind of the translator. The argument then continues that even if there is a distinction, whether in translation or in the *Vorlage*, there is no difference in the way the son of man is viewed by each version. The divinity or otherwise of the son of man cannot be decided on the choice of preposition.

The data available for a discussion on the usage of Semitic and Greek prepositions, and their equivalence between languages, are obviously extensive. By the very nature of their varied usage, firm conclusions are almost impossible to arrive at, as exceptions can generally be found to support a point of view. But the evidence of the prepositions in this particular instance should not be dismissed out of hand. A study of their use by individual authors and translators can be indicative of style and usage.

---

68. Lust, 'Daniel 7.13', p. 64.

69. Jeansonne, *Daniel 7–12*, pp. 11 and 98, sees προσηγαγον as an example of an original reading in 967, but agrees with Ziegler's emendation of ὡς to ἕως plus the genitive.

70. For example, Goldingay, *Daniel*, p. 145, and Jeansonne, *Daniel 7–12*, p. 113.

With the prepositions currently in question there is a remarkable consistency in the way the Greek represents the Aramaic throughout Daniel 2–7. The preposition עם is found 15 times. It most often has the sense of 'with/along with/among' (2.11, 18; 4.12, 20, 22, 29; 5.21; 7.13). Once it is used to describe someone talking 'with/to' another (6.22), and once it occurs in a sentence that speaks of making war 'with/against' someone (7.21). In 2.43 and 3.33 occur idiomatic uses of עם which do not have formal equivalents in Greek. The LXX translations of these occurrences do not reveal a distinct pattern. There is no LXX equivalent to the occurrences of עם in chs. 4 (including 3.33) and 5. Excluding the exceptional Semitic usage in 2.43 (דנה עם־דנה), עם is translated variously with ἅμα (2.18), μετά (2.11; 4.15), the dative (2.43; 6.22), and πρός (7.21). This analysis excludes καθ' in 7.2, because the sense of עם there presents its own problems.[71] The variety in this part of the evidence renders it unremarkable that ἐπί is found in v. 13.

However, it should be noted that each of the different ways of rendering עם in the LXX, except at v. 13, is an attempt at a particular portion of its semantic range. Such is clearly not the case at v. 13. It is also instructive to see how the LXX uses ἐπί elsewhere in Daniel 2–7. It is found 56 times, of which 26 probably have an equivalent in the MT. Of those, ἐπί represents על eighteen times, functions as an object indicator equivalent to קדם three times, and is the equivalent of prefixed ב or ל four times. It only corresponds to עם in v. 13. If there are not enough examples with which to rule on the LXX's rendering of על, there are enough instances of its use of ἐπί to say that, except in v. 13, the LXX of Daniel is consistent in its employment of that preposition. Note too that not once does θ use ἐπί as a translation of עם.

On the evidence of the above examples it is most likely that the Septuagintal use of ἐπί represents a relationship something like the one described by Aramaic על. As it is used in Daniel 2–7, על usually means 'on/upon' and describes a spatial relationship of some sort. We have already seen the many instances which are represented in the LXX by ἐπί. This is still the major use when a number of other occurrences

---

71. The עם of v. 2 is unusual. Bentzen, *Daniel*, p. 30, likens its usage there to 3.33 and 4.31, but Charles, *Daniel*, p. 175, supposes the די represented by LXX and θ to be original. The suggestion of Delcor, 'Sources', p. 303, that עם in both vv. 2 and 13 expresses temporal co-existence is intriguing but unlikely. It would be more convincing if the recurring expression of which עם is a part in v. 2 showed this variation elsewhere.

which have no equivalent in the LXX are taken into account. It can also mean 'to' (for example, 2.24; 6.7; 7.16) or 'against' (3.19, 29). The sense is still physical, and where there is a Septuagintal equivalent, it is πρός (2.24; 7.16), ἐναντίον (6.7) or εἰς (3.29/96). On the rare occasions when על has the more abstract sense of 'concerning' (2.18; 7.16, 19), the LXX uses either περί (2.18; 7.19) or ὑπέρ (7.16). The preposition also appears in 3.19 and 6.14 as part of untranslatable Aramaic idioms, and so cannot be used in the present discussion. The point of all this is to suggest that the LXX does distinguish between עם and על. From whatever angle the rendering of prepositions from Aramaic into Greek is examined, the distinction is observed except at 7.13. It must then be concluded that the difference in meaning was one that would have been understood and observed by the translator. The evidence of the prepositions also provides a strong case for the view that the difference was there in the *Vorlage* rather than produced in translation.

The uses of both עם and ἐπί are not so broad as to provide an overlap of semantic range. But that still does not tell us whether or not the different prepositions betray a theological difference.[72] In short, is the son of man 'on' (LXX) the clouds different from the son of man 'with' (MT) the clouds? An answer to those questions requires us to shift our sights beyond the prepositions to the 'clouds' (MT, עֲנָנֵי; LXX, νεφελῶν) imagery of which they are a part. Even then, as many have observed, in general terms clouds are often indicative of a theophany, and such would be the case whatever preposition is preferred at v. 13.[73] Ps. 18.11-12 and Exod. 13.21 and 19.16 are cases in point, and 2 Macc. 2.8 provides a later example. So we need to consider how the use of different prepositions affects the functioning of the imagery.

The evidence is mixed for the MT reference עִם־עֲנָנֵי. There are no exact equivalents of the phrase to be found in biblical Hebrew. However, עם is more likely than על to describe general connections between ideas or images. The statement that the son of man comes 'with' the clouds remains undefined. It is not clear whether he is in the clouds or alongside them, or simply evocative of them by the nature of his presence. He may be with or in the clouds yet remain apart from the divinity

72. Lust, 'Daniel 7.13', p. 64, sees ἐπί as a deliberate consequence of LXX's identification of the son of man with the Ancient of Days. But contrast Casey, *Son of Man*, p. 29, and Collins, *Daniel*, p. 311.

73. For example Young, *Daniel's Vision*, p. 13, and Coppens and Dequeker, *Le fils de l'homme*, p. 60.

represented by them. There are many biblical examples that express the same sort of ambivalent understanding of cloud imagery. Sometimes objects or people are covered or suffused with the divine nimbus. The cloud appeared on the mercy seat (Lev. 16.2) and on Mount Sinai (Exod. 24.15-18). In the latter example Moses himself went up into the divine presence by entering the cloud. However it is important to note that this experience of God in the cloud did not in any way make Moses divine.[74] At other times the cloud remains an object apart, as a signal that God is present in the cloud. Such is the case with the pillar of cloud in the wilderness (Exod. 13.21-22). On occasions the cloud forms a mantle for God, indicative of his majesty or otherness (Lam. 3.44). Sometimes the clouds are regarded in a more universal sense as signs of God's creative activity (Job 26.8-9). In each case, although the forms of expression vary, God is in or with, rather than upon, the cloud. Those who encounter him do so by encountering the cloud, but without being granted any of its divinity.

A further apposite reference is from Ezek. 38.9 and 16, where the imagery is given a new twist. There the divine judgment against Israel is expressed in the military activity of 'Gog of the land of Magog' (Ezek. 38.2, גוג ארץ המגוג). His armies will cover the land 'like a cloud' (Ezek. 38.9, כענן). The land is covered with divine judgment as if by a cloud, but the human agent of that judgment by no means comes to share in the divinity of the one who sent him. The best that can be said of one who comes 'with' the clouds is that he has a special place in the activity of God. Whether he is a divine figure or not remains ambiguous.[75]

When it comes to the use of 'upon (על) the clouds' there is again no directly equivalent example available. Yet a clearer picture emerges from an examination of the biblical tradition. Isa. 19.1 depicts the Lord riding 'on a swift cloud' (על־עב קל). Ps. 104.3 provides a similar picture, this

---

74. Though some Jewish interpreters came close to seeing Moses as divine. See, for example, Ezekiel the Tragedian in the second century BCE, who was obviously in debt to Greek thought forms. In his work, Moses mounts a heavenly throne and receives a sceptre (Ezek. Trag. 74-75), and the stars worship him (Ezek. Trag. 79-80). But even here the distinction between divine and human is preserved, since the literary setting of these details is a dream which Moses' father-in-law must interpret for Moses (Ezek. Trag. 83-89). See J.H. Charlesworth, *The Old Testament Pseudepigrapha* (London: Darton, Longman & Todd, 1985), II, pp. 803-804 and 812.

75. Delcor, *Daniel*, p. 154.

time of God 'who makes the clouds his chariot' (השׂם־עבים רכובו).[76] This phrase is in parallel with 'who rides on the wings of the wind' (המהלך על־כנפי־רוח). There is a similar pairing of images in Ps. 18.10-11. Each item in the pair also figures as a representation of the divine presence in Ezekiel 1, a probable source of some of the imagery in Daniel 7. The linking of cloud and chariot through the preposition על in the LXX *Vorlage* is therefore strongly resonant of divinity. Isaiah 14 is also instructive. The 'day star' (Isa. 14.12, הילל) is condemned because he aspires to be 'above the heights of the clouds' (Isa. 14.14, על־במתי עב) so that he might be like the Most High. Being above or on the clouds in this context appears to mean equality with God. The use of על and its LXX translation as ἐπί in Isaiah 19 and Psalm 104 is a further indicator that the figure in v. 13 who arrives 'on' (ἐπί) the clouds is likely to be divine.[77] The same cannot necessarily be said of the one who arrives 'with' (עם) the clouds.

A comparison of the relationship of the son of man to the assembled company (v. 16 MT, קאמיא; v. 13 LXX, οἱ παρεστηκότες) once he arrives supports that suggestion. The MT paints a picture of the son of man being presented to a superior figure by a group already in attendance: he 'was brought before him (the Ancient of Days)' (v. 13, קדמוהי הקרבוהי). After his arrival in the LXX, it is ambiguously stated that 'those standing by drew close to him' (οἱ παρεστηκότες προσήγαγον αὐτῷ). The *haphel* הקרבוהי is apparently taken by the LXX in an active sense and either the suffix on קרב or the entire word קדמוהי is ignored. The most likely of the two possibilities is that קדמוהי is treated as an untranslatable unit, and προσήγαγον αὐτῷ translates the *haphel* verb literally, without taking into account its use as an impersonal plural. As a result, the son of man is not brought forward by attendants, but stands with the Ancient of Days. It is not clear from αὐτῷ to which of the two figures the bystanders draw near in the LXX. However, in v. 14, which must be understood with v. 13, the referent of the third person masculine singular pronoun must be the son of man. It is clearly the recently arrived figure who is the recipient of authority and homage. Therefore the pronoun at the end of v. 13 probably also refers to the son of man as the one towards whom the bystanders draw near in homage. The word chosen by the LXX to express this, προσάγω, is pregnant in the present instance. It is a word with a broad semantic range, but is often

76. Young, *Daniel's Vision*, p. 12.
77. Montgomery, *Daniel*, p. 303.

used in the context of bringing offerings or prayers to God. Such is the case in the already noted Num. 7.3, and Tob. 12.12 uses the word to speak of bringing prayers to God. That meaning is not inevitable but in this context it resonates of worship directed towards the son of man.

The versions are much closer to each other in v. 14. They both agree that the sovereignty granted the son of man is derived (LXX, ἐδόθη; MT, יהיב). They also agree that the service offered him is the same sort of service that is due divinity. As I noted earlier, this is portrayed in the MT by the word פלח. Whenever the LXX translates that word in Daniel, it does so with the verb λατρεύω. We have seen in earlier chapters that that too is a word preserved for dealings with the divine. But the Greek is also not quite equivalent to the Aramaic in that it tends to suggest a cultic understanding more than is the case with פלח. This point is explicated in the discussion on Daniel 6.[78] Incidentally, in v. 14 θ chooses to translate פלח with δουλεύω, a term which we have noted is more generally applicable than λατρεύω to human relationships of subservience.

A second small shift in emphasis between the versions may also be observed in v. 14. In the MT the enduring nature of the rule given the son of man is expounded in parallel statements each with a simple negative. It 'will not pass away' (v. 14, לא יעדה) and it 'will not be destroyed' (לא תתחבל). The syntax of the LXX in the last part of that verse is a little uncertain, but the same parallel statements seem to be intended. However, the translator has chosen the emphatic negative construction of οὐ μή with the aorist subjunctive in each phrase. In so doing, the LXX captures the sense inherent in the Semitic parallel structure, but strengthens it with the emphatic negative.

When the above evidence concerning v. 13 is weighed, the son of man in the LXX seems to bear the mark of a divine figure in a way that the MT son of man does not. The ambiguity of the phrase 'like a son of man' (MT, כבר־אנש; LXX, ὡς υἱός ἀνθρώπου) is present in both versions, but the LXX's use of ἐπί and its portrayal of the heavenly audience clarifies that ambiguity. When it comes to v. 14 the MT and the LXX agree that the figure who arrives on the clouds is vested with a special authority, an authority that is eternal in scope. Indeed the homage offered him is of the sort appropriate to God. This on its own need not make him a divine figure any more than Nebuchadnezzar's response to Daniel in 2.46 makes Daniel divine, although in that case the

---

78. Barr, *Typology of Literalism*, pp. 321-23, notes this practice of imposing the dominant meaning of a word on other meanings, and the distortions that can result.

key words פלח and λατρεύω are not present. It remains an open question in the MT whether or not the son of man's authority becomes intrinsic or remains derived. The LXX has decided in favour of the first option. As a result, the divinity of the son of man perceived by the LXX in v. 14 is read back into v. 13 and so affects the translation.[79] The translator chooses options that are possible renderings of the Aramaic, but cumulatively they tend to take the meaning in a particular direction. The LXX might well also have been working with a *Vorlage* that tended in the same direction by witnessing to על instead of עם in v. 13.

Differences in Understanding of the Holy Ones

One way of treating the son of man is as an element in the vision which is later interpreted, just as the beasts are later interpreted.[80] The cue for this approach is taken from the suggestion inherent in the כ prefix that the son of man should be thought of in the same light as the beasts. They are only 'like' (vv. 4, 6, כ; v. 5, דמיה) certain animals, and the interpretation is necessary to reveal what or who they represent. In the same way the figure on the clouds is only 'like' a son of man and his referent must be discovered through interpretation. If such an approach is followed through, the son of man turns out to be the representative of 'the holy ones of the Most High' (v. 18, קדישי עליונין, ἅγιοι ὑψίστου) in the interpretation. In that case a comparison of the way each version understands the holy ones should show up differences consistent with those noted in their respective treatments of the son of man.

First mention of the holy ones comes at v. 18 in the celestial interpreter's brief summary of the meaning of Daniel's vision. The four beasts are the four kings (v. 17), and then the holy ones receive the kingdom. In the MT an expansion on the vision begins at this first mention. In the vision the rule of the son of man is 'eternal' (v. 14, עלם) which means that it 'will not pass away' (לא יעדה) and it 'will not be destroyed' (לא תתחבל). The LXX expounds this quality with the emphatic negative. In the interpretation the sovereignty of the holy ones will be

79. According to Caquot, 'Les quatre bêtes', p. 70, the LXX translation of 7.13 begins the process of transforming the son of man into 'un objet de foi'. Bruce, 'Oldest Greek Version', p. 26, attributes this to Christian influence, but his view has found little support.

80. This is the view of Bentzen, *King and Messiah*, p. 75, as part of his theory that Dan. 7 may be understood as the 'eschatologizing of Psalm 2'.

'for ever and ever and ever' (v. 18, עד־עלמא ועד עלם עלמיא). This emphatic form is reproduced exactly in the Old Greek. As with the LXX plus of v. 8, the greater emphasis of the LXX in v. 14 is perhaps an anticipation of the interpretation.

The next appearance comes when Daniel shares with the interpreter some more details of his vision of the fourth beast and its horns (vv. 21-22). The particulars are essentially the same in both versions, with the small difference that the verb used in the LXX to denote the defeat of the holy ones (προπέω) has connotations of flight not present in יכל. In each case the holy ones end up in possession of a kingdom, although its eternal nature is not specified by Daniel. In v. 25 of the interpretation also, the versions agree that the arrogant king will wear down or 'exhaust' (LXX, κατατρίψει; MT, יבלא) the holy ones.

Once we get to v. 27, however, there are notable differences in the way the versions convey their understanding of the holy ones. The most obvious is the difference in syntax, yet the variation in syntax on its own is not indicative of a variation in meaning. Both the MT and LXX contain the same number of terms conveying concepts of governance and in the same order, even though they are in slightly different relationship to one another. Moreover, they correspond to the way the LXX has translated those terms, both in ch. 7 and in the earlier narratives. The one possible exception is the LXX's use of a term more usually favoured by θ, τὴν ἀρχήν, as equivalent to מלכות.

Apart from questions of syntax, there are two particularly knotty problems presented in this verse. First there is the unique appearance of the phrase 'people of the holy ones of the Most High' (v. 27, עם קדישי עליונין), witnessed to in the MT but not directly in the LXX equivalent, λαῷ ἁγίῳ.[81] A number of commentators have struggled with this unique usage of עם in harness with the recurring construct phrase קדישי עליונין.[82] In the absence of any other guidance from the immediate context and in the face of ambivalent evidence elsewhere, I accept the argument that

---

81. The plural עליונין is unexpected. The singular עליון as in CD 20.8 is the expected reading. See E. Lohse (ed.), *Die Texte aus Qumran* (Munich: Kösel, 1971), p. 104. The plural is usually explained as a Hebraizing plural of majesty. See Montgomery, *Daniel*, p. 307, Slotki, *Daniel*, p. 61, and Young, *Daniel*, p. 158. J.E. Goldingay, '"Holy Ones on High" in Daniel 7:18', *JBL* 107 (1988), pp. 496-97, protests that Aramaic does not even do that for אלה. He sees it as a genuine plural, as part of his argument for a celestial understanding of the holy ones.

82. Delcor, 'Sources', p. 303, sees in this usage a hesitancy about identifying the son of man with Yahweh.

'holy ones of the Most High' is equivalent to 'people of the holy ones of the Most High'.[83] The second problem, one of particular interest to the present comparison, is that of person within v. 27.

In the MT sovereignty is granted (יהיבת) the people of the holy ones. The verb is a *peil* form which does not require a subject to be specified, and we have seen that the singular probably treats the preceding list (מלכותה ושלטנא ורבותא) as a collective noun. Then, after his reception of authority, all rules will serve and obey the ambiguous 'him' (לה). It is possible that the referent is עם, as this collective noun normally takes a singular verb.[84] Such is the case in 3.29 and Ezra 6.12. On the other hand it could be the court, which is the subject of v. 26 and hence the implied subject of יהיבת. When the court first appears in Daniel's early account of his vision, the Ancient of Days seems to preside over events and there is no interest in the occupants of the other thrones. The actions of the court thereby become the actions of the Ancient of Days, who is indistinguishable from the Most High. This link is not made in the interpretations, but can be carried forward into them. Hence the eternal kingdom at the end of v. 27 could also be that of the Most High. The syntax of this verse explicitly links ownership of the eternal kingdom (מלכות עלם) with receipt of worship due to divinity. In that connection the verb פלח has been explicated elsewhere. However, the same link is made in v. 14 of the vision report although the syntax is different. As we have seen, in that context the recipient of worship and possessor of the king-dom is the son of man, not the court. That makes it more likely that the third person singular in v. 27 refers to the people of the saints. The con-struction of v. 27 and its predecessors allows rather than demands this but it is consistent with what has gone before. It is also possible that the ambiguity of the verse is a deliberate link back to the son of man in the vision. This verse then becomes the culmination of the process of divinization that we have discerned. Just as the son of man was given

---

83. Casey, *Son of Man*, p. 41. Contrast Collins, *Daniel*, p. 322, who under-stands the phrase as 'the people pertaining to or under the protection of the holy ones'.

84. I am grateful to my colleague, Dr Paul Hughes, for pointing out that the same phenomenon is observable in Exod. 1 where עם בני ישראל (Exod. 1.9, 'the people of the sons of Israel'), בני ישראל (Exod. 1.1, 7, 12, 'the sons of Israel'), and עם (Exod. 1.20, 'the people') are treated synonymously. The fuller expression of Exod. 1.9 takes a singular complement (רב ועצים) whereas 'sons of Israel' is grammatically plural.

divine authority, so have the people of the holy ones of the Most High.[85] The two are now indistinguishable, a point that is later expressed by the celestial imagery of 12.3.

The LXX's grappling with an ambivalent Aramaic *Vorlage* results in several differences in the way v. 27 is rendered. The active aorist ἔδωκε appears to be an attempt at rendering יהיבת, but the active verb cannot help but raise the question of its subject in a way that the passive of the MT does not. This is most likely to be the court or the Ancient of Days. All of this authority is given 'to the holy people of the Most High' (v. 27, λαῷ ἁγίῳ ὑψίστου), a translation which preserves equivalence of elements but is clearly interpretative of עם קדישי עליונין. Elsewhere the holy ones of the Most High are plural in their grammatical function (see vv. 18, 22), but the singular expression used here makes it possible that the holy people is the referent of αὐτῷ each time it appears. As that pronoun is an indirect object for each of the verbs ὑποταγήσονται and πειθαρχήσουσιν, it must be possible that 'all authorities' (πᾶσαι ἐξουσίαι) are subject to the holy people. Thus far, the LXX follows the MT in having the Ancient of Days or the celestial court grant authority to the holy ones.

However, we must now take account of the verbs ὑποταγήσονται ('[they] will be subject to') and πειθαρχήσουσιν ('[they] will be obedient to') in the last part of v. 27 LXX. They are strange choices with which to translate יפלחון וישתמעון ('they will serve and obey'), as they appear to secularize the sense of פלח and שמע. The expected word in the Greek for פלח would have been either δουλεύω, chosen by θ, or λατρεύω, the significance of which has been discussed in detail in an earlier chapter. But a survey of these other verbs as used in other parts of the LXX is instructive. Little can be said about πειθαρχέω, as its only other certain occurrence is in *1 Esd.* 8.90. There it is used to speak of obedience to the law.

An examination of ὑποτάσσω, on the other hand, is more revealing. The word is used in an assortment of ways and translates at least five Hebrew words (כבש, 1 Chron. 22.18; שית, Ps. 8.7; דבר, Ps. 17.48; דמם, Ps. 36.7; רדד, Ps. 143.2), none of which have the same connotations of worship as פלח. In 2 Maccabees it is used in a different sense again as a term of military rank (2 Macc. 4.12; 8.9, 22). Yet in the midst of this variety there is one theme picked out by the LXX translator's choice of

---

85. See the exposition of this view by Hartman and DiLella, *Daniel*, pp. 101-102.

ὑποτάσσω. That theme is epitomized in Psalm 8, in which v. 7 tells us that God puts the works of his hands under the sovereignty (the verb is מִשַׁל) of humanity, and 'places' (שַׁתָּה) everything under his feet. The LXX translates the latter verb with ὑπέταξας. The concept of godly rule being given to a created people is also found in Pss. 17.48, 46.4 and 143.2, each time with a different Hebrew verb, but each time rendered ὑποτάσσω in the LXX. Variations on this theme are also present in Wis. 8.14 and 1 Chron. 22.18. In the former, wisdom is extolled as the means by which 'nations will become subject to me (the speaker)' (Wis. 8.14, ἔθνη ὑποταγήσεταί μοι). In the Chronicles reference David notes that God has subjected the land to the Lord and his people (ἡ γῆ ἐναντίον κυρίου καὶ ἐναντίον λαοῦ αὐτοῦ). In each case again the verb ὑποτάσσω is used.

The choice of verbs in the last part of v. 27 LXX suggests that the transfer of God's authority to his people has been understood by the LXX in terms of the tradition outlined above. The holy people therefore are simply human agents and the divinized son of man remains a separate entity.[86] This effect is reinforced by the LXX plus of the possessive plural pronouns modifying the sovereignty words. As a result of their use, the holy ones acquire the sovereignty previously exercised by the little horn. It is as if the LXX, unlike the MT, draws back from identifying the holy ones of the Most High completely with the son of man. Perhaps this relates also to the more emphatic divinization of the figure on the clouds in the LXX. The LXX is reluctant to picture the holy ones in the ranks of angels or divine figures. The son of man of the vision remains a distinct figure rather than a symbol for the holy ones of Israel. This more earthy depiction of the holy ones on the part of the LXX tallies with other translation decisions made, that together tend to take the meaning in a particular direction.[87]

Links with Other Stories: Daniel the Visionary

There are a number of explicit clues that encourage the reader to contrast Daniel as visionary with Daniel as interpreter. Once the date has been set, we are told that Daniel 'saw a dream and visions of his head

---

86. Compare Anderson, *Daniel*, p. 87, who argues the same point for MT by referring to Isa. 61.5-9.

87. Young, *Daniel*, p. 154, who is insistent that the son of man is a divine figure, considers the LXX to be a correct interpretation in this direction.

upon his bed' (v. 1, חלם חזה וחזוי ראשה על־משכבה). The reader is put in mind of Daniel's own words to King Nebuchadnezzar, 'this is your dream and visions of your head upon your bed' (2.28, חלמך וחזוי ראשך על־משכבך). Apart from the pronominal suffixes, the phrasing is almost identical. Almost the same phrase also appears in Nebuchadnezzar's account of another of his dreams (4.7, 10). At other times the sage tells of his 'visions of the night' (vv. 2, 7, 13, חזוי [עם־]ליליא) or, as a variation, of 'visions of my head' (v. 15, חזוי ראשי). The same variety of expression is seen in chs. 2 and 4 of the king's dreams. Nebuchadnezzar also saw 'visions of the night' (2.19, חזוי די־ליליא) and 'visions of my head' (4.2, חזוי ראשי).[88] It begins to look as if the roles have now been reversed.

This becomes clear when the physical effect of the dreams on Daniel is noted. After the vision he records that 'my spirit was troubled' (v. 15, אתכרית רוחי) and the visions 'frightened me' (v. 15, יבהלנני). Things were not much better after he heard the interpretation, when 'my thoughts frightened me and my colours changed upon me' (v. 28, רעיוני יבהלנני וזיוי ישתנון עלי). Nebuchadnezzar also found his 'spirit' (רוח) troubled as a result of dreams (2.1, 3), and was frightened (בהל) by his experiences (4.2). Verse 28 is an almost word-for-word reflection of Belshazzar's response to his own encounter with God (5.6, 10), except that the order is reversed and the Babylonian king also had trouble with the knots of his loins. The distinction between the Daniel of ch. 7 and of chs. 2–6 is not an absolute one. The sage also found that 'his thoughts frightened him' (4.16, רעינהי יבהלנה) as the interpretation of the dream of the tree dawned on him. There was an element of the visionary about the interpreter also. It is interesting to note that vv. 15 and 28 are both different in the LXX from the MT. As a result the literary resonances with the Daniel of earlier chapters are not present in the LXX.

Although Daniel experiences similar physical and mental symptoms to the kings when he dreams, there is an implied contrast with the way he deals with his fears. Whereas the kings are invariably thrown into a panic, the quiet response of Daniel that 'I kept the matter in my heart' (v. 28, מלתא בלבי נטרת) is of a completely different order. The same contrast this time is present in the LXX.

---

88. The use of די in 2.19 but not in ch. 7 has no significance. די is also used in ch. 7 to express a construct relationship between nouns. See vv. 4, 6, 7, 10, 19 and 27. M.H. Segal, *A Grammar of Mishnaic Hebrew* (Oxford: Clarendon Press, 1927), p. 185, says די and the construct are 'used indiscriminately' in Aramaic to express the genitive.

Links with Other Stories: Bestiality/Humanity Theme

The interplay between bestial and human also forms a link with the narrative of ch. 4.[89] In the earlier chapter King Nebuchadnezzar was explicitly denied his humanity until such time as he acknowledged the
sovereignty of the Most High (4.14). The tree which sheltered the birds
and the beasts was cut down and became one from whom the heart of a
man was removed and whose lot was with the beasts (4.12-13). When
he acknowledged God, his humanity returned to him (4.31). These
themes re-emerge in ch. 7 in a way that is reminiscent of ch. 4 but is not
a tidy equivalent of it. This time a beast is given 'the heart of a man'
(v. 4, לבב אנש) in a reversal of Nebuchadnezzar's being given 'the heart
of a beast' (4.13, לבב חיוה).[90] Even the arrogant little horn at the end of
the vision had eyes 'like the eyes of a man' (v. 8, כעיני אנשא). This makes
clear what was only implicit in ch. 4, that Nebuchadnezzar's humanity
was ultimately derived from God in the same way that the humanity of
the beasts belongs to God and is ultimately removed by the heavenly
court.[91] Later in the vision of ch. 7 the sovereignty exercised by
the beasts is removed and given to one 'like a son of man' (v. 13,
כבר אנש).[92] At this point there is no evidence of any humanity resident in
the fourth beast, which is killed and his body destroyed, or in the other
three who are allowed to live on. They are described simply as 'the
beasts' (v. 12, חיותא). Just as Nebuchadnezzar lost his humanity when he
refused to acknowledge the source of his authority, so the beasts lose
theirs at the judgment scene. We have explored above the strong
implication contained in the *peil* forms of the early part of the chapter
that the humanity of the beast derives from God. Nebuchadnezzar also
has his humanity returned to him when he sees in ch. 4 that heaven
rules. There is a further echo here from ch. 2 in that Nebuchadnezzar,
as symbolized by the great statue, ruled over 'the sons of men'
(2.38, בני־אנשא).

The interaction of these themes is not as explicit in the LXX. On one
hand, as already noted, the LXX implies the human quality of speech in

89. Jephet, *Daniel*, p. 34, and Lenglet, 'Daniel 2–7', p. 174.

90. K. Koch, 'Die Weltreiche im Danielbuch', *TLZ* 85 (1960), p. 830, notes that
the first beast in MT is the only one with a human manner.

91. Saadia, in Gallé, *Daniel*, p. 72, also links the first beast with
Nebuchadnezzar's humanity in ch. 4.

92. Bevan, *Daniel*, p. 119.

the second and third beast, and agrees with the MT in v. 8 that the little horn of the fourth beast also possesses the facility of speech. The detail of the 'human eyes' (v. 8, ὀφθαλμοὶ ἀνθρώπινοι) is also present in the LXX. So the beasts are if anything more human than in the MT, but only marginally so. They are contrasted with a son of man who is more divine than human, so the interplay between beasts and a human figure (one like a son of man) does not work in quite the same way as in the MT.

Once it comes to the link with the themes in ch. 4, the explicit vocabulary resonances of the Aramaic are absent in the LXX. It is true that the tradition of Nebuchadnezzar eating the food of the beasts and taking on some of the physical characteristics is utilized by the LXX (4.15, 33b). But the more metaphysical notion of his heart being changed to that of a beast is hardly present at all. The one exception is the reference, 'My flesh was changed as well as my heart' (4.33b, ἠλλοιώθη ἡ σάρξ μου καὶ ἡ καρδία μου). Even there the compound subject with a singular verb identifies the change of heart with physical changes. These bodily changes are emphasized by the LXX in ch. 4 more than the Aramaic. For example, in 4.16 LXX the wish is that the king's 'body be changed by the dew of heaven' (ἀπὸ τῆς δρόσου τοῦ οὐρανοῦ τὸ σῶμα αὐτοῦ ἀλλοιωθῆ). The MT equivalent is that 'his heart be changed from men' (4.13, לבבה מן־אנושא ישנון). Other occurrences of this concept (4.31, 33 MT), or the notion that the king's 'lot' (חלק) is with the beasts (4.12, 20 MT), have no equivalent in the LXX.

Indeed, the idea of some sort of isolation or exile at times replaces the MT notion of Nebuchadnezzar's bestiality (4.25-26 LXX). For example, Nebuchadnezzar relates that at the moment the Most High was acknowledged 'my understanding returned to me' (4.33, מנדעי יתוב עלי). In a section otherwise uncharacteristically close to the MT, the LXX equivalent is that 'my kingdom was restored to me' (4.36, ἀποκατεστάθη ἡ βασιλεία μου ἐμοί). The extra Septuagintal detail that Nebuchadnezzar would not 'speak with any man' (4.32, οὐ μὴ λαλήσῃς μετὰ παντὸς ἀνθρώπου) also tends in the same direction. This is part of the tendency to allegorize in ch. 4 LXX already discussed, which is seen most clearly in the LXX's description of the tree (4.10-12). The net result of these differences in ch. 4 is that the literary links between chs. 7 and 4 are not as clearly drawn. This is not only the case in terms of vocabulary and theme. As the MT stands, the pattern of symbolic vision and interpretation is shared by chs. 4 and 7. The extended allegory of ch. 4 LXX does not allow for such an equivalence of structure.

Links with Other Stories: Four Empires Theme

The autobiographical vision account and the bestiality–humanity axis in ch. 7 provide a number of links with ch. 4. The theme of the four empires provides a more obvious tie to ch. 2.[93] The relationship of the four empires in each chapter to one another has been debated at length.[94] It is not part of my present purpose to solve the historical question of whether the four kings or empires in mind are the same in each instance. It is enough to note the literary resonances that arise when ch. 7 also explores the theme of the four empires.

In general terms, the writer assesses the four empires similarly in both chapters. Nebuchadnezzar is the head of gold and clearly occupies a position superior to that of the second and third elements of the statue in 2.38-39. The vision that Daniel has is not so clear on this point, but the MT does say of the first beast that he was given the heart of a man (v. 4).[95] That does not happen for the second and third beasts, who in fact fade into the background, apart from the problematic reference to them in v. 12. Chapter 2 is more explicit that the second and third empires, the silver and bronze of the statue, are not as important as the first empire (v. 39). The same attitude to the first three empires is preserved also in the LXX. The verses of ch. 2 in question are closely translated. The details are slightly different in ch. 7, but the effect is largely the same. We have seen that the second and third empires are given a slightly higher profile by ch. 7 LXX in that they are more human than their MT counterparts (vv. 5-6), but then they disappear from the account entirely. They do not even make the difficult appearance in v. 12.

Both visions of the four empires are most interested in the fourth empire, and the eternal kingdom that eventually replaces it.[96] There are

---

93. Beasley-Murray, 'Interpretation of Daniel 7', p. 54.

94. For example Rowley, *Darius the Mede*.

95. Driver, *Daniel*, p. 81. Against this, J. Clerget, 'L'énigme et son interpréta-tion', *LV* 160 (1982), p. 44, identifies the fourth beast with the head of gold.

96. It is granted that ch. 2 sometimes treats the statue as a unity, and sometimes as a symbol of successive regimes. But problems raised by this ambivalence do not

striking similarities about the way the fourth empire is portrayed. Chapter 7 recalls the feet of iron in 2.41 when it describes the fourth beast, although this time as separate elements in the description. The beast has 'teeth of iron' (v. 7, שִׁנַּיִן דִּי־פַרְזֶל) and it does its evil work 'with its feet' (v. 7, בְרַגְלֵיהּ).[97] The number of the 'ten horns' (v. 7, קַרְנַיִן עֲשַׂר) may also recall the toes of the feet on the statue (2.42-43), although differences between the LXX and MT traditions about the toes in ch. 2 mean that that point cannot be pressed too hard. In his expanded account of the vision Daniel adds the detail that the fourth beast also had 'claws of bronze' (v. 19, טִפְרַיהּ דִּי־נְחָשׁ). The reference to iron and bronze reminds the reader of the four metal tradition central to ch. 2, without necessarily implying any logical links as far as interpretation is concerned.[98] The behaviour of the fourth beast is also reminiscent of its counterpart in ch. 2. The destructive nature of the iron empire is echoed in ch. 7 with the picture of the creature with iron teeth and bronze claws 'eating, crushing and trampling' (vv. 7, 19, 23, אָכְלָה מַדְּקָה...רָפְסָה). In particular, the verb דקק is used in both contexts (see 2.40). The divisions within the fourth empire of 2.43 are also present in the eleventh horn's humbling of three kings to make room for himself (v. 24), although the theme is less prominent in ch. 7.[99]

There is a twist in the tail of the imagery with the use of the same verb to describe what happens to the statue when it is struck by the stone not quarried by human hands. The rock 'crushed' (2.34, הַדֵּקֶת) the feet of the statue, then all the elements of the statue were 'crushed together' (2.35, דָּקוּ כַחֲדָה; see also 2.44) before being scattered to the wind. The image is reversed in that what the fourth empire does to those around it in ch. 7 has already happened to that empire in the judgment against it of ch. 2. The same sort of resonance comes through the use of the verb אכל ((vv. 7, 19, 23). The reader is put in mind of the idiom describing the treatment of Daniel and his three friends at the hands of the courtiers in chs. 3 and 6. There they 'ate pieces of him' (3.8; 6.25, אֲכַלוּ קַרְצֵיהוֹן). The irony of the slanderers' fate in ch. 6, that they are eaten by the lions, has been noted. But as well as their being eaten, the lions 'crush' (6.25, הַדִּקוּ) their bones, an extra detail that strengthens the

jeopardize the literary argument here being offered.

97. Delcor, *Daniel*, p. 147.

98. Goldingay, *Daniel*, p. 157, writes, 'There is no specific reason to suppose that the connection (between ch. 7 and chs. 2–6) is other than a literary one.'

99. Bevan, *Daniel*, p. 114. See also Montgomery, *Daniel*, p. 282.

resonance of this particular image in ch. 7 with what has gone before. The behaviour of the Babylonians has been reversed against them as part of the judgment on them, just as happens to the fourth empire of ch. 7.[100]

Related to the theme of judgment against the four beasts is the strong hint that their sovereignty is something that they are dependent on God for anyway. Just as it is taken away from them, so it was given to them in the first place. We have looked at this effect in the first part of ch. 7 in some detail. That also recalls the reminder to Nebuchadnezzar, much more explicitly than in ch. 7, that God 'has given' (2.37-38, יהב) his authority to him and will also take it away.[101] The existence of this story adds to the effect of Daniel's later vision.

As far as the broad outlines of the stories and vision go, the links discernible in the MT are also present in the LXX. The physical description of the fourth empire, its aggressive behaviour, and the divisions within it are all represented in the LXX. The ironies of judgment outlined above may also be discerned. This is not surprising given that ch. 2 of the LXX is much closer to the MT than ch. 4 LXX. But the emphasis on the derived nature of royal authority as a link between the chapters is not as clearly drawn in the LXX, largely because the distinctive use of *peil* in the early verses is not well represented in the Greek; and the particular connections through vocabulary are not present to the same extent. Neither v. 7 nor v. 19 is exactly equivalent in the LXX. The nine occurrences of דקק in the book (2.34, 35, 40, 44, 45; 6.25; 7.7, 19, 23) are translated with several different synonyms, or else not represented at all, so the thread woven by the one Aramaic word is not as evident. We have already seen that the idiomatic expression for slander in the Aramaic of 3.8 and 6.25 is not translated literally by the LXX, so the connections made by the word אכל are likewise not part of the LXX's story.

Links with Other Stories: The Final Kingdom

There are also important links between chs. 2 and 7 in their view of the kingdom that replaces the vicious fourth kingdom. The final kingdom is not developed to the same extent in ch. 2, but the key characteristics of

---

100. See Lenglet, 'Daniel 2–7', p. 176, on the smashing stone and son of man as complementary images.

101. Lenglet, 'Daniel 2–7', p. 179.

timelessness and indestructibility are conveyed in the phrases 'it will never be destroyed' (2.44, ‏לעלמין לא תתחבל‎) and 'it will be set up forever' (2.44, ‏תקום לעלמיא‎). The reign of the son of man, likewise, is 'an eternal rule' (v. 14, ‏שלטן עלם‎) which 'will not be destroyed' (v. 14, ‏לא תתחבל‎). Similar echoes are found in the LXX at this point. Just as the authority of the son of man is an 'eternal authority' (v. 14, ἐξουσία αἰώνιος), so the final kingdom of ch. 2 'will be set up forever' (2.44, στήσεται εἰς τὸν αἰῶνα). The recurrence of ‏חבל‎ in Aramaic is also paralleled in the LXX with the verb φθείρω. The kingdom represented by the crushing rock will 'not be ruined' (2.44, οὐ φθαρήσεται) and the kingdom granted the son of man will likewise 'never be ruined' (v. 14, οὐ μὴ φθαρῇ).

Further Literary Links with Other Stories

The points just focused on provide ample evidence on their own in support of the case for understanding Daniel 7 in conjunction with the stories that precede it. But there are also other instances of vocabulary that evoke the earlier stories.[102] The use of ‏קום‎ in v. 4, where the eagle was stood on its feet, recalls the parody of ch. 3 when the statue is constantly referred to as that which 'Nebuchadnezzar set up' (3.2, 3, 5, 7, ‏די הקים נבוכדנצר‎).[103] The horn that 'uprooted' (v. 8, ‏אתעקרו‎) three other horns calls to mind the tree of ch. 4 which in fact was not quite uprooted. 'Its root stock' (4.12, 20, 23, ‏עקר שרשוהי‎) was allowed to remain against the day that the king's sovereignty and the tree's greatness would be returned. 'All peoples, nations and tongues' (v. 14, ‏כל עממיא אמיא ולשניא‎) is a formula encountered time and again. Apart from the variations on it, it is found in the exact form here quoted in four of the five preceding stories (3.4, 7, 31; 5.19; 6.26).[104] The vocabulary of the LXX also creates these resonances, although in the last example there is greater variation in the way the formula appears.

---

102. Z. Stefanovic, 'Thematic Links between the Historical and Prophetic Sections of Daniel', *AUSS* 27 (1989), pp. 125-26, sets out in tabular form a number of links between the historical and prophetic sections.

103. An interesting interplay goes on between 'standing' and 'falling' in Dan. 2–7. Note, for example, that the myriads stand before the Ancient of Days (7.10) while Nebuchadnezzar's officials are required to fall before the statue of ch. 3.

104. Anderson, *Daniel*, p. 86.

Structural Links with Other Stories

There is also a sense in which the very structure of chs. 2–7 binds the vision and interpretation of Daniel to the stories about his and his companions' encounters with the sovereigns. We have noted that several of the narratives are shaped to build suspense. They begin with the king's problem, which is either caused or heightened by some sort of divine revelation, and build the expectation that what ensues will solve the problem. The suspense comes in that the meaning or purpose of the divine revelation takes a considerable time to be worked out. Occasionally it is apparently put in the background by the narrator, while he turns the spotlight onto other agenda. Only toward the end of the story is the interpretation or solution offered, or sometimes the exact nature of the problem finally explicated. In chs. 2 and 5 the reader must wait to find out what the solution to the riddles might be. In fact, the initial emphasis on the effect of the revelations on the king delays an explanation of the revelation, and its interpretation takes longer still. Even chs. 4 and 6 have elements of suspense built into them. The same kind of structure of suspense operates in chs. 2–7 as a unit. Daniel 2 begins a revelation of what must take place 'after this' (2.29, 45, אחרי דנה). The reader must wait to see the final exposition of these things in ch. 7.[105] The more active nature of the empires in ch. 7 relative to those in ch. 2 is one indication of this process.[106] In the meantime further dramas are played out between the dream of the statue and the fuller explanation of the four empires. This in itself lends a new significance to the fourth empire and the final kingdom, just as the significance of the writing on the wall was heightened by its absence from the central part of the narrative in ch. 5. The stories in between are enlisted to help explore that significance.

The same observations on structure cannot apply to the LXX. In the first place, the individual narratives are not structured for suspense in the LXX to the same extent as in the MT. This renders it less likely that a deliberate structural link between the visions of chs. 2 and 7 can be read into the LXX. There is also the complex question of what an earlier

105. Goldingay, *Daniel*, p. 158. Raabe, 'Daniel 7', p. 273, notes the details in ch. 7 that are additional to ch. 2. Heaton, *Daniel*, p. 178, calls vv. 9-14 the climax of the whole book.

106. See Goldingay, *Daniel*, p. 158, who also enumerates other differences between the regimes of chs. 2 and 7.

shaping of Daniel may have looked like. 967 places chs. 7 and 8 between chs. 4 and 5 resulting in a chronological arrangement based on the royal dating in the Old Greek tradition.[107] We noted in the chapter on Daniel 5 that this is possibly the oldest order of the Old Greek, while the MT order arises in a 'heavily redacted composition of the Semitic text'.[108] Whatever view is taken on the composition history of the respective versions, the 967 order creates a different perspective on the relationship of ch. 7 to the whole, and strikes a chord with what we have observed about the differences between the LXX and MT narratives in chs. 4 and 5.[109] In the MT ch. 7 points towards the visions, yet draws on a number of themes in the preceding stories. It also denotes a shift from concerns of exile to issues of nationhood. The organization is more thematic or genre-related than chronological. In 967 chs. 4 and 5 can be separated from each other without undue violence to continuity because the concern that binds chs. 4 and 5 in the MT, the person of Nebuchadnezzar, is largely expressed in the MT plus material and so is less prominent in the Old Greek. Chapters 3 and 4 in the LXX suggest a view of Nebuchadnezzar that owes something to the experience of the Jewish people at the hands of Antiochus IV Epiphanes. By placing ch. 7 immediately after the stories in chs. 2–4 967 follows up the theme of Nebuchadnezzar as the evil king.[110]

Conclusion

Given the nature of the material being treated, I have spent less time than previously on the shape of the narrative itself. When the chapter is treated as a literary unit, there is a definite narrative structure discernible, akin to the autobiographical dream account in ch. 4. As in ch. 2, there is little difference in the way the LXX shapes the story, which is partly why that aspect has not dominated my approach to ch. 7. A couple of exceptions have been noted, however. The Aramaic use of passive forms creates a nuance of divine workmanship lying

---

107. Geissen, *Der Septuaginta-Text*, p. 33.

108. Lust, 'Daniel 4–5', p. 53. See also Bogaert, 'Relecture et refonte', pp. 198-200.

109. The problem of a Hebrew chapter (8) with Aramaic (7 and 5) on either side of it is a weakness in the argument for the originality of 967, which has not been satisfactorily resolved.

110. Bogaert, 'Relecture et refonte', p. 206.

behind events, while the eschatological nature of Daniel's visionary experiences stands out more in the LXX than in the MT. In passing, a couple of instances have been noted where the LXX anticipates the narrative, a habit we have observed in its translations of other stories.

The bulk of the chapter has concentrated on the respective understanding and interpretation of Daniel's vision in each version. The chief difficulty in so doing is found in the number of exegetical points that need to be settled in each version before they can be set alongside each other. In particular, I have proceeded on the premise that the Ancient of Days in both versions can be thought of in the same terms as the Most High. In the MT the son of man is understood as a human figure who has divine characteristics and privileges invested in him. In the same way that the beasts symbolize four empires, the holy ones of the Most High correspond in the interpretation to the son of man in the vision. They are a group of humans who, like him, are given a divine task.

Many of the differences between the versions can be explained in technical terms and their significance should not be exaggerated. Nevertheless, partly through translation choices and partly through working with a variant *Vorlage*, the LXX does exhibit some tendencies. The LXX takes even less interest in the second and third beasts than does its MT counterpart. The son of man is an inherently divine figure, rather than one who is invested with divinity. As a corollary, the holy ones of the Most High are characterized in more earthly terms. One consequence of that is a difference between the versions in the way symbols are used.

When it comes to the literary relationships between ch. 7 and its preceding narratives, the MT and the LXX have most in common in their use of the four empire scheme which unites chs. 2 and 7. This is not surprising given that the Old Greek translation or its *Vorlage* is closer to the MT in those two chapters than elsewhere in Daniel 2–7. Otherwise, the literary resonances binding this vision narrative to the other stories are not as strong in the LXX as in the MT, sometimes because of a different Aramaic text behind the LXX and sometimes because themes become lost in translation. The evidence for a coherent structure in chs. 2–7 is also stronger in the MT . Indeed there is a suggestion from 967 that the LXX follows quite a different ordering, and we have seen hints of that ordering in the discussion of earlier chapters.

Chapter 8

DIFFERENCES IN DANIEL 1 AND 8–12

This chapter surveys in general terms how the LXX compares with the MT of the Hebrew chapters of Daniel (1; 8–12) as a way of rounding out the comparative study of chs. 2–7. The survey is primarily undertaken as a check on the conclusions reached in previous chapters, and is not intended to solve the multitude of exegetical and theological problems raised by both versions of these complex chapters. Differences in the *Vorlage* and those arising in translation are not distinguished, except in tentative terms. I begin by discussing the nature of the Greek translation, and certain renderings which could be problematic. These raise the question of the extent to which the LXX interprets its *Vorlage*, and the debate on that subject is alluded to. While there is generally close equivalence in the Greek translation, there are some marked differences in the way each version treats certain key terms, people, places and dates in the chapters under discussion. The central part of the survey focuses on these and, without engaging fully in the debate, suggests that a degree of interpretation is to be found in them. As in ch. 7, the differences often do not signify a change in meaning, but sometimes demonstrate a slightly different outlook between versions. Along the way I note a number of instances where tendencies evident in chs. 2–7 continue to be present in the LXX translation of the Hebrew chapters. The variations that arise do not affect the narrative form of the chapters in question, so that aspect will not be a part of the ensuing discussion.

The Nature of the Translation

An extremely rough generalization is that the LXX relates to the Hebrew MT in Daniel 1 and 8–12 much as it does to the Aramaic MT of Daniel 2 and 7. There is an oscillation in the degree of direct equivalence on the part of the Greek translation. Sometimes the equivalence is marked while at other times there are some notable variations. The Hebrew syntax is often tortuous, particularly, but not only, in ch. 11, and this creates difficulty for the translator. Despite those difficulties, at times the equivalence of elements in the Greek translation suggests a translator with considerable respect for his *Vorlage*.[1] Each of the chapters in question displays certain tendencies that distinguish it from its neighbours, but examples of this direct syntactical equivalence can be cited from each. Leaving aside lexical equivalence, the syntactical correspondence is striking in 8.5. The Greek includes the personal pronoun ἐγώ to represent אני, although it makes it the subject of a finite verb rather than the היה plus participle form of the MT. והנה and καὶ ἰδού correspond, as do ἐπὶ προσώπου and על־פני. Whatever the phrase might mean, the puzzling הצפיר קרן חזות is retained by the LXX with τοῦ τράγου κέρας ἕν.[2] In 9.7 the Hebrew idiom of ל with pronominal suffixes as possessive becomes the dative forms, σοι and ἡμιν, while the כ prefixed to יום is κατὰ τὴν ἡμέραν. The phrase in the last part of 10.14 is not elegantly stated in either language, but the same word order is present in each with the standard exception of γάρ. The Greek word order ἔτι ὅρασις εἰς ἡμέρας is a replication of the Hebrew עוד חזון לימים. Dan. 11.3 LXX exactly reproduces the expression משל ממשל רב ('will rule with great dominion') with κυριεύσει κυρ(ι)είας πολλῆς. Correspondence with the Hebrew emphatic in 12.5, ראיתי אני דניאל (literally 'I saw, I Daniel'), results in the unusual Greek word order, εἶδον ἐγὼ Δανιηλ. Perhaps the point is best illustrated at 11.17, where the Hebrew is nothing if not obscure. Notwithstanding slight alterations in content, the syntax of the MT is still reproduced by the Greek.

At the same time there are some marked variations to note. Both versions contain material that is not present in the other. In the MT these include the extra detail on dating and the physical description of a rebuilt Jerusalem in 9.25. At 10.9 the MT conveys the additional detail that Daniel had 'fallen into a deep sleep' (נרדם). A number of MT pluses appear in ch. 11 around the detail of the conflict between the kings of the north and the south. These involve the fate of the daughter (11.6), the presence of a multitude given over to the king of the south (11.11), mention of a ruler of the covenant (11.22), and the role played by the

---

1. It is the conclusion of Jeansonne, *Daniel 7–12*, p. 131, that 'the OG tries to render faithfully the *Vorlage* into well-constructed Greek prose'.

2. *BHS* speculates that ἕν witnesses to אחד rather than חזות.

nations of Edom, Moab and Ammon (11.41). Material in the LXX additional to the MT may be found in the added narrative detail of 8.11,
which mentions captives being carried away and the 'eternal hill' (τὰ
ὄρη τὰ ἀπ' αἰῶνος) broken up. At 9.27 the extra detail of the 'sevens'
probably equates to 9.25 MT in some way. The cryptic reference in
11.34 MT to those who stumble and are given a little help, is expanded
and intensified in the LXX. The conclusion at 12.13 is longer in the LXX,
with an extra 'rest' (ἀναπαύσῃ) and the promise that the visionary
would rise to glory.

Apart from the existence of plus material in both versions, there are
numerous small differences between the versions, which can be
explained in one of several ways. They either exist in the *Vorlage*, or
they arise in translation. Those that arise in translation can either be an
attempt at clarification or interpretation on the part of the translator, or
are explicable as some sort of misreading of the Hebrew text. It is
seldom possible to distinguish with certainty between these types of
variations, and there is an ongoing debate as to how the variations
should be regarded. A number of commentators view the LXX in these
chapters as interpretational to some degree.[3] An extreme statement in
the same direction is found in McCrystall who says that the peculiarities
of the LXX can only be accounted for as 'the activity of someone who
was translating from a deliberate standpoint'.[4] Others are more cautious
about the extent of interpretation in the LXX.[5] In concluding her
exhaustive text-critical study of Daniel 7–12, Jeansonne says that 'the
OG translator did not undertake the work with a particular agenda' and
would not have held a translation to be 'the proper forum for the theological interpretation of the readings of the sacred text'.[6] Jeansonne and
McCrystall represent opposite ends of the spectrum in this particular
debate.

Not surprisingly, the difficult nature of ch. 11 produces the most

---

3.   For example F.F. Bruce, 'The Earliest Old Testament Interpretation', *OTS* 17
(1972), pp. 37-52; A. van der Kooij, 'A Case of Reinterpretation in the Old Greek of
Daniel 11', in J.W. van Henten, H.J. de Jonge, P.T. van Rooden and J.W. Wesselius
(eds.), *Tradition and Re-interpretation in Jewish and Early Christian Literature*
(Leiden: Brill, 1986), pp. 72-80; or R.T. Beckwith, 'Daniel 9 and the Date of
Messiah's Coming in Essene, Hellenistic, Pharisaic, Zealot and Early Christian
Computation', *RevQ* 10 (1979–81), pp. 527-28.

4.   McCrystall, 'Daniel', p. 93.

5.   For example Hanhart, 'The Translation of the Septuagint', p. 342.

6.   Jeansonne, *Daniel 7–12*, p. 133.

examples of the different types of variation, but they are also present in the other chapters. Whatever the significance of the difference, the LXX characterization of the four young Jews as 'from the nation of the sons of Israel from those of Judea' (1.6, ἐκ τοῦ γένους τῶν υἱῶν Ισραηλ τῶν ἀπὸ τῆς Ιουδαίας) probably reflects some kind of expansion on 'from the sons of Judah' (מבני יהודה) in the *Vorlage*. The effect is to identify the Judahite youths with the nation as a whole, and also to identify Israel and Judah. This nationalistic tendency in the LXX of Daniel has also been discerned elsewhere.[7] It is possible that the extra phrase 'for the sons of your people' (8.19, τοῖς υἱοῖς τοῦ λαοῦ σου) has similar origins.[8] Several variations in 9.26 are unlikely to have risen in the process of translation, as both versions contain plus material. The MT has the extra modification of the leader as one 'who is coming' (הבא), as well as the final emphatic 'desolations are decreed' (נחרצת שממות). At the same time the LXX includes 'the anointed one' (τοῦ χριστοῦ) with the victims of destruction. The Hebrew of ch. 11 is so difficult that it is seldom possible to be certain whether the LXX is following a different tradition or simply making the best of a bad job. But the reference in 11.27 to two kings who 'dine alone' (μόνοι δειπνήσουσιν) seems to owe something to a variant *Vorlage*. A final example in 12.3 concerns the role of the shining ones who either 'keep/hold fast my word' (LXX, κατισχύοντες τοὺς λόγους μου) or 'turn many to righteousness' (מצדיקי הרבים).[9]

Other differences could be the result of a Greek translator clarifying an obscure Hebrew *Vorlage*. That seems to be happening where the neutral Hebrew term מראה (1.13, 'appearance') is applied to the youths by the MT. The LXX specifies the concern about their appearance that it should not be 'enervated' (διατετραμμένη). In 9.23 the LXX makes quite clear with a small plus that the decree which went out was 'from the Lord' (παρὰ κυρίου).

---

7. Clines, *The Esther Scroll*, pp. 146-47, discerns a similar movement in Esther. He identifies two Esther stories, the 'Esther tale' and the 'Mordecai tale'. The latter is central to the earlier A Text and is about a Jew, particularly a Benjamite (A Text Est. 1.1). The former, in which Mordecai is no longer a Benjamite, transforms the story to one about the Jews and events that help define Jewish self-identity.

8. But note that Montgomery, *Daniel*, p. 352, calls this a 'correct exegetical plus', an assessment with which Jeansonne, *Daniel 7–12*, p. 69, agrees.

9. The translation preferred by Charles, *Daniel*, p. 331. But Montgomery, *Daniel*, p. 473, thinks LXX has misread the Hebrew as מחזיקי דברי. It is also conceivable that the use of κατισχύω is an attempt to represent מחזיק.

However, most differences in meaning are more readily explained by the difference in semantic range of the Hebrew word and the Greek one chosen to translate it. As a result the meaning is slightly skewed.[10] The examples of this are numerous, but a small selection will be adduced in illustration. The first comes from 8.25 where the Hebrew reads, 'and suddenly he will destroy many' (ובשלוה ישחית רבים). The LXX equivalent is 'and by deceit he will do away with many' (καὶ δόλῳ ἀφανιεῖ πολλούς). Both δόλῳ and ἀφανιεῖ are possible renderings of the Hebrew, but are unusual and result in a slight difference in meaning. The expected rendering of שלוה as it is used in this context is ἐξάπινα, the choice made in 11.21 and 24. However, that meaning of שלוה is an extension of its basic sense of ease and prosperity, just as the notion of deception can be seen as an extension of the semantic range of שלוה in a different direction.[11] The result is a slightly different view of the methods of this particular king. Similarly, ἀφανίζω is usually employed to translate שמד (11.44 LXX; 7.26, 9.26, 11.44 θ), which seems to carry the sense of being reduced to nothing. By extension, its connotations are nearly always destructive. In this instance the Hebrew is שחת, a word meaning destruction or corruption or ruination. The translator has applied part of the range of ἀφανίζω in using it to translate שחת. Another small but typical example is found in the last word of 10.6 MT, המון. The sense is of the type of roar engendered by a large number of something, usually people. Hence the translator must choose whether the sound made by the being in Daniel's revelation is simply an uproar, or an uproar that implies the presence of a multitude. The LXX opts for the former with θορύβου while θ chooses the latter with ὄχλου.

A more extensive example of the same type occurs in 11.20, where the first part of the verse varies in meaning at least partly because the Greek translator has misread an ambiguous piece of Hebrew. The MT may be roughly translated, 'and one who causes an exactor (of tribute) to pass through the splendour of the kingdom will stand in his place'. The LXX reads, again roughly translated, 'and out of its root a shoot of a kingdom will stand unto standing'. In the expression על־כנו ('in his

---

10. Hanhart, 'The Translation of the Septuagint', p. 342, considers that LXX is at times interpretational in the sense that 'a decision is made between various possibilities of understanding which are already inherent in the formulation of the Hebrew *Vorlage*'.

11. See the discussion on שלוה in L. Koehler and W. Baumgartner, *Lexicon in Veteris Testamenti Libros* (Leiden: Brill, 1953), p. 973.

place'), the LXX has read כנה, 'root stock', hence the Greek ἐκ τῆς ῥίζης αὐτοῦ. Similarly הֶדֶר ('splendour') has been read as הָדָר, which can also carry the sense of fruitfulness. The result is φυτόν in the translation. The function of הדר מלכות is syntactically ambiguous, but context suggests it is the object of the participle מעביר. The same ambiguity is present in the Greek equivalent, φυτὸν βασιλείας, but this time sense requires it to function as a subject. The translator is perhaps aware that formal equivalence has not quite delivered a coherent result in this instance, so the additional phrase 'a man smiting the glory of the king' (ἀνὴρ τύπτων δόξαν βασιλέως) is designed to convey what he thinks the Hebrew may have intended. Certainly the plus corrects the meaning towards the most probable reading of the Hebrew, namely that the glory of the kingdom is in jeopardy. This one example illustrates the mixture of interpretation and misreading that is characteristic of the LXX in Daniel 1 and 8–12.

Translations of Particular Words

It is worth noting in passing that there are some surprising translations, which cannot count as misreadings or a different tradition, because the LXX is consistent in its use of them. One example of such is the translation of עת ('time') with ὥρα ('hour'), which first happens in 8.17. This seems like a more specific term than the general concept behind עת warrants. However, by translating in the same way in 9.21, 11.35 and 40, and 12.1, the LXX invests the term with a certain amount of eschatological significance for the purposes of translating the Hebrew sections of Daniel. Exceptions to this are the threefold use of ἡμέρα in 12.1 and the more conventional choice of καιρός in 12.4. Interestingly, this usage does not feature when the Aramaic עדן is translated.

We saw on more than one occasion in the central chapters of this study that the LXX had trouble with geographical or administrative terms in the Aramaic. In that connection the LXX understood χώρα less specifically than the MT understood מדינה in the Persian context. In translating the Hebrew sections also, the LXX uses χώρα in a very broad sense. Only once, in 8.2, is it used to translate מדיוה. Of its eight other uses, seven translate ארץ (9.7; 11.16, 19, 28, 40, 41, 42) and one translates אדם (11.39). This broader understanding helps to explain the inconsistent usage when the Aramaic stories were being translated.

Another apposite example is found where the MT refers to Daniel as 'treasured one' (חמ[ו]דד). Whenever the word is applied to Daniel, the LXX translates with ἐλεεινός (9.23; 10.11, 19), whereas when it describes inanimate objects the Old Greek reads one of the forms of ἐπιθυμία (10.3; 11.38, 43). A difficult Hebrew usage is the word פת־בג, which means something like 'fine food' and appears in several slightly different forms. Apart from its translation with τραπέζης in 1.5, the word is consistently represented in ch. 1 LXX with δεῖπνον (1.8, 13, 15, 16). Its one appearance in the later chapters, 11.26, has no parallel in the LXX.

Differing Traditions Represented in the Septuagint?

There are certain words or concepts that the LXX seems not to represent exactly, either because it reflects a different tradition or because it finds their meaning obscure. One such is the strange phrase ארץ־הצבי ('the land of beauty'), abbreviated in 8.9 to הצבי. On that occasion the LXX renders it as 'north', perhaps taking its cue from 8.4. It is not represented at all in the LXX Greek of 11.16 and 41. The one occasion when it is translated is in 11.45 (θελήσεως). The word צבי also appears in Ezek. 20.6 and 15, also inexactly translated with κηρίον.

Another is the term מעוז, which the MT also uses in conjunction with מבצר in ch. 11. The Hebrew writer of Daniel uses the two terms virtually synonymously, which they are where the semantic ranges of 'place of refuge' (מעוז) and 'fortified place' (מבצר) overlap. The LXX is not quite sure what to do with them, but often takes the sense of the words as expressing functions of cities. In 11.10 it translates מעוז with 'city' (πόλις). In 11.19 it uses χώρα, but paradoxically translates מדינה with πόλις in 11.24. The term מבצר is also translated with πόλις in 11.24. The portmanteau phrase מבצרי מעזים (11.39) has a double representation in the LXX. It is both πόλεων and the more literal ὀχύρωμα ἰσχυρόν. The MT speaks of a 'fortified city' (עיר מבצרות) in 11.15, and on that occasion the LXX translates literally with τὴν πόλιν τὴν ὀχυράν. Strangely the LXX equivalent of מעוז in 11.31 is ἅγιον ('holy things'), which is hardly a translation at all. There may be a lacuna in the Greek, but if there is, it cannot be the feminine πόλις, modified as it is by ἅγιον. Unfortunately 967 is unable to help at this point.

Translation of Key Terms

The LXX betrays a slightly different understanding of several key terms or concepts in its translations of the Hebrew chapters. A number of commentators have identified as significant a group called the 'maskilim' (המשכלים), the 'wise/understanding ones' or 'teachers'. The consistency with which this participial noun occurs, as well as the finite forms of the verb שכל, suggests an identifiable group in the mind of the writer.[12] θ normally translates both the nominal and verbal forms with the verb συνίημι or its cognate σύνεσις (1.4; 9.13, 25; 11.33, 35; 12.3, 10). The only exceptions are in 1.17 and 9.22. However, even θ does not recognize the uniqueness of the Hebrew term as it uses the same words to translate forms of בין, a more common occurrence in the Hebrew chapters. The LXX treats שכל even less distinctively. Whereas בין or its cognate is consistently translated by a form of διανοέομαι in the LXX (8.5, 15, 23, 27; 9.2; 10.12; 11.30; 12.8), the translator does not distinguish between συνίημι (1.17; 11.35; 12.3) and διανοέομαι (9.13, 25; 12.10) when translating שכל. It looks as though, unlike some subsequent commentators, he does not understand the term משכלים generically.

At whatever stage it may have arisen, there is also a variation in the way the LXX treats the heavenly beings as they are presented in the MT. A small but familiar example is in 1.2 where 'the treasure house of his (Nebuchadnezzar's) gods' (בית אוצר אלהיו) is 'his idol temple' (εἰδωλίῳ).[13] The difference is one that is typical in the LXX, and continues a tendency noted in its translation of the Aramaic chapters.

More problematical is the LXX's portrayal of the heavenly beings that Daniel encounters, especially in chs. 10 and 11, and where the Hebrew uses שר. That word routinely denotes earthly authorities, but here strongly implies other-worldly beings.[14] When he appears, Michael is described as 'one of the chief princes' (10.13, אחד השרים הראשנים) and

---

12. Davies, *Daniel*, pp. 121-22, and Collins, *Apocalyptic Vision*, pp. 168-69 and 210-11. Hartman and DiLella, *Daniel*, p. 309, also speak of a 'specific group'. But others such as Goldingay, *Daniel*, pp. 308-309, and Montgomery, *Daniel*, p. 471, prefer a more generalized interpretation.

13. McCrystall, 'Daniel', p. 91, attributes this rendering to the influence of Jer. 12.16-17.

14. 'Angel princes in the court of heaven', according to Caird, *Language and Imagery*, p. 238.

later as 'your prince' (10.21, שַׂרְכֶם). In 12.1 he is 'the great prince' (הַשַּׂר הַגָּדוֹל). The LXX explicitly recognizes Michael as an angelic figure in two of those instances. At 10.21 the translation is simply 'the angel' (ὁ ἄγγελος), while in 12.1 LXX Michael is 'the great angel' (ὁ ἄγγελος ὁ μέγας). In 10.13 'one of the chief princes' is expressed by εἷς τῶν ἀρχόντων τῶν πρώτων, a phrase which is not so explicit. Nevertheless, ἄρχων is a common and wide-ranging word which denotes earthly or heavenly beings according to context. In fact, its semantic range is similar to that of שַׂר, and is used accordingly by θ to translate every instance of שַׂר in Daniel (1.7, 9, 10, 11, 18; 8.11; 9.6; 10.13, 20-21; 11.5; 12.1). Unlike θ, the LXX has clarified the angelic status of Michael.

The LXX diverges more markedly from the MT at the references in 10.13, and 20 to 'the prince of Persia' (10.13, שַׂר מַלְכוּת פָּרַס; 10.20, שַׂר פָּרַס) and 'the prince of Greece' (10.20, שַׂר יָוָן). The heavenly messenger of the MT describes these beings in the same terms as for Michael, and a celestial battle seems to be implied.[15] However, the terminology of the LXX translation differs in that these princes of Greece and Persia are seen as στρατηγοί ('leaders/commanders'). This is a more explicit term than ἄρχων, and its referent is almost inevitably to political or military leadership. In Daniel it translates שַׂר in the list of officials in 3.2. It translates שַׂר three other times in the LXX (1 Kgs 29.3-4; 1 Chron. 11.6; 2 Chron. 32.21), and each time the context is secular. In the last named verse στρατηγόν is an item in the list of Assyrian leaders who are subjected to the activity of an 'angel' (ἄγγελον) sent by the Lord. Other words translated with στρατηγός are normally to do with human leaders. See, for example, its occurrence as an equivalent to סְגָן in Jeremiah 28/51 (vv. 23, 28, 57) and Ezekiel 23 (vv. 6, 12, 23). Not surprisingly, the numerous instances in the first two books of the Maccabees are all political or military. In the book of Daniel itself there are also many uses of שַׂר in the sense of a human figure, notably in relation to the eunuch of ch. 1 (vv. 7, 9, 10, 11, 18) but also in 9.6 and 8, and 11.5. There the LXX translates with the more multi-faceted ἄρχων (in ch. 1) or δυνάστης (9.6, 8; 11.15).

---

15. That is the more commonly held view. See for example Keil, *Daniel*, p. 416, Lacocque, *Daniel*, p. 156, and Montgomery, *Daniel*, p. 411. Note also Gallé, *Daniel*, p. 121, where Ibn-Ezra and Rashi both take the prince of Persia to be a heavenly figure. W.H. Shea, 'Wrestling with the Prince of Persia: A Study on Daniel 10', *AUSS* 21 (1983), p. 235, calls on Calvin in support of his view that the Prince is a human figure. He specifies Cambyses, son of and co-regent with Cyrus.

The choice of vocabulary in the LXX suggests that the Greek translator regarded the Princes of Persia and Greece as human figures, and so
interpreted an ambiguous *Vorlage* in a particular direction. This incidentally raises the same question about the nature of the interaction between
the cosmic and the human as was raised by the translation of ch. 7.
There the holy ones of the Most High were more earthly in the LXX and
the son of man more divine. Here too there is a sharper distinction made
between heavenly beings and the temporal events with which they are
concerned.[16]

The LXX version's concern for the nation and cult of Israel in the
Daniel narratives also emerges to a limited extent in the chapters now
under review. This is most evident in ch. 9. 'Your sanctuary' (9.17,
מקדשך) is localized and emphasized in the LXX with 'your holy hill' (τὸ
ὄρος τὸ ἅγιόν σου). The emphasis is even stronger at 9.19 and 24, in
both of which verses 'Zion' (Σιων) is a LXX plus in apposition to 'your
(holy) city' (עיר [קרש]ך) in Daniel's prayer. Similarly in 9.25 another
LXX plus describes Jerusalem as 'a city to the Lord' (πόλιν κυρίῳ). All
of these elements are present also in the MT, but are underscored in the
LXX. The more nationalist description of the young men of ch. 1 LXX
already alluded to is part of the same phenomenon.

The last citation above, which contains κύριος in a plus, also brings
out a characteristic of the LXX as a whole. The Septuagintal tendency to
use 'Lord' instead of or as well as 'God' has already been explored. It is
sufficient to point out the same tendency in the translation of the
Hebrew chapters of Daniel. Notwithstanding the reverse case in 9.19,
κύριος is a plus in 9.16, 23 and 25, as well as 10.12, and δεσπότης is a
substitute for אלהים in 9.17.

Treatment of People

The versions also exhibit variant understandings of several key figures
that appear in the Hebrew chapters. The first such is met at 1.20 where
the MT tells us that Daniel and his companions are ten times better
than 'all the magicians and enchanters' (כל־החרטמים האשפים) in
Nebuchadnezzar's kingdom. The LXX, however, finds them ten times

---

16. Niditch, 'The Success Story', pp. 227-28, makes a similar distinction in the
way symbols are used between chs. 7 and 8 in MT. In her view the images of ch. 8
'are far less subtle and artistically complex'. The same might be said of LXX images
with respect to the MT.

'wiser' (σοφωτέρους) than 'the wise men and philosophers' (τοὺς σοφιστὰς καὶ τοὺς φιλοσόφους) in the kingdom. A direct qualitative comparison of the type in the MT implies that Daniel occupies the same category as the Babylonian officials. The LXX is unhappy with the view of Daniel as one of a kind with the mantic officials, and shifts the category to one more in keeping with his status as an Israelite wise man. This is also an aspect of the LXX's translation of the Aramaic section.[17] The extra ἔδωκε in 1.17 works in the same way to give Daniel a role that is unique amongst the four Jewish youths, just as the LXX of 2.17-18 saw Daniel in a position superior to his three companions.

There are several variations in the dating and naming of the kings Darius and Cyrus. In 1.21 a LXX plus reminds us that Cyrus is 'king of Persia' (βασιλέως Περσῶν). Later on at 11.1 'Darius the Mede' of the MT is 'Cyrus the king' in the LXX. Moreover, the events of ch. 10 are said by the LXX to take place in the first year of Cyrus, and not the third as claimed by the MT. There is an argument arising out of the last verse of ch. 6 that the intention of the MT is to identify the figures of Darius and Cyrus with each other. Wiseman initially proposed this idea as a historical reality based on the grammar of 6.29, and more recently this identification has been supported at least as a literary device in the MT, regardless of questions about its historicity.[18] The differences signalled above make that impossible for the LXX. Even in 6.29 LXX the two figures are clearly distinguished from each other, and Darius disappears altogether in 11.1. In a move towards a correct ordering of events, the LXX puts both chs. 10 and 11 in the first year of Cyrus.[19] Nevertheless, the existence of a Median empire preceding the Persian still exists in the dating of ch. 9 in both versions. The father of Darius, whether Ahasuerus or Xerxes, is the same figure under different nomenclature. The order of empires is still implied by the chronological ordering of the chapters in 967.

Another person whose treatment differs slightly but not significantly between versions is the court official of ch. 1 with whom Daniel and his

17. In this connection Montgomery, *Daniel*, p. 138, notes that the LXX plus material of 1.20 and 3.30/97 have the same effect as each other on the role of the young men.

18. See again the arguments of Wiseman, 'Some Historical Problems', pp. 15-16, and Colless, 'Cyrus the Persian', pp. 123-25, noted in connection with Dan. 6.

19. Montgomery, *Daniel*, p. 418. According to McCrystall, 'Daniel', p. 272, the change of year in 10.1 is to bring the date into line with 1.21.

friends have most of their dealings. The difference in name, 'Ashpenaz' or 'Abiesdri' (1.3, אשפנז or Αβιεσδρι), is explicable in technical terms and is consistent throughout (see 1.11, 16).[20] Whether this figure is actually a eunuch or simply a court official, the LXX translates literally throughout with ἀρχιευνοῦχος. Until v. 10 both versions present the chief eunuch as the one with whom the young Hebrews deal directly. However, 1.11 introduces a 'keeper' (מלצר) who comes between the men and the chief of the eunuchs. The LXX becomes confused by describing Abiesdri as the keeper 'appointed by the chief eunuch' (τῷ ἀναδειχθέντι ἀρχιευνούχῳ), where earlier in the chapter he was the chief eunuch himself.

Treatment of Geographical Terms

There are some problems in the Septuagintal treatment of the points of the compass in ch. 8. In 8.4 a ram is pictured butting against the west, north and south, which implies that the power represented by the ram is an eastern one. That implication is lost in the LXX where all four points of the compass are listed. Ultimately the western power, Greece, prevails over the ram (8.7-8). Later the small horn arising out of this kingdom prevails in a southerly and easterly direction and presumably in Palestine (8.9). Somewhat illogically, the LXX in the same place records it striking against the south, west and north, the same three directions mentioned in 8.4 MT as the frontiers of the former power, the Persians. Both 8.4 and 8.9 in the MT suggest a level of intentionality in the description of direction, which for some reason has not been represented by the LXX or its *Vorlage*.[21] Why that should be so is a matter for conjecture. Jeansonne argues with some success that the explanation is technical rather than historiographic.[22] Whatever the case may be, it does not reflect a difference in how the role of the crucial fourth kingdom is viewed, even if it could hint at a different understanding of how that role was applied geographically.

There are some differences in the naming of countries, most of which do not signify a variation in the ways the versions in question understand events. There are two such in ch. 11, first where 'ships of Kittim' (11.30, ציים כתים) is translated as 'the Romans' ('Ρωμαῖοι) and secondly

20. Montgomery, *Daniel*, p. 124.
21. Jeansonne, *Daniel 7–12*, p. 108.
22. Jeansonne, *Daniel 7–12*, pp. 104-109.

where 'the Cushites' (11.43, כשים) are identified as 'Ethiopians' (Aἰθίοπες).[23] The כתים occur seldom in biblical Hebrew, and when they do they are normally transliterated by the Greek. See, for example, Num. 24.24, which has been suggested as the source of this midrashic reference in Dan. 11.30.[24] Only here is it translated as 'Romans'. In its ancient sense, the word 'Kittim' described the inhabitants of Kition on Cyprus, and was later applied to Cyprus itself and then the western coastlands and islands generally. The westerly reference also came to include Macedonia, as witnessed to in 1 Macc. 1.1 and 8.5, and later Jewish tradition identified Kittim with Rome.[25] Vermes explains both the Greek and Roman applications of Kittim as an expression used by Jewish writers from the second century BCE onwards to signify the world power of the day.[26] The LXX translator perhaps draws on that same tradition, and clarifies from his own knowledge of Antiochus Epiphanes' campaigns that Rome was intended. The biblical Cush probably refers to the southern Nile region, and was almost universally understood as Ethiopia in the LXX (for example in Gen. 2.13 and Ezek. 29.10). The translator of Daniel 11 shares that understanding. A further case involves the rendering of יון as Greece (8.21; 10.20; 11.2). As with the previously mentioned instance, this identification was so commonly understood that even θ follows it. Other biblical examples may be found in Joel 4.6 and Zech. 9.13.

Roughly the same area of land and body of people is understood by both versions in the instances above. The LXX is a little more interpretative in its treatment of 'the king of the south' (מלך־הנגב) in ch. 11. Wherever that phrase occurs, the LXX reads 'Egypt' (11.5, 6, 9, 11, 14, 15, 25, 29, 40). There is no biblical tradition about the south to explain the persistence of that identification, but towards the end of the chapter it becomes clear in the MT that the conquering northerner would include Egypt in his fiefdom (11.42-43). Indeed the syntax of 11.42 MT emphasizes Egypt among the defeated lands. It is possible that the LXX

23. Van der Kooij, 'A Case of Reinterpretation', p. 74, takes the former as an example of interpretation.

24. Hartman and DiLella, *Daniel*, p. 270. F.F. Bruce, 'Prophetic Interpretation in the Septuagint', *BIOSCS* 12 (1979), p. 23, says the ships of Kittim reference indicates that the events of 168 BCE were seen as the fulfillment of Num. 24.24. See also Hanhart, 'The Translation of the Septuagint', p. 361.

25. Hartman and DiLella, *Daniel*, p. 270.

26. Vermes, *The Dead Sea Scrolls in English*, pp. 28-29. For example, 1QpHab 6.3-5 applies the term to Rome.

translator has taken his lead from these verses and read Egypt back into the earlier references to the south.[27] As with his reference to Rome, there may also be an element of clarification towards the translator's own view of the political events behind ch. 11.[28]

The Daughter

In connection with the same events, the figure of a daughter crops up twice in the MT of ch. 11. In 11.6 the daughter of the king of the south goes north to make an alliance. In the LXX the king of Egypt goes north and an alliance is made with the same unsatisfactory results, but the role of his daughter as an instrument in the alliance is not mentioned. In 11.17 there is also a daughter, this time in both versions, but in the MT she is a 'daughter of women' (בת הנשים) where the LXX describes her as a 'daughter of man' (θυγατέρα ἀνθρώπου). In the schema of ch. 11 as a whole, each reference is generally thought to apply to a different event.[29] The first alliance took place in the mid-third century BCE when the Seleucid Ptolemy II married his daughter Berenice to Antiochus II with ultimately disastrous results. Dan. 11.17 probably refers to a later Ptolemy–Seleucid alliance with the betrothal of Cleopatra to Ptolemy V (197 BCE). Given the LXX's apparent close interest in Egypt in this chapter, it is surprising that it does not include the detail of the daughter in 11.6.[30] The difference in 11.17 is less significant, and can perhaps be explained as a misreading of הנשים for the masculine אנשים.[31] In neither case do the differences suggest a variation in interpretation of events

27. That is the view of Bruce, 'Earliest Old Testament Interpretation', p. 43. Hanhart, 'The Translation of the Septuagint', pp. 356-57, considers the LXX rendering of 11.29 shows a detailed knowledge of the Egyptian campaign of Antiochus Epiphanes.

28. Bogaert, 'Relecture et refonte', p. 200, sees a pro-Egyptian author. McCrystall, 'Daniel', p. 385, would go further and see in the 'Egypt' readings evidence of an anti-Seleucid pro-Ptolemaic translator. Jeansonne, *Daniel 7–12*, pp. 119-23, concedes no political bias in the LXX translator.

29. See for example Goldingay, *Daniel*, pp. 296-302, on the historical events behind ch. 11.

30. McCrystall, 'Daniel', p. 325, points out from 2.43 that the translator would have known about the marriage alliance. His explanation, as part of his pro-Ptolemy thesis, that the translator wished at this point to highlight the Egyptian army has received little support. See the remarks of Collins, *Daniel*, p. 8.

31. Montgomery, *Daniel*, p. 442. Note in Ulrich, '4QDan[b] and 4QDan[c]', pp. 19 and 22-23, that 4QDan[c] is in agreement with the LXX.

behind ch. 11. However, it is worth noting that 2.43 LXX is less easily suggestive of intermarriage within the fourth kingdom than its MT equivalent.

Dating in 9.24-27

The eschatological time frame proposed by both versions is similar except at one point, namely 9.24-27. The MT asserts that 70 sevens have been determined upon the people and the city (9.24). What follows immediately is a break down of the 70 into three different periods. The first is of seven sevens' and the next is of 62 sevens' duration (9.25). The following verse is devoted to events at the end of this second period, before turning its attention to the one remaining seven left out of the 70. Dan. 9.27 describes something that happens halfway through that final seven. The LXX is identical in 9.24 with its reference to 70 sevens. But in 9.25 there is no reference to the first two periods of seven and 62. Where the MT speaks of what will happen after the 62 sevens in 9.26, the LXX speaks of what will be 'after 7 and 70 and 62'. The Greek does not use the numbers to qualify any particular type of span of time, but one is presumably to be understood. Dan. 9.27 LXX includes a substantial amount of plus material. There is reference to the end of the seven, but no mention of the middle of the seven. In addition the Old Greek repeats the 77 and 62, but this time they are 77 'times' (καιρούς) and 62 'years' (ἔτη).

There are two possible approaches to this problem. The one adopted by Jeansonne is that all the differences can be explained by 'plausible misreading of the Hebrew text and by later shifting of phrases'.[32] Therefore no theological or interpretational significance can be attached to the differences. A second approach typified by Montgomery is that the 77 and 62 of the LXX in fact may represent the 139th year of the Seleucid era, and is therefore a deliberate dating of the events in question.[33] He is not certain, however, whether the translator's achievement is intentional or accidental. Bruce is less tentative and takes Montgomery's argument further when he sees deliberate theological interpretation in the LXX numbers. In his view the date 139 in the

32. Jeansonne, *Daniel 7–12*, p. 130. But note the criticism by David, 'Composition and Structure', p. 280, of her treatment of this passage.

33. Montgomery, *Daniel*, p. 395. See also David, 'Composition and Structure', p. 297.

Seleucid era would be the time when the anointed one, the high priest Onias III, was removed (171 BCE).[34]

The LXX as it stands is not particularly coherent in its use of numbers. Both versions represent 9.24 as an overview of events subsequently detailed in 9.25-27.[35] As part of its overview, the LXX agrees with the MT about the 70 sevens. It is also possible that a word has been misread as a number seven rather than a period of time, 'seven', to produce the 77, and that there has been some misplacement of material between 9.25 and 9.26, as well as some duplication of material into 9.26 in the LXX.[36] In either instance the anointed one has his locus in the cult or nation of Israel. Since the culminating action of the period in 9.24 is 'to anoint' (לִמְשֹׁחַ) the holy of holies, it is likely that the 'anointed one' (מָשִׁיחַ) of 9.25-26 MT is also understood in those cultic terms.[37] Those who attach a chronological significance to the 77 and 62 of the LXX are compelled to take a less cultic and more nationalistic, if not messianic, view of what or who is intended by the anointed one. However the difference came about, the figure understood by the LXX is markedly different from that portrayed in the MT, in a way reminiscent of the two views of the son of man in ch. 7.

Conclusion

Jeansonne makes the case well that there is no theological *Tendenz* inherent in the Old Greek translation. Her study is a cautionary reminder that significance should not be seen where none was intended. In that regard, many divergences between the MT and the LXX have technical

---

34. Bruce, 'Earliest Old Testament Interpretation', pp. 44-45. McCrystall, 'Daniel', p. 253, agrees with Bruce but identifies the date with the deposition of Jason by Antiochus IV.

35. J.B. Payne, 'The Goal of Daniel's Seventy Weeks', *JETS* 21 (1978), p. 97.

36. Beckwith, 'Daniel 9', pp. 527-28, says the LXX is an interpretation but admits that it therefore perpetrated an 'extraordinary corruption' of the text in doing so. Bruce, 'Earliest Old Testament Interpretation', p. 44, also admits 'an astonishing alteration of the original text'.

37. But Beckwith, 'Daniel 9', p. 522, notes that θ among others treats the 7 and 62 weeks as a single period at the end of which the anointed one comes. In his view this more messianic outlook was lost in MT at the time the Masoretic punctuation of the Hebrew text reached its present form. See also T.E. McComiskey, 'The Seventy "Weeks" of Daniel against the Background of Ancient Near Eastern Literature', *WTJ* 47 (1985), p. 19.

explanations, either in the *Vorlage* itself or in the process of translation. At times, as with the use of the word χώρα, they evidence the same difficulties as were encountered in our study of the Aramaic chapters. Yet, although others have sometimes taken their case for interpretation in the LXX too far, there are points at which it is difficult to escape the conclusion that the LXX represents a variant tradition. The understanding of gods as idols and the use of κύριος are typical of the LXX as a whole. The emphasis on Egypt in ch. 11 is particular to the translation of the Hebrew chapters in Daniel. The *maskilim*, whom some would argue lie behind the whole of the book of Daniel, appear to be a more distinct group or class in the MT than the LXX in these last few chapters. If there is an attempt in the MT to harmonize the persons of Darius and Cyrus into one, a case by no means proven, that has not been understood by the LXX translator who keeps them distinct while preserving the MT tradition of a prior Median empire. Other aspects of the LXX reflect tendencies already discerned in Daniel 2–7. The LXX emphasizes the Israelite nation and cult more than its Hebrew counterpart, and is still anxious to delineate between the wisdom exercised by Daniel and that of the heathen officials. Finally, the subtlety and ambiguity of the interaction in the MT between heaven and earth, symbol and symbolized, is less evident in the LXX, which prefers to keep the two separate.

Chapter 9

CONCLUSION

Reasons for Variations

The question has recurred throughout this study as to whether or not the differences in the LXX arise in translation or were present in the *Vorlage* from which the LXX was translated. It is often impossible to tell, but examples of both types of variation can be detected. In general terms, the probability is that the LXX translates the text in front of it relatively literally. I began the literary comparison on that supposition, based on the work of others, and nothing has come to light to disturb this assumption. Where there are significant differences between the texts, these are therefore likely to have arisen in the *Vorlage*. The considerable narrative differences that result must then be due in some measure to a less carefully crafted Semitic form of the stories. That in turn relates to the probability that the LXX *Vorlage* predates the form of Daniel 2–7 as preserved by the Masoretes, a point on which I will comment more fully below.

There are, however, some differences which are more likely to have arisen as a result of the nature of the translation, and these too have had an effect on the narrative as translated. Sometimes they come about simply through a disparity in semantic range between languages, but there are other times when the translator seeks to clarify what he sees as a difficulty in the Aramaic text. Sometimes the perceived difficulty is technical and at other times it is theological. One particular recurring manifestation of this is translation which anticipates subsequent developments in the MT narrative. An important example is found in ch. 7 where the son of man is treated as though the divinity endowed on him in 7.14 was already there in 7.13. Chapter 4 is also translated very much in the light of the visions in the second part of Daniel.

As a result, my conclusion differs somewhat from that of Jeansonne that there is no theological *Tendenz* discernible in the translator of the

Old Greek.[1] In focusing particularly on chs. 7–12, she finds that differences between the versions can almost always be explained as translational or textual problems, or as a different *Vorlage*. Her point is taken that most differences probably arose in the *Vorlage*, particularly in the chapters that she investigates. That is to be expected as *Vorlage* and translation of chs. 7–12 are much closer to one another in time and provenance than is the case in chs. 2–6. But there are numerous occasions in chs. 2–7 where the translator betrays a particular mind set, which also follows through into the later chapters.[2] The suspicion of kings who usurp divine privileges, and concern for the Temple sacrifices are cases in point. Even where variations arise from incompatible semantic ranges, the choices of the translator may push the meaning in a particular direction and reveal a particular viewpoint.[3] The choice of ἔσχατος to represent אחרי in ch. 2 has that sort of effect. Moreover, Jeansonne's approach does not allow for the fact that the translator's intention does not always coincide with literary result. Even when the intention is to translate the Semitic as literally as possible, the result does not always reflect literary craft in the source language. For example, by translating a *Leitwort* in his *Vorlage* with several synonyms, the translator conveys surface meaning without capturing the literary effect intended by the Aramaic repetition.

Narrative Technique

The basic difference between the narratives of the LXX and the MT is found in the role the narrator plays within the texts. In Bar-Efrat's terms, which have functioned well for this study, the MT narrator is more covert where his LXX counterpart tends to be more overt. The distinction is relative in that it expresses degrees of omniscience, and is observable in several ways.

It manifests itself in the way that human motives and emotions are portrayed. Where emotions such as Belshazzar's fear tend to be

---

1. Jeansonne, *The Septuagint*, pp. 132-33.
2. See the comment by David, 'Composition and Structure', p. 280, on Jeansonne's approach to 9.24-27 that her policy of avoiding literary criticism prevents her from detecting literary divergences.
3. For Bruce, 'Prophetic Interpretation', p. 26, 'variants... sometimes reflect new ways of understanding the prophecies in the light of changing events, changing attitudes and changing exegetical methods'.

attributed explicitly by an all-seeing narrator of the LXX, the MT forces the reader to deduce them from observable physical phenomena. The motives behind the actions of a character are also often attributed by the LXX where the MT reader is left to deduce them for himself. For example, in ch. 6 LXX the narrator consistently specifies the motives behind characters' actions. In much the same way the narrator of the LXX from time to time betrays his position outside the story by anticipating events in the narrative, while the MT narrator generally observes the temporal and spatial limitations of the participants. The confinement of the narrative to one place at a time during Darius's night of suspense in ch. 6 illustrates the point.

The covert stance thus adopted by the Aramaic narrator is characteristic of biblical narrative. The biblical authors who convey such a narrator face the challenge of how to portray point of view within the story without compromising the narrator. In Daniel the implied reader is encouraged to adopt the perspective of the narrator in several ways. Sometimes point of view is conveyed by astute deployment of key words, such as the 'interpretation' vocabulary in ch. 2 or the words relating to prayer in ch. 6. At other times, especially in the descriptions of Daniel in ch. 5, variations in dialogue are suggestive. In that connection, and typically for biblical narrative, the minor characters of the queen mother in ch. 5 and Arioch in ch. 2 function as servants of the narrator. The former's surprising defiance of convention as a comment on one of the main personalities is also a characteristic narrative device. Particularly in the highly visual ch. 5, but to a lesser extent elsewhere, variations in what Berlin analogously calls 'camera angle' are used effectively. Perhaps the most risky perspective device is the use of irony or even parody to help the reader identify with the narrative. The comedic function is most significant in chs. 3, 5 and 6.

All of these MT features result in a certain subtlety and potential ambiguity which is not as marked in the more overt narration of the LXX. One result, for example, of the LXX narrator's anticipation of motives in ch. 6 is a less ironic or comedic presentation. The character of the queen mother is treated more conventionally and therefore less significantly, and there are differences in the visual perspective created by the LXX narrator of ch. 5. Significant words or recurring syntactical patterns that convey point of view in the MT are not always present in the LXX. Sometimes that is because they were not perceived, while at other times it is because of the differing natures of the two languages. For example, that 'tree' is neuter and 'king' is masculine in Greek means that the LXX of ch. 4 cannot reproduce the ambiguity arising from the fact that both nouns are masculine in Aramaic.

A good illustration of the different approach of the LXX to point of view comes in ch. 4 when the management of dialogue is compared in each version. Although the MT narrator nearly loses control of his material where several windows of dialogue are open at once, ultimately it remains clear which point of view is being expressed. The contrary is the case in the LXX where the material becomes more important than the shape of the narrative. The meaning is no longer to be found at least partly in the form of the narrative. Moreover, the control that Nebuchadnezzar exerts over the narrative in ch. 4 is not counterbalanced by clues that his viewpoint is not the narrator's. As narrator, his description of Daniel's outward aspect in 4.19 is an exception to the generalization that the LXX narrator is more overt. Yet that in itself remains part of the problem in ch. 4 LXX, that the narrative is unable to modify the outlook of its unreliable narrator, Nebuchadnezzar.

The internal consistency and congruency with other biblical narratives of the role of the covert narrator in Daniel 2–7, and techniques related to that role, convey an impression of the MT as a more deliberate and carefully crafted account than its LXX counterpart. Apart from any other considerations, the fact that θ reflected the literary quality of the MT is likely to have played a part in its eventual displacement of the LXX version of Daniel.

Narrative Structure

The repetition noted above of key words and patterns in the MT is one factor which gives an overall structure to the chapters under investigation. There are times when the impact of these links is not as evident in the LXX. This is one aspect of the wider discussion of the way individual stories relate to Daniel 2–7 as a larger narrative unit.

In general terms, there is less divergence between the versions of chs. 2 and 7 as compared to chs. 3–6. As a result, the thematic links between these two chapters are present in the Greek as well as the Aramaic, although the play on words may not be so evident in one or two instances. The most likely explanation of this is that the timespan between the emergence of the Semitic forms of these chapters and the Old Greek translation was comparatively shorter than was the case for the intervening chs. 3–6. I consider that explanation in more detail in the context of the text-historical discussion below.

There are more striking variations of structure in other places. Chapter 5 is more independent of ch. 4 in the LXX. At the same time there is a stronger linking between chs. 3 and 4 in the LXX than is the case for the MT. Not only does the confession of Nebuchadnezzar at the end of ch. 4 draw on the material in the Additions in ch. 3, but both chapters are significantly dated by the LXX in the eighteenth year of Nebuchadnezzar's reign. The Greek translation of both those chapters is also strongly redolent of the concerns of the visions of chs. 7–12. These differences have implications for how the overall structure of the material may have been viewed by the LXX. Taking into account the additional phenomenon that there is a weaker relationship between chs. 3 and 6 in the Greek, it begins to look as though the 967 structure with chs. 7 and 8 immediately after ch. 4 was an older ordering of the LXX tradition. This links the evil of Nebuchadnezzar (chs. 3 and 4) with events in Daniel's first vision (ch. 7).

The 967 ordering also has an effect on the nature of chs. 2–7 as a narrative unit. As we have seen, the MT shapes the narrative in such a way that the promised revelation of 'what will be after this' (2.29, להוא אחרי דנה) is to some extent realized in ch. 7. The promise and the revelation form a frame for the intervening stories. This literary feature of the Aramaic, which treats historical events in the context of wider issues, is also present in the individual stories to a greater or lesser extent. It is most marked in ch. 5 where the reading of the writing is so long delayed, but there is a level of suspense in the other narratives also. The LXX linking, particularly in the 967 order, provides a much sharper focus on Jewish suffering at the hand of Gentile powers and a more negative view of Nebuchadnezzar, but is at the cost of a more subtle and multi-faceted analysis of the interaction between the earthly and the heavenly available in the MT.

Literary Merit in the Septuagint

The comments above do not mean that our translator was artless. He was limited by a less polished *Vorlage* than the MT and handicapped by his perception of the contemporary applicability of the Aramaic, yet there is a certain facility of expression about the way he translated what he saw. This may be seen in his willingness to use synonymous words and phrases, but is also evident in the occasional word or phrase or structure. The nicely balanced statement 'the vision is accurate and this interpretation trustworthy' (2.45) has later echoes in chs. 4 and 6. The irony of the plotters calling Daniel the king's 'friend' in ch. 6, or the picture in ch. 4 of a usurper making merry in the palace are further examples of a lively touch.

The Symbolic

The way that narrative form and structure differ between the MT and the LXX relates to the way the two versions treat the symbolic. In the context of the discussion of the respective interpretations of the great tree in ch. 4, I noted the lack of agreed terminology for working with these sorts of categories. There we saw, in the terms adopted for the purpose of the discussion, how the MT is more symbolic and the LXX more allegorical in its understanding of the cosmic tree. The MT understands the tree in a way that is at the same time local and universal. While the tree is a picture of Nebuchadnezzar's pride and fall, the symbol also hints at a much wider concern moving outward from the local application. The LXX concentrates more on a one-to-one correspondence between features of the symbol and aspects of the king's life, thus reducing the picture's significance to its immediate application. One effect of that is that the spheres of vision and interpretation remain distinct from one another.

That the LXX pictures a more straightforward relationship between the earthly and heavenly realms in ch. 7 is another expression of the same tendency. In the LXX the holy ones and the son of man are distinct entities, and the close correspondence between vision and interpretation is again more in evidence. The MT contains an interplay between the divine and the human which defies neat categorizations. Somehow the divine is also human, and the human divine. Apart from anything else, the academic debate over both the son of man and the holy ones demonstrates that ambiguity.

The MT characteristic, within and across narratives, of setting human history in the context of an overarching concern, and indeed of working out that concern through the portrayal of temporal events, reinforces that impression. Concerns of heavenly significance are worked out in political terms, but not in the sense that earthly realities merely reflect a heavenly battle. Because the two planes interact, the MT does not separate meaning and interpretation when dealing with divine revelation. The dream of ch. 2 needs the intervention of the Most High to be described as well as interpreted. The acts of reading and of solving the writing on the wall are functions of the same divine gift. There is no distinction between the earthly manifestation and the divine messenger behind it. The LXX coincides with ch. 2 MT in that respect, more for the reasons of text history noted earlier. However, in ch. 5 the LXX assumes that only the interpretation of the writing is a problem.

The narrative differences both express and help to bring about the different understanding of the symbolic. An ambiguous covert narrative style in the MT blurs distinctions, whereas the more overt omniscience of the LXX seeks to clarify them. The symbols of the MT turn out to be highly appropriate in a story struggling to work out the tension of being a faithful Jew in a foreign land. The symbols of the LXX and their treatment therein, on the other hand, reflect a situation where a threatened Jewish nation must struggle to maintain its distinctiveness.

Wisdom

The two versions hold differing views of Daniel as a wisdom figure, and the fact that they do so is related to matters discussed immediately above. Just as there is an interplay between the symbol and its interpretation, between the human and the divine, so there is a tension over the role of Daniel the wise man in the MT. The same tension is not present in the LXX. Apart from chs. 3 and 6, there is no court contest in the LXX, because to acknowledge the contest is to validate Daniel as 'chief' of the Babylonian wise men (4.6 MT). The contest implies an admission that Daniel is a member of the same set as the pagan court officials. The MT is prepared to engage that ambiguity, but the LXX does not wish to make such an identification. The struggles of chs. 6 and 3 centre respectively on Daniel's political wisdom and the public refusal of the three young men to engage in idolatry. Because they do not concern the mantic powers of the Jews' opponents, there is not a problem for the LXX.

This implies that there are differing views of wisdom at work in the versions. The difference is by no means absolute or consistently portrayed, but tendencies can be detected. There is a persistent thread in the LXX narratives that sees Daniel as an established wise elder in the Jewish community. His calling of the fast in ch. 2 is one place where he is so pictured. This wise man develops out of the Solomonic figure who rises to prominence in Susanna, and relates wisdom inwards to the Jewish community. The wisdom exercised in the MT of chs. 2–6 is directed outwards towards the Babylonian/Persian context in which the exiles find themselves. Both versions combine in the person of Daniel the roles of purveyor of divine revelation and exerciser of political wisdom, but the MT does not shy away from the mantic aspects or identification with heathen mantic practitioners.

The issue is a little different from ch. 7 onwards. Because there is no comparison in question, Daniel is recognized by the LXX as a visionary. It identifies its wise judge of chs. 1–6 with the visionary of ch. 7 in that the nationalist concerns link both major sections. The connection in the MT is more of a literary one as the visions of Daniel are the culmination of his mantic role in the early chapters, at the same time as being a reversal of roles from interpreter to dreamer. An exception to the LXX's less mantic perceptions in chs. 2–6 occurs at 4.19 where the LXX hints that Daniel's experience was to some extent ecstatic, although this can be explained as an anticipation of ch. 7 by the translator.

It is difficult to explain the origins of each understanding of wisdom, as there is little agreement amongst critics about the nature of wisdom or its purveyors in the book of Daniel. Müller argues with some success that an archaic manticism from the Israelite tradition, such as that evident in the dreamer Joseph, reappeared in the second century BCE.[4] For him that is a crucial element in the development of apocalyptic. In that case the LXX represents an earlier pre-apocalyptic tradition.[5] On the other hand, Whybray considers that there was no class of Israelite sages as such to counter the Babylonian wise men. Only much later does a class develop, which he identifies with the *maskilim* of the Hebrew

---

4. Müller, 'Mantische Weisheit', pp. 271-74, although that begs the question of the date of the Joseph stories. G. von Rad, *Wisdom in Israel* (London: SCM Press, 1970), p. 281, also sees the wisdom of Daniel as 'basically old', although his views on the origins of apocalyptic differ from those of Müller. J.G. Gammie, 'Spatial and Ethical Dualism in Jewish Wisdom and Apocalyptic Literature', *JBL* 93 (1974), p. 377, also views Daniel's wisdom as 'old sapiential ethical dualism'. M. Barker, *The Older Testament* (London: SPCK, 1987), p. 92, argues that such 'esoteric' wisdom in fact points to a lost tradition rooted in what she sees as the older strata of the Old Testament. Its presence in a nationalistic setting in Daniel is important to her argument for its existence.

5. As von Rad, *Wisdom in Israel*, p. 281, considered the MT also to be.

sections of Daniel.[6] By that reasoning, the LXX is more likely to be a later corrective away from the pluralist tendencies of the MT.

There is no more agreement on the relationship of Daniel to other wisdom circles. He may or may not belong to the same scribal tradition as that of Sirach 38.24–39.11.[7] Saldarini puts the wisdom of MT Daniel later rather than earlier when he equates it to that of Sirach. Collins credits responsibility for the book of Daniel to an identifiable circle known in Daniel as *maskilim*.[8] As we have seen, others disagree on the existence or otherwise of such a circle. They are not recognized by the LXX version. Some have suggested that Daniel has Hasidic origins, or is even linked to early Essenism.[9] This may have been in reaction to the more nationalist approach of the Hasmoneans as expressed in the books of the Maccabees.[10] It is even possible that such a conflict is discernible in Daniel itself if 11.34 is a slighting reference to those who give 'a little help' (עזר מעט), as compared to the ones 'who stumble' (הכשלם).[11] There is little consensus on the significance of these matters for the dating of Daniel texts. To complicate the picture further, de Vries suggests that the

---

6.   R.N. Whybray, *The Intellectual Tradition in the Old Testament* (Berlin: de Gruyter, 1974), p. 16. Similarly A.J. Saldarini, *Pharisees, Scribes and Sadducees in Palestinian Society* (Wilmington, DE: Michael Glazier, 1988), p. 254, says the wisdom of Daniel is a Palestinian usage rather than of the diaspora. Hammer, *Daniel*, p. 26, locates the 'transcendental character of wisdom' in ch. 2 with 'much of the later wisdom literature'.

7.   Saldarini, *Pharisees, Scribes and Sadducees*, p. 254, says Daniel is part of that scribal tradition, but G.H. Wilson, 'Wisdom in Daniel and the Origin of Apocalyptic', *HAR* 9 (1985), p. 373, is intent on dispelling that notion.

8.   J.J. Collins, 'Daniel and his Social World', *Int* 39 (1985), pp. 132-33.

9.   J. Blenkinsopp, 'Interpretation and the Tendency to Sectarianism: An Aspect of Second Temple History', in E.P. Sanders (ed.), *Jewish and Christian Self-Definition* (London: SCM Press, 1981), II, p. 18; Hartman and DiLella, *Daniel*, pp. 43-45; and P.R. Davies, 'Hasidim in the Maccabean Period', *JJS* 28 (1977), p. 130. The present discussion begs the important point raised by Davies as to whether or not there ever was an identifiable group called hasidim.

10.   Blenkinsopp, 'Interpretation', p. 18, and S.J. de Vries, 'Observations on Quantitative and Qualitative Time in Wisdom and Apocalyptic', in J.G. Gammie, W.A. Brueggemann, W.L. Humphreys and J.M. Ward (eds.), *Israelite Wisdom* (New York: Scholars Press, 1978), p. 274 n. 12.

11.   V. Tcherikover, *Hellenistic Civilization and the Jews* (trans. S. Applebaum; New York: Atheneum, 1970), pp. 198 and 477 n. 37, thinks the hasidim stumble and the Hasmoneans give a little help. Davies, 'Hasidim', p. 129, agrees with the general idea but not with the precise identification of groups made by Tcherikover.

MT manifests a late Essenism with a Zadokite emphasis, whereas David says that the LXX represents a form of Zadokite messianism in contrast to the MT.[12]

In light of the conflicting evidence, it is difficult to set the differing MT and LXX pictures of Daniel as a wisdom figure in a wider context. The aphoristic view of Daniel in the LXX is unlikely to reflect a translation of the later concept of *maskilim* back into chs. 2–6, as we have seen that the LXX does not seem to view them as a class. But the problem with seeing them as predecessors of the mantic apocalypticists is that the picture of Daniel as a mantic official is part and parcel of the Persian backdrop to the stories. A possible solution is that there were various Hebrew circles of wisdom in tension with each other from at least the Persian period.[13] Whatever labels we may attach to them, this tension is probably hinted at in the MT. Perhaps it also explains the differences in outlook between the versions if each one is built out of earlier divergent circles. For the moment it is sufficient to note the dual character of the LXX, sometimes suggesting an earlier and sometimes a later tradition than the MT.

It is possible that θ's replacement of the LXX is partly a reflection of this conflict of wisdom circles. That would explain the existence of a θ or an ur-θ in pre-Christian times. It also helps to explain the prevalence of θ in the post-second Temple rabbinic period, because then the values of the Hasidim prevailed over those of the Hasmoneans. And θ by then would be more acceptable as nearer to the MT, which was increasingly taking on authoritative status.

Theological or Political Concerns

It becomes evident as the early chapters of Daniel are studied that the political and theological concerns of the versions cannot be separated. Certain temporal events form a backdrop either to the production of the

---

12. De Vries, 'Observations', p. 274 n. 12. In the words of David, 'Composition and Structure', p. 297, the LXX points to 'a precise form of messianism revolving around the restoration of the legitimate high priest or at least of a legitimate successor of the Zadokite priesthood'.

13. See again the thesis of Hayman, 'Qohelet', pp. 106-107, who identifies three 'trajectories' of wisdom which develop in different directions. He considers that at least one of his trajectories, the reshaped ancient myth of secret heavenly wisdom, is discernible well before Qohelet.

stories or their translation. The attitude of each version towards these events is tied up with its theological concerns.

The absence from parts of the LXX of the court contest is not only an indication of the LXX view of wisdom. It also hints at the immediate political concerns of the two versions in the central chs. 4 and 5. The occurrence of the court contests in both chapters of the MT helps to knit together the two accounts around the person of Nebuchadnezzar. Not only does Belshazzar stand in judgment before the hand of God, he also suffers invidious comparison with his illustrious predecessor. Because the stories do not function as a pair in the LXX, from which the recapitulation on Nebuchadnezzar's career in ch. 5 is absent, the comparison is not as evident. Just as Belshazzar is not as bad as his MT counterpart, so in human terms Nebuchadnezzar is not viewed as positively by the LXX. Indeed, he becomes in the LXX an embodiment par excellence of the evil king pictured in ch. 7. However, because the LXX views Nebuchadnezzar in more nationalistic terms than does the MT, his acknowledgments of the Most High are explicit confessions of the God of Israel rather than the universalist statements of the MT. The same interest in the conversion of the king is also evident in the LXX's treatment of Darius, although there it is even more strongly stated and seems to hint at a particular tradition which thought highly of Darius. The MT remains indifferent towards him. But, particularly in the case of Darius, these distinctions should not be too boldly drawn in light of the interaction noted between the different blocks of royal confession material.

The LXX version's desire to see the kings converted to the God of Israel is part of the wider phenomenon of its interest in the national and cultic life of the Jewish people. The MT of the stories tends to address the issues in terms more appropriate to a diaspora setting. The LXX treatment of the sovereigns also reflects the alertness of the Greek version to any hint of a polytheistic outlook. Hence the suspicion of a king who may conceivably be arrogating divine authority to himself. This monotheistic emphasis also shows up in the LXX's opposition to idolatry and its adoption of the wider Old Greek convention of using κύριος as a name for God.

Text-Historical Questions

This study has proceeded on two assumptions about the composition history of Daniel 2–7. The first is that chs. 4–6, and possibly also 3–6, were linked in the MT before chs. 2 and 7 were redacted as the outer pairing in the chiasm. It was also suggested that in its present form ch. 2 is later than chs. 3–6 and perhaps not very much earlier than ch. 7. There is an earlier form of ch. 2 discernible that has more in common with chs. 3–6, before the pairing was made with ch. 7. It is not accidental that the greater difference between the MT and the Septuagintal *Vorlage* comes in what have been postulated as the earlier chapters: 4–6 certainly, but also ch. 3 where the long Additions occur. This theory of the composition of Daniel 2–7 has proved to be a workable one.

The second premise is less one of chronology and more one of literary structure, and is that presented by Lenglet: that the Aramaic chapters of the MT are arranged in a chiasm with chs. 4 and 5 as the central pair. This too has turned out to be a workable proposition within the limitations that Lenglet himself warns about. The Nebuchadnezzar material alone ensures that at one level chs. 4 and 5 function as a continuous narrative. Chapter 6 relates to them thematically to a limited extent, but has the strongest relationship with ch. 3. While there is some continuity through all the stories, it is notable that ch. 7 has the most in common with chs. 2 and 4.

In discussing the type of wisdom evident in the respective versions, I noted the difficulty in determining whether the LXX takes us to a later or earlier portrayal of Israelite wisdom. A narrative-critical comparison reveals the same tantalizing duality in the LXX when it comes to considering the composition history of both the MT and LXX. The Old Greek seems to take us both closer to an *Ursprung* and further away from the putative Persian provenance of the Aramaic.

The LXX reflects an earlier form of the story in chs. 4 and 6 particularly. The Greek dream of the great tree bears some comparison with the early story of Nabonidus's conflict and exile and possible madness. The procedures surrounding Daniel's night in the lion pit in the same version also seem to preserve an early type of trial by ordeal, the details of which are not relevant to the concerns of the MT. Against that, the administrative and courtly vocabulary of the MT tend to convey a Persian provenance which is largely lost in translation, indicating a much later translator. The looseness of the narrative connections between the stories suggests that the translator encountered them before they were redacted into the MT form, yet the LXX treats the stories of Daniel 2–6 in a manner contemporaneous with the subsequent visions of chs. 7–12. Hence the habit of reading later understandings in the MT material into a translation of earlier sections.

Aspects of the MT reveal similar problems. A Babylonian/Persian backdrop to chs. 2–6 is evident, yet such is not the case for the later chapters. At the same time it is difficult to escape the conclusion that the Aramaic/Hebrew book of Daniel is intended as a unity. The literary links across a number of form divisions ensure that this is so. The implication is that, although the concerns of chs. 2–6 are early, their incorporation into a unit with chs. 7–12 and redaction into the present shape are almost certainly late. It is surprising that the integrity of the early stories is so well preserved despite the later developments. Moreover, why has the interest in the Gentile Nebuchadnezzar been retained in the MT alongside the extremely negative view of world rulers contained in the visions?

Two further problems are raised by the nature of the versions. The first is that the version that is most obviously Maccabean, and hence Palestinian in outlook, is the Greek translation. It would have been expected that interest in translating such exilic stories into Greek would have arisen in the diaspora rather than in Palestine itself. Another question is raised by the LXX ordering witnessed to in 967. That order, allied with what seem to be intentional variations in dating, suggest that the LXX reflects a deliberate arrangement of the stories that is different from the MT. Did that occur before or after the redaction of the MT?[14] It is likely to have been earlier, or at least at the same time, given the insertion of chs. 7 and 8 into the stories, which suggests that translation may have taken place very close to when the MT reached its present form.

Historical-critical approaches have produced little agreement on these complexities. The composition history evidence produced by a literary-critical approach is hardly decisive in one direction, but some probabilities can be adduced. The evidence suggests that the earliest collation in the tradition represented by the MT was chs. 4–6, and possibly including ch. 3 as well. Chapters 2 and 7 are a later pair which complete the chiasm, although the core of ch. 2 is a somewhat earlier composition. That it received additional material at the same time as the attachment of ch. 7 to the narratives is likely. The feeling for Nebuchadnezzar and a positive view of Daniel's courtly role influenced this tradition from early

14. In the opinion of David, 'Composition and Structure', p. 94, an Aramaic collection was 'even translated into Greek, before it was expanded into a bilingual composition during the Maccabean period'. He is in agreement with Lust, 'Daniel 4–5', p. 43, against Bogaert, 'Relecture et refonte', pp. 200-201.

in the process of its formation. At the same time there must have been a differing Aramaic tradition which grew out of the same pool of stories, perhaps also originating in the Persian exile, which is reflected in the uncollected stories represented by LXX Daniel. This tradition developed a more hostile view of Nebuchadnezzar and a less mantic conception of the wisdom of Daniel. The situation could be analogous to the treatment of Nebuchadnezzar in Jeremiah 27–29, to which I have alluded on several occasions. There too the LXX has apparently preserved an early and less friendly tradition about the Babylonian king.

The stories of Daniel were finally collected during the first half of the second century BCE in Palestine, and combined with the visions as a direct result of the religious and national crisis centred on Antiochus IV Epiphanes. Whatever circle was responsible for the MT compilation, it was probably not one sympathetic to the Hasmonean or Maccabean approach. The stories were very soon translated into Greek in the light of the vision material. The Aramaic so translated came from the differing tradition earlier mentioned, perhaps also Persian in origin but representing finally a Palestinian outlook. Whether the translation was physically undertaken in Judea or the diaspora, it also reflects a Judean outlook. It is at this stage that the translator's unfamiliarity with aspects of the original setting of the stories and his interest in the Maccabean struggle reveals itself. This in part explains the constant interplay between translational interpretation and variant *Vorlage* as reasons for differences.[15] At the same time the variant ordering available in 967 was probably adopted, and the substantial Greek Additions inserted. Whether or not the Additions had a Semitic original has not been resolved. There is no physical manuscript evidence available to suggest it. The argument of those who claim such an original is dependent on the Semitic cast of the language, but does not adequately take account of the interaction between the two languages during the first and second centuries BCE.[16] That a Greek work can successfully be retroverted into Aramaic or

15. See Aejmelaeus, 'Septuagintal Translation Techniques', p. 398, who points out that 'it is possible to have both free translation and a different *Vorlage* in the same text'.

16. Moore, *Daniel*, pp. 44-46, summarizes the arguments for both points of view. While he favours a Hebrew original for the Additions, he concedes that 'not only are there very few Hebraisms that one can point to in the additions, but there is not one indisputably clear example of a Greek word or phrase which can only be explained by positing a Semitic *Vorlage*'.

Hebrew may prove nothing more than that it has been authored by a Greek speaker immersed in a Semitic mind set and under the influence of Septuagintal Greek.[17]

This analysis is put forward tentatively as the most likely explanation of sparse and conflicting evidence, and no doubt raises as many questions as it solves. There are two which seem particularly acute. First, it is surprising that a Palestinian tradition should have been translated into Greek at all. The more usual assumption is an Alexandrian origin for the translation, which could perhaps be supported by the unusual interest of ch. 11 LXX in Egypt.[18] Against this must be set the driving interest of the LXX in the Temple and cult, as well as in national life, which suggests a Palestinian setting. If the LXX is a Palestinian production, it would join a corpus of Greek works from that part of the world that includes the books of the Maccabees. Another possibility is that the translation did not take place on Jewish soil, but still reflects a Judean *Vorlage*. A parallel case is that of Sirach, a Jerusalemite work translated into Greek in Egypt. A Palestinian origin for the LXX is admittedly a weak point in the argument, and is possibly as circular as it is inconclusive.

A second concern relates to the MT. The different 967 ordering indicates that the final redaction of the MT took place well after the Persian period. In that case, the demonizing of Nebuchadnezzar in popular mythology may be expected to have begun. Why is the less hostile view retained by the MT even when the visions become attached? A literary-critical answer might be that this is a further reflection of the literary sophistication of the MT's exploration of the themes. No certain historical answer is suggested by the available evidence. It is possible, however, that this is another manifestation of the existence of different political points of view centred on the wisdom trajectories noted earlier. The MT's different treatment of the kings thereby reflects the Persian material preserved in its own particular wisdom tradition. The different attitude to the kings in the LXX does not therefore mean that it is later, but that it reflects a group with different agenda, a group that has probably co-existed with the MT viewpoint for some time.[19] The existence of two

17. See Tov, 'Three Dimensions', pp. 533-34, on the effect of translations out of Hebrew and Aramaic on the Greek language.

18. But Bogaert, 'Relecture et refonte', p. 200, considers that the translator's pro-Egyptian stance does not require that he be in either Egypt or Judah.

19. David, 'Composition and Structure', p. 95, also postulates two independent collections in the early Hellenistic period.

points of view that had long been in tension with one another also explains material in both the MT and the LXX that is exceptional to the general trend of the version. Such material would have been the result of some interaction over time between the traditions.

Prospects

Because the texts have been treated within limited parameters, there are a number of questions inevitably left unanswered. Most obviously, this study has only treated six out of the twelve chapters in Daniel. The brief survey chapter on the Hebrew sections, as well as confirming a continuity across the linguistic division in both versions, served to highlight the issues that would repay treatment in the light of the work done on chs. 2–7. Several further areas of study also beckon at the end of this narrative-critical comparison. The first relates to the history of the texts while the others are more theological.

I have paid little attention to the linguistic evidence for dating the Aramaic of the MT. However, a number of studies have recently cast doubt on Driver's famous assertion that 'the Greek words demand, the Hebrew supports, and the Aramaic permits, a date after the conquest of Palestine by Alexander the Great (BC 332)'.[20] Kitchen took issue with Driver in 1965 when he demonstrated a number of linguistic features that could indicate an earlier date for the stories.[21] Although Kitchen himself has not returned to that particular fray since, others have accumulated more evidence that supports his thesis. Coxon was cautious in his series of linguistic studies in the late 1970s but allowed that much of the evidence could point to an earlier date for the Aramaic of Daniel.[22] Other work, by such as Yamauchi and Masson, casts doubt on

20. Driver, *Daniel*, p. lxiii. See also Bevan, *Daniel*, pp. 41-42.

21. See his conclusions in K.A. Kitchen, 'The Aramaic of Daniel', in D.J. Wiseman *et al.*, *Notes on Some Problems in the Book of Daniel* (London: Tyndale Press, 1965), pp. 77-79. A much earlier move in the same direction was taken by H.H. Schaeder, *Iranische Beiträge* (Halle: Max Niemeyer Verlag, 1930), I, pp. 199-20, as cited by David, 'Composition and Structure', p. 50.

22. For example P.W. Coxon, 'A Morphological Study of the *h*-Prefix in Biblical Aramaic', *JAOS* 98 (1978), p. 416; 'The Problem of Consonantal Mutations in Biblical Aramaic', *ZDMG* 129 (1979), p. 22; 'The Distribution of Synonyms in Biblical Aramaic in the Light of Official Aramaic and the Aramaic of Qumran', *RevQ* 19 (1978), p. 512; and 'The Syntax of the Aramaic of *Daniel*: A Dialectical Study',

the particular notion that the presence of Greek words in Daniel necessitates a late date.[23] Fitzmyer on the *Genesis Apocryphon* also points to an earlier date for the Aramaic of Daniel.[24] There have of course been dissenting voices.[25] It would be useful now to consider the linguistic evidence in tandem with the literary indicators towards a greater understanding of the textual history.[26] As far as the LXX text is concerned, I have ignored the possibility that different parts of the translation may have come from different hands. That too is an area which would repay careful study and could turn out to have text-historical significance.

This literary-critical approach also begs a more thorough reflection on the tool of narrative criticism from a theological rather than simply a methodological perspective. By seeing the meaning of the narrative as in part a function of its form, and with an awareness of the implied reader and implied narrator within the text, I have used narrative criticism as a means of exploring a particular group of texts and their relation to one another. However, I have avoided the larger questions raised about the

HUCA 48 (1977), p. 122. More recently Stefanovic, *The Aramaic of Daniel*, p. 108, concludes that 'the search for features in (Daniel Aramaic) of an early date should be pursued more intensively'.

23. E. Masson, *Recherches sur les plus anciens emprunts sémitiques en grec* (Paris: C. Klincksieck, 1967), pp. 113-14; and E.M. Yamauchi, 'Daniel and Contacts between the Aegean and the Near East before Alexander', *EvQ* 53 (1981), p. 47, who concludes his essay with the hope that 'future commentaries will come to recognize that the Greek words in Daniel cannot be used to date the book to the Hellenistic age'.

24. J.A. Fitzmyer, 'Some Observations on the *Genesis Apocryphon*', *CBQ* 22 (1960), p. 279; and *Genesis Apocryphon*, pp. 19-23. See also G.L. Archer, 'The Aramaic of the "Genesis Apocryphon" Compared with the Aramaic of Daniel', in J.B. Payne (ed.), *New Perspectives on the Old Testament* (Waco, TX: Word Books, 1970), pp. 161-69, whose polemical tone should not distract the reader from his argument for Daniel Aramaic as an early eastern form of the language.

25. For example A.S. van der Woude, 'Erwägungen zur Doppelsprachigkeit des Buches Daniel', in H.L.J. Vanstiphont, K. Jongeling, F. Leemhuis and G.J. Reinink (eds.), *Scripta Signa Vocis* (Groningen: Egbert Forsten, 1986), pp. 306-307, who links linguistic questions with a redaction critical approach to the problem of bilingualism in Daniel. In his view it is not outside the bounds of possibility that classical imperial Aramaic was used in the mid second century BCE.

26. A great deal of useful work has in fact been done by David, 'Composition and Structure', pp. 270-80, in a lengthy excursus on the LXX version, although his focus is almost exclusively on 9.24-27 and 8.11b-14.

method. The relationship, if any, of 'narrative theology' to narrative criticism is a particularly important one. In that regard, Frei's analysis of 'the eclipse of biblical narrative' has motivated a number of thinkers in the field who are not necessarily in agreement with one another.[27] In fact, do the proponents of narrative criticism think in terms of a theology related to the method at all? Furthermore, in Frei's terms, what do they understand by realistic narrative and how do they apply the concept to biblical interpretation? Ought the opposite of 'historical critical' be 'realistic' or 'literary', or does the concept of narrative realism provide a way through the perceived dichotomy between the two?[28]

Frei is puzzled that the rise of the realistic novel in eighteenth- and nineteenth-century English literature occurred at the same time as the emergence of the historical-critical method,[29] which militated against a realistic reading of biblical narrative. Prickett holds a mirror up to Frei and wonders if the reverse is true. Prose realism was in fact an attempt to respond to the new ways of looking at biblical narrative.[30] His opinion is grounded on the view that realism is not a possible concept in the biblical Hebrew world.[31] Whether or not Prickett can make a case, the question he raises of the applicability of late Western categories of literary criticism to biblical stories is an important one. Narrative critics of the Bible are often indebted to European critics of the novel such as Frye, Booth or Genette.[32] Is this because the Bible has been formative in Western literature, or is there a danger of imposing external categories on the biblical narrative?[33]

A further question in need of development is the relationship of

27. See H.W. Frei, *The Eclipse of Biblical Narrative* (New Haven: Yale University Press, 1974); and 'The "Literal Reading" of Biblical Narrative in the Christian Tradition: Does it Stretch or Will it Break?', in F. McConnell (ed.), *The Bible and the Narrative Tradition* (Oxford: Oxford University Press, 1986), pp. 36-77. The various directions his students have taken is well illustrated in the volume of essays edited by G. Green (ed.), *Scriptural Authority and Narrative Interpretation* (Philadelphia: Fortress Press, 1987).

28. The review of Frei by F.F. Bruce, 'Book Review of *The Eclipse of Biblical Narrative*', *CSR* 5 (1975), p. 200, suggests that it does not.

29. Frei, *The Eclipse*, pp. 16 and 130-37.

30. Prickett, 'Poetics and Narrative', p. 7.

31. Prickett, 'Poetics and Narrative', p. 15.

32. In addition to works by Genette and Booth already cited, see N. Frye, *Anatomy of Criticism* (Princeton, NJ: Princeton University Press, 1971).

33. Auerbach, *Mimesis*, p. 23, argues powerfully for the former view.

narrative form to meaning. Alter would say that the characteristics of biblical narrative reflect the nature of the God spoken about in the narratives, his dealings with humanity, and his position in relation to space and time.[34] For him, the devices that draw the reader into the stories are themselves an expression of Jewish monotheism. While the particularity of Alter's application can be self-limiting, Auerbach treats the topic in more general terms and makes an influential case that 'The concept of God held by the Jews is less a cause than a symptom of their manner of comprehending and representing things'.[35] This question of the relationship of literary form to revelation is a huge one that is related to the foregoing material but whose treatment must wait for another time.

A final prospect raised is the equally vast topic of canon. A literary comparison of the LXX and MT of Daniel 2–7 has raised historical questions which relate to the debate over the formation of the Jewish canon. The different positions are epitomized in the conversation between Beckwith and Barton.[36] The latter argues that outside the Pentateuch the prophets and writings remained a very unsettled collection until very late. This unsettlement in itself, particularly in the prophets, suggests the presence of a protest element opposing the religious establishment.[37] Beckwith, on the other hand, holds the view that the Hebrew canon was fixed into its tripartite structure at an early stage.[38] It would be interesting to consider whether the presence of differing wisdom circles centred on Daniel from as early as Persian times could have any input into this debate.

A continuing treatment of these two contrasting accounts of the wise courtier Daniel still beckons. There are theological, historical and linguistic questions not yet answered. But a narrative-critical approach provides important clues on the student's quest for understanding of the nature of these texts and the society and faith which they reflect.

34. Alter, *Biblical Narrative*, pp. 32, 155, 158 etc.

35. Auerbach, *Mimesis*, p. 8.

36. R. Beckwith, *The Old Testament Canon of the New Testament Church* (London: SPCK, 1986); and J. Barton, *Oracles of God* (London: Darton, Longman & Todd, 1984).

37. Barton, *Oracles*, pp. 267-70.

38. Beckwith, *The Old Testament Canon*, pp. 68-71 and 123-27. He argues that Daniel, along with Esther, Ezra–Nehemiah and Chronicles, was a settled part of the Hagiographa from the second century BCE.

Appendix 1

THEODOTION

What follows is a brief chapter-by-chapter summary of the most prominent differences between θ and the MT in Daniel 2–7. The relationship of those differences to the LXX will also be noted where appropriate. As a rule, the θ translator follows the sense of the Aramaic closely but not slavishly. Differences sometimes reflect problems in translation or the need to depart from strict equivalence in the interests of sense. At times θ seems to reflect a *Vorlage* different from the MT. Occasionally there is a hint of interpretation about the version, either for theological reasons or because the translator apparently feels the need to clarify a word or phrase. The distinction between these two types of variation is not always easy to draw.

Daniel 2

Daniel 2 contains several examples of variations which arise because the Aramaic is difficult. This is likely to be the case with 'his sleep went from him' (v. 1, ὁ ὕπνος αὐτοῦ ἐγένετο ἀπ' αὐτοῦ) as a rendering of the impersonal Hebrew expression שְׁנָתוֹ נִהְיְתָה עָלָיו. θ has also interpreted דִּי at the start of v. 9 as οὖν in the interest of clarifying some tortuous Aramaic syntax. Verse 30 is similarly difficult with its hint of anacolouthon in the Aramaic, and θ, like the LXX, gets over the hurdle with a rephrasing of the sense. The use of ἐν σπουδῇ in v. 25 to translate the difficult בְּהִתְבְּהָלָה is a rendering that we also meet in 3.24/91 θ and 6.20, and is an example of the Greek taking on a wider range of meaning to match the semantic range of the Semitic original.[1]

Other differences arise when θ adopts a particular modification which is consistently observed by the translator. Such is the case with the insertion of a possessive pronoun to modify 'interpretation' in vv. 7, 9 and 16. The translator may have adopted an alternative reading of the consonantal text in vv. 7 and 16, but that cannot be the case for פִּשְׁרָא in v. 9. Similarly, θ rejects the MT modifiers of 'earthenware' (חֲסַף) in vv. 41 and 43 (דִּי־פֶחָר and טִינָא) and instead employs ὀστράκινος and ὄστρακον throughout. Another example of the same phenomenon is the habit seen elsewhere in θ of rearranging lists when they are perceived to be out of order. θ's objection on this occasion is to a perceived misplacing of 'earthenware' (חֲסַף or חַשְׁף)

---

1.   See the extensive discussion by Walters, *The Text of the Septuagint*, pp. 144-48, on this particular example.

in the lists of vv. 35 and 45.[2] At times this sort of difference may be accounted for as a dependence on the LXX by θ, but the evidence for that is mixed.[3]

In the examples cited above, θ sometimes agrees with the LXX against the MT (vv. 7, 9, 41, 43, 45), but sometimes an expression is suggestive of an independent interpretation (vv. 16, 35, 41). A particular example that is probably both an interpretation by θ and a sign of LXX influence is the phrase 'what must happen' (vv. 28, 29, 45, ἅ/τί δεῖ γενέσθαι) after these things or at the end. θ appears to have been influenced by the LXX rendering of להוא on the first two occurrences, and then reproduced that reading in v. 45 where the LXX is content with a simple ἐσόμενα. Whether or not there is a sense of compulsion lying behind δεῖ as used by the LXX has been discussed. As far as θ is concerned, repetition of the phrase may well tie in with the translator's view of what the dream of Nebuchadnezzar means.

On other occasions it is not possible to determine whether a difference has come about because the translator interprets or because his Aramaic *Vorlage* differs from the MT. A shortened form of v. 40 either clarifies a verbose Aramaic or witnesses to a time before the corrupt form available in the MT. The θ expression 'it will be shattered by itself' (v. 42, ἀπ' αὐτῆς ἔσται συντριβόμενον) is a vivid exposition of the fragility of the kingdom expressed in the MT and LXX, but a departure of this magnitude is out of character for θ, and so a different *Vorlage* is the more likely explanation. That is also the most likely explanation for θ's reading 'insight' (v. 20, ἡ σύνεσις) for 'might' (נבורתא). The grammatical difficulties represented by the isolated infinitive 'to report' (v. 27, ἀναγγεῖλαι) arise because the Aramaic element יכלין is absent from θ. This also suggests the possibility of a different, possibly corrupt, *Vorlage* of v. 27, as does the shorter form of v. 31 in θ. Perhaps the substitution of a singular first person pronoun for the plural in v. 23 (ἐγνώρισάς μοι instead of הודעתנא) reflects a different *Vorlage*, but it could be an amendment intended by θ to overcome a difficulty with the sense of the narrative.

Daniel 3

A feature of Daniel 3 is that θ includes the Additions, and in other respects also has a little more in common with the LXX than is the case elsewhere in Daniel 2–7. There are hints that θ is not quite as literal as usual in ch. 3, particularly in terms of the addition or subtraction of elements and the accuracy of semantic information conveyed by the translation.[4] This may be illustrated by the lists in vv. 2-3. In each instance the list of officials deviates slightly from the MT, but in different ways in each case. Not only are there two fewer officials mentioned, but they are not

2. See Rosenthal, *Biblical Aramaic*, p. 16, on the vacillation in biblical Aramaic between ט and ת.

3. See the discussion by Schmitt, 'Die griechischen Danieltexte', pp. 9-29, of the relationship between θ and LXX, and what he calls the 'Inkonstanz und Inhomogenität' of θ. Note that he makes a distinction that is beyond the scope of this discussion between the putative Theodotion of Daniel ("θ'") and the real Theodotion (θ'). See also Montgomery, *Daniel*, p. 170.

4. See Barr, *Typology of Literalism*, p. 294. These are two of the six modes he distinguishes in assessing the literalness of a translation.

equivalent to the officials in the MT. Moreover, the use of καί in the lists is not consistent between the two blocks of θ material and is not equivalent to the use of ו by the MT. It is generally agreed that the ו in front of 'governors' (ופחות) in both verses is deliberately placed to divide the list into separate categories of officials. No such effect is discernible in θ. This contrasts with the lists of Babylonian wisdom officials in chs. 2, 4 and 5, where θ reproduces the series almost exactly (2.2; 5.7; 5.11). The exceptional case is 4.4/7 where the third and fourth elements in the list are reversed, but in the light of other examples this is almost certainly due to an error in translation or transmission. It contrasts also with the care by which θ attempts to reproduce the MT administrative terminology in ch. 6 (v. 8, for example). In a similar vein, the use of καί in the lists of musical instruments (vv. 5, 7, 10) does not match the MT.

Of a slightly different order is the inclusion of 'bagpipes' (v. 7, συμφωνίας) in the first repeat of the musical instrument list. This is either a witness to an earlier *Vorlage* before that item had dropped out of the Aramaic text, or an attempt by the θ translator to correct a perceived corruption in the MT. The same phenomenon is observed in 5.23 where the MT varies a list by reversing the items, gold and silver, while θ preserves the order that obtained in 5.2.

The above differences could be due to a different translation practice on the part of θ from that prevailing in other chapters.[5] On the other hand, they could simply witness to a *Vorlage* more at variance with the MT. Other divergences do point towards a slightly less literal type of translation. 'King Nebuchadnezzar' is omitted in v. 2 θ. 'In that moment' (v. 8 MT, בה־זמנא) is simply 'then' (τότε) in θ. The closely literal nature of θ's translation is most likely to waver where the translator betrays his theological mind set. Such is the case in ch. 3 where θ describes the fourth figure in the furnace as 'like a son of God' (v. 25/92, ὁμοία υἱῷ θεοῦ). The MT has the phrase, 'like a son of the gods' (לבר־אלהין).

A number of smaller semantic variations point to translation difficulties. In vv. 2 and 3 the genitive plural 'regions' (τῶν χωρῶν) is used to render מדינתא, which is normally regarded as a singular. The LXX uses a singular accusative form, χώραν. In this instance the irregular non-spirantization of feminine singular determined state nouns has probably resulted in a misreading of the Aramaic consonants.[6] The Aramaic idiom שׂים...טעם, 'to have regard for somebody', provides θ with the same problems in v. 12 as in 6.14. In the latter instance it is translated 'has not subjected himself to your decree' (οὐχ ὑπετάγη τῷ δόγματί σου). In the present chapter θ renders it 'did not obey your decree' (v. 12, οὐχ ὑπήκουσαν...τῷ δόγματί σου). Both are attempts to deal literally with טעם. The verbs ῥύομαι (v. 17) and ὑπερίσχω (v. 22) overlap the semantic range of the Aramaic that they are attempting

5.   To speak of translation 'practice' rather than 'policy' or 'technique' avoids the question of how much intentionality may be assigned to the θ translator. See A. Aejmelaeus, 'Translation Technique and the Intention of the Translator', in C.E. Cox (ed.), *VII Congress of the International Organization for Septuagint and Cognate Studies* (Atlanta: Scholars Press, 1991), pp. 26-28, on the subject. The idea is expressed by Schmitt, 'Die griechischen Danieltexte', p. 7, with the German word *Übersetzungsgewohnheit*.

6.   Rosenthal, *Biblical Aramaic*, p. 13.

to translate (שׁוב and חצף respectively) even though the chosen translation tends to take the meaning in a different direction. In v. 27/94 a variation in meaning comes about when the syntax of the Aramaic is not reproduced quite accurately by θ. The word order of the MT suggests that the verbs 'gathered round' (מתכנשׁין) and 'saw' (חזין) have separate subjects in the form of separate groups of officials. The higher ranked trio from vv. 2 and 3 (אחשׁדרפניא סגניא ופחותא) 'gathered round' while the officials 'saw'. This distinction is not preserved by θ which treats the verbs as a pair with a common subject.

Other differences between θ and the MT are probably related to textual problems. The opening phrase in v. 9 MT, 'They answered and said:' (ענו ואמרין), is not represented at all in θ. The result is an unusual and compressed structure in which the verb διαβάλλω (v. 8) takes both a direct and an indirect object. Such a construction is possible but unlikely. This is closely followed by the absence again in θ of the final phrase in v. 10 MT, 'will fall and worship the golden image' (יפל ויסגד לצלם דהבא). Again the grammatical result is not impossible, but it leaves a gap in the formula that was earlier reproduced exactly in vv. 5-6. Some corruption in the text of the *Vorlage* or in transmission is the most likely explanation of these differences.

θ's treatment of some of the more vivid Aramaic images in this chapter cannot be adduced as evidence of a less literal translation practice, as they receive the same treatment elsewhere in the θ translation of Daniel. At v. 8 the Chaldeans in θ merely 'slandered' (διέβαλον) the Jews, while those in the MT 'ate pieces of' (אכלו קרהציהון) them. This is consistent with 6.25.[7] In the king's final decree the general populace is enjoined to worship God lest they be 'destroyed' (v. 29/96, ἀπώλειαν), according to θ. According to the MT they 'will be made into limbs' (חדמין יתעבד). The LXX Greek is the same as θ in v. 8, but in the second image the LXX evokes the same picture as the MT with the expression 'he will be dismembered' (v. 29/96, διαμελισθήσεται). Again the Theodotionic translation is the same as in 2.5.

More difficult to explain is a puzzling θ plus, the final phrase where Shadrach, Meshach and Abednego are deputed to rule over all the Jews who were in Babylon (v. 30/97). The final statement in the LXX about the heroes' promotion is also fuller than the MT but it gives no indication that their duties were with special reference to the Jews. Although the translation of θ in this chapter is a little less literal than elsewhere, it is still exceedingly cautious. Such a marked divergence as this one from the MT is often explicable in terms of the LXX, but such is not the case here. Whether or not it witnesses to a different *Vorlage*, it is part of the tradition of leadership within the distinct Jewish community in exile that lurks in the Greek versions. I explored this point in some detail in connection with the LXX plus of 2.18.[8] Another instance

---

7. If Goldingay, *Daniel*, p. 66, is right that this is an Akkadian expression, it was probably unfamiliar to the much later Greek translator.

8. Plöger, *Daniel*, p. 61, is uncertain whether the treatment of the three in θ is a 'restitutio in integrum', or a further promotion. Lacocque, *Daniel*, p. 61, thinks θ is an addition, perhaps in light of 1 Macc. 2.51-61. The suggestion of Koch, 'Die Herkunft der Proto-Theodotion-Übersetzung des Danielbuches', *VT* 23 (1973), p. 165, that this denotes the Exilarch of Parthian and Sassanid times is probably anachronistic.

of non-MT tradition is the date, 'in the 'eighteenth year of Nebuchadnezzar the king' (v. 1, "Ετους ὀκτωκαιδεκάτου Ναβουχοδονοσορ). But here θ reflects the LXX.

There are also differences between the two Greek versions in the Additions, although they are almost identical in the poetic material.[9] At the point where the Greek diverges from the Aramaic (v. 24), θ agrees with the LXX in focusing on the singing of the young men. However, it is more succinct in its introduction to the singing (vv. 24-25), but slightly longer than the LXX in vv. 46 and 51 of the prose material linking the two main sections of poetry.

There are occasional differences in verse order in the songs themselves. In poetic terms, these differences do not form a consistent pattern. At times they suggest a corruption of the LXX on the part of θ. This seems to be the case in vv. 67-72, where θ follows the order vv. 67, 68, 71, 72, 69, 70. This results in imagery of light and dark (vv. 71-72) interrupting images of cold and wet instead of coming after them as in the LXX. Within these verses also the phrase 'cold and heat' (v. 67, ψῦχος καὶ καῦμα) in θ differs from 'frost and cold' (ῥῖγος καὶ ψῦχος) in the LXX. It is not possible to tell whether this is a corruption on the part of θ or an attempt to link the heat of v. 66 with the cold of v. 68. In favour of the second option, vv. 71-72 have similarly contrasting pairs, but against this the imagery of heat and cold seems to follow a pattern of parallel pairs rather than contrasting ones. The relationship between the two versions is also problematic at vv. 84-85, where the LXX twice does not include 'of the Lord' (κυρίου). The result is a line that scans differently from anywhere else in the song. Has θ inserted κυρίου to correct this scanning problem? If so it has for some reason chosen to leave v. 83 alone, which is just as short on syllables. On the other hand, the LXX may have been objecting to 'Lord' twice on a line and amended accordingly. It remains a matter of speculation.

Daniel 4

There are several points in Daniel 4 θ where the translator seems to be interpreting his text. These largely relate to points of theology. In a manner typical of θ in general, the MT 'holy gods' (vv. 5, 15, אלהין קדישׁין) is rendered in the singular with θεοῦ ἅγιον (vv. 8, 18). In a similar vein, the rather secular advice to the king in v. 24/27 MT to 'abolish' (פרק) his sins in the hope of an 'extension of your prosperity' (ארכה לשׁלותך) is reworked by θ. The more godly alternative offered is the advice to the king 'to redeem your sins' (τάς ἁμαρτίας σου...λύτρωσαι) in the hope that 'God will be patient...' (ἔσται μακρόθυμος...ὁ θεός). While this translation could owe something to a broadening of semantic range of the Aramaic, it also has a theological point to it and reflects language used by the LXX. This outlook reveals itself further in θ's choice at v. 26/29 of ναός ('temple') for the more

---

9.   Note again the view of Bruce, 'Oldest Greek Version', p. 36, and Daubney, *The Three Additions*, p. 46, that this in itself suggests a common Semitic original of the Additions. Schmitt, 'Die griechischen Danieltexte', p. 27, allows that this is a possibility, but on balance (p. 29) favours the view that θ's *Vorlage* in the Additions was the Old Greek.

broadly understood Aramaic word היכל. Some sort of link with the LXX can also be discerned in the consistent use of τὸ κύτος αὐτοῦ (vv. 8/11, 17/20, 'its girth/ trunk') for חזוחה ('its appearance') in Aramaic. As another aspect of interpretation, the translator in v. 6/9 is either working from an uncorrupted *Vorlage* or is making a deliberate attempt to clarify a confusing MT, with 'hear' (ἄκουσον) instead of 'tell' (חזי).

Other minor differences can be explained either by an anachronistic understanding of the Aramaic original on the part of the translator, or by a *Vorlage* that differs from the MT. An example of the former is the variable translation by θ of יחלפון ('will pass over'). Twice ἀλλαγήσονται (vv. 22/25, 29/32) and once ἀλλοιωθῶσιν (v. 20/23) are employed, and both mean 'will change', a probable reflection of the Jewish Palestinian Aramaic meaning. An instance of the latter is the reversal of terms in the list of mantic officials at v. 4/7.

Daniel 5

θ in ch. 5 presents a similar picture. At times the translator apparently misreads the MT original. Where the Aramaic מחא (v. 19, 'spared') is represented by the Greek ἔτυπτεν ('struck down') θ has adopted the dominant meaning, although the parallelism of the Aramaic here and in 4.32 seems to require the less usual sense.[10] Sometimes a different *Vorlage* is suggested by additions or omissions of one element. A particularly strong case is the θ inclusion of 'diviners' (γαζαρηνοί) in v. 15, as this term is always a transcription of the Aramaic in θ. Another example is the inclusion of 'reporting mighty acts' (ἀναγγέλλων κρατούμενα) in v. 12.

But there is a touch of interpretation about some differences. An example that has been referred to is the rendering of the difficult בטעם חמרא as καὶ πίνων (v. 1/2). Typically, θ speaks of 'God' rather than 'gods'. In v. 11 Daniel has the spirit 'of God' (θεοῦ) in contrast to the plural of the MT, while in v. 23 Belshazzar is accused of arrogance 'against the Lord God' (ἐπὶ τὸν κύριον θεόν), not 'the Lord of heaven' (מרא־שמיא). Elsewhere the differences hint at a desire to deal with perceived redundancy in the *Vorlage*. The omission of the phrases at the end of v. 11 and beginning of v. 18 (אבוך מלכא and אנתה), as well as the final מן־יהוד in v. 13, are cases in point.

Daniel 6

Occasionally in Daniel 6, θ departs from its closely literal practices. An example of this is in v. 21 where the Greek does not represent the Aramaic ענה with ἀποκρίνω as it usually does. However, θ does reproduce the idiom at v. 14. Also in v. 13 the Greek syntax of a participle modifying a finite verb (προσελθόντες λέγουσιν) is used to convey the two verbs joined by ו in the MT (קריבו ואמרין). Although θ sometimes employs this more idiomatic form, it normally prefers an exact equivalence of elements. In that same verse also קדם does not appear in θ.

Other differences are more likely to be interpretational, as when the Greek clarifies

10. Rosenthal, *Biblical Aramaic*, p. 15.

that it is 'to his God' (v. 14, παρὰ τοῦ θεοῦ αὐτοῦ) that Daniel is praying. At times some uncertainty in the mind of the translator is discernible. Such may be the case where the difficult verb רגשׁ (v. 16) is ignored, or the nocturnal 'diversion' (v. 19, דחון) of the king is assumed to be 'food' (ἐδέσματα). Sometimes a difference occurs because the attempted literal rendering of the Aramaic does not quite reproduce the same sense in Greek. One example is the use of ἐν σπουδῇ (v. 20, 'in haste') to represent the meaning of בהתבהלה ('in trepidation'). Another example is the attempt to render literally the Aramaic מן־קדמי שׂים טעם (v. 27). The rather ambiguous די of v. 9 is translated by θ with the equally flexible ὅπως, but the result is a slightly different nuance in the way the clauses are linked. The more causative sense of the Greek almost suggests that the immutability of the law of the Medes and the Persians owes something to this particular decree.

The above examples probably arise from a *Vorlage* witnessed to by the MT. There are other differences that suggest either a different original or a conscious attempt to tidy up the MT text. The shorter Greek in both vv. 5 and 6 seems like a deliberate reduction of a verbose piece of Aramaic. The addition of 'out of the mouths of' (v. 21, ἐκ στόματος) replicates the full expression that is used elsewhere in the MT and θ (v. 23), either by oversight on the part of the translator or because פם was absent from θ's *Vorlage*. The θ plus material in v. 19, where the agency of God in the lions' pit is detailed, clearly owes something to the LXX. It is possible also that θ's suggestion of Daniel's primacy at the beginning of v. 4 (καὶ ἦν Δανιηλ ὑπὲρ αὐτούς) owes more to the LXX than to the MT.

Daniel 7

Most differences between θ and the MT in Daniel 7 may be explained as problems of translation. On occasions θ translates all the elements of the MT, but the syntactical relationships end up at variance. Such is the case in v. 19, where φοβερὸν περισσῶς seems to have been misplaced by the translator, and the subsequent description of the beast is syntactically as difficult as its MT counterpart. Another example of difficulty in translation comes where θ, in common with many translators since, has trouble with 'in its sheath' (v. 15, בנוא נדנה). He resorts to the equally obscure ἐν τῇ ἕξει μου. In none of these examples is any influence from the LXX apparent.

Even the interpretations are normally attempts to clarify the meaning, and carry no theological significance. An example of interpretation motivated by the difficulty of the MT comes in v. 6 where two changes are made in the interests of clarity. In the opening sentence the MT uses אחרי ('another') and leaves 'beast' understood, where θ says specifically 'another beast' (ἕτερον θηρίον). Similarly, the wings of a bird 'on its back' (על־גביה) are understood by θ to be 'above it' (ὑπεράνω αὐτῆς). In the first example θ acts independently of the LXX, whereas the LXX shows the same understanding as θ in v. 6 but uses slightly different vocabulary.

There is one significant instance of interpretation in v. 27 where the puzzling 'to the people of the holy ones' (לעם קדישׁי) is rendered simply as 'to the holy ones' (ἁγίοις). The LXX interprets that phrase with λαῷ ἁγίῳ, but retains an equivalence of elements in so doing. It is probable therefore that the θ minus is not due to a different *Vorlage* so much as an attempt to adjust this exceptional expression towards the more usual קדישי on its own. I have noted this habit also in other chapters where variations in repeated material are adjusted to eliminate the variation. Here the change indicates that θ views 'the people of the holy ones of the Most High' (עם קדישי עליונין) as equivalent to 'the holy ones of the Most High' (vv. 18, 22, 25, קדישי עליונין) elsewhere in the chapter.

Another possible example of interpretation on the part of θ is found in vv. 23-24. The MT says that the fourth kingdom 'will be different' (v. 23, תשנא) from its predecessors, and the eleventh king 'will be different' (v. 24, ישנא) from the ten that went before. In neither place does θ use exact equivalents in translation. According to him the fourth kingdom 'will outdo' (v. 23, ὑπερέξει) the other three, while the eleventh horn will 'surpass in evil' (v. 24, ὑπεροίσει κακοῖς) all the others. Although θ translates שניה in v. 19 with διάφορον, the variation at both instances of שנה in vv. 23-24 suggests an interpretation of the nature of the difference. However, the possibility that θ is working from a different *Vorlage* must be admitted. On this occasion his rendering of the MT verbs differs from the LXX, yet the inclusion of κακοῖς as a plus against the MT is in line with a similar plus in the LXX.

Appendix 2

SEPTUAGINT DANIEL 2–7 IN ENGLISH

What follows is an English translation of the Rahlfs edition of Daniel 2–7 LXX. Its purpose is to assist in the comparison of the LXX with the MT by representing as closely as possible in English the syntactical relationships and vocabulary of the Greek. It strives to be as literal as it can be without distorting the sense of the Greek or producing meaningless English. Stylish English is not an aim. To that end, a one-to-one equivalence of vocabulary is sought for verbs, nouns, adjectives and adverbs. Footnotes indicate where that cannot be achieved. Greek word order is also represented wherever possible. Syntactical relationships are preserved in English, except that participles are often best rendered with finite verbs, and an active form of the verb in Greek is commonly expressed in English with a passive. I do not try for exact equivalence with particles and prepositions, but vary the translation of them according to context. Ambiguous Greek is allowed to remain ambiguous in the English. καί and δέ remain as 'and' or 'but' and are not interpreted. Words in brackets represent either an English addition or a Greek element not represented in the translation.

Daniel 2

2.1   And in the second year of the reign[1] of Nebuchadnezzar, it happened that the king fell into visions and dreams and was frightened in his dream, and his sleep went from him.

2.2   And the king ordered to be brought in the magicians and enchanters and sorcerers of the Chaldeans to report his dreams to the king, and they came[2] and stood before the king.

2.3   And the king said[3] to them: I have seen a dream and my spirit was shaken.[4] Therefore I want to find out the dream.

---

1.   Also translated as 'kingdom'.

2.   Greek participles are translated with a finite verb when their mood is more appropriately expressed in English as indicative.

3.   εἶπον and λέγω are treated as synonymous. The are translated with 'say' or 'tell' or occasionally 'speak'. εἶπον is also translated with 'order' when the sense demands, but 'order' usually is reserved for ἐπιτάσσω.

4.   Also translated as 'move'.

2.4   And the Chaldeans spoke to the king in Syrian: Lord King, live forever.
          Report your dream to your servants[5] and we will tell[6] its interpretation.[7]

2.5   But the king answered and said to the Chaldeans: If you do not announce to
          me in truth the dream and explain to me its interpretation, you will be made
          an example of and your possessions will be taken into the king's treasury.

2.6   But if you make clear the dream to me and report its interpretation, you will
          acquire[8] gifts of all sorts and will be glorified by me. Explain to me the
          dream and interpret.[9]

2.7   But they answered a second time and said: O King, tell the vision and your
          servants will interpret it.

2.8   And the king said to them: In truth I know that you are buying time because
          you have seen that the matter[10] has gone out[11] from me. Therefore as I
          have commanded, so shall it be.

2.9   If you do not announce the dream to me in truth and explain its interpreta-
          tion, you will be put to death. For you have agreed to make lying words[12]
          to me until the time changes.[13] Now then, if you tell me the word that I
          saw[14] by night I will know that you will also explain its interpretation.

2.10   And the Chaldeans answered the king: Nobody on earth is able to tell the
          king what he saw, as you are asking, and no king and no power ever asks
          such a matter of a wise man or enchanter or Chaldean.

2.11   And the word that you seek, O king, is deep and awesome, and there is
          nobody who will explain this to the king except an angel, whose habitation
          is not with any flesh. Such a one is not found anywhere.

2.12   Then the king became sad and in great sorrow commanded all the wise men
          of Babylon to be led out.[15]

2.13   And it was decreed to kill them all, and Daniel was sought and all those
          with him for the sake of destroying (them) together.

2.14   Then Daniel spoke with the good counsel[16] and resolution which he had, to
          Arioch, chief of the king's bodyguard, who had been commanded to lead
          out the wise men of Babylon.

2.15   And he enquired of him and said: Why is it harshly decreed by the king?
          Then Arioch intimated the command to Daniel.

---

5.   Both παῖς and δοῦλος are translated as 'servant'.
6.   A translation of φράσω, which only appears here.
7.   'Interpretation' and 'judgment' translate κρῖμα and κρίσις as well as the forms of both
prefixed by συγ-.
8.   Also translated as 'seize'.
9.   Also translated as 'pronounce'.
10. Translation of πρᾶγμα oscillates between 'matter' and 'affair'.
11. Also translated as 'rebel', 'withdraw' and 'leave'.
12. 'Word' translates both ῥῆμα and λόγος.
13. Also translated as 'affect'.
14. 'See' and 'look' both translate ὁράω which is also treated as synonymous with εἴδω.
15. Where the active form of a verb seems to carry a passive sense, it is translated with a passive. This is true especially of the Aramaic active impersonal often represented in the Greek.
16. Also translated as 'plot'.

2.16   And Daniel went quickly into the king and petitioned that time might be given him by the king, and he would explain everything to the king.

2.17   Then Daniel went away to his house and showed everything to Hananiah, Mishael and Azariah, the companions.

2.18   And he declared a fast and prayers (and) to seek help from the Lord Most High concerning this secret, lest Daniel and those with him be given over to destruction along with the wise men of Babylon.

2.19   Then to Daniel in a vision that very night was the secret of the king made clearly manifest. Then Daniel blessed the Lord Most High.

2.20   And he spoke up and said: The name of the great Lord shall be blessed forever, for wisdom and greatness are his.

2.21   And he changes seasons and times,[17] removes kings and sets (them) up, gives wisdom to the wise and insight to those who are learned,

2.22   reveals the deep things and dark things, and knows what is in the darkness and in the light, and puts an end to it.

2.23   To you, Lord of my fathers, I confess and praise, for you have given me wisdom and prudence, and now you have intimated to me the thing I petitioned you to explain to the king.

2.24   And Daniel went in to Arioch, who had been appointed[18] by the king to kill all the wise men of Babylon, and said to him: Do not destroy the wise men of Babylon, but take me in to the king, and I will explain everything to the king.

2.25   Then Arioch in haste took Daniel in to the king and said to him: I have found a wise man from the captivity of the sons of Judea who will explain everything to the king.

2.26   And the king answered and said to Daniel, who was also called in Chaldean Balthasar: Are you able to explain to me the vision which I saw and its interpretation?

2.27   And Daniel spoke up and said to the king: (As for) the secret which the king saw, not of wise men or sorcerers or magicians or diviners is the explanation.

2.28   But there is a God in heaven who reveals secrets, who has explained to King Nebuchadnezzar what must happen at the last days. O King, live forever. The dream and the vision of your head upon your bed is this:

2.29   You, O King, lay upon your bed and saw everything which must happen at the last days, and the one who reveals secrets explained to you what must happen.

---

17.   χρόνος and καιρός are both translated as 'time' except when they occur in this hendiadys. Then they are distinguished by translating the latter as 'season'.

18.   καθίστημι is normally translated as 'set up', a phrase that reflects the two senses of 'erect' and 'promote' which are present in the single Greek word. ἵστημι is also translated with 'set up' as well as 'stand'.

2.30	But not by a wisdom which is in me above all men was this secret made manifest to me, but for the sake of it being explained to the king, it was intimated to me what you came upon[19] in your heart in knowledge.

2.31	And you, O King, saw and behold: One image and that image was exceedingly great and its surpassing appearance stood before you, and the appearance of the image was frightening.

2.32	And its head was of pure gold, the chest and arms silver, the belly and thighs bronze,

2.33	and the legs iron, the feet partly iron and partly earthenware.

2.34	You looked until a stone was cut from a mountain without hands, and it struck the image upon the iron and earthenware feet and ground them down.

2.35	Then the iron and earthenware and gold and silver and bronze were ground together[20] and became like very fine chaff on the threshing floor, and the wind cast them out so that nothing was left of them. And the stone which struck the image became a great mountain and struck all the earth.

2.36	This is the vision and we will also tell the interpretation to the king.

2.37	You, O King, are king of kings and to you the Lord of heaven has given rule and kingdom and might and honour and glory

2.38	in all the inhabited world of men, and beasts of the field and birds of heaven and fish of the sea has he given over into your hand to be lord of them all. You are the head of gold.

2.39	And after you will arise a kingdom inferior to you, and another third bronze kingdom which will be lord over all the earth,

2.40	and a fourth kingdom mighty as iron which overpowers everything and hews down every tree, and all the earth will be shaken.

2.41	And as you saw its feet partly of potter's earthenware and partly of iron, the other kingdom will be divided in itself, since you saw the iron mixed together with the earthenware pottery.

2.42	And (as you saw) the toes of the feet partly of iron and partly of earthenware, part of the kingdom will be mighty and part will be shattered.

2.43	And as you saw the iron mixed together with the earthenware pottery, there will be mingling in the races of men but they will not be in harmony nor well-disposed to one another, just as iron cannot be blended with earthenware.

2.44	And in the times of these kings the God of heaven will set up another kingdom which will be forever and will not be ruined, and this kingdom will never belong to another nation, but it will strike and do away with these kingdoms and it will be set up forever,

2.45	even as you saw a stone cut from a mountain without hands and it smashed the earthenware, the iron and the bronze and the silver and the gold. The great God has intimated to the king what will be at the last days, and the vision is accurate and this interpretation trustworthy.

---

19. Also translated as 'respond'.
20. Literally 'became together'.

2.46   Then Nebuchadnezzar the king fell on his face on the ground and wor-
       shipped[21] Daniel, and ordered sacrifices and drink offerings to be made to
       him.

2.47   And the king spoke up and said to Daniel: In truth is your God the God of
       gods and the Lord of kings, who alone makes manifest hidden secrets, for
       you were enabled to explain this secret.

2.48   Then King Nebuchadnezzar extolled Daniel and gave him great and many
       gifts and set him up over the affairs of Babylon, and brought him forward
       as ruler and leader of all the Babylonian wise men.

2.49   And Daniel petitioned the king that Shadrach, Meshach and Abednego be
       set up over the affairs of Babylon, and Daniel was in the royal court.

Daniel 3

3.1   In the eighteenth year Nebuchadnezzar the king, who administered cities
       and regions and all those inhabiting the earth from India to Ethiopia, made a
       golden image, its height 60 cubits and its breadth 6 cubits, and he set it up
       on the plain around the region of Babylon.

3.2   And Nebuchadnezzar, king of kings and lord of the whole inhabited world,
       sent to be gathered all the peoples and tribes and tongues,[22] satraps, pre-
       fects, governors and courtiers, administrators and all those in authority over
       the region and over the whole inhabited world, to come to the dedication of
       the golden image which Nebuchadnezzar the king set up.

3.3   And the aforementioned stood before the image.

3.4   And the herald proclaimed to the crowd: It is declared to you, O nations and
       regions, peoples and tongues,

3.5   when you hear the sound[23] of the horn, pipe and zither, trigon and harp,
       bagpipes and all kinds of music, you will fall down and worship the golden
       image which Nebuchadnezzar the king set up.

3.6   And anyone who does not fall down and worship will be thrown into the
       furnace of fire which burns.[24]

3.7   And at that time when all the nations heard the sound of the horn and all the
       sounding of music, all the nations, tribes and tongues fell and worshipped
       the golden image which Nebuchadnezzar set up, in front of it (the image).

3.8   At that time Chaldean men approached and slandered the Judeans

3.9   and responded and said: O Lord King, live forever.

3.10   You, O King, commanded and pronounced that any man who hears the
       sound of the pipe and all the sounding of music should fall down and wor-
       ship the golden image,

3.11   and whoever does not fall down and worship will be thrown into the fur-
       nace of fire which burns.

---

21.   'Worship' translates both προσκυνέω and σέβομαι.
22.   Also translated as 'speech'.
23.   Also translated as 'voice'.
24.   Also translated as 'heat'.

3.12 There are certain Judean men whom you set up over the region of Babylon: Shadrach, Meshach, Abednego. These men did not fear your commandment, and your idol they did not serve[25] and your golden image which you set up they did not worship.

3.13 Then Nebuchadnezzar, furious with anger, commanded Shadrach, Meshach, Abednego to be brought.[26] Then the men were brought to the king.

3.14 And when Nebuchadnezzar the king glanced over at them he said: Why, Shadrach, Meshach, Abednego, do you not serve my gods, and the golden image which I set up not worship?

3.15 And now if you are ready, upon hearing the horn and all the sounding of music, to fall and worship the golden image which I set up... But if not, know that when you do not worship you will immediately be thrown into the furnace of fire which burns. And what sort of God will rescue[27] you from my hand?

3.16 But Shadrach, Meshach, Abednego answered and said to King Nebuchadnezzar: O King, we have no need concerning this command to answer,

3.17 for there is one God in the heavens, our Lord whom we fear, who is able to rescue us out of the furnace of fire, and out of your hand, O King, he will rescue us.

3.18 And then it will be plain to you that we neither serve your idol nor your golden image which you set up do we worship.

3.19 Then Nebuchadnezzar was filled with fury and the form of his face changed, and he ordered the furnace to be heated seven times more than it was necessary to be heated.

3.20 And he ordered the most mighty men in the army[28] to bind Shadrach, Meshach, Abednego hand and foot and throw (them) into the furnace of fire which burns.

3.21 Then these men were bound, having their shoes (on) and (with) their hats upon their heads (and) with their clothing, and they were thrown into the furnace.

3.22 Seeing that the command of the king was pressing and the furnace heated seven times more than before, and the hand-picked men had bound them hand and foot and carried them up to the furnace and thrown them into it,

3.23 then the flame came out of the blazing furnace and killed the men who had bound those with Azariah, but they were kept (from harm).

3.24 Then Hananiah and Azariah and Mishael prayed[29] and sang praises to the Lord thus, for the king had commanded them to be thrown into the furnace.

---

25. 'Serve' translates both λατρεύω and δουλεύω.

26. Both φέρω and ἄγω are translated as 'bring'.

27. Also translated as 'take away'.

28. Also translated as 'host' or 'power'.

29. προσεύχομαι and δέομαι with its cognate noun are both translated as 'pray'. An exception is when the two occur as a hendiadys, in which case the latter term is translated as 'plead'.

3.25 And Azariah stood and prayed thus and opened his mouth and confessed to the Lord, together with his companions in the midst of the fire of the furnace excessively heated by the Chaldeans, and they said thus:

3.26 Blessed are you, Lord, the God of our fathers, and your name is praiseworthy and glorified forever,

3.27 for you are righteous in all that you have done, and all your works are true and your ways straight and all your judgments true.

3.28 And you have made a judgment of truth by all that you have brought upon us and upon your holy city of our fathers, Jerusalem, for you have done all these things in truth and justice because of our sins.

3.29 For we have sinned in everything and broken the law to rebel against you, and we have erred in everything and the commandments of your law we have not obeyed,

3.30 nor have we kept (them) nor have we done as we have been enjoined to that it might be well for us.

3.31 And now everything that you have brought upon us and everything that you have done to us, you have done in true judgment.

3.32 And you have given us over into the hands of our enemies, lawless and hated rebels, and to a king unrighteous and the most evil in all the earth.

3.33 And now it is not for us to open the mouth. Shame and contempt have come upon your servants and those who worship you.

3.34 Do not give us over to the end[30] because of your name and do not annul your covenant.

3.35 And do not withdraw your mercy from us, because of Abram who was beloved by you and because of Isaac your servant and Israel your holy one,

3.36 to whom you spoke and told them to multiply their seed as the stars of heaven and as the sand by the shore of the sea.

3.37 For, Master, we have been made the smallest of all the nations, and we are the humblest in all the earth today because of our sins.

3.38 And there is not at this time ruler and prophet, nor leader nor burnt offering nor sacrifice nor offering nor incense, nor a place to offer first fruits before you and find mercy.

3.39 But in shattered soul and humbled spirit may we be accepted[31] as with burnt offerings of rams and bullocks and as with myriads of fat lambs.

3.40 Thus may our sacrifice come before you today and appease you, for there is no shame for those who have relied on you and make atonement[32] before you.

3.41 And now we follow you with our whole heart and we fear you and we seek your face. Do not put us to shame,

3.42 but do with us according to your clemency and according to the fulness of your mercy,

---

30. 'End' translates both τέλος and πέρας.
31. Also translated as 'wait'.
32. See Moore, *Daniel*, p. 59, on the textual difficulties in this verse.

3.43	and rescue us by your marvelous deeds and give glory to your name, Lord.
3.44	And let all those who exhibit evil against your servants be rebuked and let them be put to shame by all the powers and let their might be shattered.
3.45	Let them know that you alone are the Lord God and esteemed over the whole inhabited world.
3.46	And the labourers of the king who threw them in did not leave off heating the furnace. And when at first they threw the three into the furnace, the furnace was red-hot because of its sevenfold intensity. And when they were thrown in, the ones who threw them in were above them and the ones underneath them stoked naphthah and tow and pitch and faggots.
3.47	And the flame leapt out above the furnace to 49 cubits,
3.48	and it spread out and burnt those of the Chaldeans found near the furnace.
3.49	But an angel of the Lord came down at once to the aid of those with Azariah into the furnace, and scattered the flames of fire out of the furnace,
3.50	and made the midst of the furnace as a moist wind whistling, and the fire did not reach them at all, and it did not distress and did not trouble them.
3.51	But the three as out of one mouth took up a song of praise, and glorified and blessed and exalted God in the furnace saying:
3.52	Blessed are you, Lord, the God of our fathers, and praised and highly exalted forever, and blessed is the holy name of your glory and greatly praised and highly exalted for all ages.
3.53	Blessed are you in the Temple of your holy glory and greatly praised and highly esteemed forever.
3.54	Blessed are you on the throne of your kingdom and praised and highly exalted forever.
3.55	Blessed are you who sees the abyss while seated upon the cherubim, and praised and glorified forever.
3.56	Blessed are you in the firmament and praised and glorified forever.
3.57	Bless the Lord, all the works of the Lord. Sing praise and highly exalt him forever.
3.58	Bless the Lord, angels of the Lord. Sing praise and highly exalt him forever.
3.59	Bless the Lord, heavens. Sing praise and highly exalt him forever.
3.60	Bless the Lord, all waters above the heaven. Sing praise and highly exalt him forever.
3.61	Bless the Lord, all the hosts of the Lord. Sing praise and highly exalt him forever.
3.62	Bless the Lord, sun and moon. Sing praise and highly exalt him forever.
3.63	Bless the Lord, stars of heaven. Sing praise and highly exalt him forever.
3.64	Bless the Lord, all rain and dew. Sing praise and highly exalt him forever.
3.65	Bless the Lord, all the winds. Sing praise and highly exalt him forever.
3.66	Bless the Lord, fire and heat. Sing praise and highly exalt him forever.
3.67	Bless the Lord, frost and cold. Sing praise and highly exalt him forever.
3.68	Bless the Lord, dews and falling snow. Sing praise and highly exalt him forever.

3.69 Bless the Lord, ice and cold. Sing praise and highly exalt him forever.

3.70 Bless the Lord, rime and snow. Sing praise and highly exalt him forever.

3.71 Bless the Lord, nights and days. Sing praise and highly exalt him forever.

3.72 Bless the Lord, light and darkness. Sing praise and highly exalt him forever.

3.73 Bless the Lord, lightnings and clouds. Sing praise and highly exalt him forever.

3.74 Let the earth bless the Lord. Let it sing praise and highly exalt him forever.

3.75 Bless the Lord, mountains and hills. Sing praise and highly exalt him forever.

3.76 Bless the Lord, all that springs forth from the earth. Sing praise and highly exalt him forever.

3.77 Bless the Lord, springs. Sing praise and highly exalt him forever.

3.78 Bless the Lord, seas and rivers. Sing praise and highly exalt him forever.

3.79 Bless the Lord, whales and all that move in the waters. Sing praise and highly exalt him forever.

3.80 Bless the Lord, all birds of heaven. Sing praise and highly exalt him forever.

3.81 Bless the Lord, quadrupeds and beasts of the earth. Sing praise and highly exalt him forever.

3.82 Bless the Lord, sons of men. Sing praise and highly exalt him forever.

3.83 Bless the Lord, Israel. Sing praise and highly exalt him forever.

3.84 Bless the Lord, priests. Sing praise and highly exalt him forever.

3.85 Bless the Lord, servants. Sing praise and highly exalt him forever.

3.86 Bless the Lord, those of righteous spirit and soul. Sing praise and highly exalt him forever.

3.87 Bless the Lord, devout and humble in heart. Sing praise and highly exalt him forever.

3.88 Bless the Lord, Hananiah, Azariah, Mishael. Sing praise and highly exalt him forever, for he has rescued us out of Hades and saved us out of the hand of death and delivered us out of the midst of the burning flame and redeemed us out of the fire.

3.89 Confess to the Lord for he is deserving, for his mercy is forever.

3.90 Bless, all who worship the God of gods. Sing praise and confess for his mercy is forever and forever and ever.

3.91 And when the king heard them singing praises he stood up and saw them living. Then Nebuchadnezzar the king marvelled and arose in haste and said to his friends:

3.92 Behold I see four men loose walking around in the fire and no ruination has come to them, and the sight of the fourth is like an angel of God.

3.93 And the king approached the door of the furnace of burning fire and called them by name: Shadrach, Meshach, Abednego, servants of the Most High God of gods, come out of the fire. Accordingly, the men came out of the midst of the fire.

3.94	And the courtiers, governors and hereditary leaders and friends of the king gathered round and saw these men, that the fire had not reached their bodies and their hair was not scorched and their garments[33] were not affected, nor was the smell of fire on them.

3.95	And Nebuchadnezzar the king responded and said: Blessed be the Lord the God of Shadrach, Meshach, Abednego, who sent his angel and saved his servants who put their hope in him, for they disregarded the command of the king and gave over their bodies to be set on fire that they might not serve or worship another god than their God.

3.96	And now I pronounce that every nation and all tribes and all tongues, whoever should blaspheme the Lord the God of Shadrach, Meshach, Abednego, will be dismembered and his house confiscated, for there is no other god who is able to rescue thus.

3.97	So then the king gave authority to Shadrach, Meshach, Abednego, and set them up as rulers over the whole region.

Daniel 4

4.4	In the eighteenth year of King Nebuchadnezzar, he said: We were at peace in my house and thriving upon my throne.

4.5	I saw a dream, and I was awe-struck and fear fell upon me.

4.10	I slept and behold: A high tree (was) growing upon the earth. The sight of it was great, and there was not another like it.

4.12	Its branches were thirty stadia in length and it cast a shadow over all the beasts of the earth under it, and in it the birds of heaven nested. Its fruit was plentiful and good and supplied all living things.

4.11	And the sight of it was great. Its crown drew near to heaven and its trunk to the clouds, filling everything under heaven. The sun and moon dwelt in it and it lit all the earth.

4.13	I looked in my sleep and behold: An angel was sent in might out of heaven.

4.14	And he shouted and said to him: Hew it down and annihilate[34] it, for it has been commanded from on high to uproot and disable it.

4.15	And say thus: Leave one of its roots in the earth, so that with the beasts of the earth on the hills he will be fed grass as the cattle.

4.16	And let his body be changed by the dew of heaven, and for seven years let him be grazed with them,

4.17	until he knows the Lord of heaven has authority over everything in heaven and on earth, and whatever he wants he does among them.

4.17a	It was hewn down before me in one day and its annihilation (took place) in one moment of the day and its branches were given over to every wind and it was dragged about and cast out. And he ate the grass of the earth with the beasts of the earth, and was given over to the guard and in bronze fetters

---

33.	Literally 'trousers'.
34.	The unprefixed form of φθείρω is also translated as 'annihilate'.

and handcuffs he was bound by them. I marvelled greatly at all these things and my sleep left my eyes.

4.18 And I arose early from my bed and called Daniel, ruler of the wise men and leader of the interpreters of dreams, and told the dream to him in full. And he showed me its whole interpretation.

4.19 And Daniel marvelled greatly and the true meaning[35] dismayed him, and fearful trembling seized him and the sight of him changed and his head shook for a moment. And he wondered and answered me with a soft voice: O King, let this dream come upon those who hate you, and its interpretation upon your enemies.

4.20 The tree planted in the earth, the sight of which was great: You are it, O King.

4.21 And all the birds of heaven nesting in it are the might of the earth and of the nations and of all tongues unto the ends of the earth. And all regions serve you.

4.22 And as that tree was lifted up and drew near to heaven and its trunk reached the clouds: You, O King, were exalted over all men who were upon the face of all the earth, (and) your heart was exalted in arrogance and might towards the Holy One and his angels. Your works were seen, how you desolated the house of the living God because of the sins of the consecrated people.

4.23 And the vision which you saw, that an angel was sent in might from the Lord, and that he said to raise up the tree and hew it down: The judgment of the great God will come upon you,

4.24 and the Most High and his angels are pursuing you.

4.25 And they will lead you away to prison and they will send you into a desert place.

4.26 And the root of the tree which is reserved, since it was not uprooted: The place of your throne will be kept for you until a time and a moment. Behold: against you are they preparing, and they will flog you and they will bring on what has been judged against you.

4.27 The Lord lives in heaven and his authority is over all the earth. Pray to him concerning your sins and redeem all your unrighteousness by acts of mercy, so that he might give clemency to you and (let you) be upon the throne of your kingdom for many days, and not annihilate you. Accept these words for my word is accurate and your time is fulfilled.[36]

4.28 And upon the completion of the words Nebuchadnezzar, who heard the interpretation of the vision, kept the words in the heart.

4.29 And after twelve months, the king was walking upon the walls of the city in all his glory, and going about upon its ramparts.

4.30 And he answered and said: This is Babylon the great which I have built, and my royal house is famous by my strong might for the honour of my glory.

35. Also treated as 'fancies'.
36. Literally 'full'.

4.31   And at the completion of his word he heard a voice from heaven: It is said to you, King Nebuchadnezzar, the kingdom of Babylon is taken from you and given to another, to a man of no account in your house. Behold: I am setting him up over your kingdom and he will receive your authority and your glory and your luxury, so that you might find out that the God of heaven has authority in the kingdom of men, and to whomever he wishes he gives it. Until sunrise another king will make merry in your house, and will gain possession of your majesty and your might and your authority.

4.32   And the angels will drive you away for seven years and you will not see, neither will you speak with, any man. You will be nourished with grass as the cattle and your food will be the green plants of the earth. Behold: Instead of your glory you will be bound, and another will have your house of luxury and your kingdom.

4.33   But soon everything will be accomplished upon you, Nebuchadnezzar, King of Babylon, and it will not fall short of any of these things.

4.33a   I, Nebuchadnezzar, King of Babylon, was bound up for seven years. I was nourished with grass as the cattle and I ate of the green plants of the earth. And after seven years I gave my soul to prayer and I petitioned concerning my sins before the face of the Lord, the God of heaven, and about my ignorance of the great God of gods I prayed.

4.33b   And my nails became as the feathers of an eagle, my hair as a lion. My flesh was changed, as well as my heart. I went about naked with the beasts of the earth. I saw a dream and fancies seized me, and much sleep seized me for a time and drowsiness fell upon me.

4.34   And upon the completion of the seven years my time of redemption came and my sins and my ignorance were paid in full[37] before the God of heaven. And I prayed about my ignorance of the great God of gods. And behold: An angel called to me out of heaven and said: Nebuchadnezzar, serve the holy God of heaven and give glory to the Most High. The throne of your nation he is giving back to you.

4.36   At that time my kingdom was restored to me and my glory given back to me.

4.37   I acknowledge the Most High and praise the creator of heaven and earth and the sea and the rivers and all that are in them. I confess and praise, for he is God of gods and Lord of lords and King of kings, for he does signs and wonders and changes seasons and times. He takes away a kingdom from kings and sets up others in their place.

4.37a   From now I will serve him, and trembling from fear of him has seized me, and I will praise all his holy ones. For the gods of the nations do not have might in themselves to turn aside the kingdom of a king to another king, and to kill and to make alive, and to do signs and great marvels and fearful things and to change immensely great matters, such as the God of heaven has done in me and has changed great matters in me. All the days of my

---

37. Literally 'filled' or 'fulfilled'.

kingdom I will bring sacrifices for the sake of my soul to the Most High as a pleasing smell to the Lord, and I will do what is pleasing before him, I and my people, my nation and my regions under my authority. And whoever has spoken against the God of heaven, and whoever is left speaking thus, I will condemn him to death.

4.37b   And King Nebuchadnezzar wrote an encyclical to the nations and regions and tongues in every place, to those who dwell in all the regions for generations and generations: Praise the Lord, the God of heaven, and offer sacrifices and offerings to him with esteem. I, king of kings, acknowledge him with esteem for he has done thus with me. In this day he seated me upon my throne and I gained possession of my authority and my rule among my people, and he restored my greatness to me.

4.37c   King Nebuchadnezzar to all nations and all regions and all who dwell in them: Let peace be multiplied to you for all time. And now I will show you the works which the great God has done with me. For it has pleased me to bring before you and your wise men that God exists and his marvels are great, his kingdom is a kingdom forever, his authority from generation to generation. And he sent letters concerning everything which had happened to him in his kingdom to all nations who were under his kingdom.

Daniel 5

Abstract: Balthasar the king put on[38] a great reception on the day of the dedication of his kingdoms, and from among his nobles he called two thousand men. In that day Balthasar, lifted up by the wine and boastful,[39] drank to all the shaped and carved gods of the nations in his place, but to God Most High he did not give praise. On this night fingers came out as of a man and wrote on the wall of his house on the whitewash opposite the lamp-stand: Mene, peres, tekel. And their exposition is: Mene, counted; peres, taken away; tekel, set up.

5.1   Balthasar the king gave a great feast for his companions and drank wine.

5.2   And his heart was lifted up and he ordered the gold and silver vessels of the house of God, which Nebuchadnezzar his father had taken from Jerusalem, to be brought and wine to be poured into them for his companions.

5.3   And it was brought and they drank from them.

5.4   And they blessed their idols made by hands, and they did not bless the eternal God who has authority over their spirit.

5.5   In that very moment fingers as of the hand of a man came out and wrote upon the wall of his house on the whitewash opposite the light in front of King Balthasar, and he saw the hand writing.

5.6   And the sight of him changed and fears and fancies dismayed him. Then the king hastened and rose from his seat and examined that writing, and the companions clamoured round him.

38.   Literally 'made'.
39.   Also translated as 'clamour'.

5.7 And the king shouted in a loud voice for the magicians and sorcerers and Chaldeans and diviners to be called, to announce the interpretation of the writing. And they came in as spectators to see the writing, and they were not able to provide the interpretation[40] of the writing for the king. Then the king set forth a command and said: Any man who shows the interpretation of the writing, this purple robe and a gold necklace will be endowed on him, and authority over a third part of the kingdom will be given to him.

5.8 And the magicians and sorcerers and diviners came in, and none of them was able to announce the interpretation of the writing.

5.9 Then the king called the queen concerning the sign and showed her it, that it is great and that no man is able to announce the interpretation of the writing to the king.

5.10 Then the queen reminded him of Daniel who was from the captivity of Judea.

5.11 And she said to the king: The man was learned and wise and superior to all the wise men of Babylon,

5.12 and a holy spirit is in him, and in the days of your father the king he showed extraordinary interpretations to Nebuchadnezzar your father.

5.13 Then Daniel came in to the king, and the king answered and said to him:

5.16 O Daniel, are you able to show me the interpretation of the writing? And I will endow a purple robe and gold necklace upon you and you will have authority over a third part of my kingdom.

5.17 Then Daniel stood before the writing and read and answered thus to the king: This is the writing: counted, reckoned, taken away. And what is written by the hand stands. And this is their interpretation.

5.23 O king, you gave a great feast for your friends and drank wine, and the vessels of the house of the living God were brought to you and you drank from them, you and your nobles, and you praised all the idols made by hands of men. And you did not bless the living God, and your spirit is in his hand and he has given your kingdom to you, and you did not bless him or praise him.

5.26-28 This is the interpretation of the writing: The time of your kingdom is counted, your kingdom is ceasing, your kingdom is cut short and completed. It is given to the Medes and the Persians.

5.29 Then Balthasar the king clothed Daniel in purple and endowed a gold necklace on him and gave authority to him over a third part of his kingdom.

5.30 And the interpretation came upon Balthasar the king, and the kingdom was taken away from the Chaldeans and given to the Medes and the Persians.

Daniel 6

6.1 And Artaxerxes the Mede received the kingdom. And Darius was full of days and esteemed in old age.

6.2 And he set up 127 satraps over all his kingdom.

40. Literally 'interpret the interpretation'.

6.3   And over them three men were their leaders, and Daniel was one of the three men

6.4   who had authority over all in the kingdom. And Daniel was clothed in purple and (was) great and esteemed before Darius the king, for he was esteemed and learned and quick-witted and a holy spirit (was) in him, and he was successful in the king's business which he managed. Then the king wished to set up Daniel over all his kingdom, and the two men he had set up with him and the 127 satraps.

6.5   But when the king wished to set up Daniel over all his kingdom, (then) the two young men prepared a plot[41] and a resolution between themselves and said to one another: Since no sin or ignorance has been found against Daniel about which a complaint could be brought against him to the king...

6.6   And they said: Come, let us set up an injunction together that no man may make a petition[42] or pray a prayer[43] from any god for thirty days except by Darius the king. But if not, let him be executed. (This was) in order that they might give Daniel away before the king and he might be cast into the pit of lions. For they knew that Daniel prayed and pleaded with the Lord his God three times a day.

6.7   Then these men approached and spoke before the king:

6.8   We have set up an injunction and a statute that any man who prays a prayer or makes a petition by any god for thirty days except by Darius the king, will be cast into the pit of lions.

6.9   And they petitioned the king that he might set up the injunction and might not change it, for they knew that Daniel prayed and pleaded three times a day, so that he might be given away by the king and cast into the pit of lions.

6.10   And accordingly King Darius set up and ratified (it).

6.11   But Daniel found out about the injunction which he set up against him, and opened the windows in his upper room facing Jerusalem and fell on his face three times a day just as he had formerly done, and prayed.

6.12   And they watched Daniel and caught him praying three times a day each day.

6.13   Then these men met with the king and said: King Darius, did you not lay down an injunction that no man should either pray a prayer or make a petition by any god for thirty days except by you, O King, lest he be cast into the pit of lions? The king answered and said to them: The word is accurate and the injunction remains.

6.13a   And they said to him: We swear to you by the decrees of the Medes and Persians lest you change the command or show favouritism,[44] and lest you detract from what has been said, and (that you) punish the man who has not

---

41.   Literally 'plotted a plot'. βουλεύω is normally translated as 'wish'.
42.   Literally 'petition petitions'.
43.   προσεύχομαι and δέομαι are also translated as 'pray'.
44.   Literally 'marvel at a face'.

upheld this injunction. And he said: I will do thus as you say, and this stands for me.

6.14   And they said: Behold: We have found Daniel your friend praying and pleading with the face of his god three times a day.

6.15   And in distress the king ordered Daniel to be cast into the pit of lions according to the injunction which he set up against him. Then the king was greatly distressed concerning Daniel, and strove to rescue him until the setting of the sun from the hands of the satraps.

6.16   And he was not able to rescue him from them.

6.17   But Darius the king cried out and said to Daniel: Your God whom you serve constantly three times a day, he will rescue you from the hand of the lions. Have courage till morning.

6.18   Then Daniel was cast into the pit of lions, and a stone was brought and placed against the mouth of the pit, and the king sealed (it) with his own signet ring and with the signet rings of his nobles, lest Daniel be carried away[45] from them or the king draw him up out of the pit.

6.19   Then the king returned to his palace and lay down without eating and was distressed about Daniel. Then the God of Daniel brought to pass[46] what he had foreseen and closed the mouths of the lions, and they did not trouble Daniel.

6.20   And King Darius got up early in the morning and himself received the satraps, and went and stood at the mouth of the pit of lions.

6.21   Then the king called Daniel in a loud voice with weeping and said: O Daniel, are you still alive and has your God, whom you serve continually, saved you from the lions and have they not harmed you?

6.22   Then Daniel heard the loud voice and said: O King, I am still alive.

6.23   And God has saved me from the lions since righteousness before him was found in me, and also before you, O King, neither ignorance nor sin was found in me. But you listened to men leading kings astray and cast me into the pit of lions to destruction.

6.24   Then all the powers gathered round and saw Daniel whom the lions had not troubled.

6.25   Then these two men who had born witness against Daniel, they and their wives and their children, were cast to the lions and the lions killed them and crushed their bones.

6.26   Then Darius wrote to all the nations and regions and tongues, to those who dwell in all his land, and said:

6.27   All men who are in my kingdom shall stand worshipping and serving the God of Daniel, for he is a God who endures and lives from generation to generation forever.

6.28   I, Darius, will be worshipping and serving him all my days, for idols made by hands cannot save like the God of Daniel has redeemed Daniel.

---

45.   Also translated as 'raise up' and 'pass away'.
46.   Literally 'made'.

6.29   And King Darius was gathered to his people[47] and Daniel was set up in the kingdom of Darius. And Cyrus the Persian received his kingdom.

Daniel 7

7.1   In the first year of Balthasar's reigning in the region of Babylon, Daniel saw a vision of the head upon his bed. Then Daniel wrote the vision which he saw in the main points.[48]

7.2   Upon my bed I saw while asleep at night and behold: Four winds of heaven fell into the great sea.

7.3   And four beasts came up out of the sea, different one from the other.

7.4   The first (was) like a lion and had wings like an eagle. I looked until its wings were plucked and it was raised up from the earth and set up on human feet, and a human heart was given it.

7.5   And behold: With it another beast had the appearance of a bear, and it stood upon one side[49] and three ribs were in its mouth, and he spoke[50] thus: Arise, devour much flesh.

7.6   And after these things I saw another beast like a leopard, and four wings extended above it and four heads (belonged to) the beast, and speech was given to it.

7.7   And after these things I saw in a vision of the night a fourth fearful beast, and fear of it was surpassingly mighty. It had great iron teeth. It ate and pounded, it trampled round about with its feet, it behaved differently from all the beasts before it. And it had ten horns

7.8   and many plots in its horns. And behold: Another single horn grew up in their midst smaller among its horns, and three of the former horns were withered by it. And behold: Eyes as human eyes were in this horn and a mouth speaking great things, and it made war against the holy ones.

7.9   I looked until thrones were placed and an ancient of days sat down, who had a garment as snow and the hair of his head as pure white wool. The throne (was) as a flame of fire

7.10   and from before him[51] went out a river of fire. Thousands of thousands attended on him and myriads of myriads stood by him. And the court sat and the books were opened.

7.11   I saw then the sound of the great words which the horn spoke, and the beast was beaten and its body destroyed and given into the heat of fire.

7.12   And he withdrew their authority from those round about him, and a time of life was given to them for a time and a season.

---

47.   This translation of γένος is exceptional, in order to capture better a significant phrase.
48.   Literally 'words'.
49.   Literally 'rib'.
50.   A possible alternative is that the verb is passive in intent.
51.   Literally 'from his face'.

7.13   I saw in a vision of the night and behold: Upon the clouds of heaven one like a son of man came and one like an ancient of days was nearby, and those standing by drew close[52] to him.

7.14   And authority was given to him, and all the nations of the earth by generation and all glory are serving him. And his authority (is) an eternal authority which will never pass away, and his kingdom (which) will never be ruined.

7.15   And I, Daniel, was exhausted by these things in the vision of the night,

7.16   and approached one of those standing (by) and sought accuracy from him about all these things. And he answered and spoke to me and explained to me the interpretation of the words.

7.17   These great beasts are four kingdoms which will be destroyed from the earth.

7.18   And the holy ones of the Most High will receive the kingdom and they will occupy the kingdom for ever and ever and ever.

7.19   Then I wanted to inquire closely about the fourth beast which was corrupting everything and (was) fearful, and behold: Its teeth (were) iron and its claws bronze. It devoured everything round about and trampled with feet.

7.20   And concerning its ten horns upon the head, and the other one which grew and three fell down before it, and that horn had eyes and a mouth speaking great things, and its appearance surpassed the others.

7.21   And that horn meant to join battle with the holy ones and put them to flight,

7.22   until came the Ancient of Days and gave judgment for the holy ones of the Most High. And the time was given and the holy ones took possession of the kingdom.

7.23   And he told me about the fourth beast: It will be a fourth kingdom on the earth which will be different from all the earth and will confuse it and grind it down.

7.24   And the ten horns of the kingdom: Ten kings will stand and the other king will stand after these, and he will be different in evil deeds from the first ones and will humble three kings.

7.25   And words against the Most High he will speak and the holy ones of the Most High he will exhaust, and he will wait[53] to change times and a law, and everything will be given over into his hand for a time and times and half a time.

7.26   And the court will sit and do away with the authority, and they will plot to pollute and destroy until the end.

7.27   And the kingdom and authority and their greatness and the rule of all kingdoms under heaven he will give to the holy people of the Most High to reign over an eternal kingdom, and all authorities will be subject to him and will be obedient to him.

7.28   Until the conclusion of the word I, Daniel, was overcome by great distraction and my state of mind altered (me) and I fixed the word in my heart.

52. Translating προσήγαγον from 967.
53. Also translated as 'accept'.

BIBLIOGRAPHY

Aejmelaeus, A., 'Translation Technique and the Intention of the Translator', in C.E. Cox (ed.), *VII Congress of the International Organization for Septuagint and Cognate Studies* (Atlanta: Scholars Press, 1991), pp. 23-36.

—'Septuagintal Translation Techniques—A Solution to the Problem of the Tabernacle Account', in G.J. Brooke and B. Lindars (eds.), *Septuagint, Scrolls and Cognate Writings* (Atlanta: Scholars Press, 1992), pp. 381-401.

Alt, A., 'Zur Menetekel-Inschrift', *VT* (1954), pp. 303-305.

Alter, R., *The Art of Biblical Narrative* (London: George Allen & Unwin, 1981).

Anderson, R.A., *Daniel, Signs and Wonders* (Grand Rapids: Eerdmans; Edinburgh: Handsel, 1984).

Archer, G.L., 'The Aramaic of the "Genesis Apocryphon" Compared with the Aramaic of Daniel', in J.B. Payne (ed.), *New Perspectives on the Old Testament* (Waco, TX: Word Books, 1970), pp. 160-69.

Auerbach, E., *Mimesis: The Representation of Reality in Western Literature* (trans. W.R. Trask; Princeton, NJ: Princeton University Press, 1953).

Auld, A.G., and C.Y.S. Ho, 'The Making of David and Goliath', *JSOT* 56 (1992), pp. 19-39.

Avalos, H.I., 'The Comedic Function of the Enumerations of the Officials and Instruments in Daniel 3', *CBQ* 53 (1991), pp. 580-88.

Baldwin, J.G., *Daniel* (Leicester: Inter-Varsity Press, 1978).

Bar-Efrat, S., *Narrative Art in the Bible* (Sheffield: Almond Press, 1989).

Barker, M., *The Older Testament* (London: SPCK, 1987).

—*The Great Angel* (London: SPCK, 1992).

Barr, J., *The Semantics of Biblical Language* (London: Oxford University Press, 1961).

—*The Typology of Literalism in Ancient Biblical Translations* (Göttingen: Vandenhoeck & Ruprecht, 1979).

Barthélemy, D., *Les devanciers d'Aquila* (Leiden: Brill, 1963).

Barthélemy, D., D.W. Gooding, J. Lust and E. Tov, *The Story of David and Goliath* (Göttingen: Editions Universitaires, 1986).

Barton, J., *Reading the Old Testament* (London: Darton, Longman & Todd, 1984).

—*Oracles of God* (London: Darton, Longman & Todd, 1986).

Bauer H., and P. Leander, *Grammatik des Biblisch-Aramäischen* (Hildesheim: Georg Olms, 1962).

Beale, G.K., *The Use of Daniel in Jewish Apocalyptic Literature and in the Revelation of St John* (Lanham, MD: University Press of America, 1984).

—'A Reconsideration of the Text of Daniel in the Apocalypse', *Bib* 67 (1986), pp. 539-43.

Beasley-Murray, G.R., 'The Interpretation of Daniel 7', *CBQ* 45 (1983), pp. 44-58.

Beckwith, R.T., 'Daniel 9 and the Date of Messiah's Coming in Essene, Hellenistic, Pharisaic, Zealot and Early Christian Computation', *RevQ* 10 (1979–81), pp. 521-42.

—*The Old Testament Canon of the New Testament Church* (London: SPCK, 1986).

Bennett, W.H., 'The Prayer of Azariah and the Song of the Three Children', in R.H. Charles (ed.), *Apocrypha and Pseudepigrapha of the Old Testament* (Oxford: Clarendon Press, 1913), I, pp. 625-37.

Bensly, R.L. (ed.), 'The Fourth Book of Ezra', in J.A. Robinson (ed.), *Texts and Studies* (Cambridge: Cambridge University Press, 1895), III.2.

Bentzen, A., *Daniel* (Tübingen: J.C.B. Mohr, 1937).

—*King and Messiah* (London: Lutterworth Press, 1955).

Berlin, A., *Poetics and Interpretation of Biblical Narrative* (Sheffield: Almond Press, 1983).

—'Book Review of *The Redaction of the Books of Esther*', *Bib* 75 (1994), pp. 106-12.

Bevan, A.A., *A Short Commentary on the Book of Daniel* (Cambridge: Cambridge University Press, 1892).

Bickerman, E., *Four Strange Books of the Bible* (New York: Schocken Books, 1967).

Black, M., *An Aramaic Approach to the Gospels and Acts* (Oxford: Clarendon Press, 1967).

Blenkinsopp, J., 'Interpretation and the Tendency to Sectarianism: An Aspect of Second Temple History', in E.P. Sanders (ed.), *Jewish and Christian Self-Definition* (London: SCM Press, 1981), II, pp. 1-26.

Bogaert, P.-M. 'Relecture et refonte historicisante du livre de Daniel attestés par la première version grecque (papyrus 967)', in R. Kuntzmann and J. Schlosser (eds.), *Etudes sur le judaïsme hellénistique* (Paris: Cerf, 1984), pp. 197-224.

—'Daniel 3 LXX et son supplément grec', in A.S. van der Woude (ed.), *The Book of Daniel* (Leuven: Leuven University Press/Uitgeverij Peeters, 1993), pp. 13-37.

Boogaart, T.A., 'Daniel 6: A Tale of Two Empires', *RR* 39 (1986), pp. 106-12.

Booth, W.C., *The Rhetoric of Fiction* (Chicago: University of Chicago Press, 1961).

Brekelmans, C.H.W., 'The Saints of the Most High and their Kingdom', *OTS* 14 (1965), pp. 305-29.

Brenner, A., *The Israelite Woman* (Sheffield: JSOT Press, 1985).

—'Who's Afraid of Feminist Criticism? Who's Afraid of Biblical Humour? The Case of the Obtuse Foreign Ruler in the Hebrew Bible', *JSOT* 63 (1994), pp. 38-55.

Brock, S.P., 'The Phenomenon of Biblical Translation in Antiquity', in S. Jellicoe (ed.), *Studies in the Septuagint: Origins, Recensions, and Interpretations* (New York: Ktav, 1974), pp. 541-71.

—'To Revise or not to Revise: Attitudes to Jewish Biblical Translation', in G.J. Brooke and B. Lindars (eds.), *Septuagint, Scrolls and Cognate Writings* (Atlanta: Scholars Press, 1992), pp. 301-38.

Brown, R.E., 'The Pre-Christian Semitic Concept of "Mystery"', *CBQ* 20 (1958), pp. 417-43.

Bruce, F.F., 'The Earliest Old Testament Interpretation', *OTS* 17 (1972), pp. 37-52.

—'Book Review of *The Eclipse of Biblical Narrative*', *CSR* 5 (1975), pp. 199-201.

—'The Oldest Greek Version of Daniel', *OTS* 20 (1976), pp. 22-40.

—'Prophetic Interpretation in the Septuagint', *BIOSCS* 12 (1979), pp. 17-26.

Burton, E. de W., *Syntax of the Moods and Tenses in New Testament Greek* (Edinburgh: T. & T. Clark, 1898).

Busto Saiz, J.R., 'El texto teodocionico de Daniel y la traduccion de Simaco', *Sef* 40 (1980), pp. 41-55.

Caird, G.B., *The Language and Imagery of the Bible* (London: Gerald Duckworth, 1980).

Caquot, A., 'Sur les quatre bêtes de Daniel VII', *Semitica* 5 (1955), pp. 5-13.

—'Les quatre bêtes et le "fils d'homme" (Daniel 7)', *Semitica* 17 (1967), pp. 37-71.

Cardascia, G., 'L'ordalie par le fleuve dans les "lois assyriennes"', in G. Wiessner (ed.), *Festschrift für Wilhelm Eilers* (Wiesbaden: Otto Harrassowitz, 1967), pp. 19-36.

Casey, P.M., 'Porphyry and the Book of Daniel', *JTS* 27 (1976), pp. 15-33.

—*Son of Man* (London: SPCK, 1979).

Cassin, E., 'Daniel dans la "fosse" aux lions', *RHR* 139 (1951), pp. 129-61.

Charles, R.H., *A Critical and Exegetical Commentary on the Revelation of St John* (2 vols.; Edinburgh: T. & T. Clark, 1920).

—*A Commentary on Daniel* (Oxford: Clarendon Press, 1929).

Charlesworth, J.H., *The Old Testament Pseudepigrapha* (2 vols.; London: Darton, Longman and Todd, 1983, 1985).

—*Graphic Concordance to the Dead Sea Scrolls* (Tübingen: Mohr [Paul Siebeck]; Louisville: Westminster/John Knox, 1991).

Chesterton, G.K., 'The Tremendous Adventure of Major Brown', in *Thirteen Detectives* (London: Xanadu, 1987), pp. 30-51, reprinted from *The Idler* (June 1904).

Clerget, J., 'L'énigme et son interprétation', *LV* 160 (1982), pp. 36-47.

Clines, D.J.A., *The Esther Scroll* (Sheffield: JSOT Press, 1984).

Coggins, R., 'The Literary Approach to the Bible', *ExpTim* 96 (1984), pp. 9-14.

Colless, B.E., 'Cyrus the Persian as Darius the Mede in the Book of Daniel', *JSOT* 56 (1992), pp. 113-26.

Collins, J.J., 'The Symbolism of Transcendence in Jewish Apocalyptic', *BR* 19 (1974), pp. 5-22.

—'The Court-Tales in Daniel and the Development of Apocalyptic', *JBL* 94 (1975), pp. 218-34.

—*The Apocalyptic Vision of the Book of Daniel* (Ann Arbor: Scholars Press, 1977).

—*The Apocalyptic Imagination* (New York: Crossroad, 1984).

—'Daniel and his Social World', *Int* 39 (1985), pp. 131-43.

—*Daniel* (Minneapolis: Fortress Press, 1993).

Cook, E.M., '"In the Plain of the Wall" (Dan 3.1)', *JBL* 108 (1989), pp. 115-16.

Coppens, J., and L. Dequeker, *Le fils de l'homme et les saints du trés-haut en Daniel VII* (Bruges: Publications Universitaires de Louvain, 1961).

Cowe, S.P., *The Armenian Version of Daniel* (Atlanta: Scholars Press, 1992).

Coxon, P.W., 'Daniel III 17: A Linguistic and Theological Problem', *VT* 26 (1976), pp. 400-409.

—'The Syntax of the Aramaic of Daniel: A Dialectical Study', *HUCA* 48 (1977), pp. 107-22.

—'The Distribution of Synonyms in Biblical Aramaic in the Light of Official Aramaic and the Aramaic of Qumran', *RevQ* 9 (1978), pp. 497-512.

—'A Morphological Study of the *h*-Prefix in Biblical Aramaic', *JAOS* 98 (1978), pp. 416-19.

—'The Problem of Consonantal Mutations in Biblical Aramaic', *ZDMG* 129 (1979), pp. 8-22.

—'The "List" Genre and Narrative Style in the Court Tales of Daniel', *JSOT* 35 (1986), pp. 95-121.

—'The Great Tree of Daniel 4', in J.D. Martin and P.R. Davies (eds.), *A Word in Season* (Sheffield: JSOT Press, 1986), pp. 91-111.

—'Another Look at Nebuchadnezzar's Madness', in A.S. van der Woude (ed.), *The Book of Daniel* (Leuven: Leuven University Press/Uitgeverij Peeters, 1993), pp. 211-22.

Croatto, J.S., *Biblical Hermeneutics* (trans. R.R. Barr; Maryknoll, NY: Orbis Books, 1987).

Dalman, G., *Grammatik des Jüdisch-Palästinischen Aramäisch* (Leipzig: Hinrichs, 1894).

Daubney, W.H., *The Three Additions of Daniel* (London: G. Bell & Sons, 1906).

David, P.A., 'The Composition and Structure of the Book of Daniel: A Synchronic and Diachronic Reading' (unpublished D.S.T. thesis, Katholieke Universiteit Leuven, 1991).

Davidson, A.B., *Introductory Hebrew Grammar: Syntax* (Edinburgh: T. & T. Clark, 1989).

Davidson, B., *The Analytical Hebrew and Chaldee Lexicon* (Peabody, MA: Hendrickson, 1981).

Davidson, M.J., *Angels at Qumran: A Comparative Study of 1 Enoch 1–36, 72–108, and Sectarian Writings from Qumran* (Sheffield: JSOT Press, 1992).

Davies, P.R., *1QM, the War Scroll from Qumran* (Rome: Biblical Institute Press, 1977).

—'Hasidim in the Maccabean Period', *JJS* 28 (1977), pp. 127-40.

—*Daniel* (Sheffield: JSOT Press, 1985).

Delcor, M., 'Les sources du chapitre VII de Daniel', *VT* 18 (1968), pp. 290-312.

—'Un cas de traduction "targumique" de la LXX à propos de la statue en or de Dan III', *Textus* 7 (1969), pp. 30-35.

—*Le Livre de Daniel* (Paris: Gabalda, 1971).

Dequeker, L., 'The "Saints of the Most High" in Qumran and Daniel', *OTS* 18 (1973), pp. 108-87.

Derrett, J.D.M., 'Daniel and Salvation History', in *Studies in the New Testament* (Leiden: Brill, 1986), IV, pp. 132-37.

Dougherty, R.P., *Nabonidus and Belshazzar* (New Haven: Yale University Press, 1929).

Driver, G.R., and J.C. Miles, *The Assyrian Laws* (Oxford: Clarendon Press, 1935).

Driver, S.R., *Daniel* (Cambridge: Cambridge University Press, 1900).

Eissfeldt, O., 'Die Menetekel-Inschrift und ihre Deutung', *ZAW* 63 (1951), pp. 105-14.

Elliger, K., *Deuterojesaja. I. Jesaja 40,1–45,7* (Neukirchen–Vluyn: Neukirchener Verlag, 1978).

Emerton, J.A., 'The Origin of the Son of Man Imagery', *JTS* 9 (1958), pp. 225-42.

Ferch, A.J., 'Daniel 7 and Ugarit: A Reconsideration', *JBL* 99 (1980), pp. 75-86.

Feuillet, A., 'Le fils de l'homme de Daniel et la tradition biblique', *RB* 60 (1953), pp. 170-202.

Fewell, D.N., *Circle of Sovereignty* (Sheffield: Almond Press, 1988).

Finkel, A., 'The Pesher of Dreams and Scriptures', *RevQ* 4 (1964), pp. 357-70.

Fitzmyer, J.A., 'Some Observations on the *Genesis Apocryphon*', *CBQ* 22 (1960), pp. 277-91.

—*The Genesis Apocryphon of Qumran Cave 1* (Rome: Pontifical Biblical Institute, 1966).

—*The Aramaic Inscriptions of Sefîre* (Rome: Pontifical Biblical Institute, 1967).

—*The Dead Sea Scrolls: Major Publications and Tools for Study* (Atlanta: Scholars Press, 1990).

Fox, M.V., *The Redaction of the Books of Esther* (Atlanta: Scholars Press, 1991).

Frei, H.W., *The Eclipse of Biblical Narrative* (New Haven: Yale University Press, 1974).

—'The "Literal Reading" of Biblical Narrative in the Christian Tradition: Does it Stretch or Will it Break?', in F. McConnell (ed.), *The Bible and the Narrative Tradition* (Oxford: Oxford University Press, 1986), pp. 36-77.

Frye, N., *Anatomy of Criticism* (Princeton, NJ: Princeton University Press, 1971).

Gallé, A.F. (trans.), *Daniel avec commentaires de R. Saadia, Aben-Ezra, Raschi, etc.* (Paris: Ernest Leroux, 1900).

Gammie, J.G., 'Spatial and Ethical Dualism in Jewish Wisdom and Apocalyptic Literature', *JBL* 93 (1974), pp. 356-85.

—'The Classification, Stages of Growth, and Changing Intentions in the Book of Daniel', *JBL* 95 (1976), pp. 191-204.

—'On the Intention and Sources of Daniel I–VI', *VT* 31 (1981), pp. 282-92.

—*Daniel* (Atlanta: John Knox Press, 1983).

García Martínez, F., *Qumran and Apocalyptic: Studies on the Aramaic Texts from Qumran* (Leiden: Brill, 1992).

Gaster, M., 'The Unknown Aramaic Original of Theodotion's Additions to the Book of Daniel', *PSBA* 16 (1894), pp. 280-90 and 312-17, and *PSBA* 17 (1895), pp. 75-94.

Gaster, M. (ed.), *The Chronicles of Jerahmeel* (London: Royal Asiatic Society, 1899).

Geissen, A. (ed.), *Der Septuaginta-Text des Buches Daniel 5–12 sowie Esther 1–2.15 nach dem Kölner Teil des Papyrus 967* (Bonn: Rudolf Habelt Verlag, 1968).

Genette, G., *Narrative Discourse* (trans. J.E. Lewin; Oxford: Basil Blackwell, 1980).

Gershevitch, I., 'Zoroaster's Own Contribution', *JNES* 23 (1964), pp. 12-38.

Gibson, J.C.L., *Textbook of Syrian Semitic Inscriptions* (Oxford: Clarendon Press, 1975), II.

Gilbert, M.P., 'La prière d'Azarias', *NRT* 6 (1974), pp. 561-82.

Goldingay, J.E., 'The Stories in Daniel: A Narrative Politics', *JSOT* 37 (1987), pp. 99-116.

—' "Holy Ones on High" in Daniel 7:18', *JBL* 107 (1988), pp. 495-97.

—*Daniel* (Dallas: Word Books, 1989).

Good, E.M., *Irony in the Old Testament* (Philadelphia: Westminster Press, 1965).

—'Apocalyptic as Comedy: The Book of Daniel', *Semeia* 32 (1984), pp. 41-70.

Gooding, D.W., 'The Literary Structure of the Book of Daniel and its Implications', *TynBul* 32 (1981), pp. 43-79.

Goodwin, W.W., *Syntax of the Moods and Tenses of the Greek Verb* (London: MacMillan, 1889).

Green, G. (ed.), *Scriptural Authority and Narrative Interpretation* (Philadelphia: Fortress Press, 1987).

Greenfield, J.C., and A. Shaffer, 'Notes on the Akkadian–Aramaic Bilingual Statue from Tell Fekherye', *Iraq* 45 (1983), pp. 109-16.

Grelot, P., 'Les versions grecques de Daniel', *Bib* 47 (1966), pp. 381-402.

—'La Septante de Daniel IV et son substrat sémitique', *RB* 81 (1974), pp. 5-24.

—'Daniel VII,9-10 et le livre d'Henoch', *Semitica* 28 (1978), pp. 59-83.

Gunn, D.M., 'Reading Right, Reliable and Omniscient Narrator, Omniscient God, and

Foolproof Composition in the Hebrew Bible', in D.J.A. Clines, S.E. Fowl and
    S.E. Porter (eds.), *The Bible in Three Dimensions* (Sheffield: JSOT Press, 1990),
    pp. 53-64.

Hamm, W. (ed.), *Der Septuagint-Text des Buches Daniel Kap 1–2 nach dem Teil des
    Papyrus 967* (Bonn: Rudolf Habelt Verlag, 1969).

—*Der Septuagint-Text des Buches Daniel Kap 3–4 nach dem Teil des Papyrus 967*
    (Bonn: Rudolf Habelt Verlag, 1977).

Hammer, R., *The Book of Daniel* (Cambridge: Cambridge University Press, 1976).

Hanhart, R., 'The Translation of the Septuagint in Light of Earlier Tradition and
    Subsequent Influences', in G.J. Brooke and B. Lindars (eds.), *Septuagint, Scrolls
    and Cognate Writings* (Atlanta: Scholars Press, 1992), pp. 339-79.

Harrington, D.J. (ed.), *The Hebrew Fragments of Pseudo-Philo* (Missoula, MT: Society
    of Biblical Literature, 1974).

Hartman, L.F., and A.A. DiLella, *The Book of Daniel* (New York: Doubleday, 1978).

Hasel, G.F., 'The Identity of "The Saints of the Most High" in Daniel 7', *Bib* 56
    (1975), pp. 173-92.

—'New Light on the Book of Daniel from the Dead Sea Scrolls', *Ministry* (January
    1992), pp. 10-13.

Hatch, E., and H.A. Redpath, *A Concordance to the Septuagint and the Other Greek
    Versions of the Old Testament* (Oxford: Clarendon Press, 1897).

Hayman, A.P., 'Qohelet and the Book of Creation', *JSOT* 50 (1991), pp. 93-111.

Heaton, E.W., *The Book of Daniel* (London: SCM Press, 1956).

Holladay, W.L., *A Concise Hebrew and Aramaic Lexicon of the Old Testament* (Leiden:
    Brill, 1971).

Hooker, M.D., *The Son of Man in Mark* (London: SPCK, 1967).

Horgan, M.P., *Pesharim: Qumran Interpretations of Biblical Books* (Washington: The
    Catholic Biblical Association of America, 1979).

Humphreys, W.L., 'A Lifestyle for Diaspora: A Study of the Tales of Esther and
    Daniel', *JBL* 92 (1973), pp. 211-23.

Jeansonne, S.P., *The Old Greek Translation of Daniel 7–12* (Washington, DC: Catholic
    Biblical Association, 1988).

Jellicoe, S., *The Septuagint and Modern Study* (Oxford: Oxford University Press,
    1968).

—'Some Reflections on the καίγε Recension', *VT* 23 (1973), pp. 15-24.

Jephet Ibn Ali, *A Commentary on the Book of Daniel* (ed. D.S. Margoliouth; Oxford:
    Clarendon Press, 1889).

Kahle, P., *The Cairo Geniza* (Oxford: Basil Blackwell, 1959).

Kaufmann, Y., *The Religion of Israel* (trans. M. Greenberg; London: George Allen &
    Unwin, 1961).

Keil, G.F., *Commentary on the Book of Daniel* (trans. M.G. Easton; Edinburgh: T. & T.
    Clark, 1872).

Kenyon, F.C., *The Chester Beatty Biblical Papyri* (London: Emery Walker, 1937).

Kitchen, K.A., 'The Aramaic of Daniel', in D.J. Wiseman *et al.*, *Notes on Some
    Problems in the Book of Daniel* (London: Tyndale Press, 1965), pp. 31-79.

Klein, R.W., *Textual Criticism of the Old Testament* (Philadelphia: Fortress Press, 1974).

Knibb, M.A., *The Ethiopic Book of Enoch* (Oxford: Clarendon Press, 1978).

—*The Qumran Community* (Cambridge: Cambridge University Press, 1987).

Koch, K., 'Die Weltreiche im Danielbuch', *TLZ* 85 (1960), pp. 829-32.

—'Die Herkunft der Proto-Theodotion-Übersetzung des Danielbuches', *VT* 23 (1973), pp. 362-65.

—'Is Daniel also among the Prophets?', *Int* 39 (1985), pp. 117-30.

—*Deuterokanonische Zusätze zum Danielbuch* (Neukirchen–Vluyn: Butzon & Bercker, 1987).

Koehler, L., and W. Baumgartner, *Lexicon in Veteris Testamenti Libros* (Leiden: Brill, 1953).

Kooij, A. van der, 'A Case of Reinterpretation in the Old Greek of Daniel 11', in J.W. van Henten, H.J. de Jonge, P.T. van Rooden and J.W. Wesselius (eds.), *Tradition and Re-interpretation in Jewish and Early Christian Literature* (Leiden: Brill, 1986), pp. 72-80.

Kutscher, E.Y., *Hebrew and Aramaic Studies* (Jerusalem: Magnes, 1977).

Lacocque, A., *Le livre de Daniel* (Paris: Delachaux & Niestlé, 1976).

—'Apocalyptic Symbolism: A Ricoeurian Hermeneutical Approach', *BR* 26 (1981), pp. 6-15.

—*Daniel in his Time* (Columbia: University of South Carolina Press, 1988).

Lambert, W.G., 'Nebuchadnezzar King of Justice', *Iraq* 27 (1965), pp. 1-11.

Lanser, S.S., *The Narrative Act* (Princeton, NJ: Princeton University Press, 1981).

Lemke, W.E., 'Nebuchadnezzar, my Servant', *CBQ* 28 (1966), pp. 45-50.

Lenglet, A., 'La structure littéraire de Daniel 2–7', *Bib* 53 (1972), pp. 169-90.

Levinger, J., 'Daniel in the Lion's Den—A Model of National Literature of Struggle', *Beth Mikra* 70 (1977), pp. 329-33 and 394-95.

Lewy, J., 'The Late Assyro-Babylonian Cult of the Moon and its Culmination at the Time of Nabonidus', *HUCA* 19 (1945–46), pp. 405-89.

Lohse, E. (ed.), *Die Texte aus Qumran* (Munich: Kösel, 1971).

Long, B.O., 'The "New" Biblical Poetics of Alter and Sternberg', *JSOT* 51 (1991), pp. 71-84.

Long, B.O. (ed.), *Images of Man and God* (Sheffield: Almond Press, 1981).

Longman, T., *Literary Approaches to Biblical Interpretation* (Grand Rapids: Zondervan, 1987).

Lotman, J.M. (trans. L.M. O'Toole), 'Point of View in a Text', *NLH* 6 (1975), pp. 339-52.

Lucas, E.C., 'The Origin of Daniel's Four Empires Schemes Re-examined', *TynBul* 40 (1989), pp. 185-202.

—'The Source of Daniel's Animal Imagery', *TynBul* 41 (1990), pp. 161-85.

Lust, J., 'Daniel 7.13 and the Septuagint', *ETL* 54 (1978), pp. 62-69.

—'The Septuagint Version of Daniel 4–5', in A.S. van der Woude (ed.), *The Book of Daniel* (Leuven: Leuven University Press/Uitgeverij Peeters, 1993), pp. 39-53.

Masson, E., *Recherches sur les plus anciens emprunts sémitique en grec* (Paris: C. Klincksieck, 1967).

Mastin, B.A., 'Daniel 2.46 and the Hellenistic World', *ZAW* 85 (1973), pp. 80-93.

Mayser, E., *Grammatik der griechischen Papyri aus der Ptolemäerzeit* (Berlin: de Gruyter, 1926).

McComiskey, T.E., 'The Seventy "Weeks" of Daniel against the Background of Ancient Near Eastern Literature', *WTJ* 47 (1985), pp. 18-45.

McCrystall, A.P.J., 'Studies in the Old Greek Translation of Daniel' (unpublished DPhil thesis, Oxford University, 1980).

McGaughey, D.R., 'Ricoeur's Metaphor and Narrative Theories as a Foundation for a Theory of Symbol', *RelS* 24 (1988), pp. 415-37.

McKane, W., 'Jeremiah 27.5-8, especially "Nebuchadnezzar, my Servant"', in V. Fritz, K.-F. Pohlmann and H.-C. Schmitt (eds.), *Prophet und Prophetenbuch* (Berlin: de Gruyter, 1989), pp. 98-110.

McNamara, M., 'Nabonidus and the Book of Daniel', *ITQ* 37 (1970), pp. 131-49.

Milik, J.T., 'Prière de Nabonide', *RB* 63 (1956), pp. 407-15.

—'Milkî-ṣedeq et milkî-rešaᵉ', *JJS* 23 (1972), pp. 95-144.

—'Les modèles araméens du livre d'Esther dans la grotte 4 de Qumran', *RevQ* 15 (1991–92), pp. 321-407.

Millard, A.R., 'Daniel 1–6 and History', *EvQ* 49 (1977), pp. 67-73.

—'The Etymology of *Nebrasta*, Daniel 5:5', *Maarav* 4 (1987), pp. 87-92.

Miller, J.E., 'The Redaction of Daniel', *JSOT* 52 (1991), pp. 115-24.

Milne, P.J., *Vladimir Propp and the Study of Structure in Hebrew Biblical Narrative* (Sheffield: Almond Press, 1988).

Miscall, P.D., *The Workings of Old Testament Narrative* (Philadelphia: Fortress Press, Chico, CA: Scholars Press, 1983).

Mitchell, T.C., and R. Joyce, 'Musical Instruments in Nebuchadnezzar's Orchestra', in D.J. Wiseman *et al.*, *Notes on Some Problems in the Book of Daniel* (London: Tyndale Press, 1965), pp. 19-27.

Moberly, R.W.L., 'Story in the Old Testament', *Themelios* 11 (1986), pp. 77-82.

—*From Eden to Golgotha* (Atlanta: Scholars Press, 1992).

—*Genesis 12–50* (Sheffield: JSOT Press, 1992).

Montefiore, C.G., and H. Loewe, *A Rabbinic Anthology* (London: MacMillan, 1938).

Montgomery, J.A., 'The "Two Youths" in the LXX to Dan 6', *JAOS* 41 (1921), pp. 316-17.

—*Daniel* (Edinburgh: T. & T. Clark, 1927).

Moor, J.C. de, 'An Incantation against Evil Spirits (Ras Ibn Hani 78/20)', *UF* 12 (1980), pp. 429-32.

Moore, C.A., *Daniel, Esther, and Jeremiah: The Additions* (Garden City, NY: Doubleday, 1977).

Mosca, P.G., 'Ugarit and Daniel 7: A Missing Link', *Bib* 67 (1986), pp. 496-517.

Müller, H.-P., 'Mantische Weisheit und Apocalyptic', in J.A. Emerton *et al.* (eds.), *Congress Volume Uppsala 1971* (VTSup, 22; Leiden: Brill, 1972), pp. 268-93.

—'Märchen, Legende und Enderwartung', *VT* 26 (1976), pp. 338-50.

Muraoka, T., 'Notes on the Syntax of Biblical Aramaic', *JSS* 11 (1966), pp. 151-67.

Murray, R., 'The Origin of Aramaic 'îr, Angel', *Or* 53 (1984), pp. 303-17.

Niditch, S., *The Symbolic Vision in Biblical Tradition* (Chico, CA: Scholars Press, 1983).

Niditch, S., and R. Doran, 'The Success Story of the Wise Courtier: A Formal Approach', *JBL* 96 (1977), pp. 179-93.

Noth, M., 'Die heiligen des Höchsten', in *Gesammelte Studien zum Alten Testament* (Munich: Chr. Kaiser Verlag, 1966), pp. 274-90.

Oldenburg, U., *The Conflict between El and Baal in Canaanite Religion* (Leiden: Brill, 1969).

Oppenheim, A.L., *Ancient Mesopotamia* (Chicago: University of Chicago Press, 1977).

Paul, S., 'Daniel 3.29—A Case Study of "Neglected" Blasphemy', *JNES* 42 (1983), pp. 291-94.

Payne, J.B., 'The Goal of Daniel's Seventy Weeks', *JETS* 21 (1978), pp. 97-115.

Perrin, N., 'Wisdom and Apocalyptic in the Message of Jesus', in L.C. McGaughey (ed.), *Proceedings* 2 (Missoula, MT: Society of Biblical Literature, 1972), pp. 543-70.

Peters, J.P., 'Notes on the Old Testament', *JBL* 15 (1896), pp. 106-17.

Plöger, O., *Das Buch Daniel* (Gütersloh: Gütersloher Verlagshaus/Gerd Mohn, 1965).

Pope, M.H., *El in the Ugaritic Texts* (Leiden: Brill, 1955).

Porteous, N.W., *Daniel* (London: SCM Press, 1965).

Powell, M.A., *What is Narrative Criticism?* (Minneapolis: Fortress Press, 1990).

Poythress, V.S., 'The Holy Ones of the Most High in Daniel VII', *VT* 26 (1976), pp. 208-13.

Prickett, S., 'Poetics and Narrative, Biblical Criticism and the Nineteenth-Century Novel', in D. Jaspar and T.R. Wright (eds.), *The Critical Spirit and the Will to Believe* (London: MacMillan, 1989), pp. 1-24.

Pritchard, J.B., *Ancient Near Eastern Texts* (Princeton, NJ: Princeton University Press, 1950).

—*The Ancient Near East in Pictures* (Princeton, NJ: Princeton University Press, 1954).

Raabe, P.R., 'Daniel 7: Its Structure and Role in the Book', *HAR* 9 (1985), pp. 267-75.

Rabin, C., 'The Translation Process and the Character of the Septuagint', *Textus* 6 (1968), pp. 1-26.

Rad, G. von, *Wisdom in Israel* (London: SCM Press, 1970).

Reeves, J., 'An Enochic Citation in Barnabas 4:3 and the Oracles of Hystaspes', (IOUDAIOS Electronic Bulletin Board, November 1992).

Reid, S.B., *Enoch and Daniel: A Form Critical and Sociological Study of Historical Apocalypses* (Berkeley: BIBAL Press, 1989).

Ricoeur, P., *Interpretation Theory* (Fort Worth: Texas Christian University Press, 1976).

Rosen, H.B., 'On the Use of the Tenses in the Aramaic of Daniel', *JSS* 6 (1961), pp. 183-203.

Rosenthal, F., *A Grammar of Biblical Aramaic* (Wiesbaden: Otto Harrassowitz, 1968).

Roth, W.M.W., 'For Life he Appeals to Death (Wis. 13.18): A Study of Old Testament Idol Parodies', *CBQ* 37 (1975), pp. 21-47.

Rothstein, W., 'Die Zusätze zu Daniel', in E. Kautzsch (ed.), *Die Apokryphen und Pseudepigraphen des Alten Testaments* (Tübingen: J.C.B. Mohr, 1900), pp. 172-92.

Rowley, H.H., 'The Unity of the Book of Daniel', in *The Servant of the Lord* (London: Lutterworth Press, 1952), pp. 253-68.

—*Darius the Mede and the Four World Empires in the Book of Daniel* (Cardiff: University of Wales Press Board, 1959).

Russell, D.S., *The Method and Message of Jewish Apocalyptic* (London: SCM Press, 1964).

Sailhamer, J.H., *The Translation Technique of the Greek Septuagint for the Hebrew Verbs and Participles in Psalms 3–41* (New York: Peter Lang, 1990).

Saldarini, A.J., *Pharisees, Scribes and Sadducees in Palestinian Society* (Wilmington, DE: Michael Glazier, 1988).

Sanders, B.G., 'The Burning Fiery Furnace', *Theology* 58 (1955), pp. 340-45.

Savran, G., *Telling and Retelling: Quotation in Biblical Narrative* (Bloomington: Indiana University Press, 1988).

Schaberg, J., 'Mark 14.62: Early Christian Merkabah Imagery?', in J. Marcus and M.L. Soards (eds.), *Apocalyptic and the New Testament* (Sheffield: JSOT Press, 1989), pp. 69-94.

Schaeder, H.H., *Iranische Beiträge* (Halle: Max Niemeyer Verlag, 1930), I.

Schmidt, N., 'Daniel and Androcles', *JAOS* 46 (1926), pp. 1-7.

Schmitt, A., 'Die griechischen Danieltexte ("θ'" und ο') und das Theodotion-problem', *BZ* 36 (1992), pp. 1-29.

Schurer, E. *The History of the Jewish People in the Age of Jesus Christ* (ed. G. Vermes, F. Miller and M. Goodman; Edinburgh: T. & T. Clark, 1986), III.

Seeligmann, I.L., *The Septuagint Version of Isaiah: A Discussion of its Problems* (Leiden: Brill, 1948).

Segal, M.H., *A Grammar of Mishnaic Hebrew* (Oxford: Clarendon Press, 1927).

Shea, W.H., 'Wrestling with the Prince of Persia: A Study on Daniel 10', *AUSS* 21 (1983), pp. 225-50.

—'Further Literary Structures in Daniel 2–7: An Analysis of Daniel 5 and the Broader Relationships within Chapters 2–7', *AUSS* 23 (1985), pp. 277-95.

—'Bel(te)shazzar Meets Belshazzar', *AUSS* 26 (1988), pp. 67-81.

—'Darius the Mede', *AUSS* 29 (1991), pp. 235-57.

Sheriffs, D.C.T., '"A Tale of Two Cities"—Nationalism in Zion and Babylon', *TynBul* 39 (1988), pp. 19-57.

Silberman, L.H., 'Unriddling the Riddle: A Study in the Structure and Language of the Habbakuk Pesher (1QpHab)', *RevQ* 3 (1961–62), pp. 326-64.

Simon, U., 'Minor Characters in Biblical Narrative', *JSOT* 46 (1990), pp. 11-19.

Slotki, J.J., *Daniel, Ezra and Nehemiah* (London: Soncino, 1951).

Smith, M.S., 'The "Son of Man" in Ugaritic', *CBQ* 45 (1983), pp. 59-60.

Stanzel, F.K., *A Theory of Narrative* (trans. C. Goedsche; Cambridge: Cambridge University Press, 1984).

Stefanovic, Z., 'Thematic Links between the Historical and Prophetic Sections of Daniel', *AUSS* 27 (1989), pp. 121-27.

—*The Aramaic of Daniel in the Light of Old Aramaic* (Sheffield: JSOT Press, 1992).

—'Daniel: A Book of Significant Reversals', *AUSS* 30 (1992), pp. 139-50.

Sternberg, M., 'Proteus in Quotation Land', *PT* 3 (1982), pp. 107-56.

—*The Poetics of Biblical Narrative* (Bloomington: Indiana University Press, 1985).

Stevenson, W.B., *Grammar of Palestinian Jewish Aramaic* (Oxford: Clarendon Press, 1924).

Stinespring, W.F., 'The Active Infinitive with Passive Meaning in Biblical Aramaic', *JBL* 81 (1962), pp. 391-94.

Stuart, M., *A Commentary on the Book of Daniel* (Boston: Crocker & Brewster, 1850).

Tcherikover, V., *Hellenistic Civilization and the Jews* (trans. S. Applebaum; New York: Atheneum, 1970).

Thompson, T.L., *The Origin Tradition of Ancient Israel* (Sheffield: JSOT Press, 1987).

Torrey, C.C., 'Notes on the Aramaic Part of Daniel', *TCAAS* 15 (1909), pp. 241-82.

—*Ezra Studies* (Chicago: University of Chicago Press, 1910).

Tov, E., 'Three Dimensions of LXX Words', *RB* 83 (1976), pp. 529-44.

—'Loan-words, Homophony and Transliterations in the Septuagint', *Bib* 60 (1979), pp. 216-36.

—'Exegetical Notes on the Hebrew *Vorlage* of the LXX of Jeremiah 27 (34)', *ZAW* 91 (1979), pp. 73-93.

—*The Text Critical use of the Septuagint in Biblical Research* (Jerusalem: Simor, 1981).

—'Did the Septuagint Translators always Understand their Hebrew Text?', in

A. Piertsma and C. Cox (eds.), *De Septuaginta* (Mississauga: Benben Publications, 1984), pp. 53-70.

—'The Unpublished Qumran Texts from Caves 4 and 11', *JJS* 43 (1992), pp. 101-36.

Towner, W.S., 'Poetic Passages of Daniel 1–6', *CBQ* 31 (1969), pp. 317-26.

—*Daniel* (Atlanta: John Knox Press, 1984).

Trudinger, L.P., 'Some Observations concerning the Text of the Old Testament in the Book of Revelation', *JTS* 17 (1966), pp. 82-88.

Ulrich, E., 'Daniel Manuscripts from Qumran. Part 1: A Preliminary Edition of 4QDanᵃ', *BASOR* 268 (1987), pp. 17-37

—'Daniel Manuscripts from Qumran. Part 2: Preliminary Editions of 4QDanᵇ and 4QDanᶜ', *BASOR* 274 (1989), pp. 3-26.

—'The Septuagint Manuscripts from Qumran: A Reappraisal of their Value', in G.J. Brooke and B. Lindars (eds.), *Septuagint, Scrolls and Cognate Writings* (Atlanta: Scholars Press, 1992), pp. 49-80.

VanderKam, J.C., *Enoch and the Growth of an Apocalyptic Tradition* (Washington, DC: Catholic Biblical Association of America, 1984).

Vermes, G., 'Appendix E: The Use of בר נשא / בר נש in Jewish Aramaic', in M. Black, *An Aramaic Approach to the Gospels* (Oxford: Clarendon Press, 1967), pp. 310-28.

—*The Dead Sea Scrolls in English* (London: Penguin Books, 1987).

—'Qumran Forum Miscellanea I', *JJS* 43 (1992), pp. 299-305.

Vries, S.J. de, 'Observations on Quantitative and Qualitative Time in Wisdom and Apocalyptic', in J.G. Gammie, W.A. Brueggemann, W.L. Humphreys and J.M. Ward (eds.), *Israelite Wisdom* (New York: Scholars Press, 1978), pp. 263-76.

Walters, P., *The Text of the Septuagint* (ed. D.W. Gooding; Cambridge: Cambridge University Press, 1973).

Waltke, B.K., and M. O'Connor, *Biblical Hebrew Syntax* (Winona Lake, IN: Eisenbrauns, 1990).

Walton, J.H., 'The Decree of Darius the Mede in Daniel 6', *JETS* 31 (1988), pp. 279-86.

Wesselius, J.W., 'Language and Style in Biblical Aramaic: Observations on the Unity of Daniel 2–6', *VT* 38 (1988), pp. 194-209.

Wharton, J., 'Daniel 3.16-18', *Int* 39 (1985), pp. 170-76.

Whitcomb, J.C., *Darius the Mede* (Grand Rapids: Eerdmans, 1959).

Whybray, R.N., *The Intellectual Tradition in the Old Testament* (Berlin: de Gruyter, 1974).

Wills, L.M., *The Jew in the Court of the Foreign King* (Minneapolis: Fortress Press, 1990).

Wilson, G.H., 'Wisdom in Daniel and the Origin of Apocalyptic', *HAR* 9 (1985), pp. 373-81.

Wiseman, D.J., 'Some Historical Problems in the Book of Daniel', in D.J. Wiseman *et al.*, *Notes on Some Problems in the Book of Daniel* (London: Tyndale Press, 1965), pp. 9-18.

—*Nebuchadrezzar and Babylon* (Oxford: Oxford University Press, 1985).

Wolters, A., 'Untying the King's Knots: Physiology and Wordplay in Daniel 5', *JBL* 110 (1991), pp. 117-22.

Woude, A.S. van der, 'Erwägungen zur Doppelsprachigkeit des Buches Daniel', in H.L.J. Vanstiphont, K. Jongeling, F. Leemhuis and G.J. Reinink (eds.), *Scripta Signa Vocis* (Groningen: Egbert Forsten, 1986), pp. 305-16.

Wright, B.G., *No Small Difference: Sirach's Relationship to its Hebrew Parent Text* (Atlanta: Scholars Press, 1989).

Würthwein, E., *The Text of the Old Testament* (Oxford: Basil Blackwell, 1957).

Wyatt, N., 'The Story of Dinah and Shechem', *UF* 22 (1990), pp. 433-58.

Yamauchi, E.M., 'Daniel and Contacts between the Aegean and the Near East before Alexander', *EvQ* 53 (1981), pp. 37-47.

Young, E.J., *Daniel's Vision of the Son of Man* (London: Tyndale Press, 1958).

—*Daniel* (London: Banner of Truth Trust, 1972).

Zevit, Z., 'The Structure and Individual Elements of Daniel 7', *ZAW* 80 (1968), pp. 385-96.

Ziegler, J., *Septuaginta: Susanna, Daniel, Bel et Draco* (Göttingen: Vandenhoeck & Ruprecht, 1954).

INDEX OF REFERENCES

BIBLICAL REFERENCES

OTHER ANCIENT REFERENCES

DATE DUE

JUN 2 5 2010			
			Printed in USA